Social Roles and
Social Institutions

Social Roles and Social Institutions

Essays in Honor of Rose Laub Coser

EDITED BY

Judith R. Blau
and Norman Goodman

Westview Press

BOULDER • SAN FRANCISCO • OXFORD

Published in 1991 in the United States of America by Westview Press, Inc., 5500 Central Avenue, Boulder, Colorado 80301, and in the United Kingdom by Westview Press, 36 Lonsdale Road, Summertown, Oxford OX2 7EW

Library of Congress Cataloging-in-Publication Data
Social roles and social institutions : essays in honor of Rose Laub
  Coser / edited by Judith R. Blau and Norman Goodman.
    p. cm.
  Includes bibliographical references.
  ISBN 0-8133-8320-X
  1. Social role. 2. Social institutions. I. Coser, Rose Laub,
1916–   . II. Blau, Judith R., 1942–   . III. Goodman, Norman.
HM131.S598 1991
306—dc20   91-13122
                                                                      CIP

Printed and bound in the United States of America

The paper used in this publication meets the requirements
of the American National Standard for Permanence of Paper
for Printed Library Materials Z39.48-1984.

10   9   8   7   6   5   4   3   2   1

Contents

Foreword

Robert K. Merton

In very nearly Buffon's aphorism, it is surely the case with Rose Laub Coser that *le style sociologique c'est la femme même*. For in the earliest as in the most recent of her abundant contributions to sociology, one can detect a distinctive, evolving style of sociological thought. As I had occasion to note of that thought style before — in a foreword to her classic monograph *Training in Ambiguity* — it is one which succeeds in "taking into account both the constraints introduced by structural contexts and the variability of behavior within those contexts." Such a theoretical orientation renders redundant George Homans's emphatic counsel to his fellow sociologists that they "bring men back in" to theoretical sociology since, in *this* mode of structural and functional analysis, individual men and women were never left out. They are always seen as making choices but choices at least constrained though not fully determined by socially structured alternatives.

Concepts of intellectual style vary. For the 18th-century French naturalist Buffon, in elucidating his now universally known aphorism, an authentic auctorial style calls for substance, thoughts, and arguments so shaded and arranged as to touch the sensibilities by addressing the mind. For Ludwik Fleck, the 20th-century Polish biologist turned innovative sociologist of science, a special "thought style is built up from earlier knowledge . . . and, epistemologically most important, from special adaptations and transformations of concepts," this conception being set out in his lately rediscovered and now consequential *Genesis and Development of a Scientific Fact* (to which Thomas Kuhn has paid tribute for having provided him with much-needed reassurance that a sociological dimension to the history of science was warranted and illuminating).

It is not for me, in this mandated *short* prelude, to single out certain papers from the grand array in this dedicatory book which do honor to Rose Coser in the fitting scholarly mode by analyzing and applying some of her many contributions to sociological knowledge. Still, reference to her sociological style of thought leads at once to the analytical papers by Peter Blau, Lewis Coser, and Judith Blau, which focus variously on one of her most significant "adaptations and transformations of concepts." These perspicuous chapters amply indicate how Rose Coser has greatly extended the utility of the concept of role-set, first by making the important distinction between simple and complex role-sets and then by linking varying degrees of complexity of role-sets to individual autonomy, personality development, and mental life. These and her other related conceptual developments have provided a multiplicity of relevance for the program of empirical research on contemporary social concerns which she has long since had under way.

That still-continuing body of sociological work, both theoretical and empirical, shows yet again that, unlike the stereotyped attributions of critics who manage to ignore the abundant evidence to the contrary, certain forms of structural and functional analysis do not in the least resemble a kind of Arcadian sociology in which everything mysteriously works together for good in society. If fresh evidence of the power of such theoretical analysis is required, one need only turn to this robust volume of scholarship as it attests the pivotal place of Rose Laub Coser in contemporary sociological thought.

Rose Laub Coser —
A Portrait

Norman Goodman

The finest compliment that can be paid to a woman of sense is to address her as such.
— Christian Nestell Bovee (1820-1904)

This volume addresses a "woman of sense" and celebrates her influence upon us and many others. It takes her ideas seriously, uses them, challenges them, and extends them. It demonstrates the significant role she has played in contemporary sociology. We believe that this is the first *Festschrift* in sociology that honors a woman, and, if so, it is long overdue. But the editors and contributors to this work did not get involved in it to honor Rose Coser solely because she is a woman. We, and they, did so because she is an extraordinary person.

Rose was part of a most remarkable set of cohorts to arrive at Columbia University shortly after World War II. This group included among others Daniel Bell, Peter Blau, Suzanne Keller, Seymour Martin Lipset, Philip Selznick, and, of course, Lewis Coser. Just to list these names is to recite the roll of a significant segment of the leading figures in sociology of the past few decades.

At this time, the United States was blessed with a sizable contingent of cosmopolitan, liberal European refugee scholars. Rose and Lew Coser exemplified the breed. They brought to the study of society keen minds, a respect for scholarship, and a dedication to the quality of human existence. Many of them, Rose and Lew especially, were not content simply to study the human condition; they felt an obligation to do what they could to better it. Growing up in an activist family that was dedicated to the service of others and to improving social conditions, Rose was provided with the early socialization experiences that flowered in her adult life. Her role in promoting equality between men and women is legendary. It has been reported that at an annual meeting of the American Sociological Association in New Orleans in 1973, Rose and Jessie Bernard climbed up on the bar of a male-only restaurant and refused to budge until they got a commitment that they and other women would thenceforth be served on an equal basis with men. Whether that story is apocryphal or not, anyone who knows Rose would readily believe it.

What is clearly not apocryphal, however, is Rose's leadership in a class action lawsuit on behalf of women faculty and staff at the State University of New York at Stony Brook. She led a determined group of women in an attempt to discuss with then president John S. Toll a comparative analysis of the salaries along with the retention, promotion, and tenure rates for men and women as well as the establishment of a presidentially appointed committee to review any complaints from women on these issues. When this altogether reasonable request was denied, a number of the women faculty and staff — led mainly by Rose Coser — reluctantly instituted a class action law suit. In the end, the litigation had mixed results: the class action suit was denied, but a number of the women pursued individual cases and, like Rose, won them. More importantly, these actions sensitized the campus, and the University Senate created a Committee on the Status of Women to examine the comparative status and career trajectories of men and women and to serve as a clearing house for relevant complaints. Once more, Rose's strong commitment and leadership in the drive for equality between men and women made a major contribution to that important social goal.

The contributions included in this volume will serve as ample testimony to Rose Coser's substantive contribution to the discipline of sociology. But these provide only a partial view of the qualities of Rose Coser that led us to take on this labor of love. There are many facets to the jewel that is Rose Coser.

In a number of her writings, Rose Coser celebrates modernity. She argues that far from overwhelming and burdening the person, the complexity of the modern world creates remarkable opportunities for individual freedom and creativity. In so doing, she essentially writes her autobiography. To paraphrase Gilbert and Sullivan, she is the very model of the modern woman; perhaps Betty Friedan had Rose in mind when she wrote about "superwoman." Although Friedan argued that it wasn't necessary or even desirable for all women to try to do everything, some — like Rose — do! She is (even in "retirement") just such a superwoman. She is "supermom," and even "supergrandmom." Despite her commitment to teaching, scholarship, and social causes, she has had the time to raise two fine children, Ellen and Steven — and later to do equally well by their spouses and children. She excels in her family roles, as she does in the variety of roles she plays. She is not only a devoted mother and grandmother, but also a warm and affectionate wife to Lew as well as his professional collaborator, editor, and even critic on occasion. They share similar social and professional values, exemplifying the principle of homogamy, and each enhances the work and life of the other. And no one who knows Rose will fail to remark about her green thumb and her quality as a "balabusteh," a Yiddish word that is not easily translatable but which refers to the compleat homemaker. There isn't anything around the house or garden that Rose can't do or make better. At Stony Brook, colleagues from all over the campus still talk longingly about the Cosers' once-a-month soirees that were personally catered by Rose.

Admirable as these qualities are, they are not the stuff of *Festschriften*. What makes Rose worthy of this respect is that she is all of these things and a top-notch sociologist to boot. Her work exemplifies the importance of formulating and testing middle-range theories, a lesson she learned well from her mentor Robert K. Merton. Whether you look at her analysis of the hospital ward, the social role of humor, or women's roles, it is obvious that she eschews both "grand theory" and "abstracted empiricism," in the words of another "Columbian." Perhaps Lew Coser had Rose's work in mind when he attacked similar extremes in his presidential address to the American Sociological Association in 1975. He argued that sociology "will be judged in the last analysis on the basis of the substantive enlightenment which it is able to supply about the social structure in which we are enmeshed and which largely conditions the course of our lives." That is an apt summary of Rose Coser's approach to sociology.

Rose carries out this vision of the discipline with a determined intellectual rigor that sets a high standard for sociological analysis. In fact, setting high standards is her hallmark. She does so not only in her published work, but also in her training of countless generations of sociologists — whether or not they are technically "her students." In fact, several of the specific contributions to this book derive directly from Rose's tutelage (e.g., those by Jeffrey Rosenfeld and Gladys Rothbell) or indirectly from Rose's encouragement to proceed with an interesting idea (e.g., for the research by Nancy Chodorow). Her exacting demands were at least as high for women as they were for men. She was no soft touch for anyone. However, she would couple these demands with a ready availability of time, knowledge, wisdom, and comfort for the dedicated and committed student — and colleague.

In the discipline and in her role as department member, Rose was and is no shrinking violet. Often one had to be prepared to defend one's position against her challenging and probing mind. While she seems to delight in intellectual combat, she never allows it to be transformed into personal conflict. Everyone who knows Rose Coser can relate an experience of intense debate with her about some issue in sociology, psychoanalysis, feminism, or social justice. But all of us who have jousted with her continue to call her friend, colleague, and even mentor — and we know that she feels the same about us. It is out of this intellectual respect and personal affection for Rose Laub Coser that this *Festschrift* was conceived and brought to fruition. We can think of no better way of thanking Rose for being who she is than to celebrate her ideas in this volume.

Introduction

Judith R. Blau

Social role is probably the most important abstraction in sociology. This is because it links the person — the thinking, acting individual — to a structured status in a set of social relations — which, in turn, is a component of a larger complex social structure. The role, the status, the set of social relations, and the social structure are in turn normatively moderated just as they generate their own distinctive cultural meanings.

Social role is an abstraction that makes sense of empirical referents — group, behavior, organizations, professions, and occupations — as well as many theoretical concepts — social networks, exchange, institutions, rules, values, orientations, socialization, deviance. And in an important sense, social role continues to unify the discipline of sociology as it remains the linchpin of contending "schools." Culturalists, structuralists, critical theorists, symbolic interactists, and contemporary functional theorists, alike, all deal with the abstraction of social role owing to its fundamental importance at every analytical point of departure — micro, institutional, or macro. Not only would it be impossible to consider sociology without this abstraction, but most fruitful exchanges with the other social sciences depend on the concept. To make the point, it suffices to indicate some of the grounds where interdisciplinary dialogues take place: anthropology (kinship and exchange), education (role models), psychoanalysis (socialization), psychology (role congruence, labeling, and attribution theories), economics (developments in managerial theory, entrepreneurship, and rational choice).

Role analysis has undergone the same transformations that sociology has and, indeed, served the discipline well through major paradigm shifts and more subtle changes in emphases since its earliest

---

Complete references to works by Rose Laub Coser cited in this section appear in Selected Bibliography, pp. 277-281.

formulations (Park 1926; Moreno [1934] (1953); Mead 1934; for a useful summary, see Turner 1986, pp. 313-338).

Coser's contributions are distinctive in that they embrace both structural as well as social psychological (and cognitive) levels of explanation. What undergirds Coser's theoretical work on social roles is a set of dialectical oppositions. One pertains to the tension between the freedoms offered by pluralistic situations and multiple involvements on the one hand, and the constraints imposed by tradition and institutions on the other. Another deals with the contradictory nature of ambiguity: just as the expectations that govern given role relations require a steadfastness and explicitness, there must be sufficient complexity of role relations in the larger social order to maintain the ambiguity necessary for individual autonomy. Still another deals with the ecology of individual identity, as it is rooted in close intimate relations and fully developed in far-flung impersonal groups.

To clarify these theoretical interests, it is first necessary to see how Coser simultaneously liberated role theory from both its micro-psychological underpinnings and from its overly deterministic structural straitjacket. Some early work (for example, Merton 1950, pp. 40-105; Goode 1960) emphasized how role relations are fostered in segmentalized relations, leading to the conclusion that complex social arrangments are stressful and alienating, whereas other approaches (for example, Goffman 1961; Garfinkel 1967) suggested that in an oppressive or nonsensical world, actors become adept at playing many roles.

Coser, in contrast, allows variability both at the level of the individual actor and at the level of the social order. She accomplishes this by situating the actor in multiple roles and multiple groups; by granting some modicum of "sense" to individual actors that enables them to use discretion in allocating time to different roles; by stressing the importance of complexity of social worlds and individuals' multiple group involvements for cognitive and emotional development; and by showing how groups are articulated in larger social structures, such as occupations, work organizations, and communities. The rich variation at several levels thus allows Coser to demonstrate that there is a plurality of forces acting on each group and each set of role relations and, thus, some indeterminacy for the actor. This is the source of free will.

Coser, drawing explicitly from the work of Georg Simmel (1955), views society as generating the bases of differentiation along social, economic, spatial, and temporal dimensions. But, nevertheless, the actor is not the hapless victim. Coser states: "The differentiation among institutions in modern society — the family, the place of work, the school — requires that individuals segment their activities so that they behave differently at different places and at different times. . . ." ("The

Complexity of Roles as a Seedbed of Individual Autonomy," 1975, p. 237). This enables Coser to examine the ways in which individuals are enmeshed in complex structures and how they are generally offered myriad opportunities to exercise discretion and exert autonomy. I stress, "generally," since Coser also pays serious attention to the conditions under which groups fail in these regards: when particularistic values intrude; when groups exert "greedy demands" on participants; when structures of dominance make unmitigated demands on occupants of particular roles; and when role partners are insufficiently nurturant. In short, supplementing the generalizations are the contingencies for group cohesion and the acquisition of individual identity.

In these various ways, Coser liberated role theory from its micro foundations, enabling her to examine the variable context in which role relations emerge and develop. This theme is developed in different ways in "Insulation from Observability and Types of Social Conformity" (1961), *Life on the Ward* (1962), "Where Have All the Women Gone" (1981), and "The Greedy Nature of *Gemeinschaft*" (1984). In these contributions, Coser shows precisely how role theory can be invigorated by a conception of social structure that is abundantly articulated, complex, and multi-leveled. In "The Greedy Nature of *Gemeinschaft*" (1984) Coser shows how the overdetermined conception of social structure is only useful in understanding impoverished and insular groups. Here also is an instance of the paradoxical in Coser's writings: close family life and community ties may be as antithetical to individualism as are highly authoritarian communes ("Jonestown as Perverse Utopia," with Lewis A. Coser, 1979).

Yet Coser's theoretical work also alerts us to the way in which social role theory can account for individual variability. This is possible because Coser does not view actor, status, role, and person as coexistent. For example, people have different points of view acquired through participation in many social circles; independence is attainable through the evasiveness of role demands, and role autonomy is achieved though the reduction of spatial restrictions ("Cognitive Structure and the Use of Social Space," 1986).

Given her training and research in psychiatry departments as well as her considerable knowledge about personality theory and cognition, Coser views the individual as too important to leave out of role analysis. For example, she provides us in "Authority and Structural Ambivalence in the Middle-Class Family" (1964) with a brilliant account of the consequences of the differentiated loci of expectations for behavioral and attitudinal conformity on the formation of childhood identity. The key insight is used in a similar way by Coser in her analysis of residents' training. Hierarchical arrangements generate sociological ambivalence for lower participants and direct attention to alternative possibilities: repression, evasiveness, or rebellion. To call superiors equals ("consultants") in these arrangements is a denial of the hierarchical arrangements and a denial of the ambivalence, and while it is a threat to the existing social order, it serves the purposes of anticipatory socialization (*Training in Ambiguity*, 1979). Needless to say, ambivalence, along with the possibilities of repression, evasiveness, or rebellion, is the rich psychic material of family life, and in her work Coser has made good use of them, framing them and interpreting them from a consistent structuralist perspective.

By loosening the concept of social structure to accommodate pluralities of overlapping and multiple differentiated structures and by being attentive to the actor, it is possible for Coser to consider the tensions between autonomy and freedom and the constraints of tradition and institutions. Freedom, for Coser, is individualized self-development, but it is not possible to achieve it outside of complex social arrangements. What imperils both the individual and social arrangements is the domination of a uniform group that makes singular demands for conformity ("The Greedy Nature of *Gemeinschaft*," 1984). She clarifies the residues of greedy demands in modern institutions, just as she indicates how individuals can be freed from these demands.

Just as understanding the basis of individual autonomy is important for Coser, so is understanding group cohesiveness. This is clear from her writings on the family and parenting. Perhaps the most detailed examination of group cohesion, however, can be found in her empirical research on hospital wards and resident training. In her paper "Laughter Among Colleagues" (1960), Coser shows how humor serves to "reduce social distance between persons occupying different positions in the social structure" and to "withdraw persons' attention from serious concerns" and to "relax the rigidity of the social structure." Thus, humor is a social mechanism that fosters group cohesion, and it does so in a way that is subtly destructive of hierarchy as it helps to restore principles of equality.

The consequences of the failure of a group to maintain continuity and a stable set of norms for participants is nowhere better illustrated than in Coser's paper "Suicide and the Relational System" (1976). When an otherwise stable social system is disturbed by turnover and normative disorder, there is an observable increase in the emotional unease of psychiatric patients, as indicated by an increase in attempted suicides. Although an unusual setting, the theoretical point is clear enough: while greedy demands made on individuals deny them autonomy and independence, individuals nevertheless need structure and the continuity of social support for identity.

The ever abiding concern here is a set of humanistic principles, wedded to straightforward commitment to empirical research and guided by the conviction that such principles — and the means to achieve them — can be understood within a sociological framework. What then are these humanistic principles? Certainly equal opportunity, autonomy, and individuation, but it is in social arrangements that these are achieved. Modern social arrangements are to be valued for their complexity and for the fact that they permit the flexible patterning of role relations, but they are social arrangements that are fostered by trust — and when trust fails, by legal protections — and by mutual regard, and when mutual regard fails, by civility. Simple, unidimensional social systems fail precisely because they succumb to greediness, autocratic control, or cultural hegemony. The point is well taken that the myriad of social circles in which individuals participate is not what alienates, it is the hegemonic control by one group that is the source of alienation in modern life. As Simmel noted, the close-knit sphere is replaced in heterogeneous modern life by many homogeneous spheres.

Coser would add that the initial dyadic and group experiences of family life remain a cultural prototype of the kind of support and mutual regard that groups must provide to individual members. It is Coser's rather sophisticated knowledge of child psychology and psychoanalysis that enables her to see more clearly than Simmel the value of group belonging and the way that identity is established in the first place. And, it is by virtue of her complex view of social structure that she can situate her humanistic values of equality and individual autonomy in her sociology. A final point on Coser's epistemological orientation is important for two reasons. First, it clarifies how Coser's diverse interests — ranging from articles on cultural symbols in the Magic Flute ("The Principle of Patriarchy," 1978) to articles on organization ("Authority and Decision-Making in a Hospital," 1958) — exhibit a theoretical integrity. Second, the point clarifies some important linkages among papers that may not be altogether obvious because of substantive and methodological differences.

As Donald L. Levine (1985, pp. 8-9) indicates, the disposition in the social sciences has been to flee from ambiguity: to discount ambiguity as an empirical phenomena; to rely on unidimensional measures; and, to ignore the constructive role that ambiguity can play in theory. As I have already discussed, Coser takes as problematic what is ambiguous or "multivocal" over what is clear and unidimensional, and she also insists that theoretical constructs be richly grounded in a variety of empirical indicators. Moreover, with regard to the nature of sociological theory itself, her work can be seen as extending the Simmelian principle that concepts and propositions exhibit transformational, if not dialectical, relationships. Thus, in different contexts we see different juxtapositions of concepts such as opportunity, status, ambivalence, greediness, and evasiveness. The tension between group cohesiveness and individual autonomy, for example, cannot be understood independent of the affinities between them. Donald Light makes a similar point in Chapter 14 when he shows that the relation (one might say, the geometrical configuration) between role insulation and structural constraints has changed in medical settings since the 1960s when Coser drew attention to the theoretical principle that governs this relation. But the initial formulation allows for new constellations and, indeed, is strengthened by them. Coser's work is capacious precisely because of her recognition of the importance of ambiguity in social life and in sociological theory. She suggests intellectual links that we would otherwise not see, and her work points to new and novel departures.

Organization and Overview of the Papers

The volume is organized in terms of the following topics: role complexity, issues relating to persisting and emergent rules, social institutions, and role realignments and structural change. This is useful for it clarifies how Coser's work ranges over the continuum from micro-sociological through macro-sociological issues. Chapters in PART ONE (Lopata, L. Coser, Rothbell, P. Blau) deal with role complexity and role impoverishment. PART TWO includes contributions by Epstein, Rosenfeld, D'Antonio, Daniels. In different ways these authors focus on the rules that place constraints on social roles and the ways in which these rules can be transformed.

With the exception of Chapter 12 by Andrea Tyree, the chapters in PART THREE (J. Blau, Nowotny, and Chodorow) relate to organizations and professions. Tyree's chapter is situated as the closing chapter in PART THREE because it broadly deals with families, ethnicity, and migration — topics which are covered in earlier chapters — and also with a topic on which Coser is currently working — how current patterns can be traced to earlier similarities and differences among ethnic groups. Because Tyree's chapter also deals with persistence and change it provides a bridge to the final section. Papers in PART FOUR by the Perrins, Light, Riesman, and Goodman are about social institutions — medicine and medical schools, higher education, and the American family — and how they spark controversy and have undergone change in some respects while they exhibit persistence in other ways.

But Rose Coser is never content with letting intellectual matters settle in such an easy manner. Thus, my discussion of these papers cross-cuts the organization of the volume as I group papers into the following topics: role-sets and role relations, sociology of gender, sociology of the family, medical sociology, and ethnicity and social change.

Role-Sets and Role Relations

An introduction to role theory is provided by Helena Lopata. Chapter 1 is an historical overview of contrasting ways to conceptualize social role and status. Lopata herself situates role theory in an interactionist perspective that highlights symbolic processes. Her approach exemplifies the influence of George Herbert Mead and other members of the "Chicago School." She stresses the negotiated nature of social relations and how people actively define and shape behavior and expectations, and how definitions of the situation are dynamic over time.

While this perspective contrasts with that of Coser's more structural approach to social roles as well as with Coser's greater attention to tensions and conflict, there are important convergencies: first, both approaches posit that participation in richly textured arenas enhances competence and self-esteem; second, recognition is given the actor's capacity to shape present and future participation in these arenas. Lopata's interactionist perspective also can be contrasted with that of other authors who might be said to be situated in the "Columbia School." Specifically, in the Mertonian tradition, Lewis Coser, Peter Blau, and Judith Blau emphasize the structuredness of social roles — their formal configurations and linkages, and that the dual role-status is articulated in larger social institutions. Lewis Coser engages this set of assumptions at the individual level, Judith Blau at the level of the organization, and Peter Blau plays out the implications of differentiation at the macro level for social relations.

Lewis Coser treats the reader to an analysis of intellectual history by tracing the underground roots of influence of Robert K. Merton (1974 [1950]) and Basil Bernstein (1974) on Alvin Gouldner (1985) and Rose Coser (esp., "The Complexity of Roles as a Seedbed of Individual Autonomy," 1975). Merton's structural conception of role-set clearly suggests that complex role relations and the occupancy of multiple status sets engenders conflict and stress. Gouldner, instead, views such experiences as the ones that foster exceptional creativity. Quoting Gouldner, Lewis Coser summarizes the basic point: creativity depends on a person's "access to multiple traditions, as well as their capacity to switch or translate from one to another." Merton's emphasis was also challenged by Rose Coser, who concluded that conflict and contradiction can serve as a "spur for individualism and free choice." In addition to Merton, both Gouldner and Rose Coser acknowledge an intellectual debt to Basil Bernstein. His work on linguistic codes had indicated that flexible styles of thought develop through contact with diverse others and wide experiences, which in turn suggested to Gouldner that complex role relations foster creativity. Similarly, Rose Coser drew attention to the importance of complex role-sets for fostering cosmopolitan perspectives. However, she also joined this conceptualization to the mechanisms individuals use to attain autonomy — perceptual and cognitive differentiation, the expansion of choices, and the more distinctive sense of identity that is attained in complex role-sets.

Another Merton student, Peter Blau, turns his attention to the structural origins of role relations. He states that it can be assumed that in-group relations are preferred over out-group ones, but there will be great diversity in social relations, nevertheless, owing to imperfectly matched population distributions with respect to the salient dimensions of interpersonal choice, such as ethnicity and education. Owing to the heterogeneity of the population — in terms of ethnicity, educational and occupational attainments, religion, and so forth — it is likely that individuals will associate with others who are in some respects different from themselves. Family relations are based on in-group ties, but given generational differences within families, Blau notes that relations will be more or less homogeneous in terms of age and that individuals of given ages will be more implicated in social relations than others. He finds, using survey data collected in China and the United States, that people in their middle years are consulted by more younger, same-age, and older persons than others; that is, they have the most age-diverse family ties. This makes middle-aged family members more cosmopolitan than younger and older family members. Thus, in spite of the considerable differences between these two societies with respect to family customs and residential patterns, as well as normative expectations about gender and generational differences, there is remarkable similarity in American and Chinese families in their patterns of social interaction. This suggests an invariant principle of family role relations that is independent of cultural context.

Chapter 9, "When Weak Ties Are Structured," engages Coser's argument in "Complexity of Roles as a Seedbed of Individual Autonomy" (1975) about the implications of occupying multiple roles and extends what Coser briefly eludes to as the connection between multiple role-sets and weak ties. Mark Granovetter's (1973) work indicates that weak ties facilitate an individual's access to resources and information and enable the person to carry out activities effectively beyond a narrow range. J. Blau examines the structural underpinnings of the development of weak ties within a bureaucratic hospital setting. Because individuals occupy many positions — statuses — simultaneously on different organizational dimensions, they are each integrated in loosely structured subnets of multiple role relations. She examines the implications of this hospital organization for accountability, therapeutic ideology, and quality care.

These chapters by Lopata, L. Coser, P. Blau, and J. Blau deal with how role complexity is achieved and explore its consequences. The other side of the coin is role impoverishment, the focus of Rothbell's chapter and also, ironically, of Daniel's chapter on privileged women. Other contributions deal with the especially constraining statuses that women occupy in families and work, but these will be discussed together.

Rothbell defines a class of social roles. We might call them singleton roles, for they have few defining attributes: the "cheap Jew," the "Jewish Mother," the "housewife." We might add, "the neighborhood gossip" (always female), the American tourist (always Texan), and the street kid (African American or Hispanic). She takes what we usually treat in cultural terms — as prejudice or stereotyping — and recasts the concept in more structural terms. Individuals to whom are attributed few role characteristics, or those who have minimal social relations, are subject to role reduction that is ongoing and reinforcing. This usefully ties in with P. Blau's discussion about older people, for whom role reduction is a likelihood, and to Arlene Kaplan Daniels's analysis of the lives of privileged women.

Daniels argues that women's place depends on their social status, and because it is inappropriate for wealthy women to work and to carry out household tasks, they must find a niche — a set of activities that are socially valued and that they enjoy. Volunteering nicely provides that niche. Basing her analysis on interviews with upper-class women, Daniels describes the ways these women resolve their ambivalence about not working, the way they distance themselves from "idle women of their own class" and achieve esteem while acquiescing to dependency on their husbands and families. Daniels has unusual skills in capturing the subtleties of social life and the dilemmas posed by the opportunities — and lack of opportunities — that face people in their different roles. It is traditional in sociology to bring *verstehen* to a study of the poor; it is more difficult in the matter of the rich, but Daniels shows how it is possible.

Analysis of Gender

Coser as sociologist enjoys the study of ambivalence, change and constancy, and ambiguity. Coser is also a "determined feminist" (as Lewis Coser notes in his chapter) and, if not named after Rosa Luxemburg, bears some resemblance to her, including her political commitment to help rectify social injustices. It is not surprising, therefore, that Coser has written extensively on gender. Issues relating to gender, as Mirra Komarovksy (1988) notes, are of interest to sociologists who think about problems of change and constancy, ambivalence, and ambiguity. Issues about gender are also about politics.

Among the contributors to this volume there is not consensus on the nature of gender differences themselves (although there is considerable agreement on other issues pertaining to institutional change and reform). The debate about gender differences and their significance relates to the contrast between Cynthia Epstein's analysis and the analyses of Nowotny, Chodorow, and to some extent, Riesman. Cynthia Epstein takes the structuralist position that whatever differences exist between women and men can be traced to institutions — families, schools, professions, and organizations. The emphasis is somewhat different for Helga Nowotny, Nancy Chodorow, and David Riesman. All agree that women are repeatedly dealt a bad hand, but Nowotny, Chodorow and Riesman also suggest that if the hands were dealt evenly women would play the game differently than men.

Although Epstein is not especially sympathetic to the position that there are "natural" differences between women and men, she develops the basic theoretical points of contention. Eschewing the idea that can be found in other contributions — that women have distinctive skills and attitudes by virtue of their innate psychic or biological characteristics, or reproductive experience — Epstein writes that "gender distinctions . . . are lodged in a persistent and ongoing context of informal social controls." Such distinctions emanate from coercive institutions, powerful gatekeepers, and subtle processes of everyday life. Epstein draws her empirical evidence from law. She traces how women have been treated differently in the courts. Paradoxically, as women have been treated more leniently in courts of law (with the possible exception of contemporary divorce law), they are treated more harshly as legal professionals. Epstein argues that policies developed in accordance with the assumptions of the "difference perspective" would merely perpetuate these inequalities. Epstein, drawing on Coser's work, proposes that a multiplicity of roles and options are available to both women and men and recommends a public policy that would equalize opportunities.

On important issues, Helga Nowotny agrees with Epstein. Science and academia fail to provide women with institutional supports that allow them to excel. Nowotny makes an interesting comparison between two Noble Prize winners who ostensibly have achieved the ultimate in successful careers, but for whom the process of achievement is quite different. The female biologist, unlike the male physicist, is denied much in the way of university support, mentoring opportunities, and access to research facilities. Instead, she has achieved success in a "protected niche of isolation."

This example motivates a thorough-going critical analysis of institutional life: the greediness of the family and the competitive and demanding (also "greedy") character of science. Women are different, owing to their greater interest in maintaining tradition, a socialized predisposition to achieve compromise rather than to engage in competitive struggles. It is to the loss of science, Nowotny maintains, that it has been unable to accommodate varieties of cultures and personalities. As a keen observer of scientists and science institutions, she reports change on both sides: a new self-assurance among young women scientists and a greater flexibility within science. Pushing the argument a bit, one can imagine that women have something to contribute to the humanization of science and its institutions — a reduction in dominance and power, a greater emphasis on consensus and collaboration, a lesser preoccupation with costly gadgetry and with military research.

Chodorow also considers the interplay between gender differences and institutions. Using archival and interview materials in a study of psychoanalysts, she points out the irony of the fact that women excelled in psychoanalysis before the field was fully institutionalized and before the feminist movement, and women's subsequent nonrecognition. In this subtle discussion, Chodorow reviews the history of psychoanalysis when female clinicians, including Anna Freud, Melanie Klein, and many others, achieved prominence. As the field became more bureaucratic, medicalized, and hierarchical, it ceased to give opportunities to women. In short, the "masculinization" of psychoanalysis drove women out or paid female practitioners scant attention. As Chodorow concludes, "my inquiry suggests . . . that women's professional identity will feel more secure and legitimate . . . as their field's theory . . . acknowledges the existence of two genders . . . and that bureaucratization and centralization may not always work in women's favor."

Although David Riesman's chapter concerns higher education, one way of considering his analysis is in the context of this debate over "difference." The issue is single-sex education (and, inferentially, similar institutions for minority students). Riesman uses his research and teaching background, as well as his considerable inside knowledge about higher education, to marshal a strong case for single-sex colleges, with special emphasis on ones for women. He draws on observations that suggest that women — without male competition and scrutiny — gain confidence, and thus excel, in these settings, better preparing them for post-baccalaureate work than coeducational settings do.

Sociology of the Family

Still cross-cutting the organization of the volume, I group here the chapters on the family: Jeffrey Rosenfeld ("The Heir and the Spare," Chapter 6), and Norman Goodman ("Marriage and the Family in the United States," Chapter 16). Rosenfeld's contribution assesses a source of ambiguity and considerable ambivalence in families: inheritance. In contrast with traditional societies where inheritance rules are institutionalized, inheritance in contemporary societies is based on a claim structure that is riddled with complexities. What is especially interesting about this claim structure is that it is cloaked with secrecy and evasiveness, and Rosenfeld links this observation to two main points. First, money is not the issue; the anxiety is about status and worth. Second, the increase in life expectancy and unpredictabilities about parental residence and lifestyle after retirement add further uncertainties to inheritance. Mining this neglected topic, Rosenfeld extracts rich conceptual material. Evasiveness, he observes, has its psychic rewards; for example, it helps parents maintain power and helps family members to avoid topics of death and illness. Moreover, evasiveness contributes to the social functioning of families in that it provides parents with flexible options and it recognizes the realities of changes in the claim structure. Yet, in recognition of the subtleties of social life, evasiveness instills competition among siblings, increases the chances of litigation, and augments family dependence on estate planning professionals.

The topic of Rosenfeld's paper on intergenerational transfer rules relates to Coser's current research, the "World of Our Mothers" project, to which I return later. After recounting the literature on the changing nature of the family, Norman Goodman in Chapter 16 summarizes the demographic, economic, behavioral, and attitudinal evidence on the dramatic changes that have occurred in the family, including age of first marriage, decline in fertility, and the increase in divorce (although the rate of increase has declined). Goodman's main point is that it is a mistake to deal with the family as if it were an imperiled institution; instead, by considering family roles and role performance as analytical concepts, it is possible to clarify how they change over time and how they vary from one context to another. This tack leads Goodman, in turn, to a reevaluation of the interface between family and jobs, the increase in "reconstituted families," and the nature of changing norms about sexuality. Evident here is a recognition that economy and culture are not always in sync, as greater options for divorce have fostered the feminization of poverty, and economic equality has not meant equality of power for women.

Sociology of Medicine

Two of Coser's books — *Life in the Ward* and *Training in Ambiguity* — deal with hospital settings; she has collaborated with physicians and psychiatrists, taught in medical schools, and helped to raise a physician, Ellen Perrin. It therefore comes as no surprise that there is so much sociology in the joint-authored contribution by two physicians. After summarizing the various sources of structural ambiguity for hospital-based training that Coser had earlier described, the Perrins note the special importance of two problems. The first is that what residents do and learn in the hospital training program is different from what they will do as practitioners. The second is that residents' roles in hospitals are defined in contradictory ways, as they are sometimes viewed as students but often compared with senior physicians. This situation prevailed in the late 1970s when Coser wrote *Training in Ambiguity*, but it has become aggravated by changes in medical delivery systems, especially the decreased rates of hospitalization and the decline in the average hospital stay. But, in spite of the fact that almost all care takes place outside of the hospital, training continues to be hospital-based. Ellen and James Perrin describe recent innovations that allow the residents to train in community-based, outpatient environments that are more realistic about the apprentice role that residents play. Such training, they argue, is congruent with the types of practice in which residents will engage as medical practitioners.

Donald Light, in Chapter 14, also reexamines the dramatic changes that have occurred in medicine within the past decades. In addition, he provides an historical overview on the sociological literature that has dealt with the sources of uncertainty in medicine and the way medicine controls uncertainty. A point of departure in the Light contribution is Coser's seminal idea that was first stated in 1966. Light summarizes this argument: ". . . . full visibility is a source of strain. People need role distance, evasiveness, denial, role segmentation, and periods of withdrawal to cope." Coser's thesis is stated in micro-social terms, but

Light reexamines it as an institutional imperative and asks how a thesis that was developed to account for practice in the 1960s stands the test of time. From being among the most powerful and least scrutinized professions, medicine is currently the among the most controlled and most scrutinized professions. Owing to extensive monitoring that has accompanied efforts to control costs and standardize care, medicine no longer affords insulation from observability. This enhanced observability, Light suggests, requires new forms of coping both by institutions and by physicians. Precise record-keeping, computerized medical records, transfer of responsibilities to paramedical specialists, and a variety of other bureaucratic mechanisms, accompanied by peer review procedures, are the structural factors that play a role in explaining the extent to which physicians in contemporary medical settings are able to secure autonomy in certain clinical matters while losing it in other areas. As Light notes, Coser's theoretical formulation initially addressed the problems of physicians within a specific historical context. However, what is of continuing importance is Coser's insight about how structural arrangements affect observation of role performances and her recognition of the tension between accountability and autonomy.

Generational Change

Coser's most recent project, "The World of Our Mothers," as described by William D'Antonio and Andrea Tyree, incorporates several of Rose's interests — gender, families, problems of discrimination, and structured opportunities. As an early collaborator in this project, William D'Antonio (Chapter 7) states that a purpose of the study of immigrant women was based on evidence that social historians had inaccurately portrayed the role of women in immigrant family life. D'Antonio and Coser assumed that women provided vital linkages between the home and the larger community and played important roles in the assimilation and acculturation processes, as they helped to resolve tensions between traditional values and those of the larger American society.

The study is comparative, including both Southern Italian and Eastern European Jewish women. D'Antonio describes the differences between these two ethnic groups in terms of occupational backgrounds, literacy rates, fertility, and differences in traditional family roles and in socialization patterns. He draws attention to the declining differences between all European ethnic groups and native Americans with respect to occupational and educational attainment, while noting that Jewish assimilation has been especially pronounced and that Southern Italian descendants have continued to embrace traditional values. D'Antonio draws our attention to the ways in which first generation immigrant women of different ethnic origins continue to influence family life patterns into subsequent generations.

The final paper I discuss is by Andrea Tyree (Chapter 12). "Reshuffling the Social Deck" is an ambitious and important contribution. It illustrates how creative social science is fostered by an ongoing dialogue between those who (as Tyree describes herself) are inclined to the "assault on aggregate data" and those who, like Coser, prefer to engage their empirical data in the field. The question that "The World of Our Mothers" project raises, as D'Antonio and Tyree both indicate, is how patterns established decades ago — whether by choice, tradition, or chance — influence current configurations. The mechanisms of persistence and change are complex and of continuing interest in sociology. The specific problem that Tyree addresses is how the current socioeconomic ranking of ethnic groups is influenced by their origins and initial experiences.

Her first objective is to identify the dimensions of occupational distributions by ethnic groups at the turn of the century. For this she uses the Dillingham Commission data supplemented with census reports for 1900. The major dimension is hierarchical, tapping a variety of closely related attributes, such as prestige, power, or literacy. The second dimension captures spatial differences and distinguishes between ethnic groups that were concentrated in rural occupations with those concentrated in urban ones. The third dimension differentiates between those occupations that were dominated by ethnic groups whose members made the initial residential and industrial choices that increased the chances that they or subsequent members of the ethnic group benefited from the union movement.

From the results of the analysis for 1900, Tyree extracts the scores for the three dimensions to predict current socioeconomic standing of ethnic groups. For all groups, their earlier hierarchical position and urban or rural spatial location are the most powerful predictors of their current standing. The higher the occupational rankings and the more urbanized the members of an ethnic group in 1900, the higher the income of their descendants. Tyree also reports some interesting exceptions, most notably for Jews.

Currently, ethnicity all by itself explains about 5% of the variance in American household income, as the social deck has undergone considerable shuffling, but Tyree demonstrates how the current ethnic hierarchy has developed from earlier ethnic group characteristics that relate to occupational ranking, urban and rural differences, and industrial variation. Such analyses complement — again, I refer to the creative dialogue — Rose Coser's work on continuity and change in families, childhood socialization, and the way in which cultural values are transmitted and transformed in the context of ethnic traditions. Puzzles about persistence and change can only be solved through these kinds of creative dialogues.

Acknowledgments

Early comments on papers and the organization of the book were provided by reviewers, including Helena Lopata. Her critical suggestions to editors and authors were so helpful that we asked her to contribute the opening chapter. Dean Birkenkamp and Ellen Williams of Westview Press were supportive of the idea of the *Festschrift* and helpful at every stage of its preparation. At Stony Brook, Jeri Lomeli and Carole Roland provided Goodman with secretarial assistance and valued help in meeting deadlines for papers and the abundant correspondence.

Several individuals from the University of North Carolina deserve special acknowledgment. We thank Rekha Mirchandani for editorial assistance and Paul Mihas for help with the final manuscript. Gary Gaddy shepherded us through the technicalities of manuscript production from start to finish. Most especially we thank Sharon Farrell for the manuscript preparation — from initial submissions, through revisions, to final copy. It was with good cheer, patience, and professional competence that she rallied on receipt of each chapter, whether it was the first, second, or third version. Lew was as helpful as one expects a *Festschrift* spouse to be; he is to be complimented on his patience and taciturnity. In recognition of Rose Coser's contributions to gender and family studies, the royalties for this book will be used to establish "The Rose Laub Coser Award for Scholarship in Women's Studies" at the Department of Sociology at the State University of New York at Stony Brook.

References

Bernstein, Basil. 1974. *Class, Codes, and Controls*. New York: Schocken Books.

Garfinkel, Harold. 1967. *Studies in Ethnomethodology*. Englewood Cliffs: Prentice-Hall.

Goode, William J. 1960. "Norm Commitment and Conformity to Role-Status Obligations." *American Journal of Sociology* 66: 246-258.

Goffman, Erving. 1961. *Asylums*. Garden City, N.Y.: Anchor Books.

Gouldner, Alvin W. 1985. *Against Fragmentation*. New York: Oxford University Press.

Granovetter, Mark S. 1973. "The Strength of Weak Ties." *American Journal of Sociology* 78: 1360-1380.

Komarovsky, Mirra. 1988. "The New Feminist Scholarship." *Journal of Marriage and the Family* 50: 585-593.

Levine, Donald. 1985. *The Flight From Ambiguity*. Chicago: University of Chicago Press.

Mead, George Herbert. 1934. *Mind, Self, and Society*. Ed. C. W. Morris. Chicago: University of Chicago Press.

Merton, Robert K. 1974 [1950] "Contributions to the Theory of Reference Group Behavior" (with Alice Kitt Rossi). Pp. 40-105 in *Continuities in Social Research*. Ed. Robert K. Merton and Paul F. Lazarsfeld. New York: Arno Press.

Moreno, Jacob. 1953 [1934]. *Who Shall Survive?* New York: Beacon.

Park, Robert E. 1926. "Behind Our Masks." *Survey Graphic* 56 (May): 135.

Simmel, Georg. 1955. "The Web of Group Affiliations." In his *Conflict and the Web of Group Affiliations*. Trans. Kurt H. Wolff and Reinhard Bendix. New York: Free Press.

Turner, Jonathan H. 1986. *The Structure of Sociological Inquiry*. 4th ed. Chicago: Dorsey.

PART ONE

Role Complexity

1

Role Theory

Helena Znaniecka Lopata

Most introductory textbooks in sociology use some variation of Linton's (1936, pp. 113-4) definition of social status as "a position in a particular pattern which is a collection of rights and duties" and social role as the "dynamic aspect of a status [that] puts the rights and duties which constitute the status into effect." Those scholars who have tried to work with this definition of social role in the 1950s and 1960s experienced problems leading to numerous variations on the theme and confusion (Lopata 1964). The classic study by Gross and his associates (1957) of school superintendents, and the thought provoking analyses of Goffman (1962) and F. Bates (1956) pointed to some of the difficulties of the Lintonian version. Biddle and Thomas (1966) devoted a large volume to role theory, in which they dissect the various major contributions to the classification and analysis of "the phenomena of role."

The fact is that the Lintonian (1936) view of role as the behavior expected of people in a certain status (position) makes actual analysis of social life difficult, if not impossible. In the first place, it does not focus on actual behavior — and life is impossible without going beyond expectations. Secondly, reference to status as a position leaves the person dangling — position in what? I have been able to distinguish what can be called "chart" positions — Davis (1949) called them "office" — in which one can locate roles, as well as status hierarchies, if we can limit status to prestige related systems (Lopata, in press). A third problem with seeing a role as dependent upon a status position is its isolated location — the role is bounded by, or limited to, the person. This is unrealistic. Social life goes on not just through the behavior of one person, but also through interrelationships among several people. The physician not only acts, but interacts with patients, nurses, specialists and others who are active participants in the role. The role cannot be limited to one person's behavior, but must include the behavior of others which provides the rights enabling those actions. Patients must come to the doctor, honestly tell their problems, allow examinations, and follow the prescriptions. Nurses and technicians assist, receptionists make appointments, and so forth. The role of physician thus encompasses more than the social person of doctor and can not be limited to her or him alone. The Lintonian definitions do not recognize this fact.[1]

Finally, the definition of role as the behavior of a person in a certain position is static, neglecting the negotiated and flexible features of actual roles carried out in the world. This is one of the problems of the whole functional approach. It focuses mainly upon the contributions of units of social systems such as roles to the functioning of the larger structure. There are other ways of looking at the relations involved in social roles. Let us briefly examine how this concept has actually been used by some sociologists.

William Goode

Goode (1960, p. 485) produced a rather unusual definition, in a footnote to his famous "A Theory of Role Strain:" "In this paper I distinguish role and status on the basis only of degree of institutionalization; all role relations are somewhat institutionalized, but statuses are more fully institutionalized." This view is certainly different from the definition of status as position and from that of role as the behavior expected of persons in that position. The Mead-Cooley symbolic interactionists would not accept the idea of a continuum between role and status — they never refer to status-taking. More on this approach below.

Talcott Parsons

Parsons (1949, 1951) used the concept of social role in several, relatively inconsistent ways. In the essay "Toward a Common Language in the Area of Social Science" (written jointly with Dunlap, Gilmore, Kluckholn and Taylor), role is seen as "the dynamic aspect of status, the behavior counterpart of the ideal or expected position defined by a status" (1949, p. 42). However, the authors point to the fact that, although any behavior expected of an incumbent of a status is included in a role, there is a core or "functional role" that is important to the welfare of others. This implies more than defense of the rights of a status. In *The Social System*, Parsons (1951, p. 25) refers to status as the positional aspect of his structural-functional framework; that is the actor's "place in the relationship system considered as a structure, that is a patterned system of parts." Yet, he writes, "On the other hand there is the processual aspect, that of what the actor does in his relations with others seen in context of its functional significance for the system. It is this which we shall call his *role*" (1951, p. 25). A final quotation from Parsons indicates the difficulty he had in defining, and we have in understanding, the concept of role: "A role then is a sector of the total orientation system of an individual actor which is organized about expectations in relation to a particular interaction context, that is integrated with a particular set of value standards which govern interaction with one or more alters in the appropriate complementary roles" (1951, pp. 38-39). Parsons comments that the alters do not have to be a defined as a group of individuals, but anyone in complementary interaction with the ego.

Parsons' various definitions move us past the rigid dependence upon status as a position and role as its determined behavior, in that he focuses on social relationships with others who are involved in a purposeful, rather than just status defending, activity. There still remains the problem of limiting role to expected relations rather than to actual interaction.

Symbolic interactionism sees social roles as interpersonal units in and of themselves, examined for their interrelationships and then, if the researcher so desires, located in the family, religious, political, or work organizations. This perspective enables us to see that the social person is involved in much more than simply responding to cultural expectations connected with a position, with greater or lesser deviation. It points to the complexity of the interaction involved in each social role.

Ralph Turner

Turner (1962, 1981) went partly in this direction by focusing on behavior that forms a meaningful unit rather than expectations, and recognizing what he calls the role-making aspects of interaction. But he did not include the related others, members of the social circle, as important for a role. Although emphasizing non-institutionalized features of role performance, he still tied it to Linton's definition of status and limited the focus to one person rather than looking at the range of relevant relationships.

Robert K. Merton

Merton (1949, 1957) and his students have opened up the concept of social role to a broader panorama which includes the people with whom the person is involved. His concept of "role-set" is defined as follows:

> . . . . that complement of role relationships which persons have by virtue of occupying a particular social status. As one example, the single status of medical student entails not only the role of student in relation to his [sic] teachers, but also an array of other roles relating the occupant of that status to other students, nurses, physicians, social workers and medical technicians (Merton 1957, p. 369).

The trouble with this formulation is that it ignores the interdependence and interaction among circle members, as Turner (1962, p. 25) points out — it reduces the role to "a single reciprocity." Several of Merton's students, including Rose Coser (1975), have accepted the concept of role-set, as have Peter Blau and Lewis Coser in this volume. I will return in a minute to Rose Coser's expansion on the implications of this idea.

Florian W. Znaniecki

In the meantime, Znaniecki (1940, 1954, 1965) had been developing an orientation toward social role that differed from Linton's anthropological view.

> I borrowed the term 'social role' from Park and Burgess twenty-five years ago and have redefined it gradually in an attempt to make it heuristically useful. . . . Every social role is performed within a *social circle* of people who accept a particular individual as a *person* presumably fit for the performance of this role. . . . These actions [*duties* of the person] together constitute his *function* as the central person of this social circle. His circle cooperates with him by granting him and actively supporting those *rights* which he needs in order to perform effectively his functions (Znaniecki 1954: 521; *emphasis added*).

Thus, Znaniecki (see mainly *Social Relations and Social Roles*, 1965) defined a social role as a set of patterned, functionally interdependent social relations between a social person and a social circle involving duties and personal rights. The person either pulls together members of the social circle or enters an already formulated one, but both the individual and the circle members must meet each others' qualifications. The circle contains everyone toward whom the person's duties are directed and everyone who grants the rights which make it possible to perform their duties. Note here that Znaniecki agrees with Parsons (1951) and Merton (1967) that circle members do not need to be organized into a group, as exemplified by the patients of a doctor. Circle segments usually include beneficiaries, colleagues and/or the work group, suppliers, and sometimes, administrators. The title of the role often carries with it its culturally defined behavior: a doctor 'doctors', professors 'profess', mothers 'mother' and so forth. However, in order to accomplish these goals, the person needs patients, students, children, as well as many other members of the social circles who provide the resources and grant personal rights. The social person has duties to each of these members, even if only to communicate needs or reward contributions. Social roles can be located in cultures, which provide sources for anticipatory continued socialization in kinship or other organizational charts and in status hierarchies.

Helena Z. Lopata

This conceptualization of social role provides a dynamic base for studying and understanding the life of a society. It also supplies the base for individual involvement in societal life. I have been working with this concept from a symbolic interactionist perspective and have found it extremely useful, elaborating on it in several ways (see especially Lopata 1966, 1971, 1979,1981, 1985, in press). In the latest work I have stressed the negotiated, relational aspects of roles, the role cluster, and the individual's social life space. Let me develop this a bit.

The individual brings to a social role those aspects of the self which are deemed necessary for the performance of duties and the receipt of rights, negotiating with the circle those aspects which differ from the cultural base on both sides. Taking as example a hypothetical American woman, we know that she is also involved in other social roles, past, present and in the anticipatory future. She is prepared, more or less thoroughly, for each role through anticipatory socialization and then carries forth the duties and, in turn, receives rights in interaction with the circle members. Each role requires her to "take the role" of several others and understand their perspectives. The more complex each role, the greater the complexity of the person involved in it, according to Kohn and Schooler (1973, 1978, 1982, 1983) as well as Rose Coser (1975). A woman can also participate in numerous roles with numerous sets of circle members, providing the base for autonomy and individuation, yet cooperative activity. This is Rose Coser's (1975a) argument in "The Complexity of Roles as a Seedbed of Individual Autonomy."

Role Clusters and Social Life Spaces

A woman's roles at any point in time are not completely unconnected; many fall into the family institution, others into the economic or professional domain. One can assume that roles which fall into the same institution bear a greater resemblance to each other than those embedded in different institutions. Looking at a woman's role cluster at any stage of her life course, we can organize it into institutional dimensions. Some women have a very rich family or professional dimension while others are involved in roles that span several institutions. In order to better understand the complexity of multiple role involvements I have adopted the concept of life space from Kurt Lewin (see Deutsch 1954) and the members of the University of Chicago Committee on Human Development, applying it to the institutional dimensions covered by a person's roles (see Williams and Wirth 1965; Cumming and Henry 1961). A multi-dimensional social life space is one consisting of multiple social roles in several institutional dimensions. It is here that I fall into step with the analyses by Rose Coser (1975a) and by Lewis Coser and Peter Blau in this volume, as well as our editors. The complexity of the social life space in which the roles are contained enables considerable complexity of personality and intellectual flexibility. In addition, women (as well as men, of course) change their social life space over the life course, as they go through each role's life cycle and move in and out of different roles. They develop, more or less consciously and successfully, hierarchal arrangements of the roles in which they are involved at any stage of life. Occasionally, or even frequently, they can simultaneously experience the peak stages of role involvement in more than one such set of relationships.

Role Conflict and Individual Complexity

Interestingly enough, the ability of American women to engage in multiple role involvements with multiple social circles has been subject to an enormous amount of negative commentary in recent sociological and popular literature. Women are portrayed as experiencing strong role conflict and stress, and as harried, nervous and unable to perform their roles adequately. There are several components to this imagery that are worrisome to a symbolic interactionist. In the first place, the focus is on women, although men are also involved in roles that can be quite conflictful. Secondly, the implication behind this portrayal is that the worst conflict is due to only certain roles that women play, those which interfere with high level involvement in the "greedy institution" of the family (see L. Coser 1974, R. Coser 1975b, Coser and Coser 1974). One of the consequences of such a view is that it tries to restrict a woman's social life space during her whole life course on the assumption that she will become a mother, and in spite of the fact that peak involvement in that role takes only a few years. It ignores women who do not become wives or mothers, or who are not deeply committed to family roles. Such restrictions are not applied to men. This view also assumes that the roles of wife, mother, and homemaker are not conflictful in and of themselves. It is only entrance into the role of employee, a profession or other occupation that is seen as producing conflict for women. In addition, the most stress producing behavior is seen as derived from entrance into the previously male dominated high status professional and managerial occupations. The "feminine mystique" of the post World War II era, so eloquently described by Friedan (1963), that we can assume helped decrease the number of women psychoanalysts in America appears to be rearing its head in recent years (as pointed out by Chodorow in this volume). A perfect example is the enormous amount of guilt allegedly experienced by women who "neglect" their infants and "latchkey" older children and husbands, as emphatically reported by the media whenever women astronauts or business executives are featured.

There is a final set of invidious assumptions underlying all the hoopla about inevitable strain and conflict from multiple role involvements of women, noted by several scholars. These hark back to the past when people lived at the brink of survival. Freud contributed to what Marks (1977) calls the "scarcity" model of energy, time and commitment, by using such metaphors as spending, draining, leaking out, or dribbling away of energy (see Lopata in press, p. 504). Baruch, Barnett and Rivers (1983, p. 140) asked themselves why the "conventional wisdom" presents women as especially stressed, unhappy and full of feelings of conflict, although the women they studied simply contradicted this image. They place the source in the mental health field, whose experts have been predicting conflicts with women's commitment to roles outside of the home. Friedan (1963) had even earlier documented the pressure toward a restricted home-based social life space on the part of psychologists and psychiatrists, anthropologists and other social scientists. One needs only to read Helene Deutsch's (1944) *The Psychology of Women* to get a feeling for the depth of this warning concerning entrance by women into the public domain. It is an interesting commentary on American society that the model of restricted energy is applied especially to women. (It also appears in reference to the elderly.) Thus, women are seen as tired from role conflict in childbearing years and following "the empty nest" stage of life.

Although quite pervasive, this imagery is contradicted by several recent studies. Several authors of chapters in the Baruch and Brooks-Gunn (1984) volume, such as Long and Porter, comment on the pleasure derived by women from multiple role involvements which actually energize them. Moen, Dempster-McCain and Williams (1989) found that multiple role involvement contributes to the longevity of women. Baruch and her associates (1983) concluded that women in complex role clusters had a strong sense of selfhood and self-worth, and feelings of mastery over their lives and independence.

Rose Coser and Role Complexity

Returning now to role theory, with special reference to social life space complexity, we can go back to Simmel (1955). As both Cosers have noted, Simmel did not find conflict inevitably debilitating. Inkeles (1983, see also Inkeles and Smith 1974) visualized modernization as providing resources for individuation and increasing independence of people. According to Rose Coser (1975a) the ability to take the role of a great variety of others participating in various social circles (she uses role-sets) increases empathic understanding. Coser also refers to George Herbert Mead's concept of the generalized other which evolves from a child's understanding of complicated games.

Role theory, especially when applied to sets of relations between a social person and participants in a social circle rather than to expected or even actual behavior of one individual conforming to demands of a position, can revitalize our examination of social life. The Znaniecki-Lopata formulations can help us analyze social life spaces or the life course, as it has helped me in the study of American women, friendship, or occupational roles. They can also help our understanding of social structures as systems of roles organized to meet defined and negotiated goals. We can study specific roles, compare them to others with similar titles or manifest purposes in different settings, identify changes in consequence of variations in social person or social circle characteristics or over time. We can analyze sets of roles in family or organizational systems. There is still much to be learned about individual and societal life through the dynamic use of social role theory.

Notes

1. Norman Goodman (personal correspondence) pointed out that even Linton (1936, p. 12) confused the issue by referring to role as behavior as well as expectations in another location in *The Study of Man*.

References

Baruch, Grace and Jeanne Brooks-Gunn. (eds.). 1984. *Women in Midlife*. New York: Plenum.

____, Rosalind Barnett and Caryl Rivers. 1983. *Lifeprints: New Patterns of Life and Work for Today's Women*. New York: McGraw-Hill.

Bates, Frederick L. 1956. "Position, Role and Status: A Reformulation of Concepts." *Social Forces*. 34: 313-321.

Biddle, Bruce J. and Edwin J. Thomas. (eds.). 1966. *Role Theory: Concepts and Research*. New York: John Wiley & Sons.

Coser, Lewis. 1974. *Greedy Institutions*. New York: Free Press.

____ and Rose Laub Coser. 1974. "The Housewife and Her 'Greedy Family.'" Pp. 89-100 in *Greedy Institutions: Patterns of Undivided Commitment*, edited by Lewis Coser. New York: Free Press.

Coser, Rose. 1975a. "The Complexity of Roles as a Seedbed of Individual Autonomy." Pp. 237-263 in *The Idea of Social Structure: Papers in Honor of Robert K. Merton*, edited by Lewis A. Coser. New York: Harcourt, Brace Janovich.

____. 1975b. "Stay Home Little Sheiba: On Placement, Displacement and Social Change." *Social Problems* 22: 470-480.

Cumming, Elaine and William E. Henry. 1961. *Growing Old: The Process of Disengagement*. New York: Basic Books.

Davis, Kingsley. 1949. *Human Society*. New York: Macmillan.

Deutsch, Helene. 1944. *The Psychology of Women*. New York: Grune and Stratton.

Deutsch, Morton. 1954. "Field Theory in Social Psychology," Pp. in *Handbook of Social Psychology*, edited by Gardner Lindsey. Cambridge, MA: Addison-Wesley.

Friedan, Betty. 1963. *The Feminine Mystique*. New York: Norton.

Goffman, Erving. 1959. *Presentation of Self in Everyday Life*. New York: Doubleday.

Goode, William. 1960. "A Theory of Role Strain." *American Sociological Review* 25: 483-496.

____. 1962. *Encounters*. New York: Bobbs-Merrill.

Gross, Neal, Ward S. Mason and Alexander W. McEacher. 1957. *Explorations in Role Analysis: Studies in the School Superintendency Role*. New York: John Wiley & Sons.

Inkeles, Alex. 1983. *Exploring Individual Modernity*. New York: Columbia University Press.

____ and David H. Smith. 1974. *Becoming Modern: Individual Change in Six Developing Countries*. Cambridge, MA: Harvard University Press.

Kohn, Melvin and Carmi Schooler. 1973. "Occupational Experience and Psychological Functioning: An Assessment of Reciprocal Effects." *American Sociological Review* 38: 97-113.

____. "The reciprocal effects of substantive complexity of work and intellectual flexibility: A longitudinal assessment." *American Journal of Sociology* 84: 24-52.

____. 1983. *Work and Personality: An Inquiry into the Impact of Social Stratification.* Norwood, N.J.: Albex.

Linton, Ralph. 1936. *The Study of Man.* New York: D. Appleton-Century.

Long, Judy and Karen L. Porter. 1984. "Multiple Roles of Midlife Women: A Case for New Directions in Theory, Research and Policy." Pp. 109-159 in *Women in Midlife,* edited by Grace Baruch and Jeanne Brooks-Gunn. New York: Plenum.

Lopata, Helena Znaniecka. 1964. "A Restatement of the Relation Between Role and Status." *Sociology and Social Research* 49: 58-68.

____. 1971. *Occupation: Housewife.* New York: Oxford University Press.

____. 1979. *Women as Widows: Support Systems.* New York: Elsevier.

____. 1990. "Friendship: Historical and Theoretical Introduction." Pp. 1-19 in *Friendship in Context,* edited by Helena Z. Lopata and David Maines. Greenwich, CT: JAI PRESS.

____. In Press. *Women's Roles, Women's Life Spaces.* Philadelphia: Temple University Press.

Marks, Steven. 1977. "Multiple Roles and Role Strain: Some Notes on Human Energy, Time and Commitment." *American Sociological Review* 42: 921-936.

Mead, George Herbert. 1934. *Mind, Self and Society.* Edited by Charles Morris. Chicago, University of Chicago Press.

Merton, Robert. 1957a. *Social Theory and Social Structure.* Glencoe, Illinois, The Free Press.

____. 1957b. "The Role Set: Problems in Sociological Theory." *British Journal of Sociology,* 8: 106-120.

Moen, Phyllis, Donna Dempster-McClain and Robin M. Williams, Jr. 1989. "Social Integration and Longevity: An Event History Analysis of Women's Roles and Resilience." *American Sociological Review* 54: 635-647.

Parsons, Talcott. 1949. *Essays in Sociological Theory: Pure and Applied.* Glencoe, Illinois: The Free Press.

____. 1951. *The Social System.* Glencoe, Illinois: The Free Press.

____, et al. 1949. "Toward a Common Language for the Areas of Social Science." Pp. 42-51 in *Essays in Sociological Theory, Pure and Applied.* Glencoe, Illinois: The Free Press.

Simmel, Georg. 1955. "The Web of Group Affiliations." Pp.125-195 in *Conflict and the Web of Group Affiliations.* Edited by Georg Simmel, translated by Kurt H. Wolff and Reinhard Bendix. New York: Free Press.

Turner, Ralph. 1962. "Role Taking: Process versus Conformity." Pp. 20-40 in *Human Behavior and Social Processes.* Edited by Arnold Rose. Boston: Houghton-Mifflin.

____. 1981. "The Real Self: From Institution to Impulse." Pp. 203-220 in *Social Psychology Through Symbolic Interaction.* Edited by Gregory P. Stone and Harvey A. Farberman. New York, John Wiley & Sons.

Williams, Richard H. and Claudine G. Wirth. 1965. *Lives Through the Years.* New York: Atherton.

Znaniecki, Florian W. 1940. *The Social Role of the Man of Knowledge*. New York: Columbia University Press.

____. 1954. "Basic Problems of Contemporary Sociology." *American Sociological Review* 19: 519-524.

____. 1965. *Social Relations and Social Roles*. San Francisco: Chandler.

2

Role-Set Theory and Individual Autonomy

Lewis A. Coser

In his theory of role-sets, Merton offered basic intellectual tools for developing a theory of individual autonomy, yet he largely left the development of such a theory to others. He argued that modern individuals tend to find themselves in a structural situation in which they are confronted with a variety of role partners. These role partners in a person's role-set are likely to have different status positions and hence are also likely to have different and often incompatible or conflicting expectations as to the attitude and behavior of the individual under analysis. This would lead to the emergence of dysfunctional consequences were there no social mechanisms allowing them to minimize conflicts and to deal with contradictions. To quote Merton (1968), "The notion of the role-set at once leads to the inference that social structures confront men [sic] with the task of articulating the components of countless role-sets so as to ensure a measure of social regularity in the role-set sufficient to enable most people most of the time to go about their business without becoming paralyzed by extreme conflicts in their role-sets" (p.42). Merton (1968) is mainly concerned "with the analytical problem of identifying the social mechanisms that produce a greater degree of order or less conflict than would obtain if these mechanisms were not called into play" (p.45). Individuals can have recourse to a series of strategies to maneuver among different role partners to their own advantage.

Merton is not primarily concerned with individual status holders but rather with minimizing disturbances in the role-set. He states that the availability of mechanisms for minimizing conflicts between role partners and status holders may assure that the individual can maintain a measure of autonomy, but his focus of analytical attention is clearly upon conditions that minimize sources of social disorder. He implies that potential disturbances may be turned to advantage by skillful role players but he is mainly concerned with minimizing structural causes of social disturbances. When he talks about mechanisms, for example, that allow the insulating of role-activities from observability, as when departmental chairpersons are expected to refrain from observing the teaching of junior members of the staff, Merton is mainly concerned with mechanisms that assure smooth functioning of the social structure of teaching than with increasing the autonomy of the young teacher (Merton 1968:428-429).

Even though he does not specifically state that his theory pertains mainly to modern society, it seems fairly obvious that Merton is above all concerned with the modern world and its contradictions and complexities. Indeed, he has provided an exciting ingredient of a full fledged sociological theory of the trials and tribulations of the world of modernity that can be compared to George Simmel's theories on the same topic. There is, however, a somewhat defensive underlying stance in this Mertonian theory. His modern actor seems a bit like a Chaplinesque character who is forever threatened by a variety of perils but nevertheless manages in the end to come to terms with all of them. Or, to put it into the vernacular; How does one manage to secure some apples without upsetting the apple cart? Merton has identified a series of mechanisms that minimize conflict and contradictions among role-partners and status holders, but he paid little attention to a person's ability to make choices and to play one member of role-set against another so as to increase his or her own freedom of action.

Two students of Merton, Alvin Gouldner and Rose Coser, who were at Columbia at almost the same time, built on Merton's work, although in rather dissimilar ways. Gouldner, as I shall show, did not choose to work directly in the Mertonian tradition yet was clearly in Merton's debt in at least one of his seminal contributions. His theory of intellectual creativity, though not mentioning Merton, has evident roots in his structural analysis. I shall deal with Gouldner's work first and then consider the work of Basil Bernstein, who had no connections with the Columbia students but developed a theory that influenced both Gouldner and Rose Coser. The last part of the paper will be devoted to an account and analysis of Rose L. Coser's work and her attempt to develop and extend Merton's theory by stressing the liberating potential of complex and multifaceted role-sets. What Gouldner, Bernstein and Coser had in common is a more positive evaluation of role-set contradictions than Merton had provided.

Alvin Gouldner on the Sources of Intellectual Creativity

The late Alvin Gouldner developed a theory of intellectual creativity that is exciting and far-ranging. It has received very little attention, partly because it is hidden in a book dealing with other matters, and partly because Gouldner did not bother to relate it to other conceptualizations in the social psychology of creativity.

Gouldner argues that creative thinkers are more likely to be bilingual or multilingual and also to be bi-or multi-theoretical. They have the ability to see things that to others are visible through only one medium or in one theoretical frame from the perspective of another. This implies a skill at *translating* back and forth between them and hence transcending the usual boundaries of language or theory. Marx, Gouldner argues, had this ability to an exceptional degree since he was in simultaneous command of a variety of languages and intellectual traditions. Spinoza also comes to mind.

Gouldner argued that persons having a variety of perspectives in their repertory have a greater chance to be intellectually productive than persons limited to one perspective. He contends that the fundamental source of major intellectual creativity "entails an ability to cross the boundaries of an intellectual tradition and thus to escape control by a single perspective" (Gouldner 1985:204). This is facilitated by involvement with multiple traditions. Freed from exclusive reliance on one particular perspective, creative thinkers can develop a set of unconventional points of view and thus reach out to what Kenneth Burke has called "perspective by incongruity." Major forms of creativity, according to Gouldner, involve a kind of intellectual deviance in so far as they imply a breaking away from customary ways of perceiving things.

What appears crucial in Gouldner's theory of creativity is the fact that it does not depend on qualities that are internal to creative persons, "but rather upon their critical assimilation of and unusual relation to established intellectual traditions, upon their access to *multiple* traditions, as well as their capacity to *switch* or translate from one to another" (Gouldner 1985:205). Gouldner's stress on multiple perspectives makes his theory a sociological rather than a psychological study. Although he did not choose to avail himself of Merton's terminology, it seems fairly obvious that he is in debt to his former teacher. When Merton talks, admittedly only in brief allusions, of increases in autonomy that come through involvement with a multifaceted role-set and with a variety of role partners, and when Gouldner argues that intellectual productivity is enhanced by involvement with many perspectives and the ability to find one's way among a variety of points of orientation that have to be mastered, it seems evident that they share a common view about the theoretical significance of multiple cross pressures and of involvement with many role partners. But while Merton's structural theory focuses major attention on mechanisms that will decrease conflicts and contradictions, Gouldner sees in them a source of intellectual creativity.

Basil Bernstein, with whom I shall deal next, is a British social scientist who does not seem to have had much connection with Columbia-type theorizing but developed a set of theoretical ideas that influenced Gouldner to some extent and Rose Coser to a larger degree.

Basil Bernstein's Theory of Linguistic Codes

Although Gouldner alludes to it only in passing, his theory of the sources of creativity is closely akin to Basil Bernstein's (1974:124-137) distinction between restricted and elaborate linguistic codes. According to Bernstein, meanings in restricted linguistic codes are likely to be concrete, descriptive or narrative. The lexicon of such restricted codes is drawn from a narrow range. Such linguistic codes are not necessarily linked to class positions, but typically the working class uses restricted and rather simple linguistic codes whereas the educated middle class favors abstract notions and elaborate codes. Bernstein also uses Parsonian nomenclature by calling his restricted and elaborate codes particularistic and universalistic respectively.

Restricted codes can be found above all in relatively small communities where members know one another; they are closely bound to specific sets of relationships between known speech partners. Elaborate codes, on the other hand, know no such restricted conditions, they are context free rather than bound to context. Elaborate codes emerge in circumstances where the speaker has enough flexibility to come to terms with different notions and had developed the capacity to address many role partners with the help of a repertory of relatively abstract ideas. Bernstein's theories are sociological rather than psychological. They are based on types of social relationships rather than on inner dispositions. To Gouldner, persons may be able to be creative if and when they acquire the ability to play a variety of roles and hence use a variety of perspectives. Bernstein argues that analytical thought must be free from traditional fetters that would limit it to the univocal perspective of specific small groups. Restricted codes, according to Bernstein, make for routine types of thought; elaborate codes and the capacity to think abstractly arise when persons are involved with a large number of people with whom they can only communicate by employing a number of multifaceted perspectives.

Rose L. Coser's Theory of Individual Autonomy

Rose L. Coser elaborates a theory of intellectual creativity and personal autonomy that utilizes not only the prior work of Merton and Bernstein, but also a number of other theorists from Piaget to Parsons and Melvin Kohn. She was a student of Merton and she has often indicated the great intellectual debt she owes to him. In particular, her frequent utilization and elaboration of Merton's theory of role-sets speaks to her intellectual line of descent.

Her 1975 article, "The Complexity of Roles as a Seedbed of Individual Autonomy", can be seen as the culminating point of a tradition that goes from Merton to Gouldner and Bernstein. It is obviously indebted to Merton but it has also close relation with Bernstein's work which is quoted frequently. It also has strong affinities with Gouldner's train of thought even though Gouldner's contributions were only published some ten years after Rose Coser's work, and Gouldner failed to quote her.

Merton's orientation to the complexities of the role-set has a somewhat defensive cast. Don't worry, he seems to be saying, the modern world is a tough and often frightening place but you can live in it if you can learn to play the game. There is no trace of such defensiveness in Rose L. Coser's contribution. She endorses the modern world whole-heartedly, and claims that individual autonomy, a quality that is highly praised in the world of moderns, is attainable only when conflicting expectations, segmented roles, clashing norms and complex role-sets exist with which the individual must come to terms. *Gemeinschaft*, so she argues, stultifies the chances of attaining autonomy by forcing all its members into common molds. "The multiplicity of expectations faced by the modern individual, she argues," incompatible and contradictory as they may be, or rather precisely because they are, makes role articulation possible in a more self-conscious manner than if there were no such multiplicity (R.L. Coser 1975:239). There is none of Merton's defensiveness in her praise of complexity, and there is also nothing of Gouldner's somewhat elitist view which has often a flavor of individualistic romanticism. It is a tough world, this determined feminist seems to be saying, but if you make use of what the structure has to offer, you can be comfortable in it. She concludes her line of thought by stating that the mechanisms that Merton has specified as helping individuals who articulate their roles in the face of multiple contradictions, serve as a spur for individualism and free choice. To Rose Coser, the contradictory messages and norms of various role partners are not a disaster but an opportunity.

Merton was mainly intent on showing that conflict and contradictions between several role partners would not necessarily have dysfunctional structural consequences. He elaborated a set of mechanisms that might serve to minimize conflict between persons and their different role partners. His main emphasis is on the structural presence of the mechanisms that may or may not operate perfectly for minimizing conflicts of expectations for individuals.

Rose L. Coser, while recognizing the importance of the mechanisms that Merton had enumerated, put her main emphasis on the freedom of choice that such mechanisms allow for the status-holder, and the ensuing increase in autonomy, even at the price of some possible social disorder. Her theory is as structural in its orientation as is Merton's, but it is largely focused on the individual status occupants and the conditions under which they can maximize their fullest potential.

Coser introduces an important distinction for role-set theory, namely that between complex and simple role sets. The fact that modern individuals, she argues, are likely to deal with a relatively large number of relationships, and that their role-partners are likely to differ considerably not only among themselves but also as to their expectations of the attitudes and behavior of the status holder, is a mark of modernity. The role-set of a person in the pre-modern world was relatively simple, but it is now complex. Complexity of role-sets, she says, has now become a common condition whereas it was limited to high-status persons in the pre-modern world. Or, to use Hegelian language, only a few people were free to choose their destiny in the pre-modern past, whereas in the modern world this is a condition open to many, if not to most.

The modern individual has choices as to his or her life path that didn't exist for ordinary persons under pre-modern conditions. The flexibility of orientations open to individuals, the variety of options available to them, create the conditions for individualism, creativity, and the capacity to deal with a variety of role partners. Abstract thinking, she argues, is possible only in complex role-sets where the individual must develop the capacity to deal with a variety of role partners who, so to speak, use different languages. It must be noted, however, that various chances for role articulation are not evenly distributed. The availability of complex role-sets does not exist at all levels of the social ladder to an equal degree. The mechanisms for role articulation are more readily available to people of relatively high rather than of low status (R.L. Coser 1975:244).

Coser argues that one who is faced with a complex role-set is in a position to gain perspective on the various attitudes of the diverse role partners by putting herself in the position of each of them as they relate to one another. "One must keep in mind that they are different from oneself and that this difference imposes some adjustment in one's own stance. It is, therefore, the more individualistic rather than the less individualistic person who can adapt to the expectations of others" (R.L. Coser 1975:257). "Complex role-sets and differentiated roles" she says "are not alienating restrictions on individuality; they are its basic structural precondition" (R.L. Coser 1975:259).

Rose L. Coser argues, and here she thinks along lines that have a good deal of affinity with what Gouldner argued later, that abstract thinking can only develop when a status-holder has the chance to deal with a complex role-set and is forced to develop the capacity to interact with a variety of role partners and to adjust to many expectations. In dyadic relations, or in narrow *Gemeinschaft* type of relations, single codes will suffice in the relation with relatively few partners, but in complex societies the concreteness of categorization of thought will have to give way to the flexible and abstract modes of discourse that can only develop in complex role-sets. Where Gouldner talks about the creative achievement of people who are provided with a multiplicity of points of anchorage, she is more specific in focusing on a particular type of intellectual achievement, the ability to think in abstract categories. Where Bernstein talks of elaborate and restricted codes, Coser analyses the structural conditions in which these codes are anchored.

Rose Coser is not arguing that people who live and work within the confinement of restricted role-sets have an easier and more satisfying life. She has written a good deal on the modern conceit and the modern nostalgia of types of *Gemeinschaft* relationships whether it is found in Toennies' work or in that of modern cultural critics who, being alienated in the world of modernity, dream Rousseauistic dreams of the beauty of communities of noble savages (R.L. Coser 1984:221-239). It is the case that people who live in societies where simple role-sets predominate may have stronger ties with their fellows, but they pay for this by using categories of thought that stay within narrow confines and fail to provide an opportunity to deal with situations that are not programmed and univocal. In simple role-sets, expectations can be more easily met and conformity more unequivocally assured, yet it is well neigh impossible for people in such circumstances to find their bearings under novel conditions. Simple role-sets suffice in a relatively static world, they do not suffice in the modern world of flux and change.

There is still another dimension to role-set theory that Coser touches upon without elaborating it in detail. Complex role-sets, by allowing the individual mental access to a variety of perspectives with a variety of role partners, also enhance the chances for the emergence of tolerance. If individuals find themselves dealing routinely with a variety of role-partners and a multiplicity of perspectives, it stands to reason that they will treat others with a measure of tolerance that is rarely to be found among people who remain wedded to limited perspectives and relatively few role partners. To the extent that persons deal with a variety of role-partners and a variety of status holders, they will be more open-minded and tolerant than persons with small role-sets and restricted perspectives. The chances for the emergence of a flexible and democratic society are considerably enhanced, though not assured, in modern democratic societies when complex relations to significant others predominate.

Rose L. Coser goes beyond Merton's pioneering work on role-set theory by stressing two intertwined notions: (1) that persons who are implicated in complex social relationships have the chance to attain more autonomy than others, and (2) that persons who are implicated in complex social relations have more chances to use more complex cognitive, ie., abstract, views of the world. This is not to deny, however, that complexity is also beset by problems of its own. Recent work on stress highlights, for example, that under some circumstances complex role-sets may lead to overloads and anxiety. Any social scientist will be ready to cite examples, but a female social scientist is likely to be aware of this even more than her male colleagues. But this is a topic of the sociology of gender which, I am sure, will be dealt with in other contributions to this volume.

References

Bernstein, Basil. 1974. *Class, Codes, and Controls, Theoretical Studies Towards a Sociology of Learning.* New York: Schocken Books.

Coser, Rose Laub. 1975. "The Complexity of Roles as a Seedbed of Individual Autonomy." In *The Idea of Social Structure: Papers in Honor of Robert K. Merton,* edited by Lewis A. Coser. New York: Harcourt Brace.

_____. 1984. "The Greedy Nature of *Gemeinschaft.*" In *Conflict and Consensus: A Festschrift in Honor of Lewis A. Coser,* edited by Walter W. Powell and Richard Robbins. New York: The Free Press.

Gouldner, Alvin W. 1985. *Against Fragmentation: The Origins of Marxism and the Sociology of Intellectuals.* New York: Oxford University Press.

Merton, Robert K. 1968. *Social Theory and Social Structure.* Enlarged Edition. New York: The Free Press.

3

Just a Housewife: Role-Image and the Stigma of the Single Role

Gladys Rothbell

> All the world's a stage
> And all the men and women merely players.
> They have their exits and their entrances.
> And one man in his time plays many parts, ...[1]

In the last three decades, American women have entered the labor force in dramatically larger numbers than during the decades between the two world wars. In particular, increasing numbers of mothers of young children have begun taking jobs outside the home. This transition in the structure of daily family life quickly became the subject of a vast popular and social-scientific literature that debated its implications for the welfare of children, for the lives of mothers and for the future of the American family.

While the debate was partially focused on the problem of the "latch-key" child, the impact of this change on mothers also became a central concern. This issue was most frequently discussed in terms of the problems created by the new duality of roles of mother and worker. The sociological concepts of role conflict (Merton 1967, p. 422ff.) and role strain (Goode 1960) provided the theoretical foundation for numerous theoretical and empirical investigations in the ensuing decades. Social scientists assessed the nature of multiple roles in terms of the problem of contradictory expectations and the stresses associated with coordinating conflicting demands of family and work roles (Akabas 1988; Arber, Gilbert and Dale 1985; Barrett 1976; Coverman 1989; Kandel, Davies and Raveis 1985; McEntee and Rankin 1983; Moore and Sawhill 1976; Statham 1986).[2]

The author wishes to thank Laura Anker, Kathy Dahlman, Norman Goodman, Dino Lorenzini, Madeline Morris, and Sheldon Rothbell for their suggestions and assistance.

But while the literature focused primarily on the *problems* associated with these changes (and the mechanisms for ameliorating them), Rose Coser perceived a silver lining in the clouds. In numerous articles, books, and lectures, she provided new insights into the positive functions of multiple roles and she demonstrated the various contexts in which multiple roles provide opportunities and advantages. Moreover, Coser illustrated the precise mechanisms by which multiple roles present opportunities for intellectual development, role articulation, increased autonomy, heightened self-image, greater creativity, enhanced prestige, access to new resources (such as "weak ties") and protection from the demands of greedy institutions (Coser 1981, 1975a, 1975b, 1964, 1961, 1956).

In these articles, Rose Coser crystallized the concept of the inherent potential benefits of multiple roles, including the possibilities for symbiotic inter-relationships between roles. She described, for example, how people in the occupational role of entrepreneur may acquire interpersonal skills which enhance their enactment of family roles, or may establish contacts which become resources for a different status. For example, in the case of the working mother this might mean that a relationship cultivated at work becomes a resource for addressing her child's problem at home. Conversely, personal experiences as a mother may inspire or illustrate sociological theories, as in the case of Rose Coser (Coser and Rokoff 1974, p. 496).

Rose Coser's analysis of the advantages of multiple roles, which I will refer to as a theory of "role-complementarity," does not contradict theories of role conflict and role strain. Rather, it refines the equation for calculating the costs of multiple roles by including a more sophisticated assessment of their rewards. As she has noted, "The many contradictions of modern life that have been analyzed in Merton's masterful writings are not a disaster, they are an opportunity" (Coser 1975, p. 259).[3]

Creating Role-Images

It is my thesis that Rose Coser's theory of the advantages of multiple roles — or role complementarity — is applicable not only to the enactment of roles in real life but also to the world of *role-images*, where individual or media produced "personalities" and group role-images are *created*. I use the term "role-image" to refer to the image that people have of the roles performed by another person or group.

Role-images are often distortions of reality because they are highly vulnerable to manipulation. Individuals or groups manipulating their own role-images are likely to utilize image enhancing devices, while those manipulating the role-images of others may sometimes resort to image diminishing mechanisms.

In either case, while the quality of attributed roles remains an important factor, it is the *quantity* of attributed roles which is often critical in determining the attractiveness of a role-image. Role-image complexity, like actual role complexity, has status enhancing potential. That is, images of groups or individuals can be enhanced or diminished by the quantity of attributed roles. If we exclude from consideration those roles or statuses which are inherently offensive or deprivational (such as prisoner or mental hospital inmate), an increase in the number of attributed roles is likely to be image enhancing. Conversely, reductions in the number of attributed roles are likely to be image diminishing. Finally, reduction to a single attributed role is likely to result in a stigmatized image.[4]

Individual Role-Images of Men: "A Family Man"

In an era of media created role-images, there is abundant evidence of deliberate manipulation to create role-images comprised of multiple roles. Candidates for political office are deliberately presented in roles outside the political realm. Their spouses and children make campaign appearances, thereby creating public awareness of the candidates in their roles as parents and spouses. Increasingly, candidates also recruit their mothers for this purpose, thereby providing public images of themselves in the role of son. Each of these stratagems attempts to capitalize on the positive image of the "family man."

Male politicians also appear as horseback riders, joggers, fishermen, golfers and regular church attenders. In addition, we are sometimes offered glimpses of old photographs in which they appear dressed in military uniform, to remind us of their earlier roles. A politician might even appear with a pet dog on national television, as in Nixon's famous "Checkers" speech. Surely a man who loves his dog, wife, children and mother, goes to church, serves in the military, and participates in sports, can't be all bad!

The greater the number of attributed roles, the greater the likelihood of identification by others through shared experience. Moreover, the image of an individual successfully enacting numerous roles supports an impression of competency and of a well balanced personality.[5]

In the constellation of roles that makes up the role-image, the absence of certain roles can cast a dark shadow on an otherwise attractive image. The nomination of David Souter for Supreme Court justice provided a good case in point. At the announcement of his nomination, *The New York Times* ran a lengthy biographical article. While the account was largely laudatory, it included the following comment:

> If there are any qualms at all about Judge Souter, it is a quiet concern over his circumscribed way of life. As a young man he was briefly engaged to the daughter of a State Superior Court justice, but he never married, and even his admirers wonder whether his solitary style has limited his empathy or human understanding. (Margolick 1990).

Individual role-images can be damaged by an impression of insufficient roles — of a "circumscribed way of life." Despite his otherwise excellent qualifications, Souter aroused distrust because of an absence of roles that represent close human relationships. In interactions with strangers, we often seek the reassuring qualities presumed to be encompassed in the role of "a family man" (Coser 1975b, p. 472).

Group Role-Images of Men: "A Cheap Jew"

Groups as well as individuals have role-images that are affected by the expansion or contraction of attributed roles. The role-image of the Jew in fiction and in ideological tracts provides a dramatic example of the manipulation of role-images to enhance or diminish group status. Historically, reductions in attributed roles have been used as a dehumanizing device. Many of the unattractive depictions of the Jew have portrayed a man devoid of roles other than that of money-hungry economic parasite. In Dickens' Oliver Twist, for example, Fagan, the Jew, has no family ties (neither family of origin nor family of procreation) and no roles beyond that of master thief. He is ahistorical, acultural, apolitical, and asexual, as well as being devoid of family roles. He is only a parasite.[6]

More radically dehumanized depictions of the Jew appear in illustrations in various editions of the *Protocols of the Elders of Zion*. These portray the Jew as tarantula, snake, and vulture. Such dehumanizing depictions eliminate all possibilities for the enactment of human roles. They allow only the role of predator, thus precluding the possibility of the Jew as a "family man."

A more recent controversial portrayal of the Jew in film provides another example of the way in which attributing multiple roles, or the failure to do so, results in role-images that are readily recognized as attractive or unattractive. Spike Lee's recent film *Mo' Better Blues* (Lee 1990b) caused a flurry of criticism for its depiction of Jewish characters in a manner considered to be "stereotypically anti-Semitic" (Ansen 1990; James 1990; Koch 1990; Markey 1990; Schappes 1990). *The New York Times* Op Ed page carried Mr. Lee's impassioned defense (Lee 1990a). The controversy centered on the issue of group role-image.

The writer-producer-director of the film, Spike Lee, is a talented, courageous black man. Most of the characters in the film are also black, with the exception of a Puerto Rican and two Jews. There is an unwritten rule of the media which invokes a higher level of critical scrutiny for characters representing a group to which the writer does not belong. Generally such characters are scrutinized with respect to the *quality* of the roles attributed to them. What is far less obvious is the need for sensitivity to the *quantity* of attributed roles. It is primarily through the portrayal of multiple roles that his black characters emerge as attractive human beings.

The major black character, Bleek, is portrayed as a child practicing music in his parents' home, as a grown man living on his own and playing ball in the street with his dad, in his own home as a married man playing with his infant son and later his older son, performing with the members of his band, in bed making love, in the park bicycling with a friend and in the hospital recuperating from an accident.

Most importantly, we see Bleek attempting to juggle the contradictory and conflicting demands of his multiple roles; and in the process we discover his values and priorities, just as he does. We see him refusing to see his girlfriend during the times he has set aside to practice music. We see him in his role as band leader when he fires his friend, Giant, upon learning that he is gambling again. We also see him in his role as friend as he pays off Giant's debt and gets him into treatment for gambling. This process of role articulation not only provides the anchor for Bleek's potentially chaotic life, but also provides the basis for the formation of his own self-image. Without multiple roles, Bleek would have no need for role articulation, fewer pressures to crystallize values and priorities, and less opportunity to form a strong self-image (Coser 1975a).

As the roles coalesce and the character grapples with conflicting demands of multiple roles, a fully drawn human being begins to take shape. We come to respect his strengths, forgive his weaknesses and empathize with his struggles.

Unfortunately, the Jewish characters, Moe and Josh Flatbush, do not benefit from a similar process. They are the owners of the nightclub in which Bleek's band performs. They are never portrayed outside of the nightclub and they never say or do anything unrelated to making money. When they refuse to increase the salaries for the band and rigidly insist on holding Bleek to his contract, they ghoulishly re-enact Shylock demanding his pound of flesh. Critics are therefore correct in perceiving Moe and Josh Flatbush as anti-Semitic stereotypes. What makes them so blatantly stereotypic is the unidimensional portrayal which relegates them to a single role — that of the cheap Jew. Spike Lee is not unique in creating stereotypic Jewish characters through unidimensional portrayals. Some Jewish film-makers, such as Woody Allen, have created stereotypic images of Jewish women by employing the same technique of relegating the character to a single role, which is then enacted in a distasteful manner (Rothbell 1989).

Individual Role-Images of Women: "Just a Housewife"

As Rose Coser has noted, we cannot enhance a woman's prestige by calling her a "family woman" (Coser 1975b, p. 472). The phrase itself sounds strange. A woman's commitment to her family is assumed and it is therefore not image enhancing, as it is for the "family man." Although there is still societal ambivalence regarding a woman's appropriate roles, it is generally true that since family commitments are assumed, female images are only enhanced by the addition of *non-family* roles.

In professional contexts, men often highlight their family roles while women try to downplay them. It is not uncommon, therefore, to hear a male colleague proudly announce that he cannot stay on for a meeting because he has to "babysit" or cook dinner. The announcement is likely to be greeted with approval, connoting recognition of the new pro-feminist male. However, should his female colleague make a similar announcement, there is more likely to be some uneasiness or silent misgivings regarding the extent of her "professional commitment."

The predominance of the family role in the role-image of women has different implications from the predominance of the work role in the role-image of men. For women it means an image characterized by primary relationships, while for men it means an image in which there are primarily secondary or instrumental relationships.

This difference is significant because, as Rose Coser has suggested, "the nature of relationships affects the thinking process" (Coser 1984, p. 231). This can happen in a number of ways. For example, the family as a greedy institution tends to restrict the mother's role-set,[7] thus depriving her of the opportunity to resolve contradictory role demands through reflection and role articulation. A predominance of primary relationships can also restrict the thinking process in other respects. By isolating individuals from more universalistic secondary relationships, it eliminates the necessity for mastering a universalistic vocabulary appropriate for the manipulation of universalistic events and relationships. As Rose Coser notes:

> In restricted role-sets the partners are satisfied with a restricted vocabulary. This is so because close relationships do not require much verbal elaboration. We all have experienced those gratifying moments when words are not needed, or when one word suffices to convey a world of meanings. . . . But meanings that don't need to be spelled out do not become clarified even for the participants, let alone communicated to outsiders, i.e., to those who do not share the close relationship. . . . Hence the nature of the relationship affects the thinking process. If only a word or two is needed to convey "a world of meanings," not only does the language become impoverished, the meanings do not become conceptualized and cannot be used as readily to influence others or to help modify the behavior of others, as interactions or conversations are supposed to do (Coser 1984, p. 230-231).

On the other hand, universalistic relationships, which we assume to be predominant for men, require the ability to communicate effectively in complex role-sets where it cannot be assumed that others share our meanings. This necessitates assessing the audience and tailoring one's speech accordingly.

This calls for abstract thinking. Indeed it is generally the case that "abstract thinking develops where universalistic relationships are salient" (Coser 1984, p. 233). Where particularistic relationships predominate, there are not the same demands for the development of intellectual flexibility. In sum:

> When social relationships are complex, that is, where we have different things in common with people occupying different positions, we can develop complex mental abilities. This is to say that the ability to think conceptually is in large part an attribute of the social structure. (Coser 1984, p. 233).

In some sense we intuitively knew this all along. That is why, as Rose Coser notes, we use words such as "parochial" and "cosmopolitan" to denote modes of thought that are related to group attributes. "Parochial" implies a limited perspective due to membership in a closely meshed group, such as a parish. On the other hand, "cosmopolitan" thinking implies a broad perspective that draws on many sources stemming from multiple relationships in complex role-sets.

Since women are assumed to have predominantly primary relationships, it follows that they will be perceived to be more parochial in their thinking, hence less able to engage in conceptualization and abstract thought. The stigmatization of the housewife role may be due in part to the predominance of primary relationships and the consequent intuitive attribution of parochial thinking.

It is for this reason that women running for political office tend to avoid publicizing domestic roles — a practice highly favored in the campaigns of male politicians. It is probably also for this reason that a certain sociology graduate director rejected the idea of part-time students "because we would be inundated by housewives." Like men, women who wish to enhance their role-images seek to portray multiple roles. However, unlike men, it is the roles involving secondary relationships that women are likely to publicize.

Indeed, a most effective way to denigrate women, whether as individuals or as a group, is to portray them in a single role, with a role-set limited to primary relationships. Precisely the opposite strategy, limiting the role set to secondary relationships, is likely to be most damaging when directed at men. While the number of roles would be reduced in both cases, the predominance of primary or secondary role-set members would vary by gender.

The negative group stereotypes of Jewish men and women provide a good case in point. While the mechanism of role reduction is utilized as a dehumanizing device in both cases, the role-image of the Jewish men is reduced to pecuniary pursuits based on the most universalistic medium of exchange — money. In the case of the Jewish women, the role-reduction is reversed. Their role-image is reduced to exclusively domestic pursuits and the highly particularistic relationships of the nuclear family.

Group Role-Images of Women: "A Jewish Mother"

A review of the declining role-image of the Jewish mother in twentieth century America vividly illustrates the negative effect of role reduction on group role-image (Rothbell 1989). Such a review also reveals the power of the *combination* of role reduction with the attribution of predominantly particularistic relationships in producing a *female* stereotypic group role-image. Finally, and not surprisingly, it reveals that members of such groups are likely to be characterized as having impaired ability to conceptualize and think abstractly.

In the early part of this century, characterizations of Jewish mothers portrayed them in a multiplicity of roles. Despite the fact that a maternal instinct was attributed to those mothers, they were also viewed as quite capable of enacting non-maternal social roles. Indeed, the belief that good mothering was natural may have diminished interest in their maternal behavior and highlighted their other roles.

By way of example, in the works of such authors as Fannie Hurst, Edna Ferber and Hutchins Hapgood, Jewish mothers appeared as Orthodox Jews, as citizens, as champions of social justice, as Socialists, Zionists, Anarchists, sweatshop workers, entrepreneurs, music lovers, union organizers, daughters, wives, lovers and idealistic, compassionate human beings. They were also, simultaneously, revered mothers. In these early portrayals, the women's experiences as mothers sometimes served to strengthen their resolve to work for political change to create a better world for all children.

The second half of the twentieth century saw a reversal of the earlier image of Jewish women with multiple roles and identities. The new stereotypical Jewish mother lost her political, religious, sexual, cultural and occupational roles, and became a parasitic, ignorant, materialistic mother whose sole occupation and pre-occupation was an obsessive smothering mothering. The stereotypic Jewish mother role became a totally defining deviant master status. That is, in the same way that stereotypic role-images of prostitutes and homosexuals limit perceptions of them to images of their sexual roles, so too the new stereotypic role-image of Jewish mothers limited perceptions of them to images of their mothering role (Rothbell 1989).

In this negative re-casting of the role-image of the Jewish mother, humor was employed as a subtle, but effective, weapon (Coser 1960, 1959). It was used in popular fiction and film, as well as in the Jewish mother joke which emerged as a new comic genre (Rothbell 1986).

Many of the Jewish mother jokes portray a woman whose total involvement with her sole role as mother leaves her ignorant of the world outside her kitchen. For example, Dan Greenberg's best selling *How To Be A Jewish Mother* (1964) provides a "Guide to Entertaining" which advises would-be Jewish mothers on "How to Discuss Current Events":

> Aside from a meeting of the Cousins Club, when it is perfectly proper to limit discussion to those members of the family that could not attend the meeting, you will probably be expected to discuss Current Events, particularly when men are present. Men do not consider the prevailing price of rib roast or the progress of your niece Edith's pregnancy to be Current Events. Therefore, *learn to speak their language* (Greenberg, 1964:32; emphasis added).

It is fascinating that the author warns his would-be Jewish mothers that men speak a different language. He echoes Rose Coser's observation that discussions of universalistic events require a universalistic vocabulary. The joke becomes the juxtaposition of the universalistic topics with the parochial responses. Greenberg continues:

> .... Memorize the following list of subjects and approved reactions and you will be well on your way to a reputation as a Well-Informed Hostess. ... THE COMMON MARKET: I go mainly to the A&P. ... MERRILL, LYNCH, PIERCE, FENNER & SMITH: Nice boys.Mike Douglas had them on last week. ... (Greenberg, 1964:30).

This humor exploits the idea that the Jewish mother cannot think abstractly. A market can only be her own local supermarket. In a similar vein, there is the Jewish mother's views on Red China:

Son: "What do you think of Red China?"

Jewish mother: "To tell you the truth, I really don't care for it on a pink tablecloth."

In addition to her inability to think abstractly, the Jewish mother is also handicapped by her inability to function in a complex role-set by taking into account the knowledge and interests of others:

Mama: "How much it costs to send a telegram?"

Clerk: "Where to Madam?"

Mama: "To my son the medical student."

These jokes limit the Jewish mother to domestic roles enacted within a constricted role-set. This already sparse role-image is still further restricted through portrayals of asexuality:

The young psychiatrist has been studying Mrs. Margolis's case for some time, and has finally arrived at a strange conclusion:" I don't want to seem rude, Mrs. Margolis," he begins, "particularly since I know that you have nine children and fifteen grandchildren. But -- well, do you mind if I ask you an intimate question?" "Esk!" "Tell me frankly, just what is your attitude towards sex?" "I love it", beamed Mrs. Margolis. "It's the finest store on Fift Evnoo."

Another joke in a book of "Jewish humor" (Spalding 1969, p. 166) implies that this ignorant asexual Jewish mother is also, in some strange sense, not very Jewish:

"What do I think of the Second World War?" asked Mama. "To tell you the truth, I saw it in the movies and I didn't like it."

In addition to displaying the ignorance of the Jewish mother, this joke also divorces her from any connection to the Second World War as it affected Jews specifically. In effect, it robs her of her ethnic identity and consequently of her group role-history.

These portrayals of Jewish mothers clearly project an unflattering group role-image. However, since they are produced almost entirely by Jewish men (Rothbell 1989), they have not been perceived as anti-Semitic. Instead, they have passed as self-deprecating humor.

Creators of *group* role-images are granted broader latitude in the role-images they create for members of their own group than they would be granted for images of other groups. But the definition of what legitimately constitutes "one's own group" is frequently unclear. While the most vocal critics of Spike Lee's *Mo'Better Blues* accused him of creating negative stereotypic images of Jews, the film was also criticized for its sexist depiction of black women (Nagle 1990). This raises questions about the appropriate criteria for viewing image creators as members of a group. Is common ethnicity sufficient, or is common gender also necessary for image creators who claim the latitude granted to self-portrayals?

Similarly, many Jewish women have been offended by the popular portrayals of Jewish women created by Jewish men. Beginning in the 1970's, some Jewish feminists set out to create their own counter-images of Jewish women. In this war of role-images, one of the most striking aspects of the new images created by Jewish women was the reintroduction of a multitude of non-mothering roles, restoring many of the former role-images of Jewish mothers, as well as adding images of Jewish mothers in new roles ranging from doctor or lawyer to astronaut, cantor and rabbi. Along with the increase in the number and the range of the roles, came an increase in the status and dignity of the images (Rothbell 1989).

Art Reinvents Life

Rose Coser's work has provided invaluable insights into the implications of multiple roles and complex role-sets. She has drawn attention to the resulting benefits of multiple roles such as enhancement of self-image and prestige, improvement of role articulation and abstract thought, acquisition of acquaintances offering the rewards of "weak ties," increased autonomy and heightened creativity.

Her insights into the social dynamics of complex roles not only shed light on actual role enactment patterns, but also illuminate the world of role-images, where *impressions* of individual and group roles are created. In both cases, multiple roles and complex role-sets create characters who are more attractive than those limited to single roles and simple role-sets. Art reinvents life.

Gender makes a difference in the application of these principles. Male images are most frequently enhanced by emphasizing family roles, while the reverse is generally true for female images. In both cases, the attractive role-image is one that includes multiple roles and complex role-sets, encompassing both primary and secondary relationships.

An understanding of the implications of multiple roles has become increasingly important as complex roles have become more prevalent in contemporary industrialized societies. Multiple roles and complex role-sets have become more pervasive as a result of the growing separation of home from work and the increasing entry of women into the workplace. These social structural changes have meant the "beginning of the end of *Gemeinschaft* society" (Coser 1985 p. 2), where people lived and died and allegedly knew almost everything about their neighbors.

In place of the *Gemeinschaft* there is increased insulation from observability (Coser 1961), providing more privacy, hence more opportunity for inventiveness in the creation of role-images. Indeed, "image management" has become something of a popular sport.

Donald Trump takes great pride in his image management skills. In his new book, *Surviving At The Top* (1990 p. 59), he describes his respect for his wife's skill in "portraying herself as the woman scorned and easily winning the public's sympathy." While he does not begrudge her the public sympathy, he wants credit as her mentor in public opinion manipulation. He boasts: "Considering the example I'd set for her in what you might call image management, I would have been deeply disappointed in her if she had done anything else."

An understanding of the social dynamics of role-complexity illuminates the processes of role reduction and enlargement, both real and imagined. With respect to role-images, role reduction can be utilized in the service of deceit and propaganda, exploiting the serious stigmatizing potential of the attribution of a single role. To the extent that the fictions employed in role-images are perceived to be real, as W.I. Thomas observed, they will be real in their consequences.

Similarly, with respect to actual roles, role reduction is seldom a welcome event. It is frequently involuntary and traumatic. Refugees who experience sudden loss of roles and role-sets often suffer severe depression (Brown 1982). Role reduction can also be deliberately employed as a subtle mechanism for establishing control over others. In the Jonestown community, for example, the deliberate role restriction of members may have been critical to the success of the mass suicide plan of Jim Jones. As Rose and Lewis Coser (1979) argue, the restriction of members' roles to a single role relationship — with Jim Jones — diminished the likelihood that members might communicate their doubts to one another and possibly plan to resist.

On the other hand, role *enlargements* are generally celebratory events for individuals as well as groups. The appearance of the first female astronaut was a cause for general celebration among women. She not only enhanced her own role-image but that of women as a group. The same was true for the first female rabbi, cantor, mayor, governor, Episcopal minister and bishop. In like manner, the first *Festschrift* honoring a female sociologist is also an occasion for celebration. It is particularly fitting that the honoree is Rose Laub Coser. She not only served as an early advocate of expanded roles for women, but also as a magnificent living exemplification of that vision.

Notes

1. In this quote from *As You Like It*, Shakespeare was referring to roles played sequentially in different life stages. As will be noted later, stereotypic characterizations not only reduce a character to a single current role, but also exclude that character's role history.
2. There is some variety in the ways in which sociologists use and define the term "role" (Biddle, 1986). My own use of the term here refers to social positions or statuses which people hold, and the related characteristic behavior patterns and assumed identities. The term "role-conflict" is used here to refer to the concurrent appearance of two or more incompatible expectations for the behavior of a person. These incompatible expectations may emerge from within the role-set of a single status, or from incompatible demands of multiple statuses.
3. Sieber (1974) provides strong supporting arguments for the advantages of multiple roles. He too questions the predominant focus on negative consequences of multiple roles, and suggests that multiple role involvements can result in enhanced physical and psychological well-being and enriched personality as a result of increased privileges, resources, rewards, ego gratifications, status enhancement and buffers against role loss.

Subsequent empirical testing of the effects of multiple roles suggest positive outcomes of increased psychological well-being (e.g., Pietromonaco et al. 1986; Vergrugge 1983; Thoits 1983, Spreitzer et al. 1979) as well as a need for a more refined specification of the conditions under which desirable outcomes are likely to occur (Arber 1985; Wilsnack and Cheloha 1987; Thoits 1983; 1986; Marks 1977).
4. Even negative former roles such as prisoner or drug addict sometimes enhance a role-image due to the personal strength displayed in overcoming the problem.

5. There is some indirect evidence suggesting that those with few social roles may indeed be at greater risk of psychological disturbance (Thoits 1983).

6. In many characterizations, the Jew has no parents, siblings, wife, sons or grandchildren in his family role-set. He has only his daughter. The Jew's daughter, like his money, represents a precious asset which he hoards and which the Gentiles will seek to acquire. This occurs in Marlowe's *The Jew of Malta* (1590) which involves Barrabas and his daughter Abigail, Shakespeare's *The Merchant of Venice* (1596) which involves Shylock and his daughter Jessica and Scott's *Ivanhoe* (1819) which involves Rebecca and her father, Isaac of York. For further discussion see Rothbell (1989, p. 944).

7. Traditional views of the mother role have imbued it with obligations which are without time boundaries, leaving no legitimate times for non-mothering roles. Fathers, on the other hand, have only been expected to perform the father role when not otherwise occupied with work and other obligations. Hence the old folk maxim, "A man works from sun to sun, but a woman's work is never done."

References

Akabas, Sheila H. 1988. "Role Overload, Role Conflict, and Stress: Addressing Consequences of Multiple Role Demands." *The Journal of Primary Prevention* (Fall-Winter): 130-140.

Ansen, David. 1990. "Spike Lee Almost Blows It." *Newsweek* (August 6):62.

Arber, Sara, G. Nigel Gilbert and Angela Dale. 1985. "Paid Employment and Women's Health: A Benefit or a Source of Role Strain?" *Sociology of Health and Illness* 7: 375-400.

Barrett, Nancy Smith. 1976. "The Economy Ahead of Us — Will Women Have Different Roles?" Pp. 155-172 in *Women and The American Economy*, edited by J.M. Kreps. Englewood Cliffs, N.J.: Prentice Hall, Inc.

Biddle, B.J. 1986. "Recent Developments in Role Theory." *Annual Review of Sociology* 12:67-92.

Brown, Geoffrey. 1982. "Issues In the Resettlement of Indochinese Refugees." *Social Casework: The Journal of Contemporary Social Work*. Family Service Association of America.

Coser, Rose Laub. 1985. "Cognitive Structure and the Use of Social Space." Presidential Address, Eastern Sociological Society Meetings, March 15-17.

____. 1984. "The Greedy Nature of *Gemeinschaft*." Pp. 221-240 in *Conflict and Consensus*, edited by W.W. Powell and Richard Robbins. New York, The Free Press.

____. 1981. "On the Reproduction of Mothering: A Methodological Debate." *Signs: Journal of Women in Culture and Society* 6:487-492.

____. 1975a. "The Complexity of Roles as a Seedbed of Individual Autonomy." Pp. 237-263 in *The Idea of Social Structure: Essays in Honor of Robert K. Merton*, edited by Lewis A. Coser. New York: Harcourt Brace Jovanovich.

____. 1975b. "Stay Home Little Sheba: On Placement, Displacement, and Social Change." *Social Problems* 22:470-80.

____. 1964. "Authority and Structural Ambivalence in The Family." Pp. 370-83 in *The Family, Its Structure and Functions*, edited by Rose Laub Coser. New York: St. Martin's Press.

_____. 1964. "Authority and Structural Ambivalence in The Family." Pp. 370-83 in *The Family, Its Structure and Functions*, edited by Rose Laub Coser. New York: St. Martin's Press.

_____. 1961. "Insulation from Observability and Types of Social Conformity." *American Sociological Review* 26:28-39.

_____. 1960. "Laughter Among Colleagues: A Study of The Social Function of Humor Among the Staff of a Mental Hospital." *Psychiatry* 23:81-95.

_____. 1959. "Some Social Functions of Humor." *Human Relations* 22:171-82.

_____. 1956. "A Home Away From Home." *Social Problems* 4:3-17.

_____ and Lewis Coser. 1979. "Jonestown As Perverse Utopia." *Dissent* (Spring):158-63.

_____ and Gerald Rokoff. 1974. "Women in the Occupational World: Social Disruption and Conflict." Pp. 490-511 in *The Family, Its Structure and Functions*, edited by Rose Laub Coser. New York: St. Martin's Press.

Coverman, Shelley. 1989. "Role Overload, Role Conflict and Stress: Addressing Consequences of Multiple Role Demands." *Social Forces* 67:956-982.

Goode, William J. 1960. "A Theory of Role Strain." *American Sociological Review* 25:483-496.

Greenburg, Dan. 1964. *How To Be A Jewish Mother*. Los Angeles: Price, Stern, Sloan.

James, Caryn. 1990. "Spike Lee's Jews and the Passage From Benign Cliche Into Bigotry." *The New York Times* (August 16):C15 and C16.

Kandel, Denise B., Mark Davies, and Victoria H. Raveis. 1985. "The Stressfulness of Daily Social Roles for Women: Marital, Occupational and Household Roles." *Journal of Health and Social Behavior* 26:64-78.

Koch, Ed. 1990. "Spike Lee Does the Wrong Thing." *The New York Post* (August 10):2.

Lee, Spike. 1990a. "I Am Not An Anti-Semite." *The New York Times* (August 22):A25.

_____. 1990b. *Mo' Better Blues*. Universal City Studios, Inc. Film produced and directed by Spike Lee.

Markey, David. 1990. "Spike Lee Misreads The History of Film." In Letters to the Editor, *The New York Times* (September 5):A22.

Marks, Stephen R. 1977. "Multiple Roles and Role Strain: Some Notes on Human Energy, Time and Commitment." *American Sociological Review* 42:921-936.

McEntee, Margaret A., Elizabeth Anne DeSalvo Rankin. 1983. "Multiple Role Demands, Mind-Body Stress Disorders, and Illness Related Absenteeism among Business and Professional Women." *Issues in Health Care of Women*, 4:177-190.

Moore, Christin A., and Isabel V. Sawhill. 1976. "Implications of Women's Employment for Home and Family Life." Pp. 102-122 in *Women and the American Economy*, edited by J.M. Kreps. Englewood Cliffs, N.J.: Prentice Hall, Inc.

Margolick, David. 1990. "Ascetic At Home But Vigorous on Bench." *The New York Times* (July 25):A1 and A12.

Merton, Robert K. 1968 [1957, 1949]. *Social Theory and Social Structure*. New York: The Free Press.

Nagle, Robin. 1990. "What About The Sexism in Spike Lee's Movies?" In Letters to the Editor, *The New York Times*, (September 15):A22.

Rothbell, Gladys. 1989. *The Case Of The Jewish Mother: A Study In Stereotyping*. Ph.D. Dissertation. Department of Sociology, State University of New York at Stony Brook.

_____. 1986. "The Jewish Mother: Social Construction of A Popular Image." Pp. 118-128 in *The Jewish Family: Myths and Reality*, edited by S.M. Cohen and P.E. Hyman. New York: Holmes and Meier.

Schappes, Morris U. 1990. "The Flatbush Brothers." In Letters To the Editor, *The New York Times* (September 5):A22.

Sieber, Sam D. 1974. "Toward A Theory of Role Accumulation." *American Sociological Review* 39: 567-578.

Shakespeare, William. *As You Like It*, Act II, Scene 7, Line 139.

Spalding, Henry D. 1969. *Encyclopedia of Jewish Humor*. New York: Jonathan David Publishers.

Statham, Anne. 1986. "Family or Career First: How Professional Women Fare in Making the Choice." *Affilia — Journal of Women and Social Work*, 1:22-38.

Thoits, Peggy A. 1986. "Multiple Identities: Examining Gender and Marital Status Differences in Distress." *American Sociological Review* 51:259-272.

_____. 1983. "Multiple Identities and Psychological Well-Being: A Reformulation and Test of the Social Isolation Hypothesis." *American Sociological Review* 48:174-187.

Trump, Donald. 1990. *Surviving At The Top*. New York: Random House.

4

Multigroup Affiliations and Complex Role-Sets

Peter M. Blau

Many old and some not-so-old social theories contrast the impersonal social relations among a conglomerate of erstwhile strangers in the modern metropolis with the integrative lasting personal relations in traditional communities — *Gesellschaft* and *Gemeinschaft* or a similar dichotomy. But this is not how the urbane Georg Simmel views the complex relations in modern society, nor how the cosmopolitan Rose Laub Coser analyzes their significance. Simmel directs attention to the importance of multigroup affiliations and crosscutting social circles for enhancing freedom from group pressures and domination, and Coser dissects the beneficial consequences of complex role-sets for intellectual development.

The concept "role-set" is Merton's (1968) refinement of Linton's (1936) analytical distinction between a status, which refers to location in the social structure, and the distinct role and role expectations that are associated with each status and govern the social relations and behavior appropriate for persons occupying this status. Merton's new insight is that not one role but several different roles are associated with every status, circumscribing different role relations with others whose location in the social structure differs. For example, a teacher is expected to act differently to students, colleagues, and the principal. A role-set is the combination of roles and role relations of a single status. Merton analyzes the instability, mechanisms for articulation, and conflicts in the role-set.

Coser (1975) enriches the concept of role-set by tracing the implications of variations in role-sets for personality development and mental life. She points out (1975, p. 241) that Simmel already notes the beneficial consequences of role segmentation for individualism and freedom, in contrast to Marx's implicit condemnation of the segregation of roles as alienating. Complex role-sets are distinguished by her from restricted ones in terms of the range of associates in different social positions and recurrent changes in role partners. The conflicting demands and expectations from role partners differently located in the social structure pose challenges which foster flexibility by learning to understand the perspectives of a variety of others and adapting to them. Meeting these challenges stimulates reflection, tolerance, and autonomy. Thus, Coser considers mental development and intellectual growth to have their roots in the social structure — the structural variability in role-sets.

Sources of Complex Role-Sets

Although the very concept of complex role-set implies that it has structural origins, Coser concentrates her analysis on its consequences and not on the specific conditions that influence the complexity of role-sets. This is the issue I raise in this paper: specifically, I ask what structural conditions and how people's choices of associates affect role-set complexity.

The population composition of the places where people live and work constitute the opportunity structures that govern whom one is likely to meet and possibly include in one's role-set of associates. If there are no Eskimos in the suburb where you live or the office where you work, the chances that your role-set includes an Eskimo are slim (though not nil, because you may have met one on your travels). This suggests several plausible social situations that increase opportunities for having a diverse set of friends and associates. The chances of having such a complex role-set are superior for people living in a large metropolis; generally for those in urban than those in rural places; and for those working in large firms. What facilitates role relations with diverse associates in these cases is not so much size itself as conditions typically accompanying it. The division of labor tends to be more pronounced in urban than rural places and in larger than smaller firms, and heterogeneity in various respects is usually greater in larger than smaller populations, as exemplified by the great diversity in many dimensions of the people in a large metropolis.

However, not all social differences promote complex role-sets. Class differences generally do not, because they imply that people make invidious social distinctions among strata and discriminate in their role relations on the basis of these class distinctions. Indeed, any ethnic distinctions and ingroup preferences involves discrimination in establishing social relations that counteract the otherwise positive influence of a diverse population structure on complex role-sets. Residential segregation intensifies this inhibiting effect of class or group differences on role-set complexity. On the other hand, both social and spatial mobility promote complex role-sets. For mobility entails not only changes in many associates but usually also having role relations with some old and some new friends, who come from two different populations — for instance, different social classes, neighborhoods, or regions.

The various illustrations of environmental opportunities for having diverse associates can be subsumed under two broad categories — two generic structural conditions that influence the opportunity to establish a complex set of role relations. First, the heterogeneity of the population of which a person is part, which is generally greater in larger populations, promotes complex role-sets. Second, social barriers between classes or groups, which typically inhibit social mobility, as well as social intercourse directly, reduce the chances of having a complex set of role relations. There is, however, a third structural influence on the opportunity to establish complex role-sets, which has not yet been illustrated, namely, how strongly various social differences in a population are correlated. If ethnic and educational and socioeconomic and residential differences are closely related, choosing a friend with whom one has one of these attributes in common often entails inadvertently selecting someone with whom one shares several of these attributes, reducing role diversity in all these respects. By the same token, weak correlations of the various social differences in a population, which represent Simmel's crosscutting social circles, promotes complex role-sets, because it makes it virtually impossible to find associates who do not differ along some lines. This is clarified by examining the influence of choice of associates.

The role-set of a person depends on the population structure in her environments, which governs the opportunities for associating with people with various characteristics; within these limits it depends on the choices of associates that she makes and that are reciprocated. (Family relations, since they are ascribed, do not depend on choices, though even for these, the *extent* of associations for adults depends, at least in part, on reciprocated choice.) Parsons' (1951, pp. 61-63 and *passim*) concepts of particularism and universalism provide theoretical criteria for distinguishing interpersonal choices. Universalistic choices are based on a criterion external to the relation itself, such as promoting the employee with the best qualifications or the highest seniority. Particularistic preferences are intrinsic to the relation itself, such as loving *your* mother or choosing friends of your own religion. Choosing associates among one's family is clearly particularistic, and so is choosing a friend of your own race or religion or any ingroup.

Much research has shown that disproportionate numbers of sociable associations, friendships, and, especially, marriages rest on particularistic ingroup choices. To cite only a few examples: Most people's closest associates are members of their own family (Marsden 1987). Friends tend to have not only the same sex, ethnic affiliation, and religion (Merton et al. 1951; Laumann 1973), but also quite similar class background and education (Hollingshead 1949; Fischer 1977). Spouses typically have national origin as well as religion in common (Kennedy 1944; Carter and Glick 1970; Alba 1976), and their education and socioeconomic status are about the same, too (Centers 1949; Hollingshead 1950; Blau and Duncan 1967; Carter and Glick 1970; Tyree and Treas 1974). In short, both homophily and (the term Merton coined for friends with the same attributes) homogamy prevail in many respects.

If the prevalent tendency is to establish interpersonal relations, particularly close ones, with members of one's kin group or another ingroup, it implies that complex role-sets are relatively rare. Homophily may be considered a rough inverse indication of complex role-sets, because if most associates are like oneself there cannot be much diversity among them. But a preferable conceptualization is to consider homophily a measure of ingroup choices that strongly influence but do not completely determine complexity of role-sets, which is more precisely measured by the degree of diversity or variability among associates (termed "range" by network analysts). Although perfect homophily (for example, if a person of Italian descent has only Italian friends) entails indeed zero diversity among associates, but zero or low homophily (if all or most friends of an Italian are not Italian) does not indicate the diversity among them (because the friends may be either all Greek or have different national backgrounds).[1] The question arises as to which attributes should be considered in determining complexity of role-sets. An answer to this question suggests some elaboration of the concept of complex role-set and discloses that such role-sets are not so rare as the profusion of ingroup choices seems to imply.

The multigroup affiliation of people and the intersection of social differences, which are especially pronounced in contemporary complex societies, imply that persons who have the same attribute in one dimension often have different attributes in other dimensions. Hence, complexity of role-sets can be measured with respect to many different attributes of people, and the decision as to which attributes should be taken into account must be based on our judgment and empirical knowledge as to which ones are expected to exert the most influence on the complexity of role-sets and its consequences. The multigroup affiliations in social structures with intersecting differences have the paradoxical implication that ingroup choices produce not only homophily in some respects but often also diversity in others. The reason is that persons whom we choose as associates because they have something in common with us — religion or education or whatever — are likely to differ from us along several other lines. The institutional structure of the family makes this inevitable for kin choices, and multigroup affiliations in intersecting structures make it most probable for some other ingroup choices. This paradox of multigroup affiliation is the reason that the strong ingroup tendencies widely observed do not suppress the development of complex role-sets in the intersecting structures of modern societies.

Homophily and Diversity of Role-Sets

To analyze the homophily and diversity of role-sets in several dimensions, we shall review some results of empirical research of the networks of a sample of the American population. The data for this network analysis were collected as part of the 1985 General Social Survey (GSS), in a network module designed by Burt (1984).[2] Respondents were asked to name "people with whom you discussed [in recent months] matters important to you" and to describe five attributes of each person named (age, sex, education, race, and religion) as well as the nature of ego's relation with each alter. The average respondent named three associates.

The inverse of homophily — how different the average alter is from ego — may be considered, as already noted, a rough indication of diversity in the role-set — how different alters are. The nature of the ego-alter relation — for instance, whether they are kin, coworkers, or neighbors — has largely parallel influences on the social distance between ego and alters and the differences among alters (see Marsden 1990 pp. 404-07). A preferable procedure, as noted, is to treat ingroup choices, which homogamy expresses, as a major influence on diversity in the role-set and distinguish indirect influences mediated by ego's ingroup choices from direct ones independent of these choices. (Since ingroup choices mathematically determine diversity for dichotomies, as indicated in note 1, it does not make sense to look for other influences on diversity in sex, race, and religion, all of which are represented by dichotomies.) Ingroup choices in age and in education have a somewhat curvilinear but largely negative effect on these two forms of diversity, respectively. Specifically, a small initial increase in ingroup choices increases diversity, but for most of their range ingroup choices decrease diversity in age and in education. As one would expect, confining role relations largely to one's ingroups finds expression in restricted role-sets.

More than one half of the associates with whom the average

respondent discusses important problems are members of his family, mostly of the nuclear family.[3] These are, of course, particularistic choices. However, the institution of the family exerts constraints that make these choices of one's most important ingroup simultaneously reduce homophily and increase diversity in some other respects. They reduce homophily in age and sex,[4] and they increase diversity in age, sex, and education, even when the influence of homophily (ingroup choices) is controlled (in the age and education analysis).[5] The reasons are not hard to find: parents and children greatly differ in age from the respondent and, even more, from one another;[6] spouses are of opposite sex; the 50 percent chance that a sibling has the same sex as the respondent is less than the 58 percent chance (in our data) that the average associate does; and rising educational levels raise the educational diversity between generations. Plausible as it is, it is an interesting by-product of the family structure that family members in one's role-set increases its diversity in various respects (not only in age and sex, which is natural, but also in factors related to either, such as education, and undoubtedly others).

Some nonkin ingroup choices in one dimension also produce intergroup choices in others, as we shall see, but not all do. Choices of consultants on important matters from a friendship clique illustrate ingroup choices that reduce diversity in the role-set. To indicate choices from a closely knit clique of friends, the measure used is the closeness of ties among *nonkin* alters only (since ties among kin also tend to be close).[7] The results show that close ties among nonkin alters are negatively related to diversity in ego's role-set. Confining persons with whom one discusses important matters to members of a closely knit clique tends to diminish their variety in age and education, and probably their range of experience and knowledge, interests and skills. In contrast, discussing one's problems with others from a variety of context expands the scope of one's role relations and improves the advice and help one can get (Granovetter 1973; 1974). Such a complex role-set furthers intellectual flexibility and self-direction and the other beneficial consequences for personality development which Coser (1975) so perceptively analyzes.

Age and Role-Sets

The network analysis reveals that older persons are more prone to discuss serious matters with others of the same religion and less prone than younger ones to discuss them with others whose education is similar to theirs. The salience of religion may grow and that of education decline with age. Alternatively, the findings may indicate that secular trends have decreased religion's and increased education's influence on social life for more recent (younger) cohorts. It is, of course, possible that a combination of changes with aging and historical trends has produced these findings.

The influences of ego's age on her choices of alters and the diversity in her role-set in terms of age are quite complicated.[8] Age has a nonmonotonic effect on ingroup choices with respect to age, in the shape of an upside-down U.[9] As people get older, they discuss issues increasingly with persons of their own age, with the curve reaching its apex at 42.8 years, virtually the exact median age (42), after which further aging increases the age difference between a person and his associates. This implies that young persons discuss problems with others who are older, though less and less so as they get older, and older persons discuss them with others who are younger, more and more so as they get older, while people in their middle years discuss them with others of their own age.

A plausible reason for this U-shaped curve is that young persons (the sample does not include any younger than 18) often discuss problems with their parents and old persons with their grown children. Indeed, this is apparently the case. For the six cohorts, from Americans in their 20s to those in their 60s, the percent who name a parent as discussant decreases regularly (58, 34, 15, 8.0, 1.9), and the percent who name a child increases in complementary fashion (0.4, 2.2, 21, 25, 30). One reason for these trends is naturally that many young people do not have children and many old ones no longer have living parents. But this cannot entirely account for the U-shaped curve, nor can any other reason for age differences in tendencies to discuss issues with children or parents, such as a disinclination to discuss problems with young children or very old parents. For the curvature persists, though in reduced form, when the influences of choice of parents and of children as discussion partners is controlled in the analysis.

A possible explanation of this pattern is that people in their middle years, who tend to be much involved in their work and careers, as well as in public and business affairs, are much in demand as consultants by both younger, less experienced, and older, no longer up-to-date, persons, as well as by others their own age. This explanation implies that persons of about median age have the most age-diverse role-sets. For if people in their middle years are popular choices as discussion partners by others who are younger, the same age, and older, it implies that their associates have the widest age range. This is indeed the case. The influence of ego's age on the age diversity of alters also assumes the shape of an upside-down U. As people grow older, the age diversity of their role-set initially increases, reaching its maximum at 42.6 years, and thereafter decreases.

Thus, the influence of ego's age on age homophily and its influence on age diversity exhibit parallel nonmonotonic curves, both first rising and then declining as ego's age increases, reaching the apex nearly at the same point, very close to median age. These results make substantive sense, inasmuch as the diversity curve supports the implication of the homophily curve; yet they conceal conflicting underlying tendencies. The results discussed are based on analyses in which other influences were controlled. In the regression of age diversity, this means that the influence of age ingroup choices (homophily) was controlled. The direct effect of ego's age on age-diversity in her role-set, reported above, forms an upside-down U. But ego's age also has an indirect effect on age diversity, via age homophily. Since age initially has a positive and later a negative influence on homophily, and homophily has a largely negative effect on diversity, the indirect effect is initially negative (+ -) and subsequently positive (- -), thus forming a U. In short, the direct and indirect effect of ego's age on the age-diversity of his role-set are both nonmonotonic but *in opposite directions*. This does not contradict the earlier conclusion that, if persons in their middle years are most likely to consult age peers whereas the youngest and oldest persons are least likely to do so, it implies that the influence of own age, independent of own ingroup tendencies, on role-set age-diversity is strongest in people's middle years, which is what the data show.

Interestingly enough, data from a sample of urban Chinese (see Blau et al. 1991) reveal essentially the same pattern of role relation with respect to age. Advancing age of young Chinese increases age homophily, reaching its maximum at age 37.8 years, after which it declines, and their age diversity similarly initially increases to a peak at age at 38.5 years and then declines. Both peaks are virtually identical with median age (38). This implies that younger Chinese tend to discuss problems with older associates and older ones discuss them with younger associates, and hence that those around median age have the most age-diverse role-sets, which the age-diversity curve confirms. This closely resembles the pattern in the United States. So does the finding in the Chinese study that discussing problems largely with members of a closely knit clique of friends makes a restricted role-set more likely. Finally, kin choices reduce age and sex homophily in the Chinese as well as the American sample, which reflects the ubiquitous age and sex differences in the family.[10]

The reason for the many parallels in two countries so different in culture, economic development, and political system may be that we have examined particularistic choices in private matters, many involving ascribed positions and family relations. These may be less affected by economic and political differences than universalistic decisions in instrumental affairs involving achieved positions and impersonal relations. The inherent generational and sex differences in the family and the homophily that prompts the formation of friendship cliques may well have opposite effects on the complexity of role-sets independent of a nation's political system and economic development.

Intersecting Structural Differences

A population structure with pronounced social differences in many dimensions exerts constraints on ingroup tendencies that produce complex role-sets, and the intersection of various social differences — Simmel's crosscutting social circles — reinforces this effect. The population composition of the social environment is conceptualized as the opportunity structure that governs the chances of intergroup relations by setting limits on ingroup preferences. A theorem, derived from two premises of the macrsociological theory I have developed, is that heterogeneity promotes intergroup relations. Research to test this theorem compared the relationship of various forms of intermarriage in the 125 largest metropolitan areas in the United States to the corresponding forms of heterogeneity, such as ethnic or industrial heterogeneity. Results supported the theorem (Blau and Schwartz 1984, pp. 43-47). Another theorem stipulates that the intersection of social differences in various dimensions promotes intergroup relations, and the implication of this theorem for intermarriage were also supported in our research (pp. 89-95). Extensive intergroup relations compose complex role-sets.

The question arises as to what sociopsychological processes mediate these structural influences on intergroup relations and complex role-sets, notwithstanding the prevailing ingroup pressures and tendencies. The theory assumes that there are ingroup preferences with respect to all socially significant differences in a population (though not that every individual necessarily has ingroup preferences in every respect), which is supported by much research for numerous attributes, as noted, as well as by our own study for all differences under investigation (Blau and Schwartz 1984:33-35). What these intervening processes are was not spelled out in this publication, but I pursued them later in class lectures along the following lines:

Since people have many ingroup preferences and are unlikely to be able to satisfy all of them in their marriages or friendships, each person implicitly establishes an ingroup preference hierarchy and seeks to satisfy her most important preferences, typically having to set aside those lower in her preference ranking for this purpose. The more pronounced the intersection of various social differences, the greater is the pressure to sacrifice some less important ingroup preferences in order to realize the most important ones. To test this inference, one can regress ingroup relations in one dimension on ingroup relations in the others on which data are available. The theoretical implication is that, though some may be positively related (and others unrelated) to the ingroup dimension selected as dependent variable, one or more will be negatively related to it, which indicates that these ingroup preferences have been relatively often set aside in order to satisfy the one represented by the dependent variable.

Mark Van Buren (1991), a graduate student at the University of North Carolina, tested this hypothesis in a paper. He selected ethnic inmarriage as the dependent variable and used the other forms of inmarriage available in the data set as independent variables.[11] The results supported the conjecture: ethnic inmarriage is negatively related to inmarriage in two respects — region of birth and industry. This indicates that significant numbers of ethnically inmarried couples are intermarried in terms of birth region and industry. The inference is that these persons sacrificed any ingroup preferences in these two respects they may have had in order to satisfy their stronger preference for marrying someone in their own ethnic group.

These results raise two further questions: one, whether these sociopsychological processes completely account for the influences of the opportunity structure; and two, what the reason is that these two ingroup preferences — region of birth and industry of employment — rather than others are set aside. Van Buren's paper provides a clue for answering the first query. He went beyond testing the idea originally suggested and introduced measures of heterogeneity as additional independent variables. He found that ethnic heterogeneity of a metropolis is negatively related to ethnic inmarriage there, which means that it is positively related to ethnic intermarriage.[12] This not only supports the heterogeneity theorem but also shows that the influence of the opportunity structure, represented here by the ethnically heterogeneous population distribution, on intermarriage persists, at least in this case, when the intervening sociopsychological process of setting aside some ingroup preferences for another is taken into account. Hence, there must also be some other influences on intermarriage. A inference derived from the theory is that the structural constraints of intersecting social differences may exert independent influences on the ingroup preferences that are sacrificed. This idea has not yet been tested.

A possible answer to the second query is that which ingroup preferences are sacrificed depends on their rank order, which is rooted in the ingroup pressures and the consequent salience of various dimensions of social differences. A measure of effective ingroup pressures, or salience, is the ratio of the observed to the expected rate of ingroup relations, independent of any influence of the population structure. This had been computed for eight forms of inmarriage in the 125 metropolitan areas under study, and the average for them is reported (Blau and Schwartz 1984, p. 35). Of the eight forms of ingroup marriage examined, birth region and industry are two of the three with the lowest salience (and the salience of ethnic background is exceeded only by that of race). These differences lend some support to the inference that less salient ingroup preferences, undoubtedly reflecting weaker ingroup pressures, are sacrificed to be able to satisfy stronger ones. To be sure, these data are not strong support for the inference, not alone because there are so few "cases" of different dimensions but especially because the least salient form of inmarriage — that referring to major occupational group[13] — was not set aside in favor of ethnic inmarriage.

Conclusions

This paper inquired into the sources of complex role-sets, whose important consequences for personality and intellectual development Rose Coser (1975) has analyzed. Two general kinds of influences on the complexity of role-sets were distinguished: people's choices of associates, and the opportunity structure of the population in which these choices are made.

The prevailing particularistic choices of ingroup associates resulting from ingroup pressures engender restricted role-sets. What, then, counteracts these oft-documented ingroup tendencies to give rise to complex role-sets? A fundamental factor is multigroup affiliation, which is found in all societies but is particularly pronounced in the complex social structures of modern societies. Multigroup affiliations frequently transform ingroup relations in one dimension into intergroup relations in others. This occurs in two ways: some institutional structures, notably the family's, make ingroup choices of their members inevitably intergroup choices in other respects; and structural differentiation of a population, provided that it involves intersecting lines of social differences, exerts constraints to sacrifice some ingroup preferences in order to realize the most important ones.

The family is a most significant ingroup, and more than one half of the persons named by the average respondent of a sample of American adults were family members. These choices of one's own kin increase diversity in age and in sex of one's role-set, which is natural given the age and sex differences in the family, and also diversity in education, owing to the secular trend of rising educational levels, which makes educational differences between parents and children likely. On the other hand, choosing to discuss important problems largely with members of a friendship clique has adverse consequences for the complexity of a person's role-set, because closely-knit cliques tend to be homogeneous in age, sex, education, and undoubtedly in other attributes. Choice of consultants from a variety of contexts, and the resulting complexity of the role-set, is likely not only to improve the advice on important matters a person gets but also broaden his experience and perspective.

Ego's age has intricate influences on her choice of alters of varying age and the age diversity of her role-set. The influence of age homophily — choosing age peers with whom to discuss important matters — on role-set diversity, though not quite linear, is largely negative, whereas that of ego's age on age homophily first rises to a peak about median age and then declines. These two influences imply that the *indirect* influence of ego's age on age diversity mediated by age homophily is initially negative but turns positive after ego's median age. However, its *direct* effect on diversity in the role-set first rises to a maximum at about median age and then declines. In short, both the direct and indirect effect of ego's age on diversity in age of his role-set are nonmonotonic, but they are in opposite directions, the direct effect being an upside-down U and the indirect one via homophily being a rightside-up U. Looking only at direct effects with other conditions controlled, however, these are seen to be parallel: as ego gets older, his age homophily first rises and then declines, and the age diversity among his associates also first rises and then declines, both peaking at median age. These intricate relationships make substantive sense. Younger people tend to discuss problems with others who are older, older people with others who are younger, and people around middle age discuss them with age peers. Thus, people in their middle years are consulted by younger, same-age, and older persons, with the result these people in their early forties have — independent of own ingroup choices — the most age-diverse associates.

The multiform heterogeneity in a differentiated population structure with intersecting social differences provides an opportunity structure for social life that furthers intergroup relations by limiting the ingroup preferences that can be realized. These influences of intergroup relations and complexity of role-sets are counteracted if social differences are accompanied by invidious distinctions and discrimination, such as class distinctions or racial discrimination, or if they entail spatial segregation. Only in extreme cases, however, do these counteracting influences completely neutralize the strong impact of intersecting social differences.

For extensive intersection implies that ingroup choices in one dimension entail for many people intergroup relations in some other dimensions.

The social process that mediates the influence of intersection and translates its constraints into intergroup relations is apparently that people realize that they cannot satisfy many ingroup preferences simultaneously and thus, at least implicitly, rank these preferences. In order to satisfy the most important ingroup preferences, they sacrifice others that are less salient, presumable owing to weaker ingroup pressures, and engage in intergroup relations in terms of these lower preferences. The extensive multigroup affiliations in the large and heterogeneous modern metropolis further the establishment of complex role-sets along many lines, though these will rarely involve alters who differ from ego and from one another with respect to the group differences that are made most salient by strong ingroup pressures.

Notes

1. Dichotomous attributes, like sex, are an exception, since for them homophily does mathematically determine diversity. Both zero and 100% ingroup choices entail zero diversity among associates, with 50% homogamy entailing maximum diversity.

2. The full analysis of the results discussed in the text, as well as the research procedures, are reported in Blau et al. (1991), which compares Chinese interpersonal networks with American ones. Although the GSS data are based on a probability sample of the adult U.S. population, our analysis, from which the results examined here derive, is confined to (the 1167) men and women in the labor force, because the Chinese sample was confined to persons in the work force. For other publications based on the GSS network data, see Marsden (1987, 1990) and Moore (1990).

3. Interestingly enough, the mean proportion of kin among associates with whom problems are discussed is smaller in the Chinese (39%) than the American sample (53%). Although the finding is unexpected, the data supply a plausible explanation: the greater employment stability in China produces more stable and closer relations with coworkers, who are much more often named as consultants on serious matters there (38%) than in this country (16%).

4. However, kin choices increase homophily in religion and race, as one would expect (see Marsden 1990:406-07).

5. Since sex homophily mathematically determines its diversity, it cannot be controlled in the diversity analysis.

6. The greater age differences between some kin associates (notably ego's parents and children) than their age difference from ego also accounts for the finding that ego's kin choices have direct effects on the age diversity of alters that reinforce the indirect effect of these kin choices mediated by homophily (which is negatively affected by kin choices and effects age diversity, for most of its range,

negatively).

7. Specifically, all kin were eliminated from every variable referring to associates; that is, the measures of homophily and diversity as well as closeness are confined to nonkin associates.

8. For age, a continuous variables, ingroup choices and diversity are measured by number of years difference (for the former, how *small* the difference between ego's age and mean age of alters is; for the latter, how *large* the average difference between all pairs of alters is). For education, differences on a six-point score are used in a corresponding manner.

9. There is no significant difference in age homophily between men and women. On the average, 59% of women's consultants are women and 58% of men's consultants are men.

10. Kin relations increase age, sex, and educational diversity in both samples, too, but they also exert other influences in the Chinese city that were not observed in the American data.

11. Mother-tongue inmarriage is the only one (of those available) that is positively related to ethnic inmarriage, which is hardly surprising in view of the dependence of a foreign mother tongue on ethnic background. (Mother tongue is coded as a dichotomy: English-other.)

12. The measures of inmarriage and intermarriage are complementary fractions adding to 1.00.

13. Despite the known substantial occupational differences between women and men, spouses are more likely than random pairs to be in the same major occupational group.

References

Alba, Richard D. 1976. *Ethnic Diversity in Catholic America*. New York: Wiley.

Blau, Peter M. and Otis Dudley Duncan. 1967. *The American Occupational Structure*. New York: Wiley.

____, Danching Ruan, and Monika Ardelt. 1991. "Interpersonal Choice and Networks in China." *Social Forces*. In press.

____ and Joseph E. Schwartz. *Crosscutting Social Circles*. Orlando: Academic Press, 1984.

Burt, Ronald S. 1984. "Network Items and the General Social Survey." *Social Networks* 6:293-339.

Carter Hugh, and Paul C. Glick. 1949. *Marriage and Divorce*. Cambridge: Harvard University Press.

Centers, Richard. 1949. "Marital Selection and Occupational Strata." *American Journal of Sociology* 54:308-19.

Coser, Rose L. 1975. "The Complexity of Roles as a Seedbed of Individual Autonomy." Pp.237-64 in *The Idea of Social Structure*, edited by Lewis A. Coser. New York: Harcourt Brace Jovanovich.

Fischer, Claude S. 1977. *Networks and Places*. New York: Free Press.

Granovetter, Mark S. 1973. "The Strength of Weak Ties." *American Journal of Sociology* 78:1360-80.

____. 1974. *Getting a Job*. Cambridge: Harvard University Press.

Hollingshead, August B. 1949. *Elmtown's Youth*. New York: Wiley.

____. 1950. "Cultural Factors in the Selection of Marriage Mates." *American Sociological Review* 15:619-27.

Kennedy, Ruby J. 1944. "Single or Triple Melting Pot?" *American Journal of Sociology* 39:331-39.

Laumann, Edward O. 1973. *Bonds of Pluralism*. New York: Wiley.

Linton, Ralph. 1936. *The Study of Man*. New York: Appleton-Century.

Marsden, Peter V. 1987. "Core Discussion Networks of Americans." *American Sociological Review* 52:122-31.

____. 1990. "Network Diversity, Substructures, and Opportunities for Contact." Pp.397-410 in *Structures of Power and Constraint*, edited by Craig Calhoun, Marshall W. Meyer, and W. Richard Scott. Cambridge: Cambridge University Press.

Merton, Robert K. 1968. *Social Theory and Social Structure*. New York: Free Press.

____, Patricia S. West, and Marie Jahoda. 1951. "Patterns of Social Life." New York: Columbia University Bureau of Applied Social Research. Mimeographed.

Moore, Gwen. 1990. "Structural Determinants of Men's and Women's Personal Networks." *American Sociological Review* 55:726-35.

Parsons, Talcott. 1951. *The Social System*. New York: Free Press.

Tyree, Andrea, and Judith Treas. 1974. "The Occupational and Marital Mobility of Women." *American Sociological Review* 39:293-302.

Van Buren, Mark. 1991. "Ethnic Intermarriage." Unpublished Paper.

PART TWO

Roles and Rules

5

The Difference Model: Enforcement and Reinforcement of Women's Roles in the Law

Cynthia Fuchs Epstein

It is in the nature of social life that the enormous ambiguity that characterizes the human condition is reduced through the social order and the conceptual frameworks that define it. Culture — concepts and language — organizes the way people experience and interpret the world. Cultural frameworks determine what people see and hear — resulting in both individual and collective selective perception. Through their society's value system, individuals learn what to regard as important and what to regard as trivial. Furthermore, insuring against random association, cultural frameworks and their values and concepts determine how people organize into groups, the enterprise they might carry out in these groups, and their social ranking.

But the very fact of social ordering, or social structure, also creates the conditions under which people create values and experience social life. Groups are situated so that they have greater or lesser understanding, learn more or less, have fewer or more resources. Some people may impose their values or manage to avoid the compulsions of others through their differential power, vision, or network of associations. Order is usually (though not necessarily) also associated with hierarchy, creating differences in power. Without this ordering of ideas and situation, the world would be a more confusing place. Thus order is gained, but the freedom created by fluidity is lost.

In much of her work, Rose Laub Coser has analyzed the intersection between ambiguity, choice, freedom and social structure. Many writers have glorified the tight social order of small communities bound by traditions, attributing to them warmth and connectedness. In such groups there is little ambiguity regarding individuals' "proper" places. Often the benefits of community are juxtaposed against the anomie and alienating qualities of large city life. According to Coser (1984, 1991), however, the very conditions that may create alienation for some in large heterogeneous structures such as cities, also create opportunity for multiple associations and freedom of choice. Indeed, this is her "defense of modernity" (Coser 1991), as she argues in her book with this name.

Aspects of modernity — the emphasis on the rights of individuals and the substitution of science for theology as a source of explanation — have certainly provided new definitions and conditions for many social roles that previously were assigned to people by tradition on the basis of their ascribed characteristics of class, race, gender and traditional group affiliations. At a minimum, the character of American culture is characterized by themes that embody the ideals of modernism, but they are vague, as are all general value schemes. Further, the "American Way" incorporates divergent and competing beliefs of groups and individuals with respect to who ought to perform various social roles and how they ought to do so. Therefore there is no perfect unanimity about the appropriate norms to accompany these roles.

The social revolutions of the modern period, including those of the 1960's and 1970's, articulated new challenges to the bases for role assignments, creating popular support as well as resistance by gatekeepers of the old order. Custom and tradition die hard, and because culture and social structure are interactive and entwined, change does not come easily, nor is it permanent. Traditional patterns of ideas and social arrangements, change and resistance to change, may move toward resolution or remain in dynamic opposition for some period of time.

It has been clear to observers that modernism affects groups differently and that its processes are experienced unevenly (Boserup 1970). Women constitute one category that seems to lag in the modernization process — they still wear the veil and traditional robes in Iran while many men dress in Western style clothes. . . . although women of different groups are affected in various ways. In some *Gesellschaft* societies, women continue to live in *Gemeinschaft* environments. Of course, all *Gesellschaft* societies contain *Gemeinschaft* pockets; the family is probably the most important. All people participate in some *Gemeinschaft* pockets, but women are particularly lodged in them (sometimes more symbolically than actually). *Gemeinschaft* groups pose attitudinal and behavioral role demands that are geared to turning members inward toward them, and they conflict with the new roles members are also permitted to pursue in the larger society (Coser 1984). Although women have moved into the public sphere in ever increasing numbers, particularly in the occupations, cultural discourse continues to focus on their roles as wives and mothers, and this has had an impact on their own discourse. Women simply are not permitted to forget their family roles, to suppress them or lay them aside. Their public roles often are linked symbolically, if not actually, to their private roles. This linkage maintains tradition although women are no longer locked exclusively into traditional role assignments by a formal rule system — the law and formal institutions. Thus, the cultural framework gears the discussion to integration of women's work roles (or other public roles) with their family roles in ways that are not applied to men (even though they are embedded in the same family *Gemeinschaft* pockets as women.) Although often there is considerable discrepancy between practice (activity in the public sphere) and attitude (orientation toward the home), selective perceptions about what women are doing and what they believe are extremely sensitive to cultural pulls toward traditional viewpoints.

However, these pressures not only affect women. Men too are affected by stereotypes that bind them to *Gemeinschaft* institutions. Some from historically disadvantaged groups may experience them negatively; but others, well situated, benefit from them. The definition of certain culturally defined enclaves as men's domains often legitimates the boundaries of *Gemeinschaft* structures such as male clubs and male-dominated professions and associations that exclude women and minority males. Thus such *Gemeinschaft* structures tend to preserve boundaries that are blurred in heterogeneous and complex modern societies.

Difference paradigms in the culture that specify separate male and female-appropriate behavior and activities resist change even when they do not appear to describe what behavior in fact occurs. Therefore, when social roles are no longer segregated into polarized clusters — as when mothers also take on roles as students or lawyers; or black men become managers and craftsmen — the difference model nevertheless remains intact.

These paradigms are woven into individual and collective perceptions and they influence personal choices and evaluations of experience. Thus difference is insisted upon, it focuses on and is reinforced by the apparent "naturalness" of different spheres, different abilities, different moralities, different orientations or different behavior for the sexes.

Perpetuation of the "difference model" and of its "sex-appropriate" roles is by no means solely the work of male bigots of another era, or of right-wing or religious ideologues. It is shared by many women and members of other disadvantaged groups and is supported by the philosophical and theoretical writings of a number of feminist writers whose belief in assumed superior attributes of women is matched by their negative evaluation of some presumed male attributes. These groups seek to maintain boundaries and to reinforce or reinstate gender and other distinctions just at a time when such boundaries are being challenged in intellectual and daily life. Of course, the same kind of boundaries are sought by men who stand to benefit from the imposition of distinctions between women and men.

In this paper I shall indicate how Coser's observations and theoretical constructs, and my own study of the processes of boundary maintenance (Epstein 1981, 1988, 1989, forthcoming), explain the continuing emphasis on difference in the institution of law (Epstein 1988). The same emphasis can be found in other spheres, among them the sciences, in which claims to objectivity are assumed. The problem in the sciences is particularly important because scientific authority is cited by occupants of most legal statuses including judges, juries, lawyers, victims and legislators. I will also analyze some of the reasons for the perpetuation of the difference model by feminist legal scholars and feminist scholars from other disciplines; and examine the consequences of boundary maintenance for women who participate in the legal profession in their various roles as practitioners, clients, and citizens.

The Underlying Difference Model and Its Contemporary Adherents

Adherents of the difference model claim there is a solid basis for identifying different traits as typical for men and women. Some assert these differences are deeply ingrained through biological determinants or the outcomes of early socialization patterns. Indeed, some have drawn support from studies by social scientists. However, there has been considerable critical evaluation of many of the studies supporting these views, and more sophisticated modes of analysis indicate there is far more similarity than difference between the sexes in cognitive abilities, personality traits, and a host of other characteristics (Epstein 1988). The overlap between men and women with respect to these characteristics is much more significant notwithstanding the occasional statistical differences; furthermore, even statistically significant differences are often acknowledged to be conditional on social situation and are variable over time. Even today, some social scientists who advocate a perspective that takes for granted that gender differences are ingrained are highly influential. These include theorists who use a psychoanalytic perspective (for example, Nancy Chodorow 1978) whose theory, like many psychoanalytic theories is difficult to test (but see Jackson, 1989); and Carol Gilligan (1982), a psychologist, whose claims that women have a different moral outlook than men is based on inappropriate studies of children and college students using poor samples (Epstein 1988; Kerber et al. 1986; Maccoby 1990; Reed 1990; Walker 1984).

Since a number of feminist legal theorists and literary critics subscribe to the claims of these social scientists and their followers, it would be useful to speculate about why the ideas of Chodorow and Gilligan remain powerful in spite of criticism and evidence that is contrary to this observations.

Boundaries and Binary Oppositions

We are reminded by Bourdieu (1984) and others that dominated groups often contribute to their own subordination because of class-differentiated dispositions and categories of perception shaped by conditions of existence; the dominant symbolic system made of binary oppositions. The polarizations that result, of course, make for boundaries that are distinct, ignoring a reality in which "blurred genres" (Geertz 1984) are more representative of social life.

Without boundaries, there is ambiguity which people individually, and in concert, tend to avoid. One of Coser's important contributions to social analysis is her identification of the process whereby people retreat from ambiguity, even when the retreat leads to conditions that restrict but provide surety, and though predictability and order may ultimately restrain freedom.

Coser also has shown how the belief systems that underlay various social arrangements contribute to people's ability to change or may deflect them from altering the course of their lives. This may happen on both an individual and a group level. For example, she has shown how a Calvinist paradigm may cause people with personal problems to blame themselves rather than the social conditions of their lives (Coser 1979). Coser's analysis is indeed fruitful in assessing the seeming paradox of women's advancement in modern life and the movement toward retreat (Kaminer 1989) by important groups of women on both the political right and left.

Both as humans and as scientists we tend to make categorical distinctions. Of course, science and other kinds of thought depend on the use of categories; but in science, like the rest of life, categories tend to become reified: conceptual boundaries, a result of social decisions, are regarded as real, and worse — as inevitable.

Particular kinds of distinctions — dichotomous models, such as those that distinguish between blacks and whites; free people and slaves; men and women — are particularly powerful in maintaining and creating differences. A number of legal writers have sought the "woman's voice" in law — presumably a model of justice based on an expression of caring and sensitivity to people's relationships that Carol Gilligan (1982) has asserted is female-linked (see Burns 1987). The particular traits specified by Gilligan are only a few of the many traits attributed to women as a result of research that poses male and female, masculine and feminine, as polar extremes. These conceptions lead to and reinforce social constructions of gender as dichotomous categories and mask the ideological components — the agenda setting components (Lukes 1974). It assumes difference as a given, rather than as a process — one with considerable rooting in law.

Consider the process. In earlier writings I sought an explanation for the creation of identity, attitudes and behavior by focusing on the socialization mechanisms that reinforce gender characterizations (Epstein 1970a). Today, that approach appears limited, and it seems certain from the research of the past two decades that the social controls ordering gender distinctions and maintaining them are of great importance (Epstein 1988). The social control perspective suggests that most gender distinctions are not lodged in early development — and certainly not in psychoanalytically derived stages — but in a persistent and ongoing context of informal and formal social controls, and is kept in place by powerful decision-makers and enforced through institutionalized norms by the conventions of ordinary behavior (such as etiquette) lodged in community and group ties and in the rule of law.

Like other coercive patterns of control, I see gender distinctions as emanating from the decisions of powerful gatekeepers and the self-monitoring of people who accept the definitions imposed on them, and rationalize them as natural or proper. Of course, we would have no social change if groups did not contest the ideas of the powerful from time to time, and certainly one result of the women's movement has been to upset conventions on gender. However, the mechanisms of control are strong and they have affected the work of scholars who regard themselves as feminists.

Theoretical and ideological frameworks create research agendas, and research findings contribute to the formulation of theory that sometimes informs political viewpoints. Both occur in a cultural context; the connection between views on gender roles and public policy is strong. Views that there are distinctive men's and women's "ways of knowing," emotions, and cognition also carry an valuative component. Thus, not only are men and women believed to possess or not to possess certain attributes, but each sex is regarded as better or worse, or as impaired or competent, depending on the attribute in question.

Law[1] (as a system of rules) and legal institutions (which include the stratification system of the profession and the social composition of the bar and courts) contribute to the social control process by providing definitions and parameters for gender distinctions and for social ordering, as well as the means of holding these distinctions in place.[2] Of course, law is also the instrument of support and legitimation of the class system and other divisions of society — by age and race, for example. Public policy and laws specify how and when the sexes may and may not mingle, and also the conditions of many of men's and women's most intimate interactions. Laws require men to support their spouses and children. Other laws prohibit women in military service from engaging in combat but require men to fight when ordered to do so. The laws may not always be enforced, and there may be infringements of them, but the knowledge that punishments are on the books for those who deviate encourages people to conform.

Law has also been an instrument for breaking down barriers and removing distinctions, as we have witnessed in the past two or three decades. But no society leaves women and men entirely free to choose the social roles they prefer or fails to punish them for deviation, although societies differ in their interest in particular infractions and in the harshness of punishment. Some groups, for example, punish the woman adulterer by denying her an invitation to dinner; others stone her to death.

Indeed, social controls, set in both an informal and formal rule system, and backed by sanctions, usually insure that men and women are regarded as different and must behave in sex-distinctive ways.

The ideological character and content of laws and their use in promulgating a particular type of social order has been emphasized by a group of legal theorists and sociologists of law in recent years. These critical scholars note that powerful groups use law to achieve their own goals while insisting that the law serves most people and is an outgrowth of natural phenomena. Some groups, (for example, the hierarchy of the Catholic Church, and religious fundamentalists) who object to laws granting women greater rights over their destiny and their bodies do so on the grounds that these rights are contrary to nature. They fail to understand that the existing laws and those of past ages are not "natural;" such matters as the distribution of property and the rights and restrictions of parties to marriage and divorce merely reflect the choices of those who devised and passed the laws.

Women have been kept "in place" by laws that restrict their right to participate in government and to control their property and their person. Recent changes in the law have broadened their options, although rights over control of their bodies (and thus, an entire range of other options) are clearly at risk today. In the past, only women who had powerful protectors or independent resources, or those who banded together in women's groups and movements, have had a chance to break away from the limits imposed on most other women. Of course, legal codes do not cover every kind of activity: custom and tradition are important too, either in supporting or in undermining these codes. But law is an important legitimator of social practice and contributes to the establishment of norms; it defines what is permitted and what is deviant. For most of legal history, law restricted women from obtaining both material and human capital resources and prevented their participation in lawmaking and other important institutions.

Furthermore, law is interpreted by those who possess power — usually men — in the judiciary, in government and in the church. And men determine the punishments of the violators. It has become clear that the cultural preferences of gatekeepers determines the way they mete out justice — whether demonstrated by the variable prosecutions of rapists, wife batterers, and employment discriminators in the United States, or by the lack of enthusiasm in India for punishing husbands who murder wives who bring insufficient dowries in India (Butalia 1985). In Western law, even statuses for which gender-free terms have long been used, ("person" for example) have been targets of efforts to genderize roles and statuses for the purpose of including or excluding men or women from particular domains.

The Differential Treatment of Women in the Courts

As is well known, in Britain before the turn of the century, male public officials and leaders held that since women need not function in the public sphere it was unnecessary to define them as "persons." Only "persons" had the right to a university education, public office, and the vote.

Without embarrassment or apology, judges painted a picture of women as too delicate, pure and refined to undertake public functions; they were accordingly classified legally alongside the insane and insolvent, and in one case, as inanimate (Sachs and Wilson 1978). Such reasoning, even after the "person" issue was resolved, restricted women's participation in the legal profession (Weisberg 1977, 1979; Fossum 1980; Epstein 1968, 1970a, 1970b, 1981, Sachs and Wilson 1978); in medicine (Walsh 1977; Lorber 1984) and in teaching (Tyack and Strober 1981). Restrictions have excluded married women from working at all in certain positions, such as airline attendant or in banking and insurance firms. In the United States, the Civil Rights Act of 1964 made such practices illegal. But, other prevalent restrictions (for example, women's role in the armed forces and limitations on employment in factory positions considered dangerous) have been upheld by law. Restrictions in the armed forces remain, although many limitations on women's employment based on "protective" codes were struck down a few years ago by the Federal court of the Eleventh Circuit.

Women's Courts

Frieda Solomon (1987) has shown that special women's courts, used for processing "women's causes," were created in almost every major urban court jurisdiction in the United States during the last years of the Progressive Era. With the best of intent, they were instigated by organized social reform movements. They provided a forum for women who wished to bring complaints against husbands and former husbands for non-support and related domestic issues, but they also dealt with "women's crimes" — prostitution-related offenses, soliciting, maintaining disorderly houses, and vagrancy. Women clients were assisted by representatives of a small number of charitable organizations and some of the few practicing women attorneys.

But these women's courts, like many other attempts to address presumed differences between men and women resulted in negative outcomes for women. Regardless of initial — statutory intent, the caseload that dominated the docket of women's courts was predominantly prostitution. As Solomon (1987) points out, the public policy demands and laws that gave rise to women's courts were part of the changing socio-economic demography of the burgeoning cities of the new industrial age and were consistent with Progressive Era attitudes toward women and morality. From Supreme Court decisions (*Muller v. Oregon* [1908]) to the most local level of government, paternalism was most often conceived as benign, but, when necessary, it had the capacity to be authoritarian.

Female defendants processed through the criminal courts were seen as having characteristics distinguishable from male criminals. Those accused of prostitution and shoplifting were seen as having "fallen" from the status of pure womanhood, they were misguided because of lack of proper education, or feeble-mindedness. The women's courts were seen as formal institutions within which informal procedures were to be used. This paternalism laid the groundwork for indeterminate sentencing for women — which often resulted in their serving longer periods in state institutions than men. In the last analysis, writes Solomon (1987), the legal structures designed to promote the salvation of women ultimately worked against them. Some of these courts were disbanded in the 1930s, but some endured and one in New York City — Part Nine of the Criminal Court of the City Magistrate's court, known as the New York City Women's Court — lasted until 1967.

Stereotypical views of women affect them elsewhere in the legal system. Even in the past few years, different standards of judgment have been applied to women (MacKinnon 1979, 1982). There is considerable disagreement in the judicial system about treating women and men equally before the law, and rulings still are based on special considerations for women. For example, evaluating the *Wanrow* decision which supported the defense of a woman confined to a wheelchair, who shot and killed an unarmed child molester, MacKinnon (1979) found the court's "special consideration" an expression of a doctrinal construction such that the sexes are "not similarly situated" with regard to the ability to defend themselves. Women defendants also face differential treatment based on cultural views of difference. One of the most widely held assumptions in studies of women on trial is that the female defendant is likely to receive a more lenient sentence than her male counterpart (Pollack 1950; Devlin, 1970; and McClean and Wood 1969). While this may occur for certain types of cases, a body of sentencing studies report harsher sentences for women than men in similar circumstances (Simon 1975; Foley and Rasche 1976; Berstein et al. 1977).

Explanations for such varying practices also differ. Those finding a pattern of leniency toward women defendants have accounted for it by male chivalry (Simon 1975; Anderson 1976; Chesney-Lind 1977); by the position of women in society (Devlin 1970); the feeling that certain forms of sentence are wholly inappropriate for women (Smith 1962; Giallombardo 1966); and, more especially, because imprisonment would separate women from their children (Sykes 1958; Goodman and Price 1967; Heidensohn 1969, 1975; Gibbs 1971). Nagel (1981) and Temin (1973), in their studies of sex differences in judicial outcomes, conclude that females whose offenses are more consistent with sex role expectations seem to experience less harsh outcomes than those whose offenses are less traditional. Phillips and De Fleur (1982) write, ". . . . if a woman is believed to have deviated from femaleness in general (i.e., she has in some fashion stepped outside gender role expectancies), she may be more likely to be believed capable of criminal activity and deserving a harsh treatment." According to these studies, the judicial outcome depends on the type of crime committed and the degree to which the crime is at variance with the female role.

Stereotypes which label women as being more in need of protection than men and more amenable to rehabilitation have sometimes resulted in longer sentences for women than for men convicted of the same crime.

Other sentencing studies show that women are sentenced in accordance with their perceived culpability and deviation from gender roles. Warren (1981) argues that for offenses against morality, women receive harsher sentences than men. Bernstein et al. (1979) points similarly to the difference in the severity of sentence depending on the degree to which the offense deviates from the appropriate gender role. According to Edwards (1984), "Women are not only on trial for the alleged crimes that they commit, but also on trial for their defiance of appropriate femininity and gender roles. For example, research has shown that gender role has had a significant impact in shaping probation officers' understanding of clients' motivation for crime, decisions made by department stores to prosecute shoplifters, police discretion to caution, and of course, judicial decision in the sentencing process."

Sociologists note that family considerations can play an important role for both men and women. But stereotypes regarding male and female family roles have different consequences for each sex. For example: Edwards suggests it is not motherhood *per se* which has an influence on allowing appeals against sentencing, but whether the appellant was a *good* mother. Evidence of "bad" mothering or evidence of children in surrogate care affects a woman's sentencing. (Men may be penalized for being bad fathers, but the qualities of good fathering are more ambiguous.) Pat Carlen (1983), in her work on women's imprisonment also makes the point that appropriate gender role, wifehood, and domesticity are factors likely to affect sentencing decisions.

The Consequences of the Difference Model in the Professional World

Before the late 1960s, women attorneys, virtually closed out of courtroom participation, sometimes found places as volunteers for the poor in the criminal courts and were among the most outspoken advocates of a permanent place for women in courts devoted to the betterment and protection of women and children. Having found this niche for themselves, it is not surprising that the first women to ascend to the bench were chosen to serve as judges in the juvenile or family courts of inferior jurisdiction (Cook 1986; Epstein 1981). As I found in my studies of women lawyers (1968, 1981), law firms' assumptions about the special personality traits of women led to their assignment to specialties which were usually the less prestigious, less lucrative, and often less interesting than those of men. Assumptions that they were less motivated and committed than men made their prospects poor for promotion to partner. Women often were regarded contradictorily as not tough enough to handle business law and the stress of the courtroom, or too tough to be collaborators and partners. They were seen as too pure to face courtroom realities, too caring to be tough-minded and too stiff and unyielding to be able to make the kinds of deals and settlements that male lawyers did through their informal professional relationships. Women who were (and are) tough faced the disapproval of both men and women colleagues and even of some feminist attorneys who faulted them for assuming a "male model" of behavior (sometimes for wearing clothing regarded as "masculine") and otherwise deviating from sex-role appropriate attitudes. Women lawyers have also been faulted for deviating from demeanor and emotion norms attached to gender roles when they are business-like in professional settings. Male colleagues assert they are stiff and evaluate them as interpersonally incompetent, and women colleagues often agree (Epstein 1981).

The viewpoint of a number of feminist legal theorists who suggest that women bring to the law a different perspective of legal and ethical concerns could be regarded as a reflection of the deep ambiguities in the culture that women face, since "caring" based on personal relationships, is regarded by them as a positive normative principle for women. It is posed as a dichotomous orientation to a "male" standard based on "uncaring" and abstracted ideals of justice. Whether women express or feel the caring ideal or not, it is certainly normatively ascribed to many of their traditional roles and thus provides a basis for developing self-concepts. Much in historical and contemporary culture underscores caring as an attribute for women in their roles as mothers, wives, as helpers of men in occupational roles, as members of the "caring" professions such as teaching and nursing, and as peace advocates. Of course, women assume many statuses with attached norms that specify ideals of justice (based on individual rights) as they do in the law (as members of Boards of Education or the League of Women Voters, for example) and engage in behavior that carries out these ideals. In practice, it is not true that moral outlooks based on caring and justice are dichotomous or mutually exclusive. However, since they have been posed that way by a core of feminist legal scholars and other feminist theorists who not so long ago could be expected to adhere to an equality model — that is, a belief that men and women react morally as individuals, not on the basis of their sex — it is useful to consider the sociological processes that might explain their position.

Using Rose Coser's analyses of ambivalence and of role distance (following Goffman) one could understand the view of these scholars as articulating their ambivalence about belonging to a male-dominated occupation. And this may add to discomfort caused by deviance from the path that women must follow, and insecurity about self concepts that often are rooted in cultural norms attached to their more traditionally female roles. Thus, these theorists may reconcile belonging to what they see as a male domain by insisting that women maintain separate integrity within it because they hold different attitudes and values that cause them to behave "as women." Thus, the ambivalence they experience may cause them to engage in role distance by performing a role but criticizing it or holding themselves symbolically apart from it.

Of course, such resolutions of whatever role conflict (Merton [1948] 1968) women experience as a result of having chosen a "deviant" course are consistent with general system mechanisms that move women to traditional patterns by making their discomfort level high for nonconformity. Other mechanisms for role conflict resolution[3] are denied women in order to press them toward a "final" resolution — that is, abandonment of the occupational role defined as causing the conflict or reduction of its scope. (Epstein [1972] 1976; 1974). Indeed another of Coser's insights sheds light on the dynamics of role integration or disintegration associated with women who hold status-sets (Merton [1948] 1968) that encompass inconsistent statuses and therefore conflicting role demands. The "concern" for the stresses these women are said to acquire is attached to their assuming nontraditional status-sets such as lawyer-mother-wife-community volunteer. Solutions suggested for women facing these stresses tend to center on reduction of their workplace commitments to part-time or flexible schedules or leaving the workplace entirely for a time, until their children are less demanding. These "solutions" have the effect of reducing women's integration in the public arena, of marginalizing them, and reducing their ability to increase the diversity of their role-sets. This consequence was noted a decade and a half ago, by Rose Coser (1975b), then writing about the Presidential veto of a bill that would give federal support for child care centers. She pointed out that rejection of this bill would prevent the mobility of women in social space or restructuring of their role relations: mothers would not have the option of movement to activities not available at home.

But even though mothers have assumed public roles in addition to their family roles, discussion of their performance is usually tied to concerns about the integration of their work with child-care responsibilities. Little attention is given to changing the nature of child-rearing and the reassignment of responsibility for it (other than to concede that men will not participate usefully). Thus the rhetoric used in public and private discourse creates controls over women's assumption of high-level jobs that translate into structural limitations and structural positioning of women.

Unlike the restrictions caused by role-demands thought to be incompatible and the restrictions on innovative ways of resolving them, continuous ambiguity undermines the perception of women in the public sphere as competent and appropriately placed. Here it is interesting to look at the further dynamics of stereotyping. Not only are women stereotyped according to their presumed personality attributes and cognitive capacities, but the stereotypes are not consistent and are often contradictory. Whatever stereotype that defines women as acting inappropriately in the nontraditional role they are assuming, is used. Thus, as mentioned before, women as lawyers may be seen as aggressive (and therefore unpleasant to consider as partners) and as passive. This is often seen in the characterizations of women judges, which also often are inconsistent. One stereotype holds that women judges are harsher than male judges; another is closer to the "caring" model and maintains that women are apt to be more lenient and empathetic than men on the bench. Yet, surveys of judicial decision-making have reflected no consistent gender differences in areas such as criminal sentences and women's rights (Rhode 1989).

Stereotypes regarding women's priorities and positions as wives and mothers affect their opportunities as professionals. Yet, there is an accumulating body of data (Zuckerman and Cole 1987; Epstein 1981, Chambers 1989) showing that some women who are successful in male-dominated professions tend disproportionately to be married and have children. Although conventional wisdom holds that marriage and children are impediments to women's career success, the seeming paradox can be explained. First, although these professional women have careers deviant from other women's, their marital and motherhood statuses show they are nonetheless conforming to social expectations regarding a normal woman's life. This may make them more acceptable working partners to men who may regard single career women as interested primarily in the social opportunities that work provides. Furthermore, since women in professional life tend disproportionately to be married to men in their own fields, their husbands often given them access to networks and business contacts they might not have independently. In some sense, then, there are not only normative aspects of women's roles that extend into their professional life, but structural elements as well that smooth their way.

Space does not permit a more extensive survey or analysis of the consequences of dichotomous thinking about gender roles in the legal system, and the integration of assumptions about men and women into the frameworks within which we analyze the various problems of inequality. Even well-intentioned dichotomizing, whether by jurists, lawyers, or social scientists, seems to lead to unintended consequences, that often have negative outcomes for women.

We need to be more alert to history, to cross cultural, cross cohort and comparative analysis which reveals the wide differences in attitudes and behavior of women in different social circumstances. Social science has increasingly provided consistent evidence that women do not inheritantly possess particular traits diferent from those of men; for example, that women are more naturally cooperative or less competitive than men in their social behavior. Women may be *assigned* care-giving roles in most societies, but their "nature" does not require it or necessarily guarantee they will provide good care in all circumstances. Their "nature" has not prevented them from engaging in acts of torture and assault when norms prescribe callousness and cruelty, as for example, manifested by Nazi women during and before World War II (Koontz 1978).

In my own studies of women in law during the past two decades (Epstein 1981), which provides information on a wide range of traits and qualities exhibited by women attorneys and judges, I could see no basis for the expectation that substantial changes could be predicted in the profession merely because of the participation of women. I concluded that "no one group ought to be burdened with the expectation of unilateral altruism." Evidence does not show that women come by altruism or caring "naturally." They may engage in such behavior, but typically as a component of traditional women's roles, normatively prescribed, and socially enforced by punishments for deviation.

As we have seen, the assignments of these role prescriptions too often has the consequences of subjugating women. Women have been vulnerable to patronizing attitudes, to discrimination, and to other forms of unequal treatment because of stereotypes that link them to these attitudes. But women's position in society as outsiders to the establishment, or in their unique roles as mothers, do not necessarily predict a common set of behaviors or attitudes. There are as many differences among women as between men and women.

Many feminist scholars today are either committed to a "difference model" or leaning towards its acceptance, because of their commitment to humanistic values, and a desire to change society. Their perspective has certainly been felt in the social science community and the legal communities which are more aware of the problems inherent in models associated with male-dominated spheres, and in attention to the role of women. But all scholars must act with caution to avoid the pitfalls that so characterized the biased analyses of the past. Models are social constructions which may hinder or expand our perceptions and knowledge. We must differentiate between those that serve our ideological agendas and those that inform us abut the nature of reality. Rose Laub Coser's work indicates that a deep commitment to humanistic social values does not preclude a sharp eye for the processes that create social reality.

Notes

1. A portion of this analysis is a revision of Epstein (1990).
2. We may note that although most, if not all, cultures hold that men and women are suited to distinctive social roles, and that these are extensions of the laws of Nature or of some Divine will, all societies take great care to establish laws — or rules where no formal body of law exists — to ensure that individuals' real roles come close to the culture's ideal roles (Epstein 1985). Nowhere does a society's watchdogs or its citizens risk leaving this process to chance.
3. Such as "delegation" and "compartmentalization," as outlined by Merton ([1948] 1968) and Goode (1960).

References

Anderson, E. A. 1976. "The 'Chivalrous' Treatment of the Female Offender in the Arms of the Criminal Justice System: A Review of the Literature." *Social Problems* 23: 349-57.

Bernstein, I.N., E. Kick, J.T. Leung, and B. Schulz. 1977. "Charge Reduction: Intermediary Stage in Process of Labeling Criminal Defendants." *Social Forces* 56: 362-384.

Bernstein, I. N. and J. Cardascia and C. E. Ross. 1979. "Defendants, Sex and Criminal Court Decisions," Pp. 320-354 in *Discrimination in Organizations*, edited by R. Alvarez and K. G. Lutterman. San Francisco: Jossey-Bass.

Boserup, Ester, 1970. *Women's Role in Economic Development*. London: George Allen and Unwin.

Burns, Michael. 1986. "The Law School as a Model for Community." *Nova Law Journal*. 10 (2).

Butalia, Urvashi. 1985. "Indian Women and the New Movement." *Women's Studies International Forum* 8: 131-133.

Carlen, Pat. 1983. *Women's Imprisonment*. London: Routledge and Kegan Paul.

Chambers, David L. 1989. "Accomodation and Satisfaction: Women and Men Lawyers and the Balance of Work and Family." *Law and Social Inquiry*. 14: 251-287.

Chesney-Lind, M. 1977. "Judicial Paternalism and the Female Status Offender." *Crime and Delinquency* 23: 121-130.

Chodorow, Nancy. 1978. *The Reproduction of Mothering: Psychanalysis and the Sociology of Gender*. Berkeley, University of California Press.

Cook, Beverly. 1986. "Legal Institution-Building in the Progressive Era: The Los Angeles Women's Court." Paper presented at the Annual Meeting of the Southern Political Science Association.

Coser, Lewis A. ed. 1975. *The Idea of Social Structure: Papers in Honor of Robert K. Merton*. New York: Harcourt Bce Jovanovich.

Coser, Rose Laub. 1966. "*Role Distance, Sociological Ambivalence and Transitional Status Systems*." American Journal of Sociology 62: 173-87.

____. 1975a. "The Complexity of Roles as Seedbed of Individual Autonomy." Pp. 237-63 in *The Idea of Social Structure: Papers in Honor of Robert K. Merton*. Edited by Lewis Coser. New York: Harcourt Brace Jovanovich.

____. 1975b. "Stay Home Little Sheba: On Placement, Displacement and Social Change." *Social Problems* 22: 470-80.

____. 1979. *Training in Ambiguity: Learning Through Doing in a Mental Hospital*. New York: Free Press.

____. 1984. "The Greedy Nature of *Gemeinschaft*." In Walter Powell and Richard Robbins, eds. *Conflict and Consensus: A Festschrift in Honor of Lewis A. Coser*, edited by W. Powell and R. Robbins. New York: Free Press.

____. 1991. *In Defense of Modernity*. Stanford: Stanford University Press.

Devlin, K. M. 1970. *Sentencing Offenders in Magistrates' Courts* London: Sweet and Maxwell.

Edwards, Susan. 1984. *Women on Trial*. Manchester, England: Manchester University Press.

____. (ed.). 1985. *Gender, Sex and the Law* London: Croom Helm.

Epstein, Cynthia Fuchs. 1968. "Women and Professional Careers: The Case of the Woman Lawyer." Unpublished Ph.D. dissertation, Columbia University.

____. 1970a. *Woman's Place: Options and Limits in Professional Careers*. Berkeley: University of California Press.

____. 1970b. "Encountering the Male Establishment: Sex-Status Limits on Women's Careers in the Professions." *American Journal of Sociology* 75: 965-983.

____. 1974. "Ambiguity as Social Control: Women in Professional Elites." In *Varieties of Work Experience*. Edited by Phyllis L. Steward and Muriel G. Cantor. New York: Schenkman.

____. 1976. "Sex Role Sterotyping, Occupations and Social Exchange." *Women's Studies* 3: 183-194.

____. 1981. *Women in Law*. New York: Basic Books.

____. 1985. "Ideal Roles and Real Roles or The Fallacy of the Misplaced Dichotomy." *Research in Social Stratification and Mobility* 4: 29-51.

____. 1988. *Deceptive Distinctions: Sex, Gender and the Social Order*. New Haven: Yale University Press and The Russell Sage Foundation.

____. 1990. "Strong Arms and Velvet Gloves: The Gender Difference Model and the Law." in *The Invisible Majority*, The Mellon Colloquium, Graduate School of Tulane University.

____. Forthcoming. "Nice Mice and Barracudas: Tinkerbells and Pinups: Gender Ideology at Work." In *Divide and Conquer: Symbolic Boundaries and the Making of Inequality*. Edited by M. Lamont and M. Fournier.

Foley, L. and C. Rasche. 1976. "A Longitudinal Study of Sentencing Patterns of Female Offenders." Paper presented at the American Society of Criminology, Tucson, AZ.

Fossum, Donna. 1980. "Women Law Professors." *American Bar Foundation Research Journal* 4: 906-914.

Geertz, Clifford. 1984. *Local Knowledge:Further Essays in Interpretive Anthropology*. New York: Basic Books

Giallombardo, R. 1966. *Society of Women: A Study of Women's Prisons* New York: John Wiley and Sons.

Gibbs, C. 1971. "The Effect of Imprisonment of Women on their Children" *British Journal of Criminology*, II: 113-130.

Gilligan, Carol. 1982. *In a Different Voice: Psychological Theory and Women's Development*. Cambridge: Harvard University Press.

Ginsburg, Ruth Bader. 1985. "Some Thoughts on the Relation to Roe v. Wade." *North Carolina Law Review* 63: 375-386.

Goode, William J. 1960. "A Theory of Role Strain." *American Sociological Review*. 25: 483-496.

Goodman, N. and J. Price. 1967. *Studies of Female Offenders*. London: H.M.S.O.

Heidensohn, F. 1969. "Prison for Women." *Criminologist* 4: 113-122.

____. 1975. "The Imprisonment of Females." In *The Use of Imprisonment*, edited by S. McConville. London: Routledge and Kegan Paul.

Horner, Matina. 1968. "Sex Differences in Achievement Motivation and Performance in Competitive and Noncompetitive Situations." Ph.D. Dissertation, University of Michigan.

____. 1972. "Toward an Understanding of Achievement-related Conflicts in Women," *Journal of Social Issues* 28): 157-175.

Jackson, Robert Max. 1989. "The Reproduction of Parenting." *American Sociological Review*. 54: 215-232.

Kaminer, Wendy, 1990. *A Fearful Freedom: Women's Flight From Equality*. New York: Addison-Wesley.

Kerber, Linda, Catherine G. Greeno and Eleanor E. Maccoby, Zella Luria, Carrol B. Stack and Carol Gilligan. 1986. "On a Different Voice: An Interdisciplinary Forum," *Signs* 11: 304-333.

Koontz, Claudia. 1987. *Mothers in the Fatherland: Women, the Family, and Nazi Politics* New York: St. Martin's Press.

Lopate, Carol. 1968. *Women in Medicine* Baltimore: John Hopkins University Press.

Lorber, Judith. 1984. *Women Physicians: Careers, Status and Power*. New York: Methuen.

Lukes, Steven. 1974. *Power: A Radical View*. London: Macmillan Press.

MacKinnon, Catherine A. 1979. *Sexual Harassment of Working Women*. New Haven: Yale University Press.

____. 1982. "Toward a Feminist Jurisprudence." *Stanford Law Review* 34: 703-737.

Maccoby, Eleanor, 1990. "The Sexes and Their Interactions: Some Explanatory Models." In *The Invisible Majority*. New Orleans: Graduate School of Tulane University.

McClean, J. D. and J. C. Wood. 1969. *Criminal Justice and the Treatment of Offenders*. London: Sweet and Maxwell.

Merton, Robert K. [1948] 1968. *Social Theory and Social Structure*, New York The Free Press.

Muller v. Oregon, 208 U.S. 412, 420, 28 S. Ct. 324, 326, 52 .Ed. 551, 555 (1908).

Nagel, I. 1981. "Sex Differences in the Processing of Criminal Defendants." Pp. 104-124 *Women and Crime*, edited by A. Morris and L. Gelsthorpe. Cropwood Round Table No. 13, University of Cambridge Institute of Criminology.

Phillips, D. M. and L. B. De Fleur. 1982. "Gender Ascription in the Stereotyping of Deviants," *Deviants* 20: 431-448.

Pollack, Otto. 1950. *The Criminality of Women*. New York: A. S. Barnes.

Reed, Kimberly A. 1990. "Different Voices, Ideal Paths: The Contradictions of Carol Gilligan," Unpublished paper, Department of Sociology, Graduate Center, CUNY.

Rhode, Deborah. 1989. *Justice and Gender*. New Haven: Yale University Press.

Sachs, Albie, and Joan Hoff Wilson. 1978. *Sexism and the Law: Male Beliefs and Legal Bias in Britain and the United States.* New York: The Free Press.

Simon, R. J. 1975. *Women and Crime.* Lexington, MA: D.C. Heath.

Solomon, Frieda. 1987. "Progressive Era Justice: The New York City Women's Court," Paper presented at the 7th Berkshire Conference on the History of Women, Wellesley, MA.

Smith, A. D. 1962. *Women in Prison* London: Stevens.

Spender, Dale. 1978. "Educational Research and the Female Perspective." Paper presented at the British Educational Research Association Conference on "Women, Education and Research," University of Leicester.

Sykes, G. 1958. *The Society of Captives.* Princeton: Princeton University Press.

Tyack, David and Myra Strober. 1981. "Jobs and Gender: A History of the Structuring of Educational Employment by Sex." Pp 131-152 in *Educational Policy and Management: Sex Differentials,* edited by Schmuck and Charters. New York: Academic Press.

Temin, C. 1973. "Discriminatory Sentencing of Women Offenders: The Argument for Equality in a Nutshell." *American Criminal Law Review.* 11: 355-372.

Walker, Laurence. "Sex Differences in the Development of Moral Reasoning." *Child Development* 55: 677-691.

Walsh, Mary Roth. 1977. *Doctors Wanted — No Women Need Apply: Sexual Barriers in the Medical Profession.* New Haven: Yale University Press.

Warren, M. Q., (ed.) 1981. *Comparing Female and Male Offenders.* Beverly Hills: Sage.

Weisberg, D. Kelly. 1977. "Barred from the Bar: Women and Legal Education in the United States, 1870-1890." *Journal of Legal Education* 28: 485-507.

____. 1979. "Women in Law School Teaching: Problems and Progress." *Journal of Legal Education* 30: 226-248.

Zuckerman, Harriet and Jonathan R. Cole. 1987. "Marriage, Motherhood and Research Performance in Science." *Scientific American* 255: 119-125.

6

The Heir and the Spare: Evasiveness, Role-Complexity, and Patterns of Inheritance

Jeffrey P. Rosenfeld

"Let's choose executors and talk of wills," says Shakespeare's Richard II. King Richard may have been willing to discuss his estate plans, but until recently, most U.S. parents were downright evasive about disposing of their wealth. Despite the time and expense which go into estate planning (and re-planning), many parents still do not tell their offspring what they will someday inherit. In fact, an estimated 32 percent of heirs only learn how much they have inherited after parents have died, and their wills are probated (Rosenfeld 1990).

Marvin B. Sussman and his colleagues first confirmed this point in 1970 in a study of inheritance patterns in Cuyahoga County, Ohio. Interviews with survivors of 659 decedents revealed that ". . . . over 70 percent [of survivors] did not know whether the decedent had made a will" (Sussman et al. 1970, p. 115) and were surprised to learn how much they had actually inherited. Ohio parents, like their counterparts throughout the United States, are reluctant to share such information with children or grandchildren (Rosenfeld 1979, p. 25-33). Ronald is a good example. This retired police officer from New York City is uneasy about being so evasive but not uneasy enough to discuss his estate plans openly.

Says Ronald, "We [i.e., he and his wife] realize it's important. But no, we haven't told the kids." William, aged 70, sounds just as guilty. He admits that, "It's something I should do. The will is more than two years

I am grateful to Marvin B. Sussman, and to the late Hanan C. Selvin, for their ideas, suggestions and criticisms. Others who helped me move beyond earlier drafts of this paper are S.A. Marino, Janet McCubbin, Ed Kick, Remi Clignet and Joseph Varacalli. They are all honest critics and good friends. Gina Costello and Ani Haratunian patiently unraveled a manuscript which had more changes and codicils than some of the wills I analyzed for "The Heir And The Spare."

old. I say to myself, 'These are my sons and they have a right to know,' but I haven't mentioned the will to them yet."

Other parents have no qualms about keeping their estate plans secret. Lena, for example, has rewritten her will three times without consulting or informing her children. French-Canadian by birth, she deliberately sought French-speaking lawyers, so that she could conceal her estate plans even more effectively. In this respect she is not much different from Reeves, a retired schoolteacher from Salt Lake City who says with a grin, "I like to keep them guessing." And so Reeves established charitable remainder unit trusts to pay for his sons' college expenses. He did so without telling either of the sons and with the stipulation that he could dissolve the trust funds if they dropped out of college.

To have a father like Reeves is to be kept permanently in the dark about inheritance issues. Here is how an heiress named Rachel describes what it was like growing up without any information about the particulars of her future inheritance. "I was told I didn't have to worry," complains Rachel, "but I was never told what the real situation was" (cited in Wojahn 1989, p. 66).

From Rachel's comment it is easy to get the impression that parents are badgered by offspring demanding to know what they will someday inherit. But the social fact is that most children do not raise such questions with their parents. "In some families," says Alan Farnham (1990:74), "the very mention of inheritance is taboo. . . . There aren't many kids who feel comfortable saying, 'Let's talk about your death and dying, Dad'. . . . It's an invasion of privacy to ask your parents how much they've got." But most heirs really should be asking because so much money is at stake. Between 1987 and 1991, a total of $778.9 billion will pass through the probate system, which represents 4.3 percent of the nation's GNP (Farnham 1990).

Yurow (1990) conservatively estimates the modal value of probated estates in 1989 at $30,000, but notes that most estates are worth considerably more.[1] In 1989, for example, the Internal Revenue Service processed 59,300 Estate Tax Returns (Form 706). The filing threshold for individuals who died in 1988 was $600,000 which means that there were 59,300 estates valued at this amount or more.[2] Many were worth quite a bit more, and it can be inferred that thousands of estates are valued at just under the taxable value every year.

More than $1 billion worth of personal and real property passes through U.S. probate courts every year; and this represents only a fraction of the wealth inherited annually. *Trusts & Estates*, the magazine read by most estate-planning professionals, puts the actual value of inherited wealth at closer to $600 billion per annum. This is based on a broader construction of inheritance which includes insurance policies, bank accounts, annuities, stock portfolios and revocable trusts in addition to the real and personal property mentioned in a decedent's will (*Trusts & Estates* 1989, p. 32). The actual percentage of wealth inherited via decedents' wills may be decreasing, but inheritance (which includes insurance policies, bank accounts, stock portfolios, etc.) is more important than ever. As Yurow (1990, p. 3) says: "It is possible to transfer the assets of an estate so that probate is virtually unnecessary and, increasingly, middle-class and wealthy persons are doing this."

Whether construed narrowly or broadly, inheritance involves the transfer of a family's wealth and is of great interest to beneficiaries for that reason. But there are other reasons why family members would be preoccupied with inheritance, even if they rarely discuss it with one another. Apart from the property and money involved, inheritance is linked with power and status in families.

Sociologists recognize that inheritance is a social as well as a legal process. Along with the redistribution of wealth there are realignments in status and power. Sussman et al. (1970, pp. 7-10) conclude from their groundbreaking study that inheritance is actually more valuable for its symbolic meaning than its economic worth, except among the very wealthy. Sociologists are beginning to explore the ramifications of inheritance for the continuity and social structure of families (Sussman and Cates 1982; Gottman 1988; McNamee and Miller 1989), and there are now theoretical and methodological breakthroughs in this area. But the important point for this essay is the fact that family members themselves recognize the role that inheritance plays in affirming their status and power as offspring, siblings, or kin. By comparing the social responses of people who contest a will and those who do not, it is possible to understand how important inheritance is.

About 20 percent of estate-litigation involves relatively small amounts of money (Rosenfeld 1982; Schoenblum 1987; Farnham 1990). In fact, court costs are as large as the disputed estates in some will-contests. In virtually all such cases it is necessary to go beyond financial issues and examine the social structure of the families involved in these lengthy and expensive court battles. Money is not the issue. Status-anxiety is. Offspring frequently contest wills to "right a wrong." They perceive that other beneficiaries would wrongly get more status, power, or control of family property if the will went uncontested. Even heirs who do not litigate and are thus "technically" satisfied with their inheritance are quite anxious about the social consequences of the intergenerational transfer. Long before probate, often while parents are still alive, the offspring are formulating their own definitions of equity: who ought to be inheriting what and why. It is all the more surprising, then, that until recently most benefactors and beneficiaries had so little to say to each other. Many parents felt uncomfortable about telling offspring what they would inherit, and offspring were often anxious about bringing up the subject as though it were bad manners to ask.

Estate-Planning as Training in Ambiguity

It is not bad manners to ask, but it involves a breach in established etiquette. The problem is anomie. These anxious offspring are experiencing a lack of norms or guidelines. And their evasive benefactors are just as uncomfortable. The problem for parents and offspring is that communicating about wealth is fraught with contradictory expectations. Evasiveness, as Rose Coser observes (1967; 1979), is actually a way of dealing with double-binding situations such as this.

Rose Coser refers to the experience of learning how to resolve contradictory expectations as "training in ambiguity" (1979). At O'Brien Hospital, where Coser did her fieldwork, the challenge was to navigate among contradictory and status-threatening demands. Residents-in-training on O'Brien's psychiatric ward had to work under the strain of being both students and doctors. They frequently showed a "trained incapacity" to deal with their double-binding roles. Rose Coser (1967:206) explains that such evasive behavior actually serves two important functions. It is an *ego defense* inasmuch as it buffers residents from the strain of being exposed to status contradictions. In addition, evasiveness serves as a *system defense* because it protects the social integration of the ward by preventing the staff from pinpointing the structural source of their stress.

Estate planning is rigorous training in ambiguity for many of the same sociological reasons. The breakdowns in communication that are so common when parents write their wills are functionally equivalent to evasive behavior on the psychiatric ward at O'Brien Hospital. These breakdowns in communication protect parents who are enmeshed in complex and demanding family systems and in this respect are ego defenses. In addition, these very same breakdowns in communication fuel the estate-planning system by encouraging parents to rely on lawyers, accountants, and other financial planners. The result is an ongoing round of annual reviews and frequent consultations with estate-planning professionals. There is no "final" plan for the children to know, only the news that there is yet another revision of Mom's or Dad's will. The result is an experience much like the "learning through doing" which was part of the problem on the psychiatric ward (Coser 1967,

1979), as well as the key to its resolution.

Will-makers must reconcile the contradictory pressures of reciprocity and utility — bequests made for reasons of love or affection — and the desire to make a "good investment" with the family's assets. In addition, the process is always adaptive to changes in tax codes and inheritance law, so that estate plans that might be workable at one point in time lose their taxable advantage later on. The result is an ongoing, incomplete process which many will-makers find confusing and intimidating. When this is superimposed upon the traditional norm that will-making is sacrosanct and confidential, the result is a breakdown in communications.

Ellen Wojahn (1989, p. 68) finds that offspring in many middle-income and upper-income families are suffering from "wealth hang-up's" as a result of such failure to communicate about inheritance. "It's amazing," says Wojahn, "how many children's wealth hang-up's are based on what should have been easy to address — namely not understanding where the money came from. To the extreme frustration of their children, many entrepreneurs persist in. . . . refusing to provide the information."

If parents are not forthcoming it is because often times they cannot be. The system itself requires that they constantly rethink their bequests, re-evaluate their beneficiaries, and rewrite their wills. Evasiveness is often the best strategy when a role imposes such contradictory expectations. The role of will-maker forces parents to decide between equity in the legal sense and the testamentary freedom to make whatever bequests they want. Wants and needs can take them far afield. Rosenfeld (1979; 1980) identifies situations when will-writers systematically included outsiders along with family members. More recently, Torrey (1990, p. 21) reanalyzed unpublished data from the IRS Inheritance Tax File for 1977 and found that the probability of making a bequest outside the immediate family was 19 percent for decedents who had been married and 60 percent of decedents who had been divorced, separated or widowed. More than traditional kinship and ascribed status are at work in these cases.

Wilbert E. Moore (1967) wrote about "serial service" as the normative force behind inheritance. But Moore's concept relies both on lineal descent and ascribed status. It overlooks significant changes which have occurred in U.S. families as a result of cohabitation, voluntary childlessness, divorce and remarriage (Rosenfeld 1990). For this reason, the concept of serial service does not address the reciprocities which now knit so many families together. Rose Coser (1982) does a better job of capturing these changes with her concept of a claim structure based on norms of reciprocity which connect the members of increasingly diverse families. The claim structure pivots on ". . . . a hierarchy of mutual services and allegiances" (Coser 1982, p. 190) and not on traditional roles and statuses. Achievement replaces ascription in the claim structure.

The concept of the claim structure helps explain why testamentary freedom does not pose a threat in most American families. Instead of siphoning wealth out of families, testamentary freedom (Sussman, 1970 p. 8) gives will-writers the option to:

> . . . . right a wrong done to an individual, to improve the family's capability of surviving as a unit. . . . testamentary freedom, in this sense, can function to support the family and social order and especially those values that undergrid intimate relationships: affection, service, reciprocity, exchange and identification.

Testamentary freedom is the power to acknowledge the existing claim structure within a family and to set priorities among claims. These decisions are formalized in the last will and testament, which is perhaps the most complex and idiosyncratic of all the documents that create and sustain American families. Families have a legal reality based on documents such as birth or death certificates and the marriage license. Only wills are revocable, which means they can be nullified and redrawn. It would be unthinkable to change the names on a death certificate or marriage license. But will-writers can and frequently do revoke their wills, add codicils, or make different estate plans. In this way estate-planning comes to reflect the changing dynamics of the claim structure — shifts in status and power resulting from divorce, remarriage, and the changing roles of women and men. This is the sociological reason why the annual review is now such an important part of estate-planning. Apart from the financial, legal, and tax advantages of the annual review, there is an important social function: to link wealth, power and status at a time when family and kinship are more complex and changeable than ever before.

Why, then, don't more families openly discuss these particulars? Rose Coser explained why years ago: evasiveness has its psychic rewards, and it also contributes to the functioning of the social system.

Evasiveness as an Ego-Defense for Will-Writers

In many families it would be easier to discuss a parent's estate-plan so that beneficiaries could prepare in advance to invest or manage the wealth they will eventually inherit. Logical and convenient though it might be, the subject does not usually arise until a parent is close to death. Part of the reason for this is that changing norms of inheritance are encouraging new types of testamentary behavior, and some of these are difficult for parents and offspring to deal with.

For example, one of the most popular bumper-stickers in our nation reads, I'M SPENDING MY KIDS' INHERITANCE. The slogan also crops up on sweatshirts and key-chains, especially in communities where older Americans live. It reflects a counternorm in our culture, one which touches on the traditional roles and relationships of wealthholders.

The traditional norm has been for wealthholders to defer their gratification and to put wealth aside for their children and/or grandchildren. Lawrence Friedman (1968), writing about "Dynastic Trusts," says that these instruments originated out of concern for future generations. This is probably true for the majority of wealthholders, yet a small but growing number of middle-class parents feel that they have already fulfilled their parental obligations and now want to focus more on themselves. Elsewhere (Rosenfeld 1980;1990), I have referred to this pattern as "Benevolent Disinheritance" because it involves giving less to one's heirs albeit not for vindictive reasons. Middle-class parents who disinherit benevolently are convinced that they have already done enough for their children.

Benevolent disinheritance is not limited to middle-class families. There are millionaires who disinherit "on principle" (Kirkland, Jr. 1986, p. 22) and put most of their wealth into charitable trusts or foundations. Their offspring only inherit a fraction of their fortunes, ". . . . enough money so that they feel they could do anything, but not so much that they could do nothing" (Kirkland, Jr. 1986:18). Often they do not tell their children about these plans. Evasiveness can actually be the best policy when parents plan to behave this way. It allows them to avoid the guilty feelings which might accompany such actions. Benevolent disinheritance is still quite rare, and only explains a small portion of the evasive behavior associated with estate-planning. Quite a bit more is explained by the fact that discussions of death or finances make people feel anxious.

Evasiveness helps parents avoid the subjects of death and finances — two issues which make people worried and uncomfortable in our culture. Parents who avoid them can temporarily sidestep the unpleasantries of death and dying. They also do not have to be concerned with what their children think of them ". . . . Now that the kids really know how much we're worth" (Rosenfeld 1979; Wojahn 1989; Farnham 1990). The illusion of the parent as immortal and omnipotent is easier to sustain by avoiding the subject of inheritance. In many respects, the system of estate-planning also depends on avoidance — the avoidance of a final estate plan.

Evasiveness as a System-Defense: The Estate Planning Profession

Estate planners encourage clients to keep their options open. They can do so by consenting to annual reviews and evaluations. And so they continue "learning by doing" as they confer annually with accountants, lawyers, and financial planners. Annual reviews may clarify the tax law, but they intensify the sociological ambivalence (Merton and Barber 1963) surrounding inheritance. The ambivalence intensifies because clients usually come to estate planners with one set of expectations and suddenly find themselves facing quite a different set. Clients bring with them a sense of reciprocity. This usually takes the form of love, gratitude, and generosity. Occasionally it can be vindictive or punitive as when a will-maker wrote:

> . . . . My only son, David, is not to receive a single penny from my estate for reasons well known to him and to my family and friends, and for the further reason that during his whole lifetime since he attained his majority he has been disobedient, ungrateful, and a constant source of humiliation, anxiety, anxiety, and sorrow (cited in Rosenfeld 1979, p. 83).

But by and large, will-makers operate within a relational framework that is familiar to sociologists. It goes by names like reciprocity (Lévi-Strauss 1957) or serial service (Moore 1967) and involves the idea of reciprocating for past behavior. Lawyers or financial planners introduce their clients to another set of criteria, however.

According to this perspective, bequests are investments which should bring the greatest possible returns. In fact, some economists insist that parents who make equal bequests to their offspring are actually favoring those children who already have some competitive advantage, be it a well-paying job, a good marriage, or solid schooling. This line of reasoning holds that inheritance is a last-ditch effort by parents to help particular offspring. Thus, farmers in one region of Illinois favor the oldest son, while those in a nearby area divide land evenly among all sons (Carroll and Salamon 1988. pp. 228-230). Behrman et al. (1986, pp. 33-54) summarize a richly textured literature which debates whether parents favor boys or girls in their trusts and estate-plans. Unequal distributions have been documented as far back as Dunham's (1963) study of probate records in Chicago. Economists are aware of this inheritance pattern but interpret it differently than sociologists do. They speak of future utility (Kessler and Masson 1989; Tomes 1981) rather than reciprocity for past actions.

The variety of trust and gift options is endless, and so are the opportunities to redo an estate plan. "Take care of your assets," says a typical mailing from one of the nation's larger insurance companies (Alliance Life Associates, Inc., 1988), "and they will take care of you." But taking care of assets means being ready to replan the portfolio of stocks, bonds, investments and real estate and being prepared to reconsider who inherits what and when.

The preoccupation with planning is reminiscent of what Phillippe Ariès has observed about attitudes toward death and dying. In *Western Attitudes Toward Death* (1981), Ariès notes that planning has become the hallmark of death and dying in modern society. Where once there was little or no preparation for death, today there is elaborate preparation as epitomized by estate planning and the professional norms of estate planners. This is a far cry from inheritance systems based on birth order and ascribed criteria like gender. Parents in such systems have no need to be evasive, and at an early age their children know where they stand. In this context it is worth recalling that Winston Churchill referred to his brother and himself as "The heir and the spare." There are indeed societies where the future is preordained by norms of inheritance, and offspring are unevasively labeled as "heirs and spares" at an early age.

Heirs and Spares: Unevasive Roles

Gary Watson (1980) has written perceptively about the impact of inheritance in societies where a family identifies the heir at birth or early during childhood. Watson shows, for example, that schooling, marriage and occupation are closely linked to heirship in Spanish Basque villages and Italian Alpine communities where inheritance of farmland is the norm.

He who inherits the ancestral estate will be schooled differently than his brothers or sisters. There is no shortage of marriage partners for a designated heir in Basque villages like Echalar or Murelage (Watson 1980, p. 9). And, of course, the heir is expected to eventually run the family farm by himself when the system is based on impartible inheritance as it is in the German-speaking Alpine village of St. Felix (Watson 1980, p. 11) or in the Irish peasant communities studied by Arensberg and Kimball (1940). The heir will also be included more in local politics and religious ceremonies, which again reflects the status-enhancing experience of being designated early in life as the heir and not the spare.

Far from being evasive, parents in a Spanish Basque village or a Swiss Alpine farming community identify and then socialize the heir differently from their other children. Even during childhood, his inheritance creates what E.H. Hughes (1945) has called a "master status" which affects all aspects of his life and even shapes his personality. This, for example, is how Watson describes childhood socialization in Spanish Basque villages:

> . . . . From infancy, he [i.e., the heir] is socialized into the role of heir. . . . Frivolity and mischievousness, permitted in his siblings, are sharply rebuked when he displays them (1980, p. 10).

If and when such rebukes occur, they are a reminder that parents cannot be evasive about inheritance when it is an ascribed status. It is a social fact which shapes a lifetime of interaction between parents and offspring.

Being an heir has its drawbacks too, and these are all the more painful because heirship is unambiguously bestowed in preindustrial societies. Thus, when farming began to decline in the Spanish Basque heartland during the 1960s, it became desirable to leave the farm and migrate to urban areas. Suddenly, being heir to the farm was a demotion rather than an honor — an albatross around the neck of he who had to inherit the land. Parents in these declining farm villages started waiting to see which son was dullest and least talented, and belatedly named this "ugly duckling" as heir to the barren farmstead.

Heirs are identified early and unambiguously when land is impartible and owning it confers honor, status and power. To be an heir is status-enhancing in such peasant societies, and it confers power and prestige throughout the life cycle. But there can be little or no parental discretion when inheritance is linked with power and status in this way. Heirship is ascribed at birth and then plays an important part in establishing educational, occupational, and migration patterns. For this reason parents cannot be evasive when they live off the land and expect to pass it on to a first-born son (Watson 1980; for historical accounts of heirship in European peasant societies see Meijers 1935, pp. 341-49). In this respect, heirship is a powerful source of social control both for parents and for offspring. Parents cannot be evasive, and offspring cannot escape the "greedy" (Coser 1984) and lifelong demands of peasant societies. The legacy of life in a *Gemeinschaft* society is an existence tightly circumscribed by relationships to family and land. This explains why it was unthinkable for Korean or Chinese peasant families to exist without sons. The Korean or Chinese family without sons could not pass along land inasmuch as girls were disqualified from inheriting. Such families were "required" to adopt sons, if only unofficially, so that there would be somebody to inherit the ancestral land. The greedy nature of *Gemeinschaft* demands that everybody have a specified status in relation to the family and to the land. Evasiveness is not an option when so much pivots on relationships which are established at birth and which link a family to the larger society. As Rose Coser observes, nothing is more certain than the expectations and obligations of the "greedy" *Gemeinschaft*.

The greedy *Gemeinschaft* is a powerful theme in Rose Coser's sociology. In her essay on role-complexity (Coser 1975, pp. 240-244) she equates *Gemeinschaft* with lack of individualism, creativity, and self-awareness. But the idea also permeates her earlier work. Mount Hermon, the hospital where Coser did the fieldwork for *Life In The Ward*, is labeled as a "tight little island" (Coser 1962, p. 3) which relies on discipline and control. "While the patient lies in his bed in the ward," she writes, "the outside world recedes from view." With it go autonomy and self-control.

Rose Coser looks to the *Gesellschaft* as the liberating source of individualism. The *Gesellschaft* offers freedom of choice and self-expression through its most important structural attribute. Coser refers to this as role-complexity and argues that in role-complexity lies freedom of choice:

> This means that in a complex role-set, where status holders have to negotiate with several different if not conflicting expectations, their behavior cannot be prescribed in detail. Life in a game of chess, behavior depends much on individual assessments of possible moves (1975, p. 31).

This process of assessment is the basis for reciprocities in a growing number of families. When Rose Coser (1982, p. 190) refers to the family as a claim structure, she means that rights and obligations can be achieved (i.e., they are negotiable) rather than ascribed. Inheritance of property is precisely one of the areas of family life where achievement is replacing ascription.

A Less Evasive Future?

Will estate-planning continue to be secretive and exclusionary? Probably, but only in families where it is expected that inheritance will pass along lines of lineal descent but cannot because those descent-lines have been muddled. The lack of norms or guidelines for transferring wealth discourages family members from discussing inheritance openly. This is often a serious problem in divorced and "reconstituted" families that include children from previous marriages. The intergenerational linkages in divorced and reconstituted families are vague and open to negotiation. As such, they complicate any interaction between benefactor and beneficiaries.

Divorce and remarriage are socially acceptable and commonplace in American society. But remarriage, as Andrew Cherlin (1984) observes, is an incomplete institution. The rights and obligations of parents and stepchildren in reconstituted families are open to negotiation and interpretation. The same holds for relationships between stepgrandparents and their stepgrandchildren. There are no social norms of inheritance for stepgrandchildren or for grandchildren who have been estranged through divorce and custody battles. Cherlin and Furstenburg (1986, p. 234), writing about the "new American grandparent," say that many older Americans must now confront stepgrandparenting issues without clearcut norms or role-models. The result is that their estate-planning is often tentative and confused — not a situation which lends itself to easy communication with heirs or beneficiaries.

The norms governing remarried parents and what they owe to children from their previous marriages are even more ambiguous. Fellows and her colleagues (1978) provide the most revealing data on how little reciprocity there is between remarried parents and their children from prior marriages. Of 745 will-writers surveyed by Fellows et al. (1978, p. 366), 23 percent said they would leave *nothing* to children from their previous marriages. An additional 29 percent of will-writers in that sample would leave only a small portion of their estate to children from their previous marriages. The attitudes of divorced parents and those of stepgrandparents are ambivalent at best. This is why divorce and remarriage may well be creating vast numbers of heirs and spares. Divorce and remarriage are weakening the intergenerational cement in many families. But other social and demographic changes have the opposite effect as they strengthen intergenerational linkages and make families more cohesive. Perhaps the single most important change is the increased life expectancy of the U.S. population. The impact has been especially pronounced in middle-income and upper-income families, the very families which were most likely to be evasive about inheritance. There will be more communication about inheritance in such families because the "graying of America" has produced new reciprocities and obligations between aging parents and their adult children.

A growing number of adult Americans are now caretakers for aging parents or in-laws as well as being parents with offspring of their own. The gerontologist Elaine Brody (1981) has referred to "women in the middle" who must be caretakers to two generations: one older and one younger. The same generational configuration has already impacted on the inheritance of wealth as an economic and social process.

More than 25 percent of Americans in their fifties have one or more parents or in-laws still living. Among adults in their forties the intergenerational linkages are even more striking. The average American 40-year-old married couple has more living parents (2.6) than children (2.2). Adults of all ages, but especially those in their fifties and sixties (when earnings are at their peak) must now create estate-plans that reflect obligations up and down the generational ladder. This explains the growing popularity of caretaker trusts in comprehensive estate-planning packages. A social consequence of these financial arrangements is the need for cooperation between parents and their children. The result is better and more frequent communication about inheritance, if only because it is the prerequisite for a caretaker trust.

The graying of U.S. families has reshaped inheritance patterns in other ways too. Older Americans, the group now living longer and requiring more daily care, tend to make larger bequests to the family members who look after them during their final years. There is not much empirical data on this subject, but the anecdotal record suggests that siblings usually expect that their aging parent will leave a larger inheritance to the brother or (as is usually the case) the sister who acted as caretaker. Where otherwise they might expect equal shares, they acknowledge that the caretaker has "earned" something extra. In this respect there is now more consensus among siblings and fewer opportunities to be evasive.

The aging of the population has reshaped inheritance patterns in yet another way. More people than ever before must divest themselves of wealth in order to qualify for benefits under Medicare guidelines. Medicare will not allow benefits for people whose income is above a certain amount. This fact, coupled with a tax code which exempts gifts (even annual gifts) valued at $10,000 or less per child, has impacted on the benefactor-beneficiary relationship. It is now commonplace for cash and property to pass from aging parents to their offspring in the form of *inter vivos* gifts or transfers. Gift-giving has become a major component of intergenerational wealth transfers in many families. In fact, some economists (Kessler and Mason 1989, p. 144; Behrman et al. 1986, pp. 51-53; Tomes 1981, pp. 947-950) argue that statistical research on inheritance fails to describe the ebb and flow of wealth in our society because it systematically ignores *inter vivos* gifts. The probate record points to equality in bequests for offspring. But inheritance may not be the most salient source of wealth for offspring. Long before the tradition of *per stirpes* (i.e., in equal shares) distribution of the estate, there was probably a history of large and unequal gifts to the children (Kessler and Mason 1989, pp. 144-147). There is less reason to be evasive about inheritance when gift-giving becomes the preferred method for transferring resources. Gift-givers will probably be more relaxed about discussing their estate-plans if only because there will be very little at stake by the time the estate is probated. A colleague of mine, now in his late 60's, jokes that, "I'm very open with my kids. They know exactly what they're going to inherit when I die: the few bucks left after I put them through graduate school, buy new cars for both of them, and make their weddings!"

Humor, as Rose Coser (1960, pp. 83-85) noted years ago, is a way of minimizing social strain. Parents who joke about inheritance with their children are using humor to deal with the ambivalence which is associated with divesting themselves of wealth. Other parents are not so lighthearted, however. Their lawyers or accountants have advised them to raise the subject. The goal is to limit or reduce the odds of estate-litigation by discussing their trusts and estate-plans. This reflects a change in estate-planning strategy which is geared to tax codes and nuances in the law, but is also having a social impact on intergenerational relationships. Many families are now discussing — if only for tax or legal reasons — what would otherwise be taboo: who will inherit what and why. "Don't play hide and seek," advises *Fortune Magazine* (1986, p. 23):

> Forget about locking your will away like some 19th-century miser. Bring the family finances into the daylight, so the children will know what they are getting and where it came from.

The legal and financial objectives are simple. Discussions with children and other family members will help iron-out misunderstandings which could otherwise jeopardize a trust or estate-plan. If only to stop the "flood of litigation" (Lustgarten 1983, p. 10 *et seq.*) now clogging our nation's probate courts, many middle-income and upper-income benefactors are discussing their trusts and estate-plans more openly.

Conclusions

There is a social component to the inheritance of wealth: communication between benefactor and beneficiaries about who will inherit what and why. Rose Laub Coser has developed a theory of society which helps interpret such behavior and locates it in the social structure.

Communication between benefactor and beneficiaries is open, forthright, and unevasive in peasant societies where status pivots on land ownership. These are classic *Gemeinschaft* societies where status is ascribed and serves as an important source of social control. The heir to the peasant farmstead is identified early, and his status determines his educational, occupational, and marital future. The pattern is more convoluted and evasive in societies like our own. The role-complexity which characterizes our day-to-day existence means that relationships are more flexible and negotiable. The prescriptive power of kinship and lineal descent (which are ascribed statuses) gives way to the influence of achieved and negotiated relationships. Inheritance has become a system of exchange based largely on the claim structure which exists in every family and not on location in the descent group. This calls attention to structural conditions under which inheritance will proceed smoothly and predictably and to when inheritance will be fraught with uncertainty, ambivalence, and litigation. There will be consensus over inheritance when there is consensus over the priority of claims in the claim structure. There is more ambiguity and strain in families where there are stepchildren and stepgrandparents, also in families where an adult has children from a previous marriage but does not have custody of them. Intergenerational linkages are poorly defined — and poorly maintained — in both of those situations. Inheritance of wealth is a source of strain for that reason.

There is a final factor reshaping the interaction between benefactors and beneficiaries: pressure from estate-planning professionals. For legal and tax reasons they are encouraging clients to be more open about their trusts and estate-plans. This bodes even more families in which offspring will know who inherits what and why. The information will come later in life, but more offspring will know if they are heirs or spares.

Notes

1. As Yurow (1990) is quick to point out, the modal amount is misleading. It does not reflect the property arrangements of most married couples. Most marital property today is jointly owned, which means it will not be probated until the surviving spouse has died. Thus the probated value of the first spouse is significantly lower because it does not include jointly owned assets or property. The value of the total gross estate, which includes jointly owned property, is much greater.

2. A significant number of decedents' estates fall just below the filing threshold in any given year. An estate valued at $600,000 is subject to the estate tax, but one valued at $599,999 would not be. Technically, a decedent must have filed a 706 Return to be considered a top wealthholder. But in actual fact, there are as many decedents with estates valued just below the filing threshold.

References

Ariès, Phillippe. 1982. *Western Attitudes Toward Death*. Baltimore: Johns Hopkins Univeristy Press.

Arensberg, Conrad M. and Solon T. Kimball. 1940. *Family and Community in Ireland*. 2nd ed. Cambridge, MA: Harvard University Press.

Behrman, Jere R., Robert A. Pollak and Paul Taubman. 1986. "Do Parents Favor Boys?" *International Economic Review* 27:33-54.

Brody, Elaine M. 1981. "Women in the Middle, and Family Help to Older People." *The Gerontologist* 21:471-480.

Carroll, Edward V. and Sonya Salamon. 1988. "Share and Share Alike: Inheritance Patterns in Two Illinois Farm Communities." *Journal Of Family History* 13:219-232.

Cherlin, Andrew J. 1984. "Remarriage as an Incomplete Institution." *American Journal Of Sociology* 84:634-650.

Cherlin, Andrew J. and Frank F. Furstenberg, Jr. 1986. *The New American Grandparent*. New York: Basic Books, Inc.

Coser, Rose Laub. 1960. "Laughter Among Colleagues: A Study of the Social Functions of Humor Among the Staff of a Mental Hospital." *Psychiatry* 23:83-91.

_____. 1962. *Life In The Ward*. East Lansing, MI:Michigan State University Press.

_____. 1967. "Evasiveness as a Response to Structural Ambivalence." *Social Science And Medicine* 1:203-218.

_____. 1975. "The Complexity of Roles as a Seedbed of Individual Autonomy." Pp 237-265 in Lewis A Coser (ed.), *The Idea of Social Structure: Essays In Honor of Robert K. Merton*. New York: Harcourt, Brace Jovanovich.

_____. 1979. *Training In Ambiguity*. New York. The Free Press.

_____. 1982. "The American Family: Changing Patterns of Control." Pp 187-204 in Jack P. Gibbs (ed.), *Social Control: Views From the Social Sciences*. Beverly Hills: SAGE Publications.

_____. 1984. "The Greedy Nature of *Gemeinschaft*," Pp 221-239 in Walter W. Powell and Richard Robbins (eds.), *Conflict and Consensus: Essays in Honor of Lewis A. Coser*. New York: The Free Press.

Dunham, Allison. 1963. "The Method, Process and Frequency of Wealth Transmission at Death." *University Of Chicago Law Review* 30:241-285.

Farnham, Alan. 1990. "The Windfall Awaiting the New Inheritors." *Fortune* 7(May):72-75, *et seq.*

Fellows, Mary Louise, Rita J. Simon, and William Rau. 1978. "Public Attitudes About Distribution at Death and Intestate Succession Laws in the United States." *American Bar Foundation Research Journal* 2:319-391.

Friedman, Lawrence M. 1968. "The Dynastic Trust." *Yale Law Review* 73:547-592.

Gotman, Anne. 1988. *Hèriter*. Paris: Presses Universitaires de France.

Hughes, Everett C. 1945. "Dilemmas and Contradictions In Status." *American Journal of Sociology* 5:353-359.

Kessler, Denis and Andre Masson. 1989. "Bequest and Wealth Accumulation: Are Some Pieces of the Puzzle Missing?" *Journal of Economic Prespecitives* 3:141-152.

Kirkland, Jr., Richard I. 1986. "Should You Leave It All To the Children?" *Fortune* 114(September 29):18-26.

Lévi-Strauss, Claude. 1957. "The Principle of Reciprocity." Pp 84-94 in L.A. Coser and B. Rosenberg (eds.), *Sociological Theory*. New York: The MacMillan Co.

Lustgarten, Ira H. 1983. "Should the Flood of Litigation Be Dammed?" *Trusts & Estates* 122 (January):10-11 *et seq*.

McNamee, Stephen J. and Robert K. Miller. 1989. "Estate Inheritance: A Sociological Lacuna." *Sociological Inquiry* 59:7-29.

Meijers, E.M. 1935. "Limits of Inheritance in the Laws of Europe." *Iowa Law Review* 20:341-69.

Merton, Robert K. and Elinor Barber. 1963. "Sociological Ambivalence," in Edward A. Tiryakian (ed.) *Sociological Theory, Values, and Sociocultural Change: Essays in Honor of Pitirim A. Sorokin*. New York: The Free Press.

Moore, Wilbert E. 1967. *Order and Change*. New York: John Wiley & Sons.

Rosenfeld, Jeffrey P. 1979. *Legacy of Aging: Inheritance and Disinheritance in Social Perspective*. Norwood, NJ: Ablex Publishing Co.

____. 1980. "Benevolent Disinheritance: The Kindest Cut." *Psychology Today* (March):80-83 *et seq*.

____. 1982. "Disinheritance & Will-Contests." Pp 75-86 in Marvin B. Sussman and Judith N. Cates (eds.), *Family Systems and Inheritance Patterns*. New York: The Haworth Press.

____. 1990. "To Heir Is Human." *Probate & Property* (July/August):21-25.

Schoenblum, Jeffrey A. 1987. "Will Contests: An Empirical Study." *Real Property, Probate & Trust Law Journal* 22:607-659.

Sussman, Marvin B. and Judith N. Cates. 1982. "Family Systems and Inheritance." Pp 1-24 in M.B. Sussman and J.N. Cates (eds.), *Family Systems and Inheritance Patterns*. New York: The Haworth Press.

Sussman, Marvin M., Judith N. Cates and David T. Smith. 1970. *The Family and Inheritance*. New York: The Russell Sage Foundation.

Tomes, Nigel. 1981. "The Family, Inheritance, and the Intergenerational Transmission of Inequality." *Journal of Political Economy* 89:928-958.

Torrey, Barbara Boyle. 1990. "A $64,000 Question: What Are the Aged Doing with Their Assets?" *Population & Development* 23:17-27.

Trusts & Estates Magazine. 1989. "Trusts and Estates: The Authority." [advertisement] 128 (October):32.

Watson, Gary S. 1980. "Intergenerational Transmission of Family Property: Some Preliminary Observations In European Farm and Peasant Communities." Paper presented at annual meeting of the Law and Society Association.

Wojahn, Ellen. 1989. "Share the Wealth or Spoil the Child?" *INC. Magazine* 2:64-77.

Yurow, Jane Handler. 1990. *Cheaper, Quicker and Simpler Probate Administration: A Policy Overview*. Washington, DC: AARP Public Policy Institute.

7

Immigrant Women and Their Children: What Kind of Legacy?

William V. D'Antonio

The invitation to contribute to this *Festschrift* in honor of Rose Coser provides me an opportunity to bring closure to a collaborative effort begun with Rose now more than a decade ago. This effort, to carry out a major oral history study of Italian and Jewish immigrant women and their children in New York and Connecticut, was cut short by my move to Washington D.C. in 1982 to become Executive Officer of the American Sociological Association. The administrative responsibilities of the office made it impossible to continue the project on any but the most minimal level during the years since then. This paper will be both a retrospective on the work we did together and a reflection on how well our ideas have withstood the test of time and more recent research.

This research had its origins in a series of conversations which Rose Coser of Stony Brook and I held during 1977-79. We found that we were both interested in the lives of immigrant women, and we had both come to the conclusion that their stories had not been adequately told. Instead our understanding of immigrant history had been based primarily upon the doings of men. Irving Howe's *The World of Our Fathers* exemplifies this historical tendency.[1] And it is also found in the way we have come to think about social mobility in American society; traditionally, we have measured mobility intergenerationally by comparing fathers' and sons' occupations. The classic example here is Blau and Duncan's *The American Occupational Structure* (1967).

Our major thesis was that immigrant women were important structural linkages for their families, and that urban American society provided roles that enabled them to help their families survive and adapt. The focus of our concern was Southern Italian and Eastern European Jewish women who arrived in this country before 1925 and who were between 13 and 25 years of age at the time. Thus, in 1990, they

The paper is truly a collaborative effort. Most of the material on Jewish families was developed by Rose, and our ideas are intermingled throughout. Thank you, Rose, for the opportunity to work with and learn from you.

would be beween 75 and 90 years of age. Our interest was in the way Italian and Jewish mothers taught their children about family traditions and learned about and linked them to American urban structures such as the school, the world of work, politics and religion.

Preliminary Considerations

Historical research on immigrant families has been slow to cast off traditional assumptions about gender roles. In their work on Philadelphia, for example, Hershberg et al. (1981, pp. 233-234) asserted that "The family deserves its recent popularity and centrality in the new historical research." But they continued to see the role of women within the family as one of maintaining the traditions and supporting the husband and father. Degler (1980) put it succinctly when he asserted that the father's role shaped the family, while the mother's role was shaped by and around the family.

Our purpose in taking a new look at immigrant family life and the process of assimilation into American society was to question Degler's assertion about the secondary role of women. It was not to gainsay the importance of the economic structure and the way it affected the family. Nor were we trying to downplay the larger structural setting that involved such variables as "housing stock; the nature and condition of the local, regional, and national economy; the number of skilled and unskilled positions available in the labor force; the location of jobs; transportation facilities; the fiscal circumstances of the local government; and the degree of discrimination encountered" (Hershberg 1981, p. 463).

We fully recognized the importance of placing the family and, in particular, women's roles within the structure of opportunities afforded by the larger urban economy. For example, the historical research carried out in Philadephia (Hershberg 1981) showed how the family determined who worked, who stayed at home and who went to school. In a way that is structurally no longer characteristic of American family life, the family then and not the individual, was the crucial decision-making unit. Thus, for example, whether a child stayed in school or not was decided by adult family members and not the child. And the assumption was that the father made such decisions.

In a variety of ways, these urban structural features have provided the context within which ethnic groups have struggled over the past 100 years to "make it." And if the role of the father has seemed most important from the perspective of the family, it has been because the father's work not only was perceived as the major factor in determining the level of material comfort that the family enjoyed, it also determined their residence location. It was assumed that location necessarily determined whether the children would stay in school or go to work.

When we acknowledge the importance to the family of these macro-structural conditions and of the father's role in the family, there seems little left to explain about how the immigrants from Europe made it during the past century. Indeed, one could be excused for coming to the conclusion that women's role in the assimilation process was at best peripheral. Rose Coser and I did not feel comfortable with that conclusion, and in the following pages I will attempt to suggest why. Suffice to say here that while most research has focused on the world of our fathers and emphasized the role of women as mothers in the home and kitchen, our focus moved beyond that to reflect on how, to what degree, and with what consequences the women might have provided vital linkages for their husbands and children to the larger community. Thus, we wanted to revise and update the immigration story by providing a different perspective on the experience of immigrants to the United States. Current research efforts in this regard provide important support for our thesis (Tropea et al. 1986; Tomasi 1985; Maglione and Fiore 1989).[2]

While the selection of Italian and Jewish women reflected in part our own backgrounds and personal interests, the selection also had important theoretical implications. In the following sections I will delineate the commonly known similarities and differences between Jewish and Italian immigrant families. It was our expectation that these similarities and differences would provide an excellent opportunity to discover the extent to which cultural variables might have interacted with macro-structural variables in the process of adaptation to American life. Lieberson (1980, pp. 15, 363-364) had aptly warned that it would be extremely difficult either to prove or disprove the impact of cultural attributes on structural factors in the struggle to get a piece of the pie. But we did not feel that a question should be avoided just because it might be difficult to answer. We wanted at least to begin to formulate the dimensions of the problem to be probed.

Receptivity to American Values

Among the key values of American society may be noted achievement, success, freedom, democracy, individualism, equality, and material comfort (Williams 1955). Degler (1980) noted how these values stood in contrast to the traditional values of immigrant families. The latter stressed group interests over those of the individual, patriarchal authority rather than equality, and group membership on the basis of ascription rather than achievement. So the relation of the immigrant family to the larger society was presumed to be a state of tension. This tension might well have been increased at least for the Italian family in which, according to Degler (1980, p. 139), "Italian women, of all immigrant women, came closest to the European pattern of being isolated in the family and having large numbers of children."

The literature abounds with the documentation of the familiar facts that (1) Jews had come to American cities from an urban environment in Eastern Europe and that Southern Italians had come from a peasant society; (2) the traditional Jewish emphasis on learning served them well at a time when increasing emphasis on education marked the development of industrial society (Glazer 1957). These factors, however, required closer analysis. Although Southern Italians did not have a tradition of learning , some Italian children did well, and they did much better even a generation later (Mariano 1921; Alba 1985, esp. pp. 59-60, 127-128). Was this merely a matter of the structural opportunities available? Did family cultural values have any impact? And did husbands and/or wives control the impact?

Presumably, Jewish families and Jewish women should have had less difficulty resolving the tensions between family and societal values than did the Italian family and Italian women. But the question still remains as to whether the important question about assimilation was structural rather than cultural or an interaction process that we still do not fully appreciate. For the present let me offer the following data from an oral history interview taken in New Haven (Izard 1975, p. 22) as part of the Ethnic Heritage Project that I directed. Mrs. Furillo (a pseudonym) recounted how at age 14 she was told by her immigrant mother that she had to go to work. She liked school and wanted to go on to high school, but her mother said: "No good school for girls. Girls don't have to know too much." Many years later, after Mrs. Furillo had become a successful businesswoman, she reported that her mother confessed her mistake to her in these words: "Look how much you have accomplished. Just imagine if I had the wisdom to let you go to school, what more you could have done."

Occupational Backgrounds and Distributions

The occupational backgrounds and histories of Jews and Italians immigrating to the United States were quite distinctive. Already in Russia in 1897, for example, almost 70 percent of all Jews were in manufacturing, commerce, or artisanry, and barely 3 percent were in agriculture (Rubinow 1907), — a sharp contrast to the *paisani* of Southern Italy. While Jews who emigrated from Russia are not a representative sample of Russian Jewry at the turn of the century (Halevy 1978), Jewish immigrants included a much higher proportion of skilled laborers than did Italians or other immigrants from Southern and Eastern Europe. Almost 40 percent of Hebrews (term used in the Dillingham Report) admitted to the U.S. between 1899 and 1910 were skilled laborers (of whom .7 percent were professionals). By comparison, only 12 percent of Italians were skilled laborers including .3 percent professionals. Conversely, among the Hebrew immigrants less than 1 in 10 were laborers or farm laborers compared with almost 60 percent among South Italians (Dillingham Commission 1911).

Information about the work of women is fragmentary. For example, one study showed that in 1910, 45 percent of Southern Italian women and about one-third of Jewish women 16 years old and over were at work. The percentage of married women who worked at that time in the men's clothing industry was far greater among Italians than among any other immigrant nationality. In that same year, of all immigrant women in the men's garment industry, of which there were some 3,000, almost 70 percent were Italian and 17 percent were Hebrews (Cohen 1977, pp. 120-143).

It is becoming clear now that women, both Jewish and Italian, worked in greater numbers than was commonly believed. Though both married and unmarried women worked in shops, married women also made money doing homework such as stitching, making flowers and threading beads. In oral histories conducted in Connecticut and New York, women who said that they had not worked after they came to this country frequently answered "yes" to the question whether they had boarders or lodgers, and often revealed, in answer to a subsequent question, that they "helped" their husbands in the store. Indeed, my grandmother got up daily with my grandfather at 4 AM to help him with his fruit and vegetable business. A review of oral histories done in Connecticut during the 1930s as part of the WPA Ethnic Heritage Program showed that it was common for Italian American women to say they were only "helping their husbands" when they were earning money. Thus they maintained the facade of the traditional patriarchal family (Yans-McLaughlin 1977, pp. 101-119).[3]

Literacy

Jews were relatively literate compared to other Southern and Eastern European immigrants; 26 percent were classified as illiterates when entering the country between 1899 and 1910. For Southern Italians the illiteracy rate was about 54 percent (Joseph 1969, pp. 190-193). Jewish women were more often illiterate than Jewish men with rates ranging as high as 37 percent (Joseph 1969, p.194).

A number of factors would seem to explain the difference in literacy between Southern Italians and Jews. First is the fact already mentioned that Italians in general came from a more rural, peasant environment than did Jews. Considering that approximately 84 percent of all Italian immigrants came from Southern Italy, and that most of them were peasants, a 54 percent illiteracy rate is not so surprising. While systematic data are lacking, we assume that the literacy rate was higher for Italian men than for Italian women (Covello 1968, pp. 512-513). Covello pointed out: "From the immigrant's point of view there was no obvious need for more than a trifling amount of formal education. . . . At best school attendance was justified only for boys — girls were never considered" (p. 523). Cornelisen's study (1977) of five Italian peasant women supports this statement, as does the earlier quotation above from Mrs. Furillo.

Furthermore, among Jewish males, "even the most ignorant knew the Hebrew text of the prayers" (Glazer 1977, p. 21). The learning of Hebrew in studying the Torah was in stark contrast with the anti-clerical stance and limited religious knowledge of most Italian men (Vecoli 1969, pp. 217-268). While the literacy levels of women were lower than those of men in both groups, it was a common practice for women, both Jewish and Italian, to do the letter writing to the old country for their families and for neighbors. The implications of this skill and social linkage are not yet fully appreciated.

A third factor which seemed to us of importance in understanding some of the early differences in adaptation to American life between Jewish and Italian families had to do with linguistic ability. Most Jews entering this country spoke at least two languages, Yiddish and the language of the country they came from — even if they could not read or write that language. And Jewish men knew ancient Hebrew as well.

Some psychological studies have shown that people who grow up multilingual have an easier time adding another language to their repertory. Whether for this reason, or some other, Jews seemed to have learned English more rapidly than any other immigrant group except the Swedes. For example, a study of foreign born industrial workers found that 75 percent of Russian Jews could speak English while this was true for only 44 percent of Southern Italians (Steinberg 1974, p. 85).[4]

Dinnerstein et al. (1979, p. 271) suggested that the difference might lie in part in the fact that in Italian families the new language was seen as a competitor to tradition. In Jewish families, however, as Warner and Srole (1945, p. 231) pointed out, the language that was spoken at home, namely Yiddish, was not considered the language representing tradition, and Russian and Polish represented the oppressive societies Jews had escaped. The language representing tradition was ancient Hebrew, with its religious meaning. Hence, according to Warner and Srole, Jewish parents did not resist the child's orientation to English.

Other studies suggest that growing up knowing several languages facilitates conceptual reasoning and may help people to adapt more readily to new societies (Lambert 1977, pp. 16-27). Bernstein (1971, p. 124) noted that "as the child learns speech or. . . . learns specific codes which regulate his verbal acts, he learns the requirements of the social structure. The experience of the child is transformed by the learning which is generated by his own apparently voluntary acts of speech." If members of a family speak two languages, "meanings will have to be expanded to the level of verbal explicitness." To the extent that this is done, the speech "induces in its speakers a sensitivity to the implications of *separateness and differences,* and points to the possibilities inherent in a complex conceptual hierarchy for the organization of experience" (Bernstein 1971, p. 128).

Warner and Srole (1945) believed that Jewish women learned English faster than Jewish men (probably because women had more opportunity than did men to learn from their children), and consequently that they were blamed by some protagonists of Yiddish culture for diluting Jewish tradition. Italian women probably also learned English faster than men, for women had to deal with public schools, community agencies and the parish church which was often controlled by the Irish clergy. Yet, the Italian language was part of a cherished tradition and helped maintain the bonds that were threatened by American urban culture (Ware 1935). Thus, the differences in the learning of languages in the Jewish-American and Italian-American families suggest that while Jews gained in their ability to adapt to the new culture and society, in part with the help of language, Italians succeeded against odds in maintaining tradition and family solidarity.

Fertility

Fertility behavior played an important part in the Jews' relatively fast adaptation to the patterns of the then developing American urban family. Within a generation of their arrival, there was a sharp decline in the rates at which Jews gave birth. First generation Russian Jews in the age group of 45-54 had a completed fertility rate of 3.5 compared with a rate for Italian Americans of 5.0 (Taeuber and Taeuber 1971, p. 449; Goldscheider 1966).

The lower fertility rate may help explain some of the Jews' achievements in education. For one, it seems that children with fewer siblings have a better chance of being achievers than children from larger families (Zajonc 1976; Lenski 1963, pp. 242-243). Moreover, evidence has been accumulating that first-born children have higher chances of being achievers than latter-born children (Kagan 1977; Breland 1974; Fortes 1974). Hence, if we assume that the average Jewish family had two children within two generations, and the average Italian family had four or five children, one half of Jewish-born but only one of four or five of Italian-born had a better chance of becoming "achievers."

More to the point of our concern with the roles of women, a lower fertility rate meant that, in contrast to most other immigrants from Southern and Eastern Europe, Jewish mothers spent a smaller proportion of their time bearing children and caring for newborns. Though they did not necessarily spend a smaller proportion of their time caring for the family, they spent less time in pregnancy and postpartum (and in the drudgery of work with newborns) and were able to give more attention to fewer children. Having fewer children also made it possible for Jewish women to spend more time outside the family — with other kin, neighbors, shopkeepers, or as members of community groups.

Family Solidarity

Jews and Italians did much to keep their families together. Yet, among Jews, intergenerational conflicts may have been more acutely felt. As Irving Howe (1976, p.80) has aptly stated, "If conflicts between generations are central to the experience of all immigrant groups, among the Jews these became especially severe because of the persuasion that, at almost any cost, it was necessary to propel sons and daughters into the outer world — or, more precisely, to propel them into the outer world as social beings while trying to keep them spiritually within the Jewish orbit." Italians were concerned about the dangers they could expect from the outer world. Schools were considered "lax" in that they kept kids out of work, provided no discipline, and at the same time provided bad company. They were a threat to a culture of "well-defined notions concerning treatment of parents, relatives, attitudes toward women, or strangers" that should be passed on only through the family (Covello 1967, pp. 262, 266).

We know little about the long-range effects of differences of patterns of family solidarity; we need to examine the way women did or did not try to reconcile solidarity in traditional terms with adaptation to the ways of the modern city. Clearly, this was much more than a matter of merely accepting or rejecting values.

In some respects, Italian and Jewish mothers resembled each other. The stereotyped image of what has been called "the overprotective mother" applies equally to Italian and Jewish mothers. In both Jewish and Italian families, mothers protected their children against what they perceived to be a hostile environment. Strong mother-son relationships seemed, however, to have had different consequences: among Jews they most likely helped the sons accept the achievement criteria of the crystallizing American middle class; among Italians they helped the family maintain solidarity and tradition. The common traits as well as the different consequences derived to a large extent from patriarchal authority in the two cultures, and the differences would seem to stem from structural arrangements rooted in tradition and adapted to the confrontation with the host society.

In both families, the authority of the father often created resentment in the sons who turned to their mothers for solace and protection. In both families, the mother's presence, even if she herself was occupied with gainful activities in the home such as stitching or flower-making, made herself available for this purpose. In both families, the frustrations — of a different order, to be sure — that wives experienced in relations with husbands often made them turn to their sons for affective gratification. And in both families, the image of the mother was glorified as one who deserved respect and one to whom a son owes something — be it obedience or respect for her wishes. Yet, to the extent there was a primacy of orientation, the Jewish mother seems to have pushed her son to adapt to expectations emanating from American society. The Italian mother seems to have helped her son live up to the demands of family solidarity. This difference comes from apparently different patriarchal family structures as these manifested themselves in the adaptation of tradition to the exigencies of the new American ways.

The Italian Family

The Italian father was likely to have limited participation in the daily life of the family. He was particularly concerned with being an economic provider and in rallying the help of the family members whose activities he controlled for this purpose (Yans-McLaughlin 1971; Yans-McLaughlin 1977; Lopreato 1970; Capozolli 1987). The good son, and the good daughter as well, obediently contributed to the material survival of the household. This seemingly material concern of the children was imbued with a moral commitment that was symbolic of their attachment and their sense of responsibility to the family. This had priority over all else, including expectations emanating from the larger society, such as education. The following statement by an Italian-born parent (Covello 1967, p. 306) expresses well the moral concomitants of material considerations: "I believe in children working at an early age so that they learn responsibility and duty toward their parents and toward their family. That is what we mean when we say in Italian, to live like *Cristiani*."

Covello went on to comment that "such a parental attitude is typical and denotes the unavoidable subordination of schooling to the economic interests of the family." Yet it also indicated that economic interests were made part of an ethic of reciprocity, in which children learned that what parents did for them ought to be returned, at least in part, for the sake of justice and family solidarity.

Obedience of wife and children was an important ingredient of family solidarity. "The inferior status of the female in Southern Italy did not grant the young wife, in accordance with the communal mores, any voice in the affairs of her husband." (Covello 1967, pp. 192, 202-203). The family was considered a collectivity under the father's stern leadership. "Within the confines of a marriage unit, the position of the father seemed on the surface to be unquestioned. The family tradition vested him with authority that embodied all the prerogatives of a patriarchal ruler" (Covello 1967, p. 192).

Yet, women had both rights and leverage to assure their own influence. In Southern Italy, there was one "right that substantially altered the commonly accepted role of the wife as 'property.' Tradition recognized the right of the wife to possess property which she could dispose of at her 'own will' and customarily, the dowry remained the personal property of the wife" (Covello 1967, pp. 206-207). Moreover, the mother symbolized the collective character of the family more than did the father. If the mother died, the family would be broken up, but if the father died, the mother kept the family together (Covello 1967, p. 208).

This may have been because the blood ties between mother and children were more clearly recognized than those between father and children.

There were other reasons as well for the husband-father not to be entirely sure of the legitimacy of his authority. As Covello (1967, p. 192) further pointed out: "Within the household his prestige was determined not solely by father-right alone, but by the status of his health, age and ability to work and to provide for the family." One of his respondents made this observation: "When my father got old we obeyed our mother more than before. . . . My brother, who became head of the family, had to take orders from her. . . ." (Covello 1967, p. 214).

The research done by Anne Parsons (1969, p. 93) with Italian families in Naples and in America provided further evidence that women had more prestige and influence than the idealized family structure would lead one to believe. If ability to work was one of the bases for sustaining authority, for those families who migrated away from the land (whether to Naples or to New York, like the families investigated by Anne Parsons) where work was hard to find, the father's authority in the household was undermined. "For nearly half the men (in Naples) interviewed, it was the mother who stood out as by far the more prominent of the two parents. . . ." This is related to "the occupational instability of both father and son, together with a greater prevalence of working mothers and working wives. Where the father's occupation is more steady, ... paternal authority seems to be more effective in producing an impression for the son that father is the stronger figure. . . ." (Parsons 1969, p. 93).

Under adverse conditions, it was up to the mother to piece together, apportion, and control the meager incomes of the family. "Under conditions of scarcity, the food-giving maternal role gains overwhelming importance" (Parsons 1969, p. 91). This gave her power while it simultaneously made her dependent on the children's contributions. Thus she helped maintain the traditional mores according to which children must help their parents at the same time as she gained in prestige (Moss and Thompson 1959; Tentori 1956; Campisi 1948).

The mother was the protector of her children. "In return for the respect she receives, the mother will always defend her children against outsiders (and one should add, within the family as well); she will accept the obligation not only to feed them as children, but to give them whatever they ask for throughout life if this is at all possible" (Parsons 1969, p. 92). One of Anne Parson's male respondents in Naples stated, "A mother would always forgive her son, even if he were an assassin, even if he were Chessman" (Parsons 1969, p. 78). Russo (1987) made the point that Francis Ford Coppola, in the movies Godfather I and II, presented the ultimate stereotype of the norms and values that characterized the Italian family and the roles of husbands, wives and children.

Ours was a beginning effort to challenge the stereotype. Maglione and Fiore (1989) provided provocative evidence from their study of more than 100 daughters of immigrant Italian women of the myth of their subservience, as well as of the tensions caused by the gap between the male dominated cultural ethos and the actual family structure.

Religion, the School, and the Opportunity Structure

In Southern Italy, the school, the police, and to some extent even the church, were seen as outside and therefore hostile agencies to South Italian peasants, as the novels by Silone and Levi have so dramatically suggested (Silone 1962; Levi 1947). The opposition of Italian-born parents to the American school system was due to their suspicion of anything foreign to tradition, just as in the past anything emanating from the central government or from the North was seen as antithetical to their interests. This, and the peculiar position of the church in Italy ever since the middle of the 19th century, explains the suspicion with which the clergy was viewed by the Southern Italian peasant. After emigration Italians continued to attend mass on the high holy days (if then), to be baptized, married and buried in the church, and to take a major part in the *festa* in honor of the patron saint of their particular town; Italian mothers were expected to pass on this religious tradition to their children. The madonna remained a powerful symbol for both men and women in South-Italian society — a symbolization which added to the respect that was owed to mothers. According to Covello (1967, p. 139), in the past, religious education was almost entirely the prerogative of the older women within the family, and it consisted primarily in the memorization of prayers and stories about the lives of saints.

American cultural patterns created conflicts for the children; their parents were convinced that their own ways were better, and mothers especially were convinced that they knew how to protect and feed their children. The following incident, in which a mother explained why she came to her son's school, illustrates the point: "I came (to school) to find out whether Tony eats his sandwich I give him each morning or whether he throws it away. You people in school have no interest in that. You will even probably tell him that he doesn't have to listen to his mother. . . ." (Covello 1967, p. 315).

This protectiveness by mothers seemed to emanate from a conflict in standards between her and the school. This is made clear by a story recalled by a young man who was trying to avoid the ridicule of other children: "Lunch at elementary school was a difficult problem for me. To have a bite I either stole some money from home or took it from my shoe shining on Saturdays and Sundays. . . . To be sure, my mother gave me each day an Italian sandwich, that is half a loaf of French bread filled with fried peppers and onions, or with one half dipped into oil and some minced garlic on it. Such a sandwith would certainly ruin my reputation; I could not take it to school. . . . My God, what a problem it was to dispose of it, for I was taught never to throw away bread, which I still think is a very nice custom" (Covello 1967,p. 339). [As an aside, I also can recall those sandwiches, which I personally liked to eat, but was embarassed by, because everybody else seemed to be eating bologna or peanut butter sandwiches on white bread.]

It is always difficult to adopt new ways, and probably more so for the older than for the younger generation. It becomes more difficult still if the new ways challenge one's values, and it is even worse when they do not seem to promise any rewards. The fact is that the opportunities that parents saw for their children did not come from schooling, at least not in the short run. Stories abound of parents saying they "sacrificed everything to send (the daughter) to high school and college" and then found that she could not get a job, and that it was much easier to get a job through one's godfather than by staying in school (Covello 1967, pp. 317-321). And children realized that they could not cut themselves loose from their families if they were going to need jobs. Italian mothers apparently believed that their children, just like they themselves, would do better to maintain the support of their families than to count on opportunities outside. Thus, where conflicts arose, the solidarity of the family came first.

The Jewish Patriarchal Family

In the traditional Jewish patriarchal family, the man's superiority was unquestioned. He engaged in religious activities, most of which involved worship with other men away from home. The wife-mother's religious obligations were focused on the home, the kashruth and the lighting of candles for the sabbath. Beyond this, the man was supposed to care for his family if possible, and the woman was supposed to take care of the household which included the care of children. But so prestigious was the husband-father role that the Jewish man did not lose status with his peers or in his community if he did not earn money, especially if he spent his time studying the Talmud. He reminded himself of his secure status by thanking God every morning for not having been born a woman. Not all Jews who immigrated were religious, but their emphasis on learning led them to the study of secular philosophies, and if they were not so literate, they were yet entitled to reading the paper after work or to spending their time with peers in the coffee house while their wives prepared the meals.

In regard to children, Jewish men were mainly concerned with the children's internal dispositions, that is, their concern was with the type of behavior that expressed the highly valued attitude of wanting to be a good Jew, especially for the boys (Coser 1974, pp. 362-373). Jewish fathers were less interested in girls. Mothers, while not indifferent to their children's Jewishness, were more occupied with the details of everyday behavior. Fathers were little concerned with the behavioral details of their wives or of their children. As long as she kept a "good house" and the children showed their allegiance to "Jewishness," they remained proud fathers and husbands without having to control the family's daily lives.

The Jewish Woman's Structural Position

This division of structured interest had important consequences for the role of women. Due to their husbands' frequent absences from the home (even if they were not at work) and their focus on the "higher things in life," women tended to remain in control over practical matters as well as over the daily lives of their children. Insulated from the structured interests and from the close observability of the patriarch in their own and their children's everyday behavior, they had much leeway to come and go and were often in the position to make important decisions about everyday life.[5]

We know from anecdotal accounts that many Jewish women made the decision for the family to emigrate. And in this country, they seem to have been the ones to mediate their children's transition from family life to life in the school and neighborhood, trying to protect them as well as they could from the dangers of the streets. Henry Roth (1934) makes the point well: the mother was able to protect her child not only from outside dangers to some extent, but also from the brutality of the father, and she did this without questioning his status or superiority.

The traditional Jewish family that gave women the responsibility for dealing with all aspects of daily life while their husbands were occupied elsewhere became similar to the evolving structure of the nucleated American middle-class family during industrialization. Here also men going to work no longer needed their wives as partners; as Judith Blake (1974) has said, they became independent of their wives in their work.

Yet, there was some difference between the Jewish immigrant family and the newly emerging modern American family: in the latter, women were likely to become completely dependent economically on their "absent" husbands, as Blake also pointed out. In the traditional and the immigrant Jewish family, men were independent of their wives in their religious and status-giving activities, and in their work if they were not self-employed, and they were also absent from the home during the day. But they were dependent on their wives for their daily needs, and if they were self-employed in small businesses, they depended on the wives even more. The Jewish women who minded the store were familiar sights. Jewish women were not completely dependent on their husbands economically since traditionally it was not considered shameful for women to work to supplement their husbands' income or substitute for it.

With smaller families Jewish women were able to be hospitable to co-religionists and new immigrants as they continued to enter the country. It is through the women's initiative that the well-known *Landsmannschaften* — groups of Jews who came from the same town — were created. As Rudolf Glanz reported, these associations of people who came from the same *shtetl* had started as informal gatherings in the homes of a *landsfroy* where, in addition to the family, friends considered as belonging to the family also showed up. Glanz(1976, p. 84) further commented: "It was the initiative of the women in their founding that was remembered vividly in the memories of the members. . . . The later rich sphere of women's activities in the organizational world of the *landsmannschaften* reached widely beyond the family aspect of its origin."

Differences in Attitudes Toward the Socialization of Boys and Girls

There is hardly any material available about the difference in attitudes toward and expectations from boys and girls in the Jewish family. Jewish mothers were, of course, like all mothers, passers-on of the tradition that boys ought to venture out and continue in their father's steps, and that girls ought to become homemakers and mothers like themselves. Their mothering no doubt helped to maintain and reproduce gender differences (Chodorow 1970).

There is more material available on the differences between boys and girls in Italian families than in Jewish families. Among others, Covello's book is a goldmine as is Anne Parsons focus on gender differences in Italian families. Italian girls were an object of honor for the family. Their sexual purity was a *sine qua non* for such honor. To this end, they were closely supervised by fathers, and even more so by brothers. While

Jewish girls were left freer to come and go, both Jewish and Italian girls worked in factories and were active in trade unions, even though Italian girls were more likely to be met by watchful brothers at the end of the working day (Foner 1979). These differences between Italian and Jewish girls were attenuated by circumstances and number of generations in the United States. Rising expectations for education and the ever increasing participation of women in the labor force has tended over the years to diminish ethnic differences.

In the next section, I will illustrate from recent research the extent of continuity and change in the differences. The primary focus will be on research that suggests that traditional Italian family values and structures continue to influence behavior and attitudes of second and third generation Italians in New York City, which houses the largest concentration of Italian Americans in the United States. Other research suggests that the very success that Jews have enjoyed has become a cause of concern to certain leaders who fear that continuing assimilation may threaten the future of Jewish identity through family life.

Educational and Marital Measures of Change

Post World War II studies of educational, occupational and income attainment have consistently shown that European white ethnic groups have made dramatic progress. For the most part, they have achieved middle and upper middle class mainstream status, with the achievement of Jews most notable. The latter have shown the highest rates of success in these three common measures. While Italian American attainment has also been dramatic, especially in the third generation, there is evidence of a lag. For example, Lieberson (1980, p. 164) reported that as late as 1960, second generation Italian American women under the age of 45 averaged between .5 and 1.1 years less schooling than did their counterparts whose origin was the USSR (for purposes of this discussion I am presuming that the great majority of immigrants from the USSR were Jewish). While the attainment differentials for the age cohorts 45-54 and 55-64 were even larger, the fact that the pattern persisted even among the younger cohorts suggests that there may well have been continuing differential impact of the family on attainment, given that the societal structures were otherwise equally accessible.

Alba (1985, pp. 59-60) noted how the different rural (Italian) and urban (Jewish) backgrounds and cultural norms led Jews to move much more quickly to take advantage of educational opportunities in the United States. The differences continued to be significant into the 1930s. However, when Alba compared the educational attainment of Italian

American women born post 1950 with that of women of British ancestry from the 1979 Current Population Survey, he found that the differences had disappeared.

Research from the 1980 Census provided support regarding the relative stability of the Italian American family. McKenney et al. (1985) reported that Italians had a higher proportion of married couples than the general U.S. population, a lower divorce rate, and a higher proportion of families with children under 18 and both parents present. As expected, these patterns were more evident among single ancestry and older Italian-Americans than among multiple ancestry and younger Italian-Americans. As with findings from a variety of earlier studies on many ethnic groups, marrying out of the ethnic group leads to lower levels of stability as measured by these variables. We may expect the 1990 Census data to show further decline in traditional family patterns (Alba 1985; Lieberson and Waters 1988).

In recent years groups like the American Jewish Committee have become concerned about the consequences of assimilation of Jews into American society. Along with high attainment in education, occupation and income, have come increasing rates of out-marriage, divorce and fertility rates at or below replacement levels. Dashevsky and Levine (1983) acknowledged that it takes courage to be optimistic about the future of the Jewish family in the face of assimilation of third and fourth generation Jews into American life. We cannot know from these data what role Jewish immigrant women played in helping to bring about such assimilation, but we do note that the patriarchal, traditional ways of Jewish family life were no match for the patterns of change made available by the opportunity structures of American society.

Continuity and Change: The Case of CUNY Students

Evidence of the continuing influence of the traditional Italian American family is found in a report prepared by Dr. Richard Gambino, Director of Italian American Studies, Queens College. Gambino (1987) reviewed several studies that compared Italian American with other racial-ethnic groups in the City University of New York (CUNY) system.

Italian Americans constitute about 18 percent of the New York City population, making them the largest single ethnic group in the city. They also constituted 20 percent of the CUNY student population during the late 1970s and early 1980s. During this time a number of studies were carried out that measured and compared student attitudes, values, and achievements. The following findings are instructive relative to this paper:

Mothers of Italian American students were less likely to have attended college than the mothers of other whites;

Italian Americans were more likely than minorities and other whites to be the first generation of their families to be attending college;

Almost 30 percent of minorities and other whites aspired to the doctorate or a professional degree, compared with only 18 percent of the Italian American students;

Italian Americans were more likely than minorities and other whites to attend a community college rather than a four year college;

Italian Americans were "younger than other CUNY students, more likely to be single, and more likely to be living with their parents;"

Italian American students "More than other CUNY students tend to regard college as vocational training rather than as broader education;"

Italian American females "suffer greater stress and anxiety than both their male counterparts and than other males and females in general;"

"Although almost every Italian American female student studied felt she had complete freedom in planning her educational and vocational future, Italian female students presented concerns about conflicts with their parents regarding whom they associate with in their personal lives;"

Finally, Gambino noted that the several studies he had reviewed showed that "Italian Americans of all generations and cirucumstances have a pronounced propensity to 'cope' with their problems, i.e., endure them, rather than attempt actively, let alone aggressively to solve them."

While all the evidence shows that the children and grandchildren of Italian and Jewish immigrant women have moved pretty much into the mainstream of American life, there continue to be some differences in the ways they have done so. Jewish women and their husbands may have embraced them so heartily that at least some among Jewish community leaders fear the demise of Jewish identity. On the other hand, Italian American wives and husbands have attempted to maintain family ties even while adapting to the urban structures. For some young Italian Americans in the nation's largest city, with the largest number of Italian Americans, the process calls for continued concern and attention.

Summary

Rose Coser and I carried out a comparative overview of the Italian and Jewish women and their family life, both as seen through the available research literature and as seen through the commonly accepted stereotypes also existing in the literature. We found that the roles played by immigrant women in the adaptation of their families, and especially of their children to American life, have been given less than adequate attention. Rather, the focus until recently has been on the opportunity structures provided by urban, industrial society and the way that men and fathers adapted to it. The family itself has been understood to be shaped by those facts. On top of that, the traditional cultural patterns brought over from Europe further insured that the women would remain at home and in the kitchen. This latter role was also consonant with the role of white, native American wives in the era before World War II. Our own personal experiences with Italian and Jewish immigrant women and their daughters led us to question the portrait that has emerged in the historical literature. Oral histories carried out in New York and in Connecticut and a reading of the oral histories taken in Connecticut in the 1930s by the WPA Writers' Project provided important evidence that a reassessment was in order.

There is no doubt that the village and peasant societies of Eastern and Southern Europe were characterized by cultures and social structures that locked people in and left little room for change. But it is equally clear that immigrants, both men and women, adapted to the opportunity structures of urban, industrial America. Our effort was to learn more about how and to what extent cultural differences between Jews and Italians might lead to different patterns of adaptation within the family and to different modes of adjustment to American values and structures.

It may well be, as Degler (1980) has insisted, that family and society are in tension because of the different value orientations and social structures within which they operate. But Lewis Coser makes clear in his essay in this volume that Rose Coser endorses the modern world with all its tensions. In his words, Rose saw the modern world as offering a range of "conflicting expectations, segmented roles, clashing norms and complex role-sets. . . . which the individual must come to grips with." The evidence suggests that Jewish and Italian immigrant women and their daughters have themselves endorsed the modern world, but with variations that continue to influence family life patterns into the third and fourth generations.

Notes

1. Irving Howe's book by this title is the most famous account of Jewish immigrants. It pays only passing attention to women. Other examples are Oscar Handlin's *The Uprooted*, and Nathan Glazer's *American Judaism*.
2. Maglione and Fiore (1989) interviewed more than 100 daughters of Italian immigrant women in a sample of respondents who volunteered for interviews and oral histories dealing with family, religion, ethnicity, education and politics. The histories and interviews were carried out from 1984-89 in the Northeastern part of the United States. While they described their fathers as powerful and authoritarian, the women did not see their mothers as subservient. They saw them rather as "quiet influencers and dominant forces" who focused on the centrality of the family in their daily lives. They also recognized how the family could and did threaten to stifle them in its warm embrace.
3. Virginia Yans-McLaughlin (1977) writes about the gap between women's actual work experience and cultural perceptions.
4. The data are based on large surveys of wage earners in 37 principal branches of mining and manufacturing in the United States. Adapted from the Dillinham Immigration Commission 1911, vol. 23, p. 197.
5. On the problem of role articulation in relation to insulation from observability and of differential structural interests among role-partners, see Merton (1968, pp. 425-433); see also Rose Laub Coser (1961).

References

Alba, Richard. 1985. *Italian Americans: Into the Twilight of Ethnicity*. Englewood Cliffs: Prentice-Hall.

Balch Institute. 1985. Atti del Convegno. *Le Societa in Transizione: Italiani e Italoamericani negli anni ottanta*. Philadelphia: PA. The Balch Institute.

Bernstein, Basil. 1971. *Class, Codes and Control. Vol. I* London: Routledge and Kegan Paul.

Blake, Judith. 1974. "The Changing Status of Women in Developing Countries." *Scientific American* 231:134-147.

Breland, H. M. 1974. "Birth Order, Family Configuration, and Verbal Achievement." *Child Development* 45: 1011-1019.

Campisi, Paul J. 1948. "Ethnic Family Patterns: The Italian Family in the United States." *The American Journal of Sociology* 53: 443-49.

Cantor, Milton and Bruce Laurie (eds.). 1977. *Class, Sex and The Woman Worker*. Westport: The Greenword Press.

Capozolli, Mary Jane. 1987. "Nassau County's Italian American Women: A Comparative View," Ch. 23 in *The Melting Pot and Beyond: Italian Americans in the Year 2000*. Proceedings of the XVIII Annual Conference of the American Italian Historical Association. Jerome Krase and William Egelman (eds.). Staten Island, N.Y.: 209 Flagg Place.

Chodorow, Nancy. 1978. *The Reproduction of Mothering*. Berkeley: University of California Press.

Cohen, Miriam. 1977. "Italian American Women in New York City, 1900-1950: Work and School." Pp. 120-143 in *Class, Sex and the Woman Worker*, edited by M. Cantor and B. Laurie. Westport: Greenwood Press.

Cornelisen, Ann. 1977. *Women of the Shadows*. New York: Vintage Books.

Coser, Rose Laub. 1974. "Authority and Structural Ambivalence in the Middle Class Family." Pp. 362-73 in Rose Laub Coser (ed.), *The Family: Its Structures and Functions*. New York: St. Martin's Press.

___. "Insulation from Observability and Types of Social Conformity." *American Sociological Review*. 26: 28-39.

Covello, Leonard. 1967. *The Social Background of the Italo-American School Child: A Study of the Southern Italian Family Mores and Their Effect on the School Situation in Italy and America*. Leiden: E.J. Brill.

D'Antonio, William V. 1985. "Comments on the Papers by McKenney et.al., and by John Seggar," pp. 57-60 in *Italian Americans*, edited by S. Tomasi. New York: The Center for Migration Studies.

___ and Joan Aldous. 1983. *Families and Religions: Conflict and Change in Modern Society*. Beverly Hills: Sage.

Daniels, Cynthia R. 1986. "No Place Like Home: A Pictorial Essay on Italian-American Homeworkers in New York: 1910-1913." Pp. 93-114 in *Support and Struggle*, edited by Joseph Tropea et al. Staten Island: American Italian Historical Association.

Dashefsky, Arnold and Irving M. Levine. 1983. "The Jewish Family: Continuity and Change," pp. 163-190 in *Families and Religions*, edited by William V. D'Antonio and Joan Aldous. Beverly Hills: Sage.

Degler, Carl. 1980. *At Odds*. New York: Oxford University Press.

Dillingham Immigration Commission. 1911. *Report to the U.S. Senate*.

Dinnerstein, Leonard, Roger L. Nichols, and David M. Reimers. 1979. *Natives and Strangers*. New York: Oxford University Press.

Foner, Phillip S. 1979. *Women and the American Labor Movement*. New York: The Free Press.

Fortes, Meyer. 1974. "The First-Born," *Journal of Child Psychology and Psychiatry* 15: 81-104.

Gambino, Richard. 1987. *Italian-American Studies and Italian-Americans at the City University of New York: Report and Recommendations*. Italian American Institute: City University of New York.

Glanz, Rudolf. 1976. *The Jewish Woman in America: Two Female Immigrant Generations, 1820-1929*. New York: KTAV Publishing House, Inc. and National Council of Jewish Women.

Glazer, Nathan. 1957. *American Judaism*. Chicago: University of Chicago Press.

Goldscheider, Calvin. 1966. "Trends in Jewish Fertility." *Sociology and Social Research* 50: 173-186.

Halevy, Z. 1978. "Were Russian Jews Representative?" *International Migration* 16: 66-73.

Handlin, Oscar. 1951. *The Uprooted*. Boston: Little, Brown, and Co.

Hershberg, Theodore. 1981. (ed.) *Philadelphia*. New York: Oxford University Press.

___ et al., "A Tale of Two Cities: Blacks, Immigrants, and Opportunity in Philadelphia, 1850-1880, 1930, 1970," pp. 461 ff. in *Philadelphia*, edited by Theodore Hershberg. New York: Oxford University Press.

Hornby, P.(ed.). 1977. *Bilingualism: Psychological, Social and Educational Implications*. New York: Academic Press.

Howe, Irving. 1976. *The World of Our Fathers*. New York: Harcourt, Brace, Jovanovich.

Izard, Holly. 1975. Interview, Connecticut Ethnic Heritage Project. March 17.

Joseph, Samuel. 1969. *Jewish Immigration to the United States from 1881-1910*. New York: Arno Press and the New York Times.

Kegan, Jerome. 1977. "The Child in the Family," in *Daedalus* (Spring): 33-56.

Lenski, Gerhard. 1963. *The Religious Factor*. Garden City: Doubleday.

Levi, Carlo. 1947. *Christ Stopped at Eboli*. Trs. by F. Fenaye. New York: Farrar, Straus and Giroux.

Lieberson, Stanley. 1980. *A Piece of the Pie*. Berkeley: University of California Press.

___ and Mary Waters. 1988. *From Many Strands*. New York: Russell Sage.

Lopreato, Joseph. 1970. *Italian Americans*. New York: Random House.

Maglione, Connie. A. and Carmen Anthony Fiore. 1989. *Voices of the Daughters*. Princeton, N.J.: Town House Publishing.

Mariano, John. 1921. *The Italian Contribution to American Democracy*. Boston: Christopher Publishing House.

McKenney, Nampeo, Michael Levin and Alfred J. Tella. 1985. "A Sociodemographic Profile of Italian Americans," pp. 3-31 *Italian Americans*, edited by L. Tomasi. New York: Center for Migration Studies.

Merton, Robert K. 1968. *Social Theory and Social Structure*. New York: The Free Press.

Moss, Leonard W. and Walter H. Thompson. 1959. "The South Italian Family: Literature and Observations," *Human Organization* 18: 35-41.

Parsons, Anne. 1969. *Belief, Magic and Anomie: Essays in Psychosocial Anthropology*. New York: The Free Press. p. 93.

Pesenti, Paul. 1990. "Family Values and Psychological Adjustment Among Female Italian and Jewish Immigrant Nursing Home Residents." Ph.D. Dissertation, Seton Hall University, School of Education.

Roth, Henry. 1934. *Call It Sleep*. New York: Cooper Square Publishers.

Rubinow, Israel. 1907. "The Economic Condition of Jews in Russia." *Bulletin of the Bureau of Labor* #72. Washington, D.C.: Government Printing Office.

Russo, John Paul. 1986. "The Hidden Godfather," Pp. 255-282 *Support and Struggle*, edited by J. Tropea et al. Staten Island: American Italian Historical Association.

Silone, Ignazio. 1970. *Fontamara*. Waltham, Mass: Ginn-Blaisdell.

___. 1963. *Bread and Wine*. New York: New American Library.

Steinberg, Stephen. 1974. *The Academic Melting Pot*. New York: McGraw-Hill.

Taeuber, Irene B. and Conrad Taeuber. 1971. *Peoples of the United States in the Twentieth Century*. Washington, D.C.: U.S. Department of Commerce and Bureau of the Census.

Tentori, Tullio. 1956. *Il Sistema di Vita della Communita Meterana*. Rome.

Tomasi, Lydio (ed.) 1985. *Italian Americans: New Perspectives in Immigration and Ethnicity*. New York: The Center for Migration Studies, 209 Flagg Place, Staten Island, New York.

Tropea, Joseph L., James E. Miller, and Cherly Beattie-Repetti. 1986. *Support and Struggle: Italians and Italian Americans in a Comparative Perspective*. Staten Island: American Italian Historical Association.

Vecoli, Rudolph. 1969. "Prelates and Peasants: Italian Immigrants and the Catholic Church. "*Journal of Social History,* (Spring): 217-268.

Vezzosi, Elizabetta. 1986. "The Dilemma of the Ethnic Community: The Italian-Immigrant Woman Between 'Preservation' and 'Americanization', in America of the Early Twentieth Century." Pp. 83-92 in *Support and Struggle,* edited by J. Tropea et al. Staten Island: American Italian Historical Association.

Ware, Caroline F. 1935. *Greenwich Village.* New York: Harper and Row.

Warner, W. Lloyd and Leo Srole. 1945. *The Social Systems of American Ethnic Groups.* New Haven: Yale University Press.

Williams, Jr., Robin M. 1955. *American Society.* New York: Knoff, Ch. 2.

Yans-McLaughlin, Virginia. 1977. "Italian Women and Work: Experience and Perception," Pp. 101-119 in *Class, Sex and the Woman Worker,* edited by M. Cantor & B. Laurie, Westport: Greenwood Press.

___. 1977. *Like the Fingers of the Hand.* Princeton: Princeton University Press.

___. 1971. "Patterns of Work and Family Organization Among Buffalo's Italians." *Journal of Interdisciplinary History* 2: 299-314.

Zajonc, R. B. 1976. "Family Configuration and Intelligence." *Science* 192 (16 April): 227-236.

8

Gender, Class, and Career in the Lives of Privileged Women

Arlene Kaplan Daniels

The early feminist studies sketched out some of the issues women face in gender-stratified societies. The idea that women share a common lot and face common problems has received powerful impetus from such research as the socio-linguistic studies of Fishman (1978), Zimmerman and West (1975), and West (1984). This research suggests that men and women show their understanding of their relative positions in a gender-stratified society irrespective of context or class positions. For example, men control conversations and interrupt women more frequently than the reverse, even when women are higher-status professionals. But pioneering studies of the special problems of women of color and women who are gay, handicapped and working class have also shown how they are different from what has been assumed to be the common lot — the problems of middle-class white women who are heterosexual. Recognition of these problems requires reformulation of just what (if anything) is common in the lot of women. From that perspective, much of the attention given to the common problems of women really reflects the interests and biases of white middle-class women (Ferree 1985; Hooks 1981). Their place in the social structure offers them special opportunities as well as subjecting them to general problems and limitations facing women in gender-stratified society.

Perhaps the lesson to be learned from these arguments is than the search for common issues may be less important at this time that an examination of the diversity of women's issues. The problems and priorities of women of color, of women of different social classes may require different kinds of analyses (Hartsock 1987). Any of the analyses must be based on knowledge of what a group of women experience and what their place is in the social order within which that experience becomes meaningful. Such an analysis takes into account not only the different kinds of subordination women experience but also the ways that the traditional work women do maintains and reproduces the social system. In order to learn about these matters, we need to discover how the women themselves define statuses, experience change, think about the reproduction of social structure. Their understanding appears in their descriptions and judgments, collected through interviews and in observations of their behavior. Empirical analyses of this kind can reveal different aspects of women's place in the larger gender-stratified system. For example, since the relationship between work outside the family (paid or unpaid) and responsibility for the family is traditionally a "woman's" issue, we may discover different aspects of that connection as we range across social class. This issue is the one of interest here, in an examination of the "appropriate" work for privileged women in American society. Privileged women — those of the upper-middle and upper classes who do not have to earn their own living or help support their families — are expected to find work, if they wish it, that is compatible with placing family responsibilities first. Traditionally, volunteer work and associated philanthropic activities fill that bill.

In the most traditional view, volunteer work is the only work that privileged women can do. The *amour propre* of their fathers and husbands would not permit any income-producing work from wives. It might take energy and time away from a wife's efforts at furthering her husband's career and it might suggest he is insufficiently prosperous. The work of volunteering and philanthropy, on the other hand, can add to his renown. The costs of volunteering, and the fund-raising efforts that philanthropy requires, may serve to show how wealthy or prosperous is the husband who can subsidize a wife in such activity.

The purpose of this paper is to show how such particulars as wealth, belief in traditional values, a place in the network of upper-class society can offer both scope and barriers to a work-career identity for women of the upper-middle and upper class who rise to positions as civic leaders through their efforts at volunteering. In the following discussion, then, we examine the particulars of upper-class or privileged women's lives and their effect on a vision of the world — and the life contingencies that strengthen or modify it — to see how gender, class and career provide the limitations (like adherence to traditional ideas about women's place) and opportunities (like the resources that come with wealth and social connections) within which women see the possibilities of self-expression in a career. The pursuit of a career in civic service offers these women their chance for independence and public regard not otherwise accessible. Developing and rising in this kind of a career provides a clearly legitimate channel for the energies and aspirations of women who don't wish to challenge the conventions about women's place. The concept of career, in this context, provides the unifying thread that ties together the work of family, class maintenance, service to the community and individual aspirations.

The Study

This study is based upon systematic interviews with seventy women in their homes or offices and additional interview-observations of them and their friends during a five year period (1971-1976) at luncheons, social gatherings and philanthropic events. After that period, and continuing to the present (1991), I have seen or phoned some of them, and gathered news of the rest, in visits back to the research site, at least twice yearly. These are women who know each other through family and friendship connections, through community service or through both. They are volunteers who have risen to civic leadership in the major metropolitan area in and around what I shall call Pacific City, a large and relatively old, established urban area in the northwestern section of the United States. They were chosen through the reputational sampling method. Three women, acknowledged widely as civic leaders (so identified in local media, holders of many distinguished local and national awards, officers and advisors on many prestigious boards) were the first interviewed and they helped choose the remaining sample on the basis of their long experience in civic activities.

Focused interviews (Merton and Kendall 1946) permitted the discussion of selected topics rather than requiring answers to a pre-determined set of very specific questions. Interviews varied in length from one to four hours, sometimes requiring two or three appointments to complete. Illustrative quotations in the text are verbatim, unless sections or phrases are bracketed to indicate paraphrase. All identifying characteristics of the respondents or their city have been changed or removed to assure confidentiality.

The resulting group presents a mix of the upper and middle classes in Pacific City. Some of the women come from old families in this or other cities; some are from newly prosperous families (new rich or solely dependent upon a professional or businessman husband's income for their affluence); and a few are from ordinary middle-class homes where they are financially secure but not notably prosperous. They are predominantly older women. At the time the study began in 1970, only one was under 40: twenty-eight women were between 40 and 50; seventeen were between 51 and 60; seven were in the 61 to 70 range, and

seven were 71 or older. The major interviews were completed by 1976. In
the ensuing years, seven of the women have died. They are a privileged
group of women, then, in their class background and hold the traditional
values for women in the period (before the women's movement) in
which they were raised and raised families themselves.

These women are well-educated: eighteen have had some college;
forty-seven hold bachelor's degrees and fifteen of these have advanced
degrees as well. They exhibit the life style of the upper-middle or upper
classes — living in comfortable, or even opulent surroundings. Most (53)
have never held a salaried job or else have worked only for a year or
two before marriage, although a few (3) have begun to work for pay
after a long volunteer career. An additional six women in this group
have worked some part of their lives at salaried positions and eight more
have had paid careers in addition to their volunteer experience — after
a husband's illness, widowhood or divorce.

Every woman in the study has been married; thirteen are divorced
and twenty-one have been widowed (six of these twenty-one have
remarried). Most of these women (63) have had children, ranging in
number from one to ten, with the average at about three. The husbands
of these women are mainly business men of various sorts: seven are
brokers in stock, insurance, food and merchandise; five are investment
analysts or counsellors; thirty-three are in business firms — generally the
family company and often as the chair of the board. But substantial
numbers are doctors (14) and lawyers (11). Some of the professional men
as well as the business men come from what Aldrich (1988) calls "old
money". This group is predominantly Protestant (40); but with a number
of Jews (18) and Catholics (12) among them.

The World of Privileged Women

The lives of privileged women are played out against the background
of a normative order — a set of expectations about how one ought to
behave, think and feel about one's place in the world. This is the world
that they explain or project as they talk about themselves in the
interviews. The elements of the world combine in various ways to
produce what the women often call "their vision" of their
responsibilities. These responsibilities both guide and limit the direction
women feel they can take. The four aspects of that vision to be presented
are: responsibility to family; responsibility to class interests; noblesse
oblige; and responsibility to self. These values are not mutually
exclusive, but blend and interact with one another in the expression of
any individual woman's construction or explanation of her behavior and

wishes. Noblesse oblige, for example is a special aspect of class interests. Responsibility to family, in any one person's view, may be seen as part of or separate from class interests.

The interaction of the interests represented by these categories is highlighted in the discussion of weighing contingencies. As women reflect on the opportunities and limitations their specific circumstances provide, we see the constraints placed upon them by their privileged position. The concluding analysis shows what we learn from a consideration of gender, class and career in the lives of women who are not only privileged, but energetic, resourceful and ambitious. The women create niches of opportunity for themselves which offer status and recognition in career development. In this entrepreneurial endeavor they find both the satisfaction of growing public regard and personal self-confidence. However, they do not alter the traditional views about women's proper place; for their activities fit within the understandings of what are appropriate activities for women of their class.

Responsibility to Family

A general characteristic of women in this study is their expression of loyalty to their parents and their in-laws; most generally, these are expressions of pride in and affiliation with their forbears and relations. They see their lives as embedded in an extended family. In large part, they see themselves as responsible for continuity and maintenance in that family. Sometimes this affiliation directs their volunteer interests — for example a woman who devoted all her volunteer interests for a number of years to a cause espoused by her mother-in-law. In many cases this pride combines with acceptance of philanthropic activity as part of an ethnic heritage. As one woman stated, "my grandfather started the community chest here and my father was head of just everything. This is a proud part of the Jewish tradition — to give." The sense of responsibility for family also appears in statements about the necessity to look after family interests. "My family is very important to me," one woman stated. "I have a very elderly mother and some sisters who are not really capable of business. And I manage a family farm as well as everything else."

This responsibility includes both personal care as well as business oversight, as revealed by the following comments: "My mother passed away recently and before [that] I helped care for her and the apartment houses;" "Showing loyalty to parents may require subordination of self on occasion;" "I can get along with any people. Anyone can push me around. . . . I was the only child of domineering parents." It may even mean deferring to parents over the wishes of one's husband. Strong ties to parents and an acknowledgement of their authority underlies one woman's statement: "My father wanted me to have an education and when I finished college he said: "Go get your M.A." And my husband said: "No!". . . . I did what my father said."

However, such conflicts were reported rarely. Instead, these women focussed on the ways they could take cues and gain support from both husbands and families in developing a sense of what they should do: how they might behave. The instructions are taken even when they are resented. One woman reported ruefully that her new mother-in-law accosted her immediately after the wedding ceremony with a box of thank you notes and a list of presents. The bride was told to respond to all gift givers at once. My informant said she was taken aback, cowed and resentful, but she obeyed, even though the work ruined her honeymoon.

Women also learn what work might be proper for them to do. Most accept their responsibilities even if a few chafe at the limitations. Clearly, paid work was not an option for most of these women. A typical remark was, "I never thought of working. My husband didn't want me to work." Working women who married into this group changed their goals accordingly — from advancement in a salaried career to volunteering: "When I married I came into a family in which the women do not work." So she got into public relations through volunteer work.

Responsibilities to one's husband require that everything be arranged so as not to inconvenience him. One woman's remark highlights a situation that I commonly encountered: "Dick is absolutely unwilling to help in the house. Even when I've been laid up and sick." The priorities of husbands are not questioned and women, sometimes explicitly, point out that a husband's wishes must come first: "I was fortunate to have help. And I was careful not to abuse the [time spent on] volunteer activity with Jack. . . . I didn't want my relationship with Jack threatened."

One sign of this priority is the care given to deciding whether or not to accept a major (generally prized) appointment. As one woman told me about her colleagues: "They consider very carefully when they take the job. . . . of Junior League President. If the husband hasn't enough security to be prince consort for one year, they wouldn't take it." These considerations are not only pressing for the younger women (in their late thirties and early forties) of the Junior League, they also are issues for women to consider at retirement age. An older woman mentioned, "[My husband] was pushing for my retirement these last years because he is semi-retired. I think I would have encountered greater resistance if I had gone another year."

But the most pressing times for setting priorities and resolving conflicting pressures from family and volunteer work demands come when women are young and so are their children. I encountered such comments as the following from younger women: "In early years women do have conflicts about the time away from home. You have to be thinking about priorities and how you will manage." Sometimes these same questions of setting priorities can arise later in life as well: "Before I retired from [my major volunteer commitments] I worked a full day — 9 to 4:30. . . . but I was still volunteer enough that if my grandchildren were coming to visit, I would say I can't come in."

One way to resolve conflicts created by taking time away from family for volunteer work is to raise children to be volunteers also. They come to see the importance of their mothers' work and so the resentment about mother's time spent away from the home is dissipated. One volunteer said, "My son once made a caustic comment. . . . 'Why can't you be like other mothers and play bridge and golf?'" "Yet he is the one. . . . most into community activity, although all [the children] have done volunteering." In fact, the mother's work may be a source of pride ("The children are proud of what I do and boast about it.") and imitation "The children respect you if their parents are active in their community. They will want to. . . . emulate their parents."

Women often spoke both of husband's and children's supportiveness, pointing out how children had grown into leadership positions in the city themselves. The care women take in training their children and the pride mothers show at children's accomplishments in civic service point to the work women do to introduce their children to one aspect of their class position and its responsibilities. Elsewhere (Daniels 1987a) I have shown how upper-class patterns of behavior and sense of entitlement are encouraged in children through their participation in private schools and special recreational activities organized primarily by their mothers. At the same time, children see how much of the work of promoting these schools and activities depends upon volunteer effort. The consequence of this encouragement can be seen when children, in turn, take their place on the governing boards of private schools as well as engaging in other volunteer activity in the city. As we shall see in the discussion of noblesse oblige, the sense of responsibility for community service and the sense of a privileged position are closely connected.

Responsibility to Class Interests

Volunteer work is an appropriate activity for an upper-class woman; working for pay is not.

The thing you give up [by salaried employment] if you rise in the volunteer hierarchy is status. Jane Stone is a pretty good example. Jane [was divorced and] took a job at the museum and lost status. But she is a real high-class person. She is now married to [a wealthy socialite] and so she immediately became upper-upper class. . . . It seems to me impossible for [most] women. . . . to own enough to live in a way that would be upper class. So [they are] handicapped by working and not [having] enough money. As a volunteer you can walk into any office and they will be afraid not to see you. An employee can be shunted off — even though in both cases you have come for fund raising.

But ordinarily, women do not discuss class generically. In contradistinction to findings by others (see, especially, Ostrander 1984), this group of women resist discussion of class interests. They resist the idea of a ruling class or a power elite. They see class in terms of husband's expectations and in terms of family and friendship networks in which they want to participate. There networks stand for "the community" in their eyes. Though much of the networking can be seen as supporting class interest — work for what are termed private schools, but, which they call the independent schools, for example. Women sometimes work with their husbands at fund raising — co-chairing a drive for example. Or women see their volunteer work as a positive support to a husband ("I did join the Junior League. . . . I thought it would be good for my husband's business. He's in insurance.") The loyalty that women feel to their families can be seen in the kinds of organizations they choose for their volunteer experience. Those who choose the Junior League (or accept when they are chosen by it, since the League is invitational) are implicitly accepting a conventional role for privileged women. Even when the League ventures into social reform projects (trying to improve education in ghetto schools, for example) rather than cultural projects which clearly do not challenge the status quo in any way (preserving historic houses, for example) it functions as a socializing agency for privileged women — teaching them how to take responsibility in the city and where to find suitable friends — just as the women do for their children through the medium of private schools and related organizations.

The Junior League is an absolute mirror of where consensus in society is. The members may look daring — [A few] years ago all the projects were about black people because society has covertly decided it was time. It wasn't two years until they elected a president who was a far right winger. . . . She felt that she wanted to bring the League back. But she didn't have to protect the League from extremes. The members won't do anything extreme. One reason is that the leadership has to sell projects to the members and their husbands. The members are thinking about their stuffy old stockbroker fathers. Such men are proud to say: "Guess what my daughter has gotten into." But they are not interested in anything that might change society. It has to be something that society is smiling on. . . . that can't hurt you. Nothing that will separate [the women] from their husbands and fathers.

The perspective provided by this woman suggests the range of the interests privileged women may express. The community organizations chosen for service offer their recruits direction within the boundaries of the understandings shared by husbands and fathers. These men, as representatives of the local power elite, provide the sanction for the directions taken and the causes espoused. The organizational activity, particularly in associations that serve as training ground, like the Junior League, may offer more the appearance than the reality of wide-ranging initiative. The activities to help the poor, for example, are designed to ameliorate lives rather than empower them (see Odendahl 1990 for a persuasive argument in support of this view of philanthropy). These aspects of the social structure within which they are embedded are either negligible or invisible to the women studied. The women who serve generally concentrate on the opportunities to learn and to help rather than these limitations. The activities of the Junior League and those of other organizations merge in the perspective of these women as they see the benefits of the contacts created by belonging to a network. That network, of course, is part of the class system that they do not see. It reveals, however, both the advantages (in providing direction and entry) and the limitations (in structuring possibilities by encouraging some, eliminating others) that a relatively tight network provides. The following woman made her way in Pacific City through the entry to the Junior League provided by her mother-in-law. But that aspect of the entry is not what she emphasized: "I transferred out here, not realizing that my husband's family was against working [wives]. But there are advantages. The number of friends in a new community that you make as a volunteer." Another woman does recognize the importance of connections in finding a place as a newcomer. As she states it, "I moved up here and didn't know a living soul. So I called my sorority group. From that, I was invited to join [a] board." The network of friends and associates may help keep a woman from becoming too engrossed in volunteer work. "I have five extra close friends. . . ." stated one woman. "They drag me out if they think I am tired in my volunteer activities. For instance, they made me buy season tickets to the symphony. And so every week we will go to lunch first and then to the [matinee performance]." Or it may pressure her into greater volunteer commitments.

> When I first went on the board it was because Madeline Aubrey called me and asked me to do it. I was new here then. . . . So I would ask my husband. . . . He said you might as well accept right now because if Madeline Aubrey wants you to do something, you are going to be pressured into it. I have been on the. . . . board for seven years. I have been president for ever so long. The nominating committee met at Madeline's and nominated me again. I said thanks a lot. But. . . . the president before me. . . . really scrambled everything up. Everyone wanted to resign. . . . I said to Madeline, "Why, to save this even I would be willing to run for president!" Within two minutes, I was president. When I found out I had been run again, Madeline told me how she had been the president for two or three or four years and when there was no one suitable to replace her, had stayed another year. And she said I could too. So that was that.

The parts of the network — formal, as in the Junior League organization, and informal, as in the circle of family and friends — help define the mixture of community and class interests that women consider suitable in developing a volunteer career. In understanding the meaning of their work as career (once it is discussed explicitly with them) — within the rationale for commitment to unpaid work — these women are aided by their view of noblesse oblige.

Noblesse Oblige

Privileged women who make a career of volunteering give full support to the idea of noblesse oblige. The term, for them, refers to altruistic service performed by those who have the resources for those who don't. McCarthy (1982, p. ix) focusses on the historical connotations of the term in the new world — as the duties of the rich to the society enriching them. The idea serves to commit people to their cities and invigorate their commitment to an ideal where the concerned citizens take responsibility for maintaining needed social and cultural institutions. A less recognized aspect of the term is the implied condescension of those who "have" toward the "have-nots." The latter are not equal partners with the privileged; they are expected to appreciate what they are offered without questions. Both aspects of the term can be found in the responses of women who talk about their volunteer work. The altruistic spirit is captured in the following remark: "I really work harder now than at the paid job [formerly held before marriage] because my conscience bothers me more. I even dream about it at night." Altruism also appears in the reluctance to take a desired, salaried job: "I didn't want to take a job away from others during the depression when I didn't need it." However, the altruistic service of the privileged women, like their work for the private schools that their own children attend, may have its self-interested side. Some of the work for cultural institutions of historic preservation may be quite directly in the interests of their own class. For example, one woman became active on the National Trust for Historic Preservation when a house owned by her family came under its jurisdiction. She said the owners "are relations of ours so we care about it personally as well as in terms of our interests in preservation." The patronizing or condescending aspect of noblesse oblige may be seen in the approach to welcoming newcomers into their midst. The search for potential black members of the Junior League, for example, is tinged with that aspect.

> We are now looking for black members. One of the New Jersey Leagues was the first to take in a black member. After much debate nationwide, the League decided not to lower standards in order to find black women to serve. . . . The ladies who we meet who are black and are suitable are all over 33, so we have to wait for their children.

Condescension can also be seen in the attitudes of Protestant women to the Jews among the volunteers. I heard one woman refer to another civic leader as "one of our best Jews." On another occasion, a woman explained her black maid's weakness with some condescension. Although an old family retainer, this black woman could not be trusted with alcohol. The cabinet had to be locked during her work day, accordingly. Anecdotes about how this weakness was discovered (the husband's scotch had been watered) were related with amusement, pity and also assurances about the efficiency and loyalty of the individual in question otherwise. In another instance, a woman boasted of her rapport with the leaders of a black youth project in a nearby ghetto. "I was one of the few whites to go there to develop conferences and fairs," she said. "And they have a hearty respect and a confidence and trust in me," she reported. In speaking of one of the young black leaders she said: "Joey is an utter gentleman when he comes to see me." In another instance, a woman reported surprise and new insight from the response of a girl in youth guidance. This volunteer staffed the library cart and offered to lend the girl one of the volunteer's own books. She said the girl was overwhelmed by the idea that the volunteer would lend a personally owned book. In this case, the inference is that the girl rather than the volunteer feels that there is great distance between them. These kinds of remarks and attitudes suggest the great distance perceived by these women between themselves and others in the community with whom they work. These women are self-conscious about the differences between themselves and those who are different and, by implication, lesser. The impetus to accomplish "good works" in the service of community or civic welfare helps bridge the gap. The distances produced by consciousness of class differences are also mitigated or overlooked in the pursuit of career.

Responsibility to Self

The efforts of these women to build careers have been discussed extensively elsewhere (Daniels 1988). Here I wish to consider the efforts these women have made to develop their own capacities and to make a mark, have an influence on society. It is from these efforts that their careers as volunteers and civic leaders develop. Sometimes these efforts are spurred on by some personal misfortune — for example, a life-threatening or disfiguring illness from which recovery is slow.

> When. . . . the children were still small. . . . I was attacked with [a potentially crippling disease]. . . . Nobody knows what caused it. . . . I took two years to recover. . . . My mother took the children while I was in the hospital for two months. . . . I was just knocked out. . . . I had to recover from that myself. [One day on a picnic with husband and children] I fell down and when I got up, I said, "Nobody but you is going to get over this. . . ." I just said I would have to get into things. [I began researching topics and giving lectures for an organization that asked me.] That was how I began getting out of myself. I also thought I ought to do some community work. . . . And I worked a lot at the League of Women Voters.

In other cases it is the eagerness to distance themselves from idle women of their own class which spurs these women on. They particularly want distance from bridge players, as this comment illustrates: "Bridge players waste their talents. A friend from college, she is three or four years older than I am, and one of the best bridge players. . . . She was a [university] graduate. She was so bright. Why should she do it? She never did a worthwhile thing since." Besides, such activity is tiresome: "I have to be doing something. I can't play bridge all day." Even when they enjoy games like bridge, women repress the desire to engage in activities associated with idleness or upper-class pretensions. As one person told me, "Myself won't allow me to be a dilettante or a bridge-player lady or a lady of the manor." The exigencies of life in high society seemed revolting to some.

I thought I needed to do something that would involve my intellect and emotional ability. I wanted to keep working. I didn't want to find myself — as soon as I had a notion of what a purely social life would be — you are in agonies if not invited to a party. . . . This was ruled out as far as I was concerned.

Instead, these women wanted to be useful. They wanted to be knowledgeable and respected in their community. And they pointed with pride to the accomplishments that indicated their success.

I started out in Girl Scouts, the P.T.A., the old Community Chest, chairman of the council committees. All were agencies in the city. That's where I got the background. Then I went on to the Social Planning Committee in the Community Chest. [Then] I said I would like to be chairman of the [Ghetto] District Committee. That involved the Housing Authority and Redevelopment, the schools and the health department. The young people from social services they sent, these are all now part of the power structure in all the agencies. My advantage [as current chair of an important commission] is I can just call any of these people. I knew them all from the Ghetto District Committee. I still was a part of Pacific City aging and youth programs. I was selected for the White House Conference on Youth and then. . . . the White House Conference on Aging. . . . Afterward I was selected as an outstanding woman of Pacific City.

The record of accomplishment increased their self-esteem. This was summed up by one woman in the following way: "I found out I could do something, I could get some self-identity and some self-confidence." The sense of self-esteem and pride in accomplishment can be encouraged or constrained by circumstances in the lives of privileged women that do or do not provide opportunities for experience, growth, and the display of talent with its attendant rewards. These circumstances show the interplay of personality or disposition, place in the social structure (the city and its power elite), and particular events that shape a woman's career as volunteer and civic leader. The circumstances are then explained or interpreted within the ideological framework of how a woman in that position ought to feel about the opportunities or setbacks in her life. The traditional understandings about her priorities (family and class interests first, opportunities for self-development and fulfillment only afterward) become costly for the individual woman who is ambitious, hard-working and able. The ability to sacrifice one's own interests without a second thought may be beyond some of the more ambitious women and so they pay a price in disappointments, squelched hopes as the cost of maintaining the system. The cost is one element to consider in weighing contingencies, thinking about alternatives.

Weighing Contingencies

These women are very conscious of their privileged position. They see
volunteer work, with its opportunities to set one's own hours, choose the
kinds of work most complementary to individual talents and interests, as
part of that privileged position. The privileges can even provide the
opportunity to criticize the status quo. To wit, "I couldn't do it if I didn't
have a rich husband — have the freedom to speak against the system."
The privileges also supply a secure and even luxurious base from which
to decide what work to do and when to do it. "[My husband and I] went
to college together. He was so proud of me. . . . He left me well off. . . .
so I would be able to go on living as I did before. I go to Europe every
year." But the privileges can also blunt keenness of ambition and
commitment to regular work. As one woman frankly states: "I wasn't
really equipped to do the kind of job I could hire someone to do. . . . I
don't want to give up the lovely long time I spend at the hairdressers,
the florists, going to Magnin's, planning my meal or cooking. I love all
these things."

Women are also limited, unlike ambitious men of their own class, by
their understanding of responsibility to children. In traditional cultural
expectations this responsibility falls to women; their husbands do not
share it. Women with children have to wait until the family is well
launched before showing a clear interest shaped by commitment and
ambition in civic service. The period of attending to family (when
children are not yet in school, for example, or when they or aging
relatives require special attention because of personal difficulties and
illnesses) generally combines with the waiting period when
apprenticeship, trial and error experience in volunteer work that is liked
or disliked, growing numbers of contacts and opportunities to display
talents and develop a reputation all establish the credentials of the future
leader. The waiting period also shows deference to the ideological
framework within which these women work. Family responsibilities
come first when necessary. These women have the opportunity and are
expected to meet family responsibilities unlike many women in the labor
force who must work but feel guilty about the pressures that take them
away from family. That necessity is most intense when children are little
and so family requirements are demanding: "I didn't really start serious
volunteer work until, how old is Harriet now? Until twelve years ago.
Before that, the only thing I did was collecting door to door with a box."

Volunteers are excused by their organizations when children are ill, or
husbands insist on attentions. Volunteers are also expected to give only
limited service when children are small. The waiting period also shows

deference to the idea that traditional women are not ambitious. As one woman put it: "I didn't have a passion to stay in the public eye." The ideal is that they are willing to work modestly in the background until undeniable excellence forces them to the attention of community and civic leaders looking for successors. Women speak of this period as "working in the vineyards." And they speak of the regrettable (if necessary) advance from one-on-one service to administration (leadership positions).

> We found that our members who were good at the ground level stuff didn't stay there long. For example, those that organized the waiting room and taking care of. . . . the kids rose to an administrative level very quickly. . . . You start out thinking you will do the wonderful dirty work [one-to-one service like tutoring] and no phone calls, no organizing and no meetings, but our talents really lie in administrative work.

Most, however, also express relief at advancing out of the other aspect of ground level work — the repetitive and boring tasks (like envelope stuffing, telephone solicitation) that one woman called "the grubbies" of volunteering.

The ideologically engendered expressions of deference to family priorities, denial of ambition, willingness to work in the background all appear within a context that raises questions about whether or not these ideas are held only in lip service or, at the very least, ambivalently. The women in this study work hard, raise great sums for charities, put in long hours, devote themselves to their organizations. It is sometimes difficult to see this commitment as a secondary interest, pursued in the interstices left by family responsibilities, and without ambition for recognition.

Some women do seize opportunity for more visible and recognized careers in paid employment when circumstances permit. They may actively search out paid employment when a husband's death or a divorce provide the legitimation of ambition. Two women in this study seized opportunity in this way when a death and a divorce, respectively, freed them to capitalize on skills they had developed in the volunteer world. They were unusual in their ability, ambition, perseverance — which enabled them to take advantage of opportunities that came their way through contacts developed in volunteering. They were also unusual in that they achieved positions of prominence, authority and high financial reward, equivalent to male executives in corporations and city government. These exceptions show the force of the rule that women do not attain high-status salaried careers. The women were anomalous and were singled out for special attentions because of their unusual careers.

Another two women found paid opportunities as executive staff in foundations when circumstances forced them to search — after the death of their husbands. They were women who said they would have been content in (even preferred) the life of a volunteer leader in these foundations if circumstances had permitted. Their positions were not quite so eminent nor well-paid as the first two, involving staffing for volunteer agencies or foundations. These reluctant workers show the force of the rule. They had stepped outside their usual world and were uncomfortable there.

The problem of finding paid work that will be commensurate with the skills, authority, prestige and income associated with the lifestyle of volunteer leader positions is worrisome for the recently divorced who must now make their own way. The following woman's complaint underscores the limitations of a career based on the status of privileged woman volunteer.

> I enjoy doing it and I hope I did a reasonably good job (providing a service developed out of volunteer work). But I don't make enough money at it to feel I should spend full time. So after looking around, [I] talked to friends, interviewed for volunteer-related jobs such as fund drive coordinator or executive director [of a public relations firm], I decided I couldn't make enough money at any of these things. . . . After a very expensive private school education, the twenty-one years of motherhood, and volunteerism, I am over qualified and undertrained to support myself. . . . I'm an executive and don't want to be a secretary and am not good at shorthand and typing. When we were growing up, the goal was to get married. . . . There was no thought of a career or taking care of oneself. In fact it was unseemly for a girl of my social background even to think of it. . . . My mother says to me today: "Marry a rich husband" and not get a job that is fulfilling or interesting. . . . I have enough regard so I wouldn't sell myself to some cat.

The problems facing women who have never worked are made acute by the growing prevalence of divorce and the increasing acceptance of women's right to remunerated work. Even among the well-to-do, women may have to find work after divorce. They may also be spurred onward by expectation and precept as more and more women enter the labor force. While some women say they enjoy their privileged position and do not question it, others in this study say they now regret that they weren't born later — in time to realize that they could assert their right to employment in the family business, for example. That wish is exacerbated for those, like the woman just quoted, who must find employment. The alternative to employment (selling oneself "to some cat") is increasingly unpalatable when other possibilities are thought to exist, even though they may not be possible for most women. Under these conditions the notion of career becomes more salient, combining the desire for self-expression with the need for independence.

Conclusions: Careers in the Lives of Privileged Women

The concept of career is one these women are eager to embrace (Daniels 1988) for it gives seriousness and suggests pattern to what might otherwise seem a number of unrelated, fragmentary occurrences. The concept is also analytically useful for it permits an observer to see how work, family and class responsibilities can be woven together in the lives of privileged women.

The women who do this weaving are a special segment of their privileged class: the most energetic, committed, responsible and hardworking. They set themselves apart from the stereotype of idle socialites and create a working life that combines their various interests and responsibilities — including their family obligation — under the general title of volunteer. They pursue the work entailed in a systematic and forceful manner so that, in time, they are singled out for special recognition as leaders. In many ways their careers are like those of other entrepreneurs and professionals who make a niche for themselves by offering some unique product or service. For the women of this study, their product is a combination of class reproduction and civic service. The concept of career offers a framework for understanding the importance of this activity of family and class maintenance mixed together with philanthropic endeavors as an important contribution to society. With this understanding, we enlarge the common view of "real" work as paid work in the public sphere to include one of the previously unexplored areas of the work women do. (See Daniels 1987b for an extended discussion of invisible work.) An examination of the activities of these privileged women from their own perspectives shows us what we can learn about how they contribute to the existing class and gender expectations while finding a way of life (a career) for themselves. In this process they transcend the stereotypes they wish to keep at a distance and make a substantial contribution to the society.

It is understandable, then, why women in this study are quick to embrace the concept of career. But the concept of a career can also be used to obscure the contradictions and tensions posed for these women as they develop work experience. The traditional understandings about family and class priorities create costs for women who are ambitious and yearn, sometimes, to give their own work prominence in the family hierarchy. Further, the problems of increasing divorce and desires for independence among women generally cast doubts about the viability of careers that are not easily transferable to financially remunerative ones. Finally, however women strive for the "career" image, they are always faced with the comparison between their own efforts and those of many colleagues who fit the commonly held stereotype of idle (or dilettante) affluent woman without salaried employment. At the same time, these women also consciously or implicitly distance themselves from less privileged women and, more generally, from any who fall in the category of those to be helped. Thus the career of the volunteer leader requires some fine distinctions and some genteel avoidance of issues which may cause discomfort if too openly confronted.

When we think of these contradictions we may draw out some suggestions for further study of the interplay of gender class and career within the social structure. What are the constraints and contradictions for privileged men in their careers? How do these concepts of gender, class, and career interact in the lives of working-class men and women and men and women of color? The discussion presented in this paper is meant to begin our consideration of such comparisons.

References

Aldrich, Nelson W. 1988. *Old Money: The Mythology of America's Upper Class*. N.Y.: Knopf.

Daniels, Arlene Kaplan. 1987a. "The Hidden Work of Constructing Class and Community." Pp. 220-235 in *Families and Work*, edited by N. Gerstl and H. Gross. Philadelphia: Temple University Press.

_____. 1987b. "Invisible Work." *Social Problems* 34 (December):403-413.

_____. 1988. *Invisible Careers*. Chicago: University of Chicago Press.

Ferree, Myra Marx. 1985. "Between Two Worlds: West German Research on Working Class Women and Work." *Signs: A Journal of Women in Culture and Society* 10 (3):517-536.

Fishman, Pamela M. 1978. "Interaction: The Work Women Do." *Social Problems* 25 (April):397-406.

Hartsock, Nancy. 1987. "Rethinking Modernism: Minority vs. Majority Values." Presented at the Conference on Gender and Politics, April. Evanston, IL: Northwestern University.

Hooks, Bell. 1981. *Ain't I A Woman*. Boston: South End Press.

McCarthy, Kathleen D. 1982. *Noblesse Oblige*. Chicago: University of Chicago Press.

Merton, Robert K. and Patricia L. Kendall. 1946. "The Focussed Interview." *American Journal of Sociology* 51 (May):541-557.

Odendahl, Teresa. 1990. *Charity Begins at Home: Generosity and Self-Interest Among the Philanthropic Elite*. New York: Basic Books.

Ostrander, Susan. 1984. *Women of the Upper Class*. Philadelphia: Temple University Press.

West, Candace. 1984. *Routine Complications*. Bloomington, Indiana: Indiana University Press.

Zimmerman, Don H. and Candace West. 1975. "Sex Roles, Interruptions and Silences in Conversation." Pp. 105-129 in *Language and Sex*, edited by B. Thorne and N. Henley. Rowley, Mass.: Newbury House.

PART THREE

Social Roles and Social Institutions

9

When Weak Ties Are Structured

Judith R. Blau

In "Complexity of Roles as A Seedbed of Individual Autonomy," Rose Laub Coser (1975) writes, "Merton has stood Durkheim on his head; rather than having the individual confronted with ready-made social norms that are external, coming down in toto, so to speak, for Merton individuals have to find their own orientations among multiple, incompatible, and contradictory norms" (1975, p. 239). Yet, in this brilliant and powerful essay, Coser orthogonalizes the Mertonian perspective — she turns Merton 90 degrees, not the full 180 — as she accepts his theoretical position that status sets and role sets are complementary structures while she rejects Merton's pessimistic interpretation of their social-psychological import.

In Merton's (1968) original formulation, role set is the arrangement of relationships that people have by virtue of occupying a given status. For example, the elementary school teacher deals with a variety of other status occupants, notably, students, parents, the school nurse, other teachers, and the principal. But this elementary school teacher also occupies other statuses, such as parent, spouse, church deacon, and member of a bridge club. In Merton's analysis, overlapping and complex role-sets and status-sets involve incompatible expectations and contradictory norms. In this tradition, others (for example, Thoits 1983) contend that demands created by excessive role entanglements and the demands of multiple statuses will lead to stress and psychological overload.

The ethnographic research on which this paper is based was carried out with support by NIMH about a decade ago. I am grateful to Richard Alba for his help with a formal test of the hypotheses derived from that research. However, the theoretical formulation that motivated that empirical analysis is largely derived from Rose Laub Coser's important contribution to role analysis and is published here for the first time. I am thankful to Mark Granovetter for his comments on a very early paper that incorporated some of the ideas elaborated here, and to Peter M. Blau whose work on the macro-antecedents of social relations has greatly influenced my thinking about these issues.

Instead, Coser, starting with the dual assumptions that multiple involvements foster independence and that role segmentation promotes tolerance and a cosmopolitan orientation, argues that overlapping and complex role-sets are the structural bases of autonomy, individualism, and free choice. Implicitly, Coser posits that what mediates between complexity of role relations (or multiple-status incumbency) and individualism is an intervening condition, namely that no institutionalized status nor role relation exerts a "greedy" or exclusive claim on the individual (L. A. Coser 1974). In the language of network theory, social ties must be weak, not strong (Granovetter 1975), for role and status complexity to foster behavioral and intellectual independence.

There are two issues posed here. First, what are the circumstances under which weak ties can be sustained in a complex organization in which, most typically, hierarchy, departmental fragmentation, and strong occupational groupings together create strongly knit and highly autonomous isolated groupings and fractionate the organization? Secondly, how can an organization otherwise constituted achieve the advantages typically promoted by bureaucratic mechanisms, notably, accountability, coordination, and clarity of responsibility? Advocates of organizational democracy have been concerned with these issues, but instead of dealing directly with the nature of power-holding, which is a typical and reasonable tack to take (for example, Abrahamsson 1977; Rueschemeyer 1986), I focus instead on the nature of the networks in which relations are imbedded. In this paper, I describe the nature of interpersonal relations within a large residential hospital for children. Its unique structural arrangements have given rise to a pattern of complex status-sets and role-sets which have interesting implications for organizational structure, organizational democracy, and, most importantly, the quality of treatment and care.

Description of the Hospital

The Children's Psychiatric Hospital has a staff of 250 and is a relatively large bureaucracy that is accountable to a formidable array of public and private bureaucracies; it is, for example, under the aegis of the State Department of Mental Hygiene, a teaching hospital for a major private medical school, engaged in a number of collaborative programs with the City's Board of Education, the City's Division of Social Services, and with the State's Division for Youth, which shares responsibility for custody of youthful offenders in a branch facility of the hospital. On the face of it, this institution is not the most likely place to look for organizational innovation.

The hospital provides long-term residential treatment for about 50 youngsters, day care for another 200, and a variety of programs housed outside of the hospital, including a school facility, a unit for juvenile court offenders, satellite clinics, a group home for hard-to-place adolescents, and public school consultation. Although the diversity of programs is considerable, the largest in terms of number of patients and staff effort are the residential and day-care programs that are located at the hospital. It should be noted, however, that program assignment does not compartmentalize staff; most of the 250 employees devote the bulk of their time to youngsters served by the residential and day programs, and the remainder of their time is divided, on a rotating basis, to one of the other programs. In this way centrifugal forces of program diversity and geographical dispersion have not fragmented staff into autonomous units.

The criteria for patient admission to both the residential and day care programs include probable psychosis and the inability to be placed in any other institution or foster home. The level of impairment is high: patients have serious emotional problems, often confounded by organic abnormalities, retardation, and high levels of family pathology. The catchment area for the hospital is one of the most impoverished in the United States and ranks high on all indicators of urban pathology. As is often the case for public institutions, this is the last "dumping ground," and most youngsters have been through a circuit of clinics, hospitals, and special schools. The average stay for residents is three years.

In any setting such as this, achieving the overall objective of effective treatment is riddled with uncertainties and fraught with frustration. Because little is known concerning "cures" for psychoses of childhood, and particularly because these psychoses are confusingly masked with a variety of cognitive and behavioral disorders that are irritating and difficult to deal with, comparable institutions elsewhere are marked by high levels of staff turnover and low morale. This is decidedly not the case at the Children's Hospital, and a main reason, it is argued, is the nature of the institutional structure.

Typically, large public residential hospitals are highly bureaucratic and rigidly structured owing to their embeddedness in multiple other organizations, perplexingly complex issues of accountability, sharp distinctions among the professional departments (members of which often exert monopolistic claims on patients and defend discipline-based approaches to treatment), and high rates of turnover within the nonprofessional departments (for a summary see J. R. Blau 1983). In contrast, small well-financed, private residential facilities, such as the Orthogenic School, represent the opposite extreme (Bettelheim 1975). In attempting to provide a family-like environment for young patients, there is a high degree of equality among staff accompanied by a uniform approach to the treatment of youngsters.

The Children's Hospital conforms to neither model. It is not a stereotypical complex organization with ideological fragmentation, nor is it a family-like arrangement with consensus about treatment. The ideology is "whatever works [behavior modification, play therapy, psychoanalytical approaches, family therapy], use it." This ideology is consistent with the structural arrangements of overlapping status sets and complex role relations. The best way to describe the seemingly chaotic pattern of staff relations is in terms of a differentiated set of crosscutting subnets. Although it required about two months of full-time field work to discover these subnets, they were confirmed in the remaining ten months of observation and empirically corroborated in a formal analysis of staff questionnaire responses (Blau and Alba 1982).

Dimensions Defining Subnets

The lattice of subnets is best understood, not in terms of the formal characteristics by which organizations are usually described — occupations, specialties, hierarchical strata, departments, units — but rather in terms of analytical dimensions that roughly correspond to major areas of work. These dimensions delineate subnets of work relations. The high degree of network complexity has obliterated the formal and bureaucratic structure. It was a deliberate policy at the time the hospital opened in 1969 to fragment and decentralize authority. As the institution grew, it inevitably became formalized along certain lines, but the steady development of overlapping structures — hierarchies, teams, functional groupings — ultimately led to the disappearance of any semblance of a neatly differentiated formal structure and to the emergence of an intricate web of subnets based on working relations. There is, of course, a formal organization plan, but it cannot be represented in a two or even three dimensional space, because individuals occupy positions in several hierarchies, functional groups, programs, and departments. These subnets of working relations define the contours of independent dimensions that refer simultaneously to what staff do and to the organization's formal configuration. It should be pointed out that not all of the system's constituent parts are ever active simultaneously; that many are potentially active at any time is illustrated by one answer given to the question, "To whom do you report?" — "That depends. For what?"

The *administrative dimension* chiefly involves activities that deal with supervision of staff, coordination, and decision-making. It consists of two components — discipline-based departments and committees that cut across departments. The first consists of six major departments and two minor ones. Departments are identified by disciplines, but not rigidly since a substantial number of staff either have interdisciplinary backgrounds or they work in areas that bring them into extensive contact with members of two departments. For example, educational psychologists are members of the Departments of Education and of Psychology. There are also nurses who, by virtue of specialized training in psychology, participate in an experimental program in token economy and attend Psychology Department meetings as well as meetings of the Department of Nursing. The second component of the administrative structure is comprised of committees that are interdepartmental, inter-program, and interdisciplinary. There are fifty-one recognized committees, the sheer number of which indicates the intensity of contact and communication. (To illustrate, an ad hoc committee was formed to develop strategies for dealing with "creative rule breaking." This followed an incident when a youngster rode a unicycle in the hospital corridors; his reasonable defense was that bikes were not allowed.)

The second dimension of working relations centers on *child care* and includes all staff interaction related to the direct supervision and education of youngsters. This dimension is defined by the units into which direct service is organized, namely the residential units, program areas (art, recreation, home economics, shop, dance), class rooms, remedial programs, day school, group home, and unit for juvenile offenders. The child care structure is multidisciplinary and multi-departmental, for it involves teachers, recreation therapists, nurses, aides, and other specialists, such as psychiatrists, psychologists, and social workers, although to a somewhat lesser extent. Just as departments and committees are important for patterning complex work relations, so are child care activities. Nurses maintain close contact with the teachers, oversee homework, and sometimes stay with an individual child in the class room (on a one-to-one basis). Similarly, teachers and recreation staff members have daily contact with nurses and aides in the residential units. But contacts involving direct care and management of children also encompass the clinicians. A psychiatrist, the director of the Children's Service, makes daily visits to the residential unit; a psychiatric social worker helped to initiate and now teaches a dance program that brings her into structured interaction with members of the recreation staff.

The third dimension pertains to *clinical practice*. It has two components. The first of these is comprised of multidisciplinary teams, each of which is responsible for the planning and coordination of the treatment of eight individual youngsters. A member of the team is formally assigned responsibility for individual therapy with one or two of the eight youngsters. Although all members of a team meet weekly as a group, there are frequent informal consultations in smaller groups to resolve particular issues.

The second component of the clinical structure is the complicated web of clinical supervision that takes place in dyads of supervisor and supervisee as well as in groups of peers (e.g., all therapists who work with autistic youngsters) who meet to review general clinical issues. Not all members of the staff are involved directly in clinical supervision, although the majority are because of the policy that all new staff and all staff who maintain a one-to-one relation with a particular youngster — even for a day — have a clinical consultant. For example, the Director, who is a psychoanalytically trained psychiatrist, has a clinical consultant by virtue of the fact that he sees two youngsters in individual therapy sessions. This is also the case for anyone who is assigned to do a "one-on-one" for a day.

Organizational Consequences

Two salient features of this hospital's social structure have paradoxical consequence of considerable interest. First, each dimension of work is independent of the others, which is to say that an individual's status and participation on one dimension is largely unaffected by that person's status and participation on the others. Second, all members have various and diverse forms of specialized responsibilities on all dimensions. Since the dimensions are independent of one another and participation is highly specialized and segmentalized, it is a striking paradox that the organization has achieved a remarkably high level of integration. The paradox is resolved by the fact that individuals, owing to their multiple bases of participation, are members of overlapping subnets. What initially appeared to me to be organizational anarchy is actually an extraordinarily complex social system that achieves internal integration and sustains itself through a process of linking and unlinking intricate sets of overlapping roles and statuses. This is an illustration of the principles of the structural model outlined by Rose Coser (1975). And, as I will describe, the consequences of these structural arrangements for staff relations and the care and treatment of youngsters are consistent with those predicted by that model.

The three formal dimensions of *administration* (departments and committees), *child care*, and *clinical practice* (teams and clinical supervision) are sufficiently independent to create a complex lattice of interaction that successfully integrates the diverse occupational categories of staff — psychiatrists, fellows in child psychiatry, psychiatric social workers, medical and dental specialists, recreation therapists, art therapists, teachers, music therapists, clinical and educational psychologists, nurses, aides, occupational therapists, and learning disability specialists. Communications and decisions flow horizontally, vertically, and obliquely through different structural subnets. Perhaps it is the extreme example that helps to demonstrate the salience of these dimensions. Obviously enough, the Director of Personnel has mostly casual contact with the staff who work with youngsters, for his job involves processing payroll, insurance, and related activities. His immunity from the structural constraints of overlapping networks, however, is by no means complete, for his regular participation in helping to run the children's ice cream sales, barbecues, and picnics makes him a meaningful, although peripheral, member of the complex social system. It comes as no surprise that all 250 staff members are on a first name basis, but that these loose links that span great distances acquire a moral value is nicely illustrated by a comment of the Director. After nearly a year of field work, I met with him to discuss the unanticipated broadening of the field investigation. He suggested without a sign of sarcasm that I had missed a knowledgeable and highly valued staff member — Sara, an aide on the evening staff and unofficial barber for the youngsters.

A point must be made here about the way in which the complex structure has lessened, if not eliminated, mechanisms of control that are believed to be generic to bureaucracies of this size. With the differentiation into hierarchies and the proliferation of specialists, it is imperative in comparable institutions that certain staff be assigned full-time managerial responsibilities that involve the coordination of work and overall supervision. Typically, policy and major decisions emanate from the top strata. However, in the Children's Hospital, there is neither an administrative unit nor management as such. The Director divides his time between "the kids" and working with groups and agencies external to the hospital. While it is said he provides charismatic clinical direction to the hospital, it is the consequences of his early managerial decisions at the time the hospital opened that are important now rather than any continuing conspicuous leadership. Aside from the personnel and budget officers, there is actually no segment of staff that could be identified as administration. It is a widely-shared joke that members of the executive staff (a committee made up of department heads, program directors, and heads of clinical services) are the last to be informed of any major problem and how it has been resolved; its purpose, I was told by several of its members, is to keep the records for the State agencies. While this may be slightly exaggerated, it is the case that policy and operational plans originally evolve through subnets of working relations, and that changes can be initiated from any segment of the hospital.

My comparative field work and interviews in other hospitals and clinics, although admittedly not as extensive, indicate there is a considerable amount of overt conflict in the Children's Hospital. Conflict is open and frequent, yet does not lead to irrevocable breakdown and fragmentation. While rage and indignation can dominate a committee meeting, the disputants may later be observed on the playground in a friendly game of basketball with some kids. Litwak (1961) has observed that in complex organizations that deal with nonuniform and uncertain tasks, there is a considerable degree of contradiction built into social relations that leads to a high degree of conflict and dynamic change. However, there are structural mechanisms in this setting that not only give rise to conflict, but also help to resolve it. To give a parallel example, Coleman (1957) notes that within communities when there is multiple group membership, an individual may be in conflict with another on a particular issue but an ally on another. Whether at the community or institutional level, participants in a multiply differentiated structure will have role relations with one another on a variety of dimensions. There is every incentive to resolve issues and to compromise on certain points. This is not a matter of shared values or, in this instance, shared professional ideology, but it is dictated by self interest: too much is lost in many areas of endeavor if two individuals break off role relations in any particular network. And the same structural mechanism that dilutes conflict also makes it likely. For the high level of work commitment that is achieved through the integration in weak nets is simultaneously and paradoxically expressed by an eagerness to articulate one's own convictions and, simultaneously, an ability and willingness to see the other person's point of view. As Coser (1975) notes, such intellectual flexibility is the special by-product of social structures that make different and competing demands on individuals.

Thus, while commitment is a significant aspect of the institutional climate, issues change, and there is a continuous realignment of staff. This is not only the case for issues on which people agree or disagree, but also for power relations. Power does not coalesce around unified blocks, and it tends to be highly elusive as it accrues to coalitions that form across the three dimensions of structure rather than within a given dimension. A main reason is that in order to establish support for an ongoing program or to secure legitimacy for a new one — and, in general, to keep building consensus — it is necessary to coopt individuals in highly diverse and strategic locations. Of course there are differences in the amount of influence individuals have, but influence tends to be area-specific, and the differences are highly unstable as coalitions form and subside, as negotiations are initiated and then succeed or fail. Superiors, equals, and subordinates alike must be consulted for advice and continued support, and different ones must be consulted as the issues change. Through this process whereby alignments continuously form and reform through exchange and cooptation, institutional life derives its tenacious integrity.

Subnets and Weak Ties

A good deal of the literature pertaining to the delivery of health services in the public sector is a polemical account of the inadequacies of organizations to coordinate the efforts of staff (see, for example, Joint Commission on Mental Health of Children 1973). As already indicated, these organizations mimic the structures of public bureaucracies with whom they deal (see DiMaggio and Powell 1983), while the diversity of health specialties they house aggravates the coordination problems inherent in hierarchical organizations. The main alternative, as already noted, is the small residential facility that exhibits the features of an isolated community, exemplified by Bettelheim's Orthogenic School (Bettelheim 1975).

Let us now recast the bureaucratic and family-like institutions into network imagery. Interestingly enough, both exhibit forms of strong ties, but for quite different reasons. By definition, the high degree of structuredness in bureaucracies entails segments of strong work, or instrumental, relationships (supervisor-supervisee; executive staff; department members; work group) in an otherwise "soup" of nonstructuredness. But in the small treatment facility, ubiquitous and close ties provide a matrix of primary group relations unifying the entire structure. These strong ties strikingly resemble patterns observed in communes, summer camps, and monastic orders. Relations in such contexts are based on close bonds of mutual identification and ingroup identity rather than on instrumental relations. The point here is that both contrasting types, the bureaucratic one with highly structured social relations and the one represented by the Orthogenic School with cohesive primary bonds, entail primarily strong rather than weak ties.

The concept of "weak ties" was first used by Granovetter (1973) to describe relations among acquaintances in a relatively open system of contact networks that are not institution-bound. However, it can also be used to describe the nature of social relations at the Children's Hospital, a closed social system in which neither homogeneous work groups nor strong friendship relations could be identified. A variety of questions were asked (both in interviews and in questionnaires) to determine the nature of relationships. To those questions that ask about work contacts, the individuals reported contacts that ranged over specialties, departments, programs, hierarchical levels. But interestingly enough, when asked about their friends the typical answer was, "Everyone I work with." Individuals' avoidance of close dyadic ties suggests that extensive weak networks can remain viable only when close ties are prohibited. The differentiated structure makes "greedy" demands (see L. A. Coser 1974) on the allegiance of the staff, and close friendships as well as other strong ingroup preferences are viewed with suspicion. Segmentalized participation on multiple task dimensions prohibits strong ties and strengthens weak ones. The reason is that when dimensions of structure intersect and staff are integrated in subnets of multiple crosscutting role relations, close bonds with some threaten working relations with others.

Granovetter's (1973) discussion of the advantages of weak over strong ties can be briefly restated, in part to emphasize why individuals are motivated to establish and maintain such links and also to lay the foundation for a discussion of the dynamics of exchange. First, an individual's access to opportunities and resources can only be fully exploited if he or she is linked with others in diverse positions with different knowledge, whereas strong ties tend to involve closed circles that limit access to such opportunities and resources. Second, because information is so widely diffused throughout the hospital structure, it is imperative for staff to sustain bridging inter-group connections, further weakening bonds of ingroup solidarity. We have already hinted that the bridges that link the lowest paid aides working in a satellite clinic and the psychiatrist-director help to insure loyalty to the institution. They also serve to promote the aide's identification with professional standards as well as the director's empathic understanding of the difficulties posed by continuous work with profoundly disturbed youngsters. The high level of commitment is revealed by frequent reports that aides are working 50 hour weeks (though paid for 40).

Multiple Statuses and Multiple Cross-Cutting Role Relations

A consequence of the independence of these task dimensions is that staff occupy multiple statuses, and there are sufficiently low correlations among dimensions to integrate each staff into a variety of overlapping subnets. For example, an art therapist is a member of a discipline-based department; will serve on at least one committee; has responsibilities in one of the minor programs, such as the group home; is a member of a clinical team assigned to a group of youngsters; has responsibilities on one of the residential units (say, helps out during lunch); may see a youngster in weekly individual sessions that results in a relationship of clinical supervision. And each of these positions involve him or her in a different social network.

To begin with the most elementary step, in Merton's (1968) terms, the art therapist has a role set — multiple role relations with various others. (As a team member, the art therapist is in contact with a nurse, aide, recreation leader, teacher, psychiatric social worker, psychiatrist, and psychologist.) But because the therapist occupies different positions on various dimensions — what Merton calls a status set — he or she has for each of these statuses a role set, or role relations with others in different positions. Because these others also occupy several statuses in the hospital, the art therapist is linked with them in other role relations. This means that any given two individuals have more than one set of role relations in the different statuses they occupy. My conceptualization differs from Merton's in that he refers to different institutional settings (father and psychiatrist), whereas a status set, as used here, has the distinctive property of joining a given pair in many ways in the hospital setting owing to its multidimensional character. It is the "seedbed of complexity," as Coser (1975) would argue. Whereas Merton focuses on the role sets that a person occupying one status has with others in different social sectors, it is the case, where sectors are confounded and interpenetrate, that the role relations a given person has with any other are derived from multiple statuses; all persons are directly and indirectly linked with nearly all others in a variety of ways.

Sometimes, the same two persons have two different role relations with another, and in one of them the person is subordinate and in another the same person is superordinate, a direct consequence of the fact that status in one dimension is relatively independent of status in another. To illustrate, a psychiatrist may be the clinical supervisor of a recreation specialist (psychiatrist is superordinate); the psychiatrist may be a member of a committee on hospital safety that the recreation specialist chairs (psychiatrist is subordinate); and they may share joint responsibility for the in-service training program at the group home (a peer relation). An institutionalized way of upending status differences is the standard practice for a member of the nursing staff to chair the morning rounds.

Simmel (1950) notes that having high status on one structural dimension and low status on another reduces the invidious differences in power and prestige. Multiple crosscutting role relations have this effect. When a nurse chairs the committee on diet on which the pediatrician serves as a member, the strongly entrenched norms of traditional deference and authority are inappropriate. The distinction Goffman (1959) makes in discussing the moral division of labor in psychiatric hospitals is between those who do the "dirty work" of patient care and those who do the "clean work" of therapy. Of course there is a division of labor in the Children's' Hospital — psychiatrists do not routinely help youngsters with their baths at night and aides do not have private therapy sessions with youngsters — but the structural arrangements continually erode the traditional moral division of labor between those who do clean and those who do dirty work. Thus, psychiatrists sometimes do help give baths (as well as break up fights and change the bed linen of the incontinent child), whereas psychiatrists in traditional hospitals do not.

The Nature of Social Exchange

Because crosscutting multiple role relations extend outwards to encompass many diverse others, debits and credits of exchange flow through chains of subnets. Suppose the evening program committee includes, among others, an evening nurse and a psychologist (since there is an overlap in shifts, day staff can meet in the mornings with night staff and in the late afternoon with evening staff). Because the psychologist is also the clinical supervisor of a social worker, the nurse may seek the support of the psychologist in order to influence the social worker concerning a youngster's visiting privileges. The social worker's compliance creates a debt of obligation that the nurse may later discharge by supporting the new system of privileges for children that the Social Work Department is backing and about which members of the Nursing Department are generally ambivalent. These bonds of indirect exchange are interlaced with those of direct exchange — in this example, through the indebtedness of the nurse to the psychologist. When information and knowledge are greatly fragmented and dispersed, staff must participate in intricate exchange networks if they are to get their own work done. An important consequence of these networks of exchange and reciprocity is that indebtedness serves to strengthen bonds of social integration and to promote involvement in institutional life (P. M. Blau 1964).

An equally, if not more, important consequence of such networks is that they insure a high level of information redundancy, which helps to make the treatment, care, and management of an individual child consistent in spite of the fact that the child has daily contact with many staff members. Such redundancy may not be particularly valuable in a work organization geared to the production of "things," but is highly desirable for an organization serving clients. What we know about socialization implies that this is particularly true for youngsters.

Lévi-Strauss (1969) has distinguished between restricted exchange that divides groups into pairs of exchange units and generalized exchange in which there are many subgroupings. A distinctive feature of generalized exchange is that individuals (groups) supply services to individuals (groups) who are different from those from whom they receive benefits. Moreover, individuals give to differently constituted groups compared to those in which they are recipients. Thus, it is not the dyadic bond of reciprocity that is so important in generalized exchange but the cross-cutting chains of obligation and indebtedness. Trust must reside in the structure of interpersonal relations rather than in given personal ones.

As already noted, the sources of motivation in the Children's Hospital are clearly not those usually observed by students of organizations. They do not stem from the gratification the professional derives from specialized practice, nor from the ability to exercise power over others, nor from the satisfaction of having close friends as co-workers. The explanation for the observable high level of motivation is best sought in the concept of generalized exchange, for participation in subnets of weak ties generates social trust and obligation that become generalized as moral mandates in a matrix of exchange relations.

The Structure of Weak Ties and Humane Care

The structure I have described directly promotes high quality of daily care in two important ways. First, it establishes a system of checks and balances: there is constant surveillance owing to the density of contacts that protects the child from both the zealous application of psychoanalytic theory by the inexperienced psychiatric resident and from manipulation or harsh punishment by a member of the nursing staff. Since such surveillance is part of the structure and systematically built into each staff member's set of statuses, it is not viewed by staff as meddlesome interference or "territorial invasion." More importantly, visibility and surveillance are effective because various facets of a person's work are observed by others whose different statuses give them different perspectives. This helps to achieve the exposure of incompetence rather than the protection of it, which many view as endemic to bureaucratic organizations.

Second, the structure helps to bring about a prevailing view of youngsters that attributes to them individuality and dignity. While in other hospitals I observed staff refer to children as a diagnostic category — "the suicidal schizophrenic" — or with sarcasm — "the dream machine" — staff in the Children's Hospital have an authentic and multi-faceted understanding of each youngster as a unique individual. Rose Coser's (1975) analysis of the implications that multiple role relations have for individuals' orientations is especially germane to the point. She states:

> *Social structures differ in the extent to which they make demands on an individual's effort at differentiation.* Complexity of role set. . . . make[s] demands on the status-occupants to negotiate, exercise judgment, reconcile, compromise, and take account of the intentions, of their role partners (Coser 1975, p. 254; emphasis in original).

Because of the fragmentation of staff into disciplines in most comparable settings, the child is typically viewed by each staff member more or less independently of others. Thus, for the psychiatrist, the child is a diagnostic category; for the nurses, a behavior problem; and for the teacher, a case with a learning disability. But when staff have diverse and multiple connections throughout the social structure, they have a much broader understanding than when they have merely restricted connections, as Coser indicates. In the Children's Hospital, staff members are directly linked with youngsters through their own several statuses but also indirectly through the various other staff members with whom they have working ties. Consequently, every staff member, regardless of specialized field, knows each child as an individual. However bizarre the symptoms and irrational the youngster's behavior might be, there is an overriding concern with that youngster's basic personality and needs. Without a moment's hesitation, to the question, "What's important to you in your work with these particular youngsters?" staff members replied without hesitation, "The whole kid," or "As if they were my own." Surely by this, the individual expresses a genuine optimism about the youngsters' chances for a normal life, and — in more realistic terms — the advocacy of each child's right to respect and an individual identity.

References

Abrahamsson, Bengt. 1977. *Bureaucracy or Participation*. Beverley Hills: Sage.

Bettelheim, Bruno. 1975. *A Home for the Heart*. New York: Bantum Books.

Blau, Judith R. 1983. "Sociological Theories." Pp. 135-146 in *Psychiatric Administration*, edited by John A. Talbott and Seymour R. Kaplan. New York: Grune and Stratton.

Blau, Judith R. and Richard D. Alba. 1982. "Empowering Nets of Participation." *Administrative Science Quarterly* 27: 363- 379.

Blau, Peter M. 1964. *Exchange and Power in Social Life.* New York: Wiley.

Coleman, James S. 1957. *Community Conflict.* New York: Free Press.

Coser, Lewis A. 1974. *Greedy Institutions: Patterns of Undivided Commitment.* New York: Free Press.

Coser, Rose Laub. 1975. "Complexity of Roles as Seedbed of Individual Autonomy." Pp. 237-264 in *The Idea of Social Structure: Papers in Honor of Robert K. Merton,* edited by Lewis A. Coser. New York: Harcourt Brace Jovanovich.

DiMaggio, Paul J. and Walter W. Powell. 1983. "The Iron Cage Revisited: Institutional Isomorphism and Collective Rationality in Organization Fields." *American Sociological Review* 48: 147-160.

Goffman, Erving. 1959. *Asylums.* Chicago: Aldine.

Granovetter, Mark S. 1973. "The Strength of Weak Ties." *American Journal of Sociology* 78: 1360-80.

Joint Commission on Mental Health of Children. 1973. *Mental Health From Infancy Through Childhood.* New York: Harper & Row.

Lévi-Strauss, Claude. 1969. *The Elementary Structures of Kinship.* Boston: Beacon Press.

Litwak, Eugene. 1961. "Models of Bureaucracy which Permit Conflict." *American Journal of Sociology* 67: 177-84.

Merton, Robert K. 1968. "Continuities in the Theory of Reference Groups and Social Structure." Pp. 422-440 in *Social Theory and Social Structure,* edited by R. K. Merton. New York: Free Press.

Rueschemeyer, Dietrich. 1986. *Power and the Division of Labor.* Stanford: Stanford University Press.

Simmel, Georg. 1950. *The Sociology of Georg Simmel.* Trans. and ed. by Kurt H. Wolff. Glencoe, Ill: The Free Press.

Thoits, Peggy A. 1983. "Multiple Identities and Psycholoical Well-being." *American Sociological Review* 48: 174-187.

10

Mixed Feelings: Women Interacting with the Institution of Science

Helga Nowotny

Where Have All the Women Gone?

With this question Rose Laub Coser opened a conference held in King's College, Cambridge in 1976 on the topic of "Women in Decision-making Elites in Cross-national Perspective." The papers reported on the situation of women in various elites in the United States and selected European countries. A recurrent general theme was to analyze the tracking system that often blocked women on their way to high status positions. It appears — then and now — that women were tolerated as members of elites only to the extent that their participation was not perceived as immediately threatening to those in power (Fuchs Epstein and Laub Coser 1981). In her own contribution at this conference, Rose Coser was particularly interested in elucidating the general process that clusters women at the bottom of social strata: the higher the rank, prestige or power within an occupation or profession, the smaller the proportion of women. Whatever the sphere in which they appear, women tend to be lower level participants.

Within academia — whether one analyzes physics, medicine or sociology — or whether one turns to countries like the United States and Britain, or to the Soviet Union and Poland, Rose Coser shows that the same monotonous pattern prevails both on the micro level and on the macro level: the higher the prestige of a position, the smaller the proportion of women. "It follows," she concludes, "that it is not enough to call for increased participation of women in such elite occupations as medicine or law. If existing trends were permitted to exert themselves,

This paper is an extensively revised version of my paper, "Gemischte Gefühle: Über die Schwierigkeiten des Umgangs von Frauen mit der Institution Wissenschaft," in Karin Hausen and Helga Nowotny (eds.), *Wie männlich ist die Wissenschaft*? Frankfurt/Main: Suhrkamp, 1987.

women in these professions would tend to drift into lower positions —
into the routine work of general practitioners, as they do in the Soviet
Union, or of law firms. . . . Instead, it is by making a claim to equal
admission to top positions that women, or other excluded minorities,
challenge the closed ranks of the system — that they challenge its
institutions of exclusiveness, which are not based only on achievement,
as claimed, but on monopolization of privilege" (Coser 1981).

In the ensuing time since this paper, women have both made
important steps forward in their struggles for equality and have suffered
set-backs. Scholarly research in this field has undoubtedly experienced
unprecedented growth. In many countries women's studies have become
institutionalized, albeit often on a precarious scale. In the area of interest
to Rose Coser herself, academia, and especially in social studies of
science and the history of science, gender relations have become the
focus of continuing attention. Here as elsewhere, however, mainstream
research has failed to take up many of the intriguing questions raised by
feminist scholarship (Fox Keller 1988; Rose 1990). Furthermore,
disappointingly enough, the mechanisms singled out by Rose Coser
through which women tend to vanish the closer they come to positions
of power, privilege and prestige, remain as effective as before. In
scientific careers, the status sequences (to use the term coined by Robert
K. Merton) that designate and institutionalize the movement in which
recruits move upwards on the career track still present formidable
hurdles for women and decrease their numbers significantly. The precise
nature and location of the hurdles varies with the institutional system. In
a recent empirical study performed in Germany — which can be said to
be similar to other studies of this kind — two of the barriers to women's
upward mobility are clearly identified (Joas 1989). The first is the
dissertation stage, the prerequisite for entering a university career.

The second barrier arises when nearing the *Habilitation*, the
prerequisite for applying for a professorship. Women, it turns out, are
not as ready as their male colleagues to commit themselves to a future
academic career in a relatively early stage. They take longer to finish
their dissertations, but they are also less often "invited" by their
professors to work on their *Habilitation*, i.e. they have not been sought
out as candidates.

The end result is once more the familiar pattern identified a decade
earlier by Rose Coser: like the sediment of a good wine, women remain
at the bottom in less qualified, less well paid positions which, moreover,
are often synonymous with temporary ones. It is as though a scientific
career contained several *rites de passage* which are fraught with special
dangers for women. Their occurrence has also been verified by many

other empirical studies investigating the "fairness" of chances that the institution of science holds out for women. While they often fail to prove the existence of *overt* or *direct* discrimination practices, they have to admit that more subtle, indirect and hidden discrimination occurs (Cole 1979; Tuchman 1980). Science, despite its claims to being universalistic in outlook and committed to a meritocratic ethos, appears to treat women differently than men. But the reverse case can also be stated: women "behave" differently from men, if "behavior" is taken to include biographical patterns and life courses that do not "fit" the male standard model of a scientific career and the dominant strategies of managing it.

In what follows I will investigate the relationship of women to the institution of science and examine how this institution treats them. It is a relationship still shaped by differential career structures and opportunities which I will illustrate through the extreme, but authentic cases of two Nobel Prize winners. Next I will turn to several lead questions about why these differentials persist. Is science a "greedy" institution in the sense in which both Lewis and Rose Coser used this term? Is the family yet another "greedy" institution with its claims on women who might therefore become caught between two such institutions? What about the alleged incompatibility said to exist between the arduous demands of a life devoted exclusively to science and a more or less normal family life? Why do gender-related publication rates continue to persist although research shows some very interesting differences? Towards the end I will enter the less tangible but nonetheless crucial realm of games that scientists play and strategies which are used within the institution of science. Can women alter the rules? Can they learn to play in a different way? And most importantly, perhaps, can the institution of science learn to treat its most precious resource — men and women — in a way that also allows women to fully unfold their creative potential?

Two Exemplary Scientific Careers: HIS and HER Institutions

HE is a physicist, of world renown, writing his autobiography during the spare time left by his ongoing research and before finally devoting himself full time to the problems of humankind. He presents reminiscences of a brilliant career in a superb way. No dramatic ingredient of a fulfilled male scientist's life is left out. The picture that he draws encompasses the various phases of this career including the fervent ambitions of a very young physicist who joins the Royal Air Force in their endeavor to defeat Fascist Germany, the exciting collaboration with Robert Oppenheimer in Los Alamos after the war and other remarkable stages of an academic career. In between he finds much to report on what contributes to the career's singular brilliance in the recollections of colleagues and friends on the inimitable atmosphere of the time they spent together filled with intellectual intensity and moulded by the feverish activity of a research group that continuously faces competition from other groups working on similar problems. It is, in a sense, an autobiography typical of the period of scientific heroism as experienced in the USA in the post war period. All that brilliant scientific minds could imagine in those days seemed to be readily translatable into experimental work. There seemed to be no lack of research funds, no unsolvable institutional obstacles. If necessary, even the setting up of a space station powered with nuclear bombs could be planned. The colonization of space, in those early days still a fantastical dream, is presented as a thoroughly serious and realistic project; even more, it is presented as being the starting point of a mission designed to protect humankind against itself. Only those who thought in such categories (and who know the pertinent formulas of the laws of nature) might finally be granted an appointment with the supreme boss of all research managers: the book closes appropriately with a dream of a quasi-religious experience of God.

The second biography is about a woman: SHE is a biologist and of world fame after being awarded the Nobel prize. She does not write her own autobiography. Perhaps she is too modest, perhaps she considers other things to be of greater importance. But she concedes to have a woman scholar write about her. Interviewing her seems to have not been easy. The picture which her biographer draws with much empathy and respect is that of a shy person whose private life sphere seems to be totally subordinate to her scientific work and hence of no interest. This work to which she has devoted herself with arduous seriousness and commitment over many years, done largely alone without colleagues and assistants, consists in cultivating, observing, and experimenting with the genetic characteristics and mutations of corn. It has become the center of her whole life. As her biographer puts it, she has developed the ability to be alone. The theoretical structure of the scientific field she works in has undergone enormous changes during her life time, and she has contributed actively and decisively to them, but her institutional position has always remained a precarious one. Notwithstanding the fact that her colleagues acknowledged her from the very beginning and that renowned scientists sided with her, the access she has had to institutions has remained very limited and the conditions she has been offered often proved to be unacceptable to her. With unwavering consistency and severity towards herself she has made her way on the margins of the institutions. When she at last finds a protected niche, she patiently —

and almost imperceptibly — continues working on her discoveries until her experiments and observations start to yield a coherent pattern. As the reader may sense, the drama of this life occurs inside this woman. Outwardly, there is nothing spectacular about her existence apart from the fact that it was very unusual at that time for a young woman to devote herself entirely to science. The life she leads is inconspicuous: it lacks ragged comradeship, playing with danger, and ambitious competition. The institution takes no notice of her and remains indifferent towards her. She, on her part, takes revenge: from a certain point of her life onwards she starts ignoring the institution. The niche she is granted is inexpensive, but to her it is precious, something she cannot be without. The heroism of this woman lies in her devotion, in her unshakeable belief in what she is doing and — to use the old fashioned but apt term — in her sacrifice.

Certainly, biographies and autobiographies, by whomever they are written, are a literary genre that follows their own stereotypes and narrative codes. Certainly, these two careers with their differences in discipline, place and time, with their different places in the various phases of intellectual and institutional changes do not permit generalizations especially as they are only two cases.

Nevertheless, the scientific institutions, as they are presented here, accept and treat HIM and HER unequally. HE is spoilt, SHE is tolerated, and HE and SHE behave differently. HE experiences the institution as a mobile and exciting place offering optimal prerequisites for his intellectual development and sufficient emotional warmth. It is an instrument by means of which he may realize his ideas, raise research funds, and mobilize collaborators. SHE, in contrast, is initially rejected and offered conditions she is not prepared to accept — yet the institution as source of work is still absolutely necessary, something she cannot do without. Though SHE at last belongs to the recognized experts of her discipline, she is denied an institutional basis, she lacks research funds she may use to implement to her ideas. She is not given the possibility of directing the research work of others. The only assets she has are her indefatigable commitment and her scientific reputation which, however, never seem to be completely secure. Unlike HIM, she and her daughters may not appear for the appointment with God, since she has deliberately renounced having a family. If such an appointment with God occurs at all, it is more likely to take place as a mystical encounter in the maize field.

It is only once that SHE experiences the implications of her social isolation quite drastically: in trying to report on her pioneering discoveries she does not succeed in making herself understood. Her presentation fails to convey the message she wants to get across. HER defeat is complete, and it takes her a long time to get over it. About HIS defeats we do not hear much. When the space project has to be stopped, innumerable technical reasons are made responsible for it, and the institution willingly accepts HIS new ideas. . . .

For readers who have not guessed as yet our "Who Is Who": HE is Freeman Dyson (Dyson 1981, 1984; Kevles 1979). SHE is Barbara McCintock (Fox Keller 1983; Richards & Schuster 1989).

Science — A Greedy Institution?

Institutions regulate human action and cooperation; they organize interests around goal-oriented action. Like any other social organization, they are subject to historical change. Form, content, means, goals and objectives as well as members' motivations and the reward structure adapt themselves continuously to existing and expected resources, and goals are reformulated in accordance with changes in a wider social context. The institution of science is organized around the production of knowledge. As a type of organization, science has equally undergone considerable change. Seen in a historical perspective, men, unlike women, have the advantage that two of the oldest types of organizations that coordinated social interests were male-dominated or exclusively run by men: the priesthood and the military. Owing to their theocratic and hierarchical nature, they became the prototype for many forms of institutions, including science and technology.

Institutions develop their own system of rewards and sanctions that induce and appropriately channel the motivation of members so that the organization's goals can be optimally achieved. Many institutions regulate recruitment by setting up their own admission criteria and their implementation. The internal relationships of members vary greatly and depend on structure as well as the relationship between means and goals. Within the institution of science there exists a peculiar mixture of cooperation and competition. In order to produce and legitimate knowledge, it has to be shared. Common, public knowledge, to become valid, must be validated by consensus. Very subtle mechanisms operate to ensure that the production of knowledge remains pluralistic, thus guaranteeing the principles of openness and the possibility for critical verification.

One of the recurrent difficulties that women experience in their interaction with the institution of science stems from the pressure exerted by the competition for which they are inadequately socialized. As long as science was in its early handicraft phase, meaning that it was organized around the production of knowledge and instruments in a guild-like, family-centered enterprise, female family members as wives, daughters or sisters — could participate, at least as helpers. When scientific production became increasingly industrialized in the second half of the 19th century and the prerequisites for admission became bureaucratically regulated through formal certification processes, women were no longer admitted. Women eventually won the arduous and long struggle to gain access to universities with the result that they find themselves as a suspiciously regarded minority in a male-dominated institution claiming to function according to meritocratic criteria and a universalistic ethos. In practice, however, science has remained gender-blind insofar as it continues to ignore that the social preconditions and life circumstances as well as the standard life biographies still differ for men and women in the wider society — to the detriment of women.

Hence, the difficulties women encounter in their interactions with the institution of science may also be attributed to the fact that the cooperation-and-competition model is an alien form of organization for them. They are less accustomed than men to move in hierarchically structured organizations where the individual is expected to be fully subordinate to the organization's goals and where performance is achieved through competition as well as through cooperation. The organizational model society deemed adequate for women in the past was neither that of the priesthood, nor that of the military, nor even that of a bureaucracy. Rather, it was the family as an organizational type where social ties, defined through kinship and neighborhood, while offering only restrained choices, were accorded priority against any impersonal, but functionally legitimated constraints. Affection and unquestioned commitment to family members were deemed to be of greater importance than was systematically learning confrontation and negotiation with non-family members. In the family model of organization, interests and their confrontation become systematically blurred or their explicit manifestation tabooed. The group's solidarity is promoted by cooperation inside and confrontation outside, while the balancing of rivalry is at best permitted among siblings.

The historical allegiance of women to the family model as an ideal form of organization continues even today to provide a strong source of ambivalence for women in their scientific everyday life. Women scientists who today are no longer willing to relinquish their claim to having a family and a scientific career experience even stronger the divergent expectations of the dominant organizational modes of cooperation and competition. For women scientists, these modes are not clearly separable and assigned to two different spheres of their lifes, marked by different priorities and urgencies, as is the case for men. Rather, they have to come to terms with both anew every day.

Lewis A. Coser once called "greedy" those institutions that demand total commitment from their members (Coser 1974). While the mechanisms through which such commitments can be obtained vary greatly, the structural feature they have in common is that individuals are cut off from current or future priorities to the outside and thus made dependent on the institution that claims their moral allegiance and the totality of their efforts. Rose Coser took up this notion and developed it further in analyzing the "greedy" nature of any Gemeinschaft-type of group or organization.

Members of such a relatively closed group are oriented toward one another cognitively and emotionally. Since relationships are generally satisfying, people do not look much for outside sources of gratification or to outside resources for achieving specific ends. By introducing another distinction, that of centripetal and centrifugal configurations, she reaches the conclusion that Gemeinschaft ties are ineffective since they restrict members so that they hardly have resources to face the outside world. This illustrates, paraphrasing Mark Granovetter (1973), the weakness of strong ties. They are likely to hamper adaptation to crises and to the problems emanating from the outside world, while centrifugal groups bound by weak ties are much more successful in their overall achievements of coping (Coser 1985).

While science has some features that seem to make it a prime candidate for a "greedy" institution such as the strong cognitive ties that bind members to each other and the sharp demarcation which exists between lay persons and scientists, it it nevertheless a highly centrifugal type of organization which successfully manages its outside environment to achieve its own goals. The family, on the other hand, is a "greedy" institution which — at least when compared to science — is much more subject to centripetal forces. Does this mean that women in science are caught between two greedy institutions which both make claims on their allegiance and commitment and force them to oscillate continuously between the different ways in which weak and strong ties are organized?

The Myth of Incompatibility or Why Do Women Scientists Publish Less?

Greedy institutions are also jealous institutions. They insist on the undivided loyalty of their members; they expect and demand their unquestioned commitment and motivation in order to achieve the organizational goals. A well tried and highly efficient means for securing the loyalty of members is the creation and maintenance of myths. Myths may conceal seemingly incompatible contradictions by denying that they exist or by regulating their existence in favor of one interpretation or demand. Myths, however, are contingent in their effectiveness on being believed, i.e. they cease to work when people see through them. The myth which the institution of science has invented to secure its members' high level motivation and commitment is the myth of incompatibility. It states that science is such a unique and demanding vocation that it cannot be reconciled with other time and energy consuming activities. Those who wish to belong to this institution hence have to make choices.

Empirical social science research has for some time tried to unravel the causes for the different scientific productivity of women and men. Many American, as well as European, studies show that differences are significant. So far, however, the assumption that family obligations adversely affect women's publication patterns can not be proven as correct. Other structural obstacles, such as lack of access to research resources, lack of research assistants, increased teaching obligations, seem to be more decisive factors, although perhaps less accessible to quantitative social research. Thus, two American sociologists, Harriet Zuckerman and Jonathan Cole, have interviewed a group of eminent scientists, women and men of comparable age, rank and research field, on the likely interlinks between marriage and having a family on the one hand and scientific productivity on the other hand (Cole and Zuckerman 1989). What they came across was a uniform pattern with regard to the presumable incompatibility of scientific work and family obligations. Both women and men were unanimously of the opinion that the demands of science, i.e. the necessary commitment and undivided attention, may hardly be met by women with children. Being forced to divide their commitment, so the widespread belief was, women publish less than their male counterparts. Exceptions to this rule would either be super women or women who have sacrificed their family life.

However, social reality challenges these current assumptions. The scientists interviewed by Cole and Zuckerman were invited to interpret a graphic presentation of their own publication record against the background of a foil listing the most important biographical events in their life such as marriage, divorce and child birth. Women scientists did not discern any connection between the ups and downs of their publication record and significant events in their lives. They tended rather to make internal and external scientific factors responsible for their ups and downs. With advancing age and rank the publication pattern increasingly converges both between the sexes and between married and single women. Cole and Zuckerman conclude that scientific productivity is not dependent on whether or not scientists are married and have a family. Different production patterns are to a much greater extent conditional upon the social structure of science, the access to scarce resources, the social position of the scientist within a laboratory, the scientific field problem choice and state of the field.

Nonetheless, success takes its toll on women who want to be both — scientists and mothers. The time at their disposal is far scarcer; the small talk at the work place, in the laboratory has to be curtailed, and informal contacts with colleagues on the whole are reduced to an essential minimum. The priorities of the most productive women scientists are work and family while the priorities of men scientists are work and careeroriented activities. Women have a price to pay for maintaining a high level of productivity. It occurs at the expense of their informal interaction with colleagues, which in turn may also have repercussions on their professional prospects.

More recently, an interesting — and somewhat puzzling — relationship between scientific productivity, marriage and parenthood became apparent. A number of different studies have shown that unmarried and childless women publish less than women with children. This seems to be a general phenomenon, independent of country studied. In a Norwegian study, for instance, Kyvik (1990) found that his data to a large extent resemble the results of former studies. First, married and divorced persons are more productive than single persons. This applies to both men and women, but the positive effects of being married are greater for men than for women. Second, women with children are more productive than women without children. Childless men, in contrast, are as productive as men with children. Third, caring responsibilities for small children are very important in explaining women's lower publishing productivity. Women with children under ten produce significantly less than their male colleagues in the some position. If men and women with older children are compared by academic rank, women are just as productive as men. Also Joas (1989) found that among women and among men with children, the percentage of those with scientific productivity above average is higher than that of their peers without children (although the difference among women is far smaller).

Such data invite a number of speculative interpretations. They range from assigning women with children better health and more energy, supportive husbands and a more stable social life to characterizing marriage as neutralizing the effects of gender by facilitating cooperation between men and women (Fox and Faver 1985; Luukkonone-Gronow and Stolke-Heiskanen 1983; Reskin 1978). Certainly, more detailed data would be necessary to securely support these interpretations. But let us return to the question of greedy institutions, the greedy nature of *Gemeinschaft*, the strength of weak ties and the weakness of strong ties. Both science and the family have their own elements of greediness, and women may be caught between the two. The two institutions differ notably, however, in the nature of ties they encourage with the outside world. Science encourages all those ties which are helpful to science. It is a very powerful centrifugal type of institution in the sense that it actively encourages setting up actors-networks which reach far beyond its own cognitive and institutional domain. The family, while showing patterns of both centrifugal and centripetal family types, nevertheless is much more centripetal when compared to science.

The fact that married or divorced women gain an advantage in scientific productivity over unmarried women may mean that the greedy institution of science has successfully incorporated the greedy institution of the family by subjecting and utilizing family life to meet its high productivity demands. This should prove to be especially strong in dual scientific career patterns, such as the one exemplified by Marie Curie and her daughter Irene Joliot-Curie's marriage and in Nobel Prize patterns. Out of the nine women Nobel Prize winners, six were married, all of them with children. The strength of weak ties has been joined with the weakness of strong ties by subjecting the latter to the former and by the fact that science uses all the resources it can muster towards its own ends including the family ties of its members. Once it became clear that women can no longer be excluded from full membership status, they too were expected to arrange their private lives in a way that will be beneficial to science and scientific productivity. By contrast, a scientific career without family life at one life period or another could mean that these women remain in the second-citizenship class, since they are perceived as lacking additional resources and ties to be utilized for the benefit of science. In her study about the world of high energy physicists (where women also remain at the margins), Traweek reports that the massive level of support expected by those engaged in scientific research extends also to their families. The families are part of the culture of high energy physics and the stages of a career in physics mold the family, much as one might expect in other institutions such as the military, religious groups, or arts. Those who are not married by the end of graduate school or those who are divorced can expect discussions about their private life to be elaborate. Liasons are discouraged as an unworthy distraction of vital energies, and students learn very early "that a successful physicist is a married physicist." The subjection of family life to science is strongly internalized. Thus, the mother of one physicist reported that her son had told her of his plans to get married because he did not want to bother with a social life that would "distract from his work" (Traweek 1988).

It fits into this pattern that women are expected to be impressed with their husband's work and highly supportive. In an interview with the wives of the four Nobel Prize winners of 1970, they all agreed that it was their highest goal in life to keep the mundane concerns away from their husbands. They thought that they had developed a high capability for following the moods of their husbands, for being enthusiastic when required and for cheering them up when depressed. "What I really understand" Margaret Gell-Mann said, "are not his ideas, but what is the matter with him" (Nowotny 1982). The greedy institution of science is at work and successfully so. Women, finally admitted to its rank, nevertheless are still expected to fulfill their supportive role. Dual career couples, although increasing in numbers, find themselves on a tight-rope walk when it comes to genuinely giving equal weight to both of their careers.

Mutual Learning Processes: A New Synthesis of Life and Work

In the every day life of the institution the difficulties of reconciling different ways of life and biographical life courses are experienced much more acutely by women than by men. The real tragedy of many women in science is the fact that they get stuck at the bottom, that they remain in the lower ranks. There, the institution takes on a different face; power differentials appear more marked, bureaucratic regulations more oppressive, rules are formal and strict. In the upper ranks of hierarchy, everything becomes less formal, and life as well as success is easier. But it is a long way to get there. Men stay better informed about the importance of informal networks, and their access to them remains more open. They aptly make use of them by cultivating what they have been accustomed to since childhood: competitiveness and cooperation with those of the same sex.

Women are either short of time or experience difficulties in keeping relationships with their male colleagues on the level of friendship when there is some subliminal erotic attraction underneath. Closely linked to these difficulties is another one resulting from the different experiences that women have in society. Unlike men, they are reluctant to recognize and admit that the rules that prevail in an institution have been socially constructed and hence can be changed. The attitude of women towards rules is highly ambiguous, as is their relationship to power: although women tend to be more observant and more trustful of rules than men, they are also less hesitant to circumvent and ignore them when they deem it necessary. This is why men reproach them frequently for believing either too strongly in authority or for being too subversive, incalculable and too extreme in their reactions. Here too, only long-standing interaction with the institution is able to lead towards a more nonchalant attitude and a better understanding of the nature of rules, how they are made, and under what conditions they may be changed.

A third difficulty to be found in the same complex of experiences arises from a related point of view. Men more easily recognize the nature of play inherent in their scientific activities and are all too ready to let themselves be carried away. They learn to recognize the blurred transition from play to fight and in particular the transition from cooperative game to antagonistic competition. They discover how to manage the constant oscillation between them early on. Quite to the contrary, play to women often appears as frivolous, a luxury they cannot or think they cannot afford. That is why they consider fighting repugnant, something which is definite or final and hence to be avoided as long as possible. To men, fighting is merely a game that has become serious and that — though fraught with specific dangers — is very likely to proceed according to rules which they have become familiar with through frequent exercise. Women, however, when forced to fight, frequently resort to weapons men regard as unfair and disproportionate, because they do not belong to the weapons arsenal sanctioned by the rules of male games. To women, fighting means passing through a YES/NO situation, comparable to a zero-sum game whose players can only be winners or losers. To men, a fight is seldom something final; it is but a phase of a long lasting dispute in which the losers of today may be the winners of tomorrow or vice versa in which it is important to have allies, since coalition partners may not be gained in a decisive phase only. Here too, the extended game-perspective dominates — fights as an iterative procedure that keeps changing in its gradualness and choice of means.

Competition thus emerges as a sort of mixture between games and fights, the driving force of performances which otherwise would not be achieved, at least not in this form. Women are suspicious of the competitive nature of science because it strongly counteracts with their willingness to cooperate and their wish to harmonize interhuman relationships. Without having to fall back on individualized experiences of socialization, the structural parameters are manifest: competition among men as the practice of rules and as the permanent source for changing them. Wherever rules appear to be constant, deeply rooted in the social nature of family communities and anchored in the structure of affection that is required, there is no room for competition because the place of those who extend affection and of those who receive it, has been firmly marked out and set.

The institution too, can and has to learn to make use of the cultural diversity it is offered by its minority members. The future of institutions is always precarious, dependent upon the degree of adjustment to altering outer and inner conditions. Monocultures of all sorts are always vulnerable. The institution of science has doubtless already undergone a number of transformational shifts in its organizational structure. The lofty ideal of the individual engaged in a lonely scientific struggle has long since given way to a mega-enterprise which increasingly differentiates and in which flexible management assumes the place of old and obsolete hierarchical structures. To the extent that scientific creativity is subject to institutionalized conditions and can at all be planned in advance, programmed and managed, the subjacent creative power — the scientific imagination — forges ahead. Owing to the divergence of their experiences, women are an important new cultural resource which might provide the institution with greater diversity and increased potential for adjustment. The attitude of women — to take one example from technology — differs from that of men whose obsession with technical things sometimes seems monomanic. They are less susceptible to what somebody who ought to know, viz. Robert Oppenheimer, once called "technological sweetness." This renders women uninteresting in those branches of research (such as military research) which fully use this obsession. But to paraphrase Bernal, does it only take good men to do good science? (Nowotny 1985).

Finally, mention should be made of the dramatic changes that have occurred within successive generations of women scientists, changes which for an institution have occurred over an astonishingly short stretch of time. To the women scientists of the first generation who paradoxically owed everything to themselves and every position they had gained to a man, the questions raised in the present contribution would simply have seemed absurd. Though socially dependent on the benevolence of their teachers and exclusively male colleagues and well aware of the male dominated structures determining recruitment and professional advance, women all the same (or perhaps because of that very fact) believed in the sexual neutrality of an institution in which they wanted to achieve and which they wanted to serve. Their scientific zeal and the tremendous price they had to pay for their choice appear as inhumanly severe by present day standards. Nevertheless, we cannot but be profoundly touched by them. The women scientist of today notwithstanding all the differences in national context and academic discipline, and given the fact that many of their legitimate demands are for from being met, are more sober and more self confident than the women scientists of previous generations. They have learned, to resume Rose Laub Coser's admonition cited at the beginning, to challenge the closed ranks of the system. But it is not only figures, quotas and policies, however important they are, that count. What is increasingly coming to the fore are challenges to the content of the scientific enterprise as well as to the social mechanisms that helped men succeed over the ages in imprinting their point of view on what counted as science. Male dominated science, while often pretending to be universal, led to serious distortions of research approaches, problem choice and research findings, as feminist scholarship is increasingly proving. If the claim to universality of the institution is to be taken seriously, it will be necessary for the corrective phase of deconstruction which has set in now to be followed by something that is capable of transcending its present shape and content.

The novel self image of women scientists today makes itself manifest in a dual way: first, by way of consciously experimenting with life forms that seek to link scientific work and creativity with the female nexus of life. Perhaps it is the paradoxical privilege of today's generation of women engaged in scientific work that they have to experience both, the myth of incompatibility which tells them that science wants everything from them, and the myth of femininity, of being bound up with life, its unpredictability and its potential subversiveness towards artificially created structures, in a way that men cannot experience and that transcends science. Perhaps everything that proves to be difficult to them when interacting with the institution of science, simultaneously accounts for their strength: their knowledge of more comprehensive forms of existence, their search for a new synthesis of life and work. Viewed from a long-term perspective of the evolution of humankind, the individual and his and her interaction with institutions, the contradiction between these two kinds of myths can be interpreted as a struggle over the cultural forms of expression of human creativity, a struggle over their societal preconditions and their channelling. The second sign of the new self assurance of women scientists leads them to cautiously start a conversation with men where women demand much more from them than men have hitherto been used to. What at first sight may look like an illicit blending of the rules of conversational discourse — illicit according to the traditional rules of scientific discourse — is in reality an anticipation of making visible the deep structured layers of the scientific imagination. These layers, although continuously being utilized by the institution of science, are rarely laid open. The question of how a hitherto male dominated institution may learn to fully embrace their potential cannot leave it at that. It demands an answer capable of pushing the institution towards an expansion that amounts to no more, but also no less, than a novel design in accordance with the full human potential of both women and men.

References

Cole, J.R. and Zuckerman, H. 1987. "Marriage, Motherhood and Research Performance in Science." *Scientific American* (February): 83-89.

____. 1979. *Fair Science: Women in the Scientific Community.* New York: Free Press.

____, and Zuckerman, Harriet. 1985. "The Productivity Puzzle: Persistence and Chance in Patterns of Publications of Men and Women Scientists," in *Advances in Motivation and Achievement,* edited by Marjorie Steinkamp and Martin D. Maehr vol. 2, *Women in Science,* Greenwich, Conn.: JAI Press, 1985.

Coser, Lewis A. (ed.) 1974. *Greedy Institutions.* The Free Press.

Coser, Rose Laub. 1974. "The Housewife and her Greedy Family" in *Greedy Institutions,* edited by Lewis A. Coser. The Free Press.

____. 1981. "Where Have All The Women Gone? Like The Sediment of a Good, They Have Sunk to The Bottom," in *Access to Power: Cross-National Studies of Women and Elites,* edited by Fuchs Epstein, Cynthia & Rose Laub Coser. London: George Allen & Unwin.

____. 1985. "The Greedy Nature of *Gemeinschaft*" in *Conflict and Consensus,* edited by Walter W. Powell and Richard Robbins. The Free Press.

Dyson, Freeman. 1981. *Disturbing the Universe.* London: Pan Books.

____. 1984. *Weapons and Hope.* New York: Harper & Row.

Fox Keller, Evelyn. 1983. *A Feeling for the Organism. The Life and Work of Barbara McClintock.* New York: W.H. Freeman & Co.

____. 1988. "Feminist Perspectives on Science Studies." *Science Technology and Human Values.* 13, 384: 235-249.

Fuchs Epstein, Cynthia & Rose Laub Coser (eds). 1981. *Access to Power: Cross-National Studies of Women and Elites.* London: George Allen & Unwin.

Hausen, Karin and Helga Nowotny (eds.) 1987. *Wie männlich ist die Wissenschaft.* Frankfurt/Main: Suhrkamp.

Joas, Hans. 1989. "Die Denachteiligung der Frauen in der Wissenschaft" in *J.D. Bernal's The Social Function of Science 1939-1989,* edited by H. Steiner. Berlin: Akademie Verlag.

Kaufman, D.R. 1978. "Associational Ties in Academe: Some Male and Female Differences." *Sex Roles* 4: 9-21.

Kevles, Daniel. 1979. *The Physicists.* New York: Vintage Books.

Kyvik, Svein. 1990. "Motherhood and Scientific Productivity." *Social Studies of Science* 20: 149-60.

Luukkonen-Gronow, T and V. Stolte-Heiskanen 1983. "Myths and Realities of Role Incompatibility of Women Scientists." *Acta Sociologica* 26: 267-80.

Nowotny, Helga. 1982. "Wie männlich ist die Wissenschaft? Eine wissenschaftssoziologische Analyse," *Wissenschaftskolleg Jahrbuch* 1981/82. Berlin: Quadriga Verlag.

____. 1985. "Does It Only Need Good Men To Do Good Science?" in *Science as a Commodity,* edited by Michael Gibbons and Björn Wittrock. Harlow: Longman.

Richard, Evellen & Schuster, John. 1989. "The Feminine Method as Myth and Accounting Resource: A Challenge to Gender Studies an Social Studies of Science." *Social Studies of Science* 19: 697-720.

Rose, Hilary. 1990. "Talking about Science in Three Colours: Bernal and Gender Politics in the Social Studies of Science." *Science Studies* 1: 5-19.

Traweek, Sharon. 1988. *Beamtimes and Lifetimes. The World of High Energy Physicists.* Cambridge: Harvard University Press.

Tuchman, Gayle. 1980. "Fair Science Reviewed." *Social Policy II* (May/June): 59-64.

11

Where Have All the Eminent Women Psychoanalysts Gone? Like the Bubbles in Champagne, They Rose to the Top and Disappeared

Nancy J. Chodorow

In her 1981 article "Where Have All the Women Gone? Like the Sediment of a Good Wine, They Have Sunk to the Bottom" and elsewhere (R. Coser and Rokoff 1982; R. Coser 1982), Rose Coser documents discrimination against women and helps us understand how subtle are the role ambiguities and sociological and cultural traps that constrain and shape women's lives as workers, professionals, mothers, and selves. In the context of such demonstration, what are we to make of a field like psychoanalysis, in which there have been numbers of leading women practitioners since the inception of the profession? Coser was extremely encouraging about my doing a study of women psychoanalysts and knew well of their relative eminence, though she did not share my assumptions about the ease with which women had become psychoanalysts and risen to eminence in their field.[1] Her skepticism was understandable given her research on psychiatric training and culture (Coser 1979), her own professional history, and her modes of sociological understanding. "Women in the Occupational World" (Coser and Rokoff 1982) and "Stay Home Little Sheba" (1982) stress the difficulties women have in meshing their child care responsibilities with work outside the home and the particular difficulties of integrating a

Research support was provided by the Russell Sage Foundation and the National Endowment for the Humanities, and in its earliest phases, by the Center for Advanced Study in the Behavioral Sciences. I also received support from the Universities of California at Berkeley and Santa Cruz and the Institute of Personality Assessment and Research, University of California, Berkeley. I am grateful to Alida Brill, Rose Laub Coser, Lewis Coser, Sanford Gifford, Nathan Hale, Malkah Notman, Sherry Ortner, Avril Thorne, Barrie Thorne, and Robert Wallerstein for aid and advice. I thank Andrea Press and Karin Martin for research assistance and Ilene Philipson for editorial help.

profession, seen as a calling, with any other set of primary responsibilities. Even more pessimistic, "Where Have All the Women Gone?" (1981) argues that the more women in an occupation, the worse the discrimination against them, and that the higher the prestige of a profession or rank within it, the smaller proportion of women will be found there. Feminization of a field leads to its decline in prestige and in market value. Moreover, sensing this relationship, and in the absence of a feminist movement, women who are successful actively tend to keep other women from entering that field or advancing.

In spite of her scepticism about my assumptions about the opportunities for women in psychoanalysis, Rose Coser was encouraging and supportive. This chapter reports on the research that began from our early discussions. First, I specify psychoanalysis as an ambiguous profession in terms of its status and of its incorporation of women practitioners. I then document briefly the trajectory of women's participation in psychoanalysis. Through this documentation, I discover that women's participation, initially high, declined in the United States. As I next look at a variety of factors that facilitated women's participation and enabled many to rise to eminence, I pay special attention to those shifting and ambiguous cultural and social processes that may also help us to understand how women's participation declined and their prominence decreased.

An Ambiguous Profession

In the sociological literature on high status occupations, such as those in medicine, law, academia, science and engineering, central questions concern the factors that keep women out and prevent their success. Originally, answers were typically provided in what we might call "supply" terms — family, socialization, and life history factors. Later answers were formulated in what we might call "demand" terms — organizational and structural factors such as discrimination, exclusion of women from male collegial networks and mentoring relationships, marginalization, tokenism, cultural masculinization of the professions, the incompatibility between professional demands and the demands of family life.[2]

In contrast, the literature that deals with female-dominated, lower status professions, such as teaching, social work, nursing and library work, focuses on other issues: how professions "tip" from being predominantly male to female; how they feminize stylistically as they feminize numerically; and, how hierarchies emerge that elevate men into positions of higher power and prestige.

Psychoanalysis borrows features from both the high status and low status professional categories and, thus, is itself sociologically ambiguous. It is a relatively high status profession: the fields from which it draws in medicine — psychiatry and pediatrics — may be low status on the medical totem pole, but they are relatively high status in the society at large when compared to social work and clinical psychology. It is predominantly male and has been throughout its history, yet it does not seem to have excluded women nearly to the extent of comparable professions, and it has enabled women to achieve striking eminence.[3] It is, moreover, a profession that — even according to some of its male practitioners — calls forth feminine capacities and has linkages to women's traditional roles. It has not "tipped," even during periods when the percentage of women has been high, and did not respond to the increasing presence of women by elevating men disproportionately to positions of importance.

A study of psychoanalysis then, must focus on gender equality and similarity rather than, as in the more usual case, on gender inequality and difference. How was this relative equality produced and reproduced culturally, organizationally and socially? What were women's experiences of role expectations and role conflict? What was the significance of gender consciousness within these processes?

In the United States since 1970, women's professional participation in a range of fields - such as law and dentistry - has increased remarkably. A large part of this increase has been a direct consequence of the feminist movement and the impact of this movement on both "supply" and "demand" factors: on women's assumption that they can and should have meaningful careers, and on institutional admissions and employment policies. In the field of psychoanalysis, however, there was no conscious effort to include women, and no women battling for inclusion *as women*. In order to extend the literature on women in the professions, we can ask: how do women come to participate on a relatively equal basis and to achieve importance and prominence in a field as part of that field's "natural," or unintended, development — as a consequence of gender neutral structural, organizational, and cultural features of that field?

A sociologically ambiguous and culturally ambivalent situation, however, often produces ambiguous outcomes (see Coser 1966; 1979). As my research progressed, it became clear that a longstanding *decline* in women's participation in the field of psychoanalysis also needed to be explained. I also discovered a somewhat mixed professional cultural reception of early eminent women psychoanalysts. Sociological ambiguity and cultural ambivalence also affected the role of culture and consciousness in the creation of gender relations and the role of gender relations in the creation of culture and consciousness. As a major part of its base of knowledge and practice, psychoanalysis includes psychologies of gender and sexuality, and it conceptualizes development in relation to gender-differentiated parents. Prevalent cultural conceptions, and especially feminist conceptions, of psychoanalysis might lead us to speculate that it would be a field particularly *inhospitable* to women, or one that women would avoid, as it seems to argue sexist and even misogynist views of women's lives. A study of psychoanalysis and its women practitioners, then, calls out for an investigation of the issue of professional knowledge and for an understanding of the relations between the field's theories of gender and its women practitioners: How did the early women practitioners react to a theory that seems to devalue them? Did the unusual gender ratio and gender relations in the field play a role in the creation of psychoanalytic theory? How did a field with a radically dichotomous understanding of male and female personality and capacities admit women and men as presumably equally capable practitioners? Freud's (1933 p. 117) claim that his feminine collegial detractors were "more masculine than feminine" does not provide a satisfactory or complete answer, for feminists or sociologists, to this question.

As I discuss elsewhere (Chodorow 1989a), I found that professional gender consciousness was strikingly absent among the the women trained between the early 1920s and mid-1940s.[4] Such absence of gender consciousness might have been, as Coser (1979) would put it, a "patterned mechanism of defense" that helped to resolve major contradictions, or what we might see as structurally and culturally induced ambivalence. But I also considered the combination of initial gender equality and low gender salience that my interviewees' expressed when they interpreted their professional lives to warrant further investigation.

My research, intertwining life historical, ethnographic, and phenomenological with structural and organizational questions about professional history, biography, gendered knowledge and the culture and social organization of a profession, focused on how practitioners construed meaning in their lives, interpreted their situation, experiences and theories. It could not, and does not provide, objective, causal answers to questions about participation. What I came to understand as conditions for entry and success in the field are to some extent those seen subjectively by interviewees, who provided various aspects of a mosaic of social, cultural and personal factors, what the anthropologist Sherry Ortner (unpublished) calls a "plot structure" of interviews, to some extent extrapolations from their descriptions of experience about conditions that produced such experience, rather than systematic data for a ranking of factors of significance.

Participation and Eminence

Many women were prominent in the early history of psychoanalysis. Readers may think immediately of Anna Freud and Melanie Klein, who created child analysis and developed classic theories of child development. They both also made major contributions to theory — Anna Freud to psychoanalytic understandings of the defensive functions of the ego and Melanie Klein to elucidating the range of mental processes that have made hers the most important alternative theory to Freud's within the world psychoanalytic scene. Margaret Mahler's studies of separation and individuation revolutionized psychoanalytic understanding of child development. Edith Jacobson developed a foundational theory of the self and the object world. Phyllis Greenacre wrote several volumes contributing to psychoanalytic understanding of creativity, body imagery, psychoanalytic biography, reconstruction, and early childhood experiences. Frieda Fromm-Reichman's writings on theory and technique have been widely read within and outside the field. Helene Deutsch, Therese Benedek, Jeanne Lampl-de Groot, Marie Bonaparte, Karen Horney, and Judith Kestenberg pioneered and elaborated a psychology of women. These women and others were training analysts and teachers, writers and theorists, clinicians, conference participants, organizational leaders. Grete Bibring, Elizabeth Zetzel, Annie Reich, and Marianne Kris are considered brilliant clinicians, theorists of the psychoanalytic process, teachers, and contributors to training. Karen Horney, with Clara Thompson, initiated the most important dissident movement in American psychoanalysis. Since I began this research in 1981, there has emerged a veritable industry of biographies, autobiographies or studies of early women psychoanalysts.[5]

This prominence of women during the period of psychoanalytic institutionalization and consolidation must not obscure its history. During the earliest years of the field, of course, before the end of World War I, women were patients, not analysts. The Vienna Society admitted its first woman member in 1910, and there were at most one or two women in Budapest, Berlin, London, New York, and Boston during the 'teens. Starting about 1920 with the establishment of training institutes in Europe, European and American women entered the field at increasing rates.[6] In Continental Europe, membership was 25 percent female by

1930, when the first large cohort of trainees had completed training, and peaked at 35 percent in 1935. Similar patterns can be found in England. In the United States, where training institutes didn't begin until about 1930, membership was 14 percent in 1930 and peaked at 28 percent in 1941.

Nazism, Freud's death in 1939 and World War II mark a historical and psychological break in psychoanalysis, and simultaneously herald the beginning of women's declining participation in the United States. In those European countries where it had first developed, the field and its community were destroyed. Institutes closed and most analysts emigrated to England or the United States. In England, the profession continued to expand, fueled perhaps by intense controversies between Kleinians and the followers of Anna Freud. But it was in the United States that the greatest growth occured, as psychoanalytic training became a virtual requirement for serious psychiatrists. However, even as the field came to have prominence and power in U.S. medical schools, hospitals, and the culture as a whole in the 1950s, and as women of the second generation participated in and helped to lead this rise in prominence and power, the number of women entering the field decreased. As these eminent women retired, women's power and visibility in the field also declined. The leading women, as I suggest, rose to the top and disappeared. They were not replaced, or, more actively, did not reproduce their own presence. Numbers help to clarify the picture. In Europe the percentage of women psychoanalysts declined to 25 percent in the 1950s (although now it is around 40 percent). There was a precipitous decline in England from 50 percent in 1950 to a still-high 30 percent in the early 1970s, though now it now again close to 50 percent. The decline in the U.S. is apparently slower in its recovery. By the early 1980's only 11 percent of psychoanalyists were women. However, there is some evidence in the United States, as women's professional participation in general increased, as women doctors go disproportionately into psychiatry, as non-medical clinicians were able to become psychoanalysts, and as the status of psychoanalysis within psychiatry and within the culture decreased, that the field by the late 1980s was refeminizing. Yet now it lagged in terms of numbers and gender consciousness behind many other professions.[7]

Women Psychoanalysts: The Supply Side

Both supply and demand factors seem to have facilitated women's early entry into psychoanalysis and rise to importance. In Central Europe after World War I, women became psychoanalysts as part of a general growth in women's participation in the labor force. The post-war poverty in Vienna and the death of large numbers of men meant that daughters of the professional and business classes went to work, and many became doctors. Several of the early women analysts came from this milieu.[8]

A cultural ethos of equality, or comradeship, between women and men was simultaneously encouraged by the Socialist Youth Movement and the Social Democrats; and, several European second generation analysts, both men and women, met as early as their *gymnasium* years or in medical school and were part of a small face-to-face group which gravitated collectively toward the two most progressive and exciting movements of their era, psychoanalysis and socialism (Sterba 1982; Jacoby 1983). More generally, many of the early women psychoanalysts who trained in Europe, whether themselves European, American or English, came to the field through participation in other radical and relatively gender-egalitarian intellectual or political communities that took psychoanalysis seriously. In addition to European social democrats, socialists or communists, New York socialists and cultural radicals, perhaps hearing Adler or Ferenczi lecture at the New School, went to Vienna for training. In England, women like Joan Riviere, Alix Strachey and Karin Stephen (Virginia Woolf's sister-in-law) shared the cultural rebelliousness (and, possibly, gender rebelliousness) of their male Bloomsbury colleagues and partners.

In England and America, where psychoanalysis was not well known outside of a few small cultural enclaves, women came to psychoanalysis serendipitously, finding Freud's books in the library stacks at Bryn Mawr or Wellesley, or as they searched for professional training. Of that small number of women who managed to get medical training, many became psychiatrists (or pediatricians) and many of these, as well as a few psychologists and social workers, found themselves looking for a more humane and successful treatment and understanding of neurotic illness and psychology more generally. Pediatricians and school teachers who wanted to address the emotional as well as physical needs of children went to Vienna to learn about child analysis.[9]

The subject matter of psychoanalysis was also seen by many interviewees as a "supply" factor. Its theoretical and clinical concerns — sexuality, child development, family, gender and generation — were compatible with traditional feminine concerns: children and women are central and not peripheral to psychoanalytic understanding, and women see themselves and are seen as particularly good at understanding both. Individual writings and interviewees attest to a belief that women are sometimes thought or think themselves to be more able to intuit or imagine what an infant is feeling. Psychoanalytic practice felt, as some put it, "natural for women" or a "mothering profession," as it required passive sitting, intuition and empathetic understanding.[10] As one interviewee put it, "analysts are passive men [because of how you have to sit and sit and wait and wait] and aggressive women [because of the drive it takes to become a woman professional and analyst]."[11] Sexuality, of course, is not in any simple way a feminine concern, and certainly was not so during the period of the development of psychoanalysis. Yet a few interviewees stressed that Freudian theory and practice treated women as desiring sexual beings, not as sex objects. Somewhat related to this was the perception by both men and women analysts that women and men often elicit a different transference, and that many patients need to work on the issues that the transference to women, or "maternal transference," elicits.

But it is not enough that women wanted to become analysts, or that they felt it was compatible with their feminine identity. As "Where Have All the Women Gone?" and other discussions of women in the professions and work world note so well, the common fate of women desiring professional entry and feeling that their training, situation, or orientation is compatible with professional requirements, is affected by the realities of discrimination, incompatible role demands of work and family, invidious cultural stereotyping, and exclusion. By looking at the institutional, organizational and historical conditions that facilitated women's participation — the "demand," or acceptance factors, the facilitating conditions and role expectations — we are better able to understand the unusual sociology of gender in psychoanalysis.

Women Psychoanalysts: The Demand Side

Some acceptance factors, as some supply factors, must be seen as serendipitous — due to historical chance, but not sociologically interesting. First, the Central European Social Democratic governments of the 1920s made gender discrimination in university admissions illegal: anyone with a *gymnasium* degree had to be admitted to medical school (although professors could and did sometimes refuse to seat women in lectures). One Austrian woman estimated that one-third of the students in her medical school classes in the 1930s were women. Second, several interviewees pointed out that Freud liked and respected women, that his tensions and splits were always with men, and that he passed the mantle to his *daughter* (Tartakoff 1972; Spiegel 1977).[12] There is a certain Freudocentrism in attributing all psychoanalytic history to Freud's personality, but there is also some truth here: psychoanalysis *is* a field that passes the mantle, as a craft within families and, through the transference and training, in the psyches of analysands and trainees. Third, Anna Freud's example as a former nursery school teacher, along with an infusion of social democratic educational goals and encouragement by analysts August Aichhorn, who pioneered the use of psychoanalytic methods with delinquents, and Siegfried Bernfeld, who was a leader in the Socialist Youth Movement and an advocate of the development of socialist educational policy, also led European and American teachers, most of whom were women, into psychoanalysis. Fourth, anti-semitism and Jewish quotas in Hungary and Poland drove some aspiring doctors to medical training in Vienna, where they got swept into the psychoanalytic ferment. Finally, because of Nazism and World War II, many of the medical and lay psychoanalysts trained in Central Europe emigrated to the United States and England just at a time of both growing general cultural recognition of psychoanalysis and dramatically increasing demand for psychoanalysts and psychoanalytic trainers, especially in the United States.

Rose Coser in *Training in Ambiguity* (1979) and Lewis Coser in *Refugee Scholars* (1984) discuss this historical convergence in relation to the generally favorable reception of refugee psychoanalysts. Women trained before the war — many in Central Europe, where there was not as much medical or professional discrimination — came to the United States at an opportune time to take positions of responsibility in hospitals and to become training and supervising analysts in the institutes that could now barely meet demands for training. In England, both immigrant and native women were available to fill almost the entire cohort of trainees during World War II and to staff the War Nurseries that formed the core of the Hampstead Clinic. Thus, in both Europe and the United States, women had entered what they understood to be an interesting but not such high status field for a number of reasons, partly in fact because discrimination had kept them out of the academy and out of more prestigious branches of medicine. After World War II, and for reasons unrelated to women's presence, psychoanalysis grew substantially in size and importance, taking its women practitioners along.

Two features of psychoanalysis in its early Central European days especially seem to have encouraged women's participation. First, in the 1920s and 1930s in Europe, psychoanalysis still saw itself more as a movement than as a profession — the psychoanalytic "movement" was a term commonly used by practitioners — and it wanted adherents. Many social movements during their charismatic, transformative periods tend more to encourage women's participation than during periods of consolidation and bureaucratization, and psychoanalysis was no exception.[13]

Second, psychoanalysis was also excluded, or institutionally independent from, mainstream institutions like the academy and government, both of which excluded women. Although discrimination against women in admission to medical and professional schools in Central Europe was illegal, such a rule did not exclude *de facto* discrimination. Women did not get academic, government or administrative appointments (and these three were often related). As psychoanalysis was not tied to the academy or government, it was therefore an avenue of potential career development for women.[14]

Another sort of institutional arrangement, particularly in America, seems to be related to women's participation. As I indicate earlier, by the end of the 1920s, and especially in the 1930s, a small number of American women went into psychoanalytic training as a direct continuation of their training in psychiatry. Particular psychiatric institutions seem to have constituted generative, or what Henry Murray calls, "creative environments" for the development of interest in psychoanalysis as well as environments that were inclusive and encouraging of women, providing collegial networks as well as leaders who supported women. In these institutions a number of women and men who were friends from medical school, college, and other residencies crisscrossed and mutually influenced and supported each other's entrance into psychoanalysis.[15] Just as the Wagner-Jauregg Clinic in Vienna, the Schloss Tegel Sanatorium in Berlin and the Tavistock Clinic in London gave many European and English psychiatric psychoanalysts their early training, St. Elizabeth's Hospital, Sheppard-Pratt Hospital and the Phipps Clinic in Washington and Baltimore and the Institute for Juvenile Research in Chicago did the same in America, and many psychiatrists and psychiatric residents went back and forth among them.

The autonomy and movement identity of the profession were reflected in the informality of psychoanalytic training during the early period. The field was not bureaucratized and did not have universalistic rules of admission which de facto excluded women; rather, entrance into training and even practice was particularistic and inclusive, opening the way to women from many fields and backgrounds, including from the position of educated woman analyzand.[16]

Although the profession later became more bureaucratized and institutionalized, and, as I indicate below, the American medical requirement made it hard for women, it retained for some time countervailing qualities that continued to facilitate women's participation and recognition. Psychoanalysis retained (and retains) aspects of a craft mentality. This began as its founder passed the mantle to a chosen set of colleagues, and continued as the profession has been passed within families and as training analyses and supervision serve to create professional geneologies and individual apprenticeship relations that influence the psyches as well as the practices of trainees.[17] Within psychoanalysis, commitment to work and commitment to colleagues did not conflict with each other, as Coser (1981) suggests is most often the case in modern professions. Training analyses and supervision, each constituting long, in-depth, intense particularistic relationships, worked to universalize mentorship, individualize trainees, and guard against group stereotypes or caricatures, including gender stereotypes. Such particularism facilitated women's participation and helped women experience their participation as individuals, and not as women.[18] This contrasts with portrayals of other professions in which personal mentorship has been more unevenly distributed and has been shown to play an important role in socializing and promoting men, and excluding women, even when these women have been formally admitted to training.

A local organization and face-to-face quality of psychoanalytic culture favorably affected women's participation, and complemented its craft organization and universal mentoring. This contrasts with how we think of the professions in which there can't be real local stars. In the academy, recognition is clearly national and international; in law and medicine, there may be local organizations, but to participate in training institutions and to get on national committees, practitioners must publish and attain national recognition. The cultural geography of psychoanalysis, by contrast, worked toward (though it did not guarantee) inclusion of women, once an analyst was trained. Because the training is relatively late in one's professional career, and because a psychoanalytic clientele tends to be located in urban centers, most analysts were likely to be located near an institute and society, where they could go to meetings and symposia, get involved in institute work, and so forth. More than most professions, organization was not just national or international, selecting out a very few for recognition. Because of the centrality of training, the local institutes remained (and remain) important and were centers of identity and interaction for members.

Although psychoanalysts themselves are unusually cosmopolitan, the organization of their profession, unlike that of many other modern professions, is unusually local and in some ways like a craft, even a family craft. Theoretical and intellectual contributions were and are recognized nationally and internationally and accord their author high esteem and recognition, and some people have made national and international reputations through organizational involvement and political leadership. When asking interviewees about important women in the profession, however, I was surprised to find that most named women who had played an important role in their local institute or women whom they had known or worked with in some other place. Even Anna Freud tended to be overlooked by those who had not trained or worked with her. Melanie Klein was never spontaneously mentioned by an American interviewee, nor Karen Horney or Frieda Fromm-Reichman by interviewees in England. The local organization in psychoanalysis continues the face-to-face quality that begins in training and works further to stress personal qualities, and not stereotypic caricatures, of practitioners. The path to recognition always began locally, that is, in clinical work. Clinical success led to appointment as a teacher or training analyst, the highest form of local recognition, and training analyst status led to local organizational participation, invitations to participate in national scientific meetings and occasionally to national organizational participation.

The Valuation of Clinical Work

This path through local recognition reflects a central aspect of psychoanalysis that facilitated women's participation and recognition. There was (and is) the continued valuation of, and the participation of virtually all analysts in, the profession's core activity, that is, clinical work. Most forms of validation followed from the recognition that someone was clinically skilled. Even theory creation, to be credible, should be based on clinical evidence and skilled clinical understanding.

Women were considered to have particular skills and capacities as clinicians and thus benefited from such an emphasis. Interviewees pointed to the clinical acumen of women in general and talked about this acumen in particular women. Honorific symposia and memorial statements also reflect such an emphasis, as when psychoanalytic couples are memorialized: the husband is seen as the theorist or astute organizational leader, the wife as the good clinician or teacher. "Working mainly as a clinician, Dora used to enjoy saying that 'Heinz writes enough for both of us,'" says an obituary for Dora Hartmann — which goes on to add that she did publish four psychoanalytic papers and seven papers in pediatrics before she became a psychoanalyst (Bernard 1974). "Edward Bibring was best known as the theoretician and Grete was a superb clinician," claims a memorial tribute to an analytic couple in which the wife, Grete Bibring served as Chief of Psychiatry at Boston's Beth Israel Hospital and Clinical Professor at Harvard Medical School, and produced a bibliography twice as long as that of her husband

(Valenstein 1979, p.6; Gifford and Menashi 1979, pp. 16, 17). This bias suggests that women can and should be great psychoanalysts but they should also be women, something I discuss below. Nonetheless, while the great theorist or the President of the International Psychoanalytic Association was seen as *more* prestigious, or *more* recognized, the great clinician was and is also recognized.

Because of the great valuation of clinical work, teaching and training, that is, the passing on of the craft (what I have called elsewhere, professional generativity) were also universally valued. These were seen as the only way to transmit clinical acumen. And possibly because of unacknowledged gender assumptions concerning generativity, as well as because of actual evaluation of skill, women were eagerly sought out as supervisors and leaders of case conference seminars. They were also appointed to the prestigious status of training analyst in favorable disproportion to their numbers (Chodorow 1986).

Writing and theory creation were, as in the academy, the main direct avenues toward extralocal eminence. Many women were great theorists — Greenacre, Klein, Jacobson, Anna Freud, Mahler, Zetzel, Fromm-Reichman, Horney and others and are certainly accorded equal stature and importance with the "great" men. There were proportionately more women than in most fields that value writing and research, although several of my interviewees themselves regretted not writing more and claimed that women, and especially women with family responsibilities, hadn't written proportionately as much as men (also see Schuker 1985). But psychoanalysts have had a certain ambivalence toward theory, except that produced by Freud. Theory is not seen to be close enough to real clinical experience, so that other forms of recognition remained important. Many people who hardly wrote at all and did not see themselves as writers were asked to participate on panels in national meetings, or became officers of local and national organizations.

There were, then, a variety of routes to recognition in the field, rather than only one route — a variety of "hats" analysts could wear. Some of these hats — clinical work and teaching and training — were particularly consonant with women's recognized or assumed skills. This situation contrasts with that of several other professions. In the academy, teaching is the core activity practiced by most academicians in contrast to research, but it is is by no means as valued. It is what women might be seen and might see themselves as doing better than research, and it is also what a woman academician must do when she has only a few hours a day for professional work because of her domestic responsibilities. If these few hours fall at that time in her life cycle when she is also beginning her career, she is less likely to gain tenure. And teaching does not necessarily prepare her or provide the foundation for better research, as clinical work does for the psychoanalyst. We find that the proportion of women decreases as we move from the teaching colleges to the research universities. It also contrasts with the "women's professions" like teaching, nursing, or social work, in which higher status is accorded to those who move away from the core activity, from teaching, nursing or casework into administration, for instance.

Being a successful clinician alone may not be enough for real eminence in psychoanalysis. But it has formed the basis for selection of teachers and training analysts, placed analysts in a position where they can have great influence on the next generation of analysts, provided cases for writing and theorizing, and spawned invitations to speak at meetings and symposia. Several early women psychoanalysts in fact wrote and spoke extensively about teaching and training. In describing one woman analyst renowned for her extraordinary clinical abilities, an interviewee said, "[She] only wrote about three articles, but every analyst in New York passed through her hands."

Gender in Professional Knowledge and Practice

I have been discussing aspects of the organization and culture of psychoanalysis that made it receptive to women's participation and that helped to generate the low gender salience I found in women interviewees' sense of professional self. But gender was not simply ignored. The ways that gender was and wasn't salient in professional knowledge, professional practice and personal life also facilitated professional participation for women.

Just as its theoretical focus on gender, child development and family and its interpersonal, reflexive method was attractive to women so that women gravitated to the field, so, reciprocally, male practitioners felt that women could make special contributions to understanding of these central issues and encouraged their contributions. The women agreed. Horney, who exclaimed, "At this point I, as a woman, ask in amazement, and what about motherhood?" (1926, p.60), Deutsch, who wrote two volumes and many papers on the psychology of women, Klein and Anna Freud, who contributed volumes on child psychology and child development, Mahler, who systematized ego psychological understandings of early child development, all confirm the feminist supposition that women's presence in a field of inquiry changes and broadens the character of knowledge to include a more complete picture of the world as it is comprised of both males and females (and children as well as adults).[19]

Psychoanalysis seems to have facilitated an unusual relation of family and work that minimized the conflicts so well documented throughout the literature and rightly emphasized by Rose Coser.[20] Most directly, because it was a relatively solo profession and because recognition and advancement in this field come relatively late in one's career, a psychoanalytic career meshed with women's traditional family life cycle. Women may have cut back their practice when their children were young, but they were still able to engage in clinical work that served as the foundation for later recognition and advancement.

The relation between family and work, however, was more complex. As I discuss elsewhere, they were theoretically separate, in that the personal didn't equal the theoretical: women tended not to apply the psychoanalytic theory of femininity to their own familial and maternal lives, and a firm assertion of natural sex differences and traditional roles in the domestic sphere complemented a commitment to gender-blindness and equal treatment in the professional sphere (Chodorow 1989a). But they were also socially connected. Interviews elicited an ethnography of the field that included, in addition to a face-to-face professional culture and local cultural geography, a meshing of professional and social culture. There was an actual family culture, as I have implied: many of the early women analysts were married to analysts and interviewees spoke easily of "psychoanalytic couples;" sisters and cousins became psychoanalysts. Many of the offspring of the great psychoanalytic couples are analysts, psychiatrists, and psychotherapists. In the Central European psychoanalytic milieux and in the generative psychiatric institutions of England and America, people lived in a psychoanalytic social world that formed an intertwining personal and professional network, mitigating the salience of gender as it sustained professional commitment and enriched professional life. Political commitments, shared refugee experience, Austro-Jewish cultural identity, all contributed to this experience. Psychoanalysis, then, provided a setting of role complementarity rather than role conflict.

The Disappearance of the Eminent Women

Women's participation in the field remained relatively stable and high in Europe and England, but it plummeted in the United States. The actual women who achieved prominence and eminence, of course, simply got old, retired, and died. But eminent women as a *category* rose to the top and disappeared. Even today in the United States, after the strong push for professional inclusion spurred by feminism, the proportion of women psychoanalysts is less than that of women in many other fields, and only in the last few years have there begun to be a few prominent women organizationally, more than a few women training analysts except in one or two institutes, and few active women writers.[21] How do we account for this? I would look at historical, cultural and structural-organizational factors.

The decline in the United States can be dated from the late 1940s and 1950s, a time when gender ideology and gender relations were influenced by what has been called a feminine mystique. The culture was saturated with psychoanalytically justified arguments against women's professional participation and for women's commitment to home and family. Training for womanhood in schools and colleges steered girls away from those science and math courses that might have led to medicine, and most medical schools, internships and residencies retained unchallenged gender quotas. In both England and America, residency programs (as well as psychoanalytic institutes) gave preference and encouragement to veterans.

These factors help us to understand the decline in women's participation and prominence in psychoanalysis, but I believe that we miss a more fine-tuned understanding of this field if we stop with such a general account. I look at cultural and then structural-organizational aspects of psychoanalysis that, together with historical understanding, provide this more illuminating account. On the cultural side, I can only point to what I would consider lines of fault, often unspoken assumptions and attitudes about gender that were in a kind of tension with the ideology and practice of equality and the generally low gender salience I found in professional consciousness. I put these forth not as explanatory, but as suggestive of a slippery and shifting grounding of gender practices and a sporadic unease about female presence and power.

Gender-blindness became a taken-for-granted, unnoticed visual lens: women I interviewed said "it didn't matter and I didn't notice," when queried about the fact that their analyst and all of their teachers and supervisors were women; they claimed to have been preoccupied while in training and afterwards much more with the theory of the unconscious and dream interpretation than with the theory of femininity (my own experience suggests that such a claim would be consonant with the emphases in psychoanalytic training and culture today as well).

Unlike the women, men with whom I spoke were quite often aware of the prominence of women, as they talked of being the only man in Anna Freud's seminar or at the Putnam Center in Boston and of the powerful women whose presence dominated the Boston, Washington, or London Societies. One man, trained in Boston during the 1950s, described his own defensive reactions as he (disparagingly and anti-maternally) thought of the senior Boston women as a group of "Bubbies." An English man from the Independent Group (the predominantly native British "object-relations" group allied neither with Klein nor Anna Freud) referred to the Kleinian "phalanx of women who all wore black." Self-assured, outspoken, influential Grete Bibring was considered by both men and women a "queen bee."

Like the middle-class mothers Rose Coser (1984) describes, women were supposed to be committed and involved, were indeed lauded for their skill, commitment and involvement, but they were not powerful. As at least one woman interviewee noted, women were relatively uninvolved in organizational and political matters, reflecting assumptions that they belong in empathetic-nurturant and generative, but not in political roles. My own research found that women were strikingly underrepresented in positions of organizational power. One man was careful to point out, discussing one of the few women who did rise to the very top of the American Psychoanalytic Association (as Chair of the Board of Professional Standards), that this woman was "absolutely dedicated to education" and that there was "not an ounce of politics in her body" (Chodorow 1986, p.51). Similarly, as I have noted, women saw themselves, and the profession saw them, as strong clinically and in training, but not theoretically.

Child analysis both encouraged women's participation and indirectly contributed to their devaluation. Several child analysts speak and write of the lower status accorded child analysis, a lower status seemingly connected to the lower status of women and children in our culture, to the lower status of child specialties in medicine, and to the fact that many child analysts were not M.D.s.[22]

In becoming professionals, women psychoanalysts did not think that they were challenging basic notions of women's nature, and indeed, they often conceptualized psychoanalysis itself as a womanly endeavor. Moreover, their move away from tradition (usually not conceptualized as feminism) was in the public (professional, economic, political) realm. They did not feel the need to transform or uproot the domestic sexual division of spheres, where they continued to take major responsibility for child and home care and for entertaining (particular early women psychoanalysts were famous party givers), and they believed that women have special nurturant capacities (Chodorow 1989a).

Women's presence may have been implicitly contested or commented upon culturally in another way, through historically important psychoanalytic debates that are not in the first instance about gender or women. It must be stressed here that these debates are certainly about more than gender and that men and women hold both positions in each controversy. Countertransference — feelings and reactions of the analyst to the patient — had long been considered as a sign of a problematic psyche, training, or psychoanalytic stance. In the early 1950s, a spate of analytic writings began to reevaluate the importance of the countertransference rather than, as traditionally, ignoring or denigrating it. It is fair to say that women — Margaret Little (1951), Annie Reich (1951), Frieda Fromm-Reichman (1950), Lucia Tower (1956), Paula Heimann (1950), Mabel Blake Cohen (1952), Edith Weigert (1954) — were prominent in this revaluation. One can speculate whether this was accidental, or a product of any number of plausible alternatives: a female psyche with a greater sense of self-in-relationship; women's lesser comfort with removing themselves from the subject-object relationship in scientific practice; tendencies toward a slightly different therapeutic stance on the part of at least some women analysts; women's more self-conscious focus necessitated by belonging to a marked gender. In any case, we have learned to consider such debates about the place of the self in social, psychological or scientific inquiry as at least partially about gender, about masculine detachment, abstraction and removal of the self and feminine concreteness, involvement, and the self's presence (see Keller 1983 and 1985; Harding and Hintikka 1983; Reinharz 1984; Collins 1990).

There is also the problematic scientific status of psychoanalysis, modeled on Freud's medical doctor-patient model and his desire to create a natural science of the mental apparatus, but in fact embodying an interplay of subjectivity and objectivity in both analyst and analysand. A self-identified science ("our science") that in fact emerges reflexively from an interpersonal situation based on interpretation and inference, psychoanalysis falls ambivalently between stereotypic masculine and feminine styles, and this dual status has been and continues to be a subject of major debate. In this context, debates about analytic stance beginning with the Freud-Ferenczi split in the 1920s can be read partially as debates about how "feminine" (responsive, empathetic, actively present) versus how "masculine" (uninvolved, rationally interpretive, distantly ungratifying) the analyst and analytic interpretation should be.

A related clinical debate revolves around whether the focus of interpretation should concern the self in its internal and external object-relational world or intrapsychic conflict among aspects of the firmly bounded individual's psychic apparatus and signalled as the individual ego's resistances and defenses (Chodorow 1989b). A final debate, with more explicitly gender-linked overtones, concerns "analysability" — whether only those at the "oedipal" level (those emotionally engaged with the father) are analysable, or whether those whose problems are of "preoedipal" (mother-child) origin, are analysable.

I believe that a comparison with other fields where similar debates have occured along with examination of the their intellectual content and emotional tone suggest that all these issues in the domain of theoretical and clinical debate are latently gender-related, mulled over almost unconsciously by *both* men and women concerned with status and respectability. Just as psychoanalysis since Freud has been sensitive to its medical, scientific and cultural status, one post-Freudian element in that sensitivity may well have been an unease with technical and theoretical, as well as numerical, feminization, because of the unusual prominence of women.

One is on firmer ground examining those organizational and structural features of psychoanalysis that led to the decline of women's presence in the field. The increasing status of the profession in the 1940s and 1950s, with the bureaucratization and institutionalization that accompanied it, seem to have had a dual effect on women. For those already in the field, it meant that what had been training and practice in a more marginal, revolutionary, field now seemed to pay off in status and power. For those wishing to enter the field, bureaucratization and institutionalization did not institute universalistic gender-blind norms that enhanced women's chances to enter the field. Rather, they reduced, even if they did not eliminate, the importance of personal relationships in training and the face-to-face quality of professional life.[23] According to accounts by younger women interviewees, as well as recent writings, mentoring could become particularistic, mitigating the universalism of the training analysis and supervisions, and the appointment of training analysts became increasingly politicized.

More precisely, statistical comparisons suggest that the uniquely American requirement that analysts be medical doctors prevented women from accomplishing required preprofessional training and thus served to exclude women from the profession. In Europe and England, there was no medical requirement, and a greater percentage of women than of men practitioners are not physicians. Close to 100 percent of male analysts and over 90 percent of female analysts in the United States are physicians, whereas in Europe and England, which have a much higher proportion of women analysts, about two-thirds of female analysts are physicians in contrast to a little over two-fifths of male analysts. The percentage of women practitioners in the United States remained high only as long as European-trained analysts continued to practice and European-trained doctors to emigrate. From 1950 onwards, when American medical school discrimination confronted the feminine mystique, women's membership plummeted. In spite of the leadership and eminence of women in the field, equal if not disproportionately female in such centers as Boston, Chicago and Washington-Baltimore, the exclusion of women from medical school served as de facto discrimination against women going into psychoanalysis.

We can enrich our understanding of even these "objective" historical and structural features of the organization of gender in psychoanalysis by reintroducing considerations of culture and consciousness. Psychoanalysis is a small field, and even with medical discrimination and a feminine mystique, there were probably enough women psychiatrists to keep the numbers of women entering the field relatively high. Some people — and I believe that feminist sociologists (including myself) — have argued that gender should no longer be salient in social organization. Early women psychoanalysts, influenced by social democratic and first wave suffragist norms, would probably have agreed. The case of psychoanalysis, with its initial high participation of women followed by precipitous decline, may demonstrate the potential limits to equality in a situation of low gender salience.

It is striking that in the mid-1950s, there were psychoanalytic institutes virtually run by powerful women that were accepting few women candidates. Coser (1981) suggests in "Where Have All the Women Gone?" that women's access to power and professional participation depends on those few women who succeed having a feminist consciousness. My study of early women psychoanalysts specifies, I believe, one variant of this. These powerful women were not, as the women Coser had in mind, refusing to stress women's rights and intentionally, whether consciously or unconsciously, trying to exclude women. My interviews with some of those few women who did receive training during the 1950s suggest that they felt supported and appreciated by older women with whom they worked. These older women, however, lacked feminist consciousness in another sense. Because of their own life histories, self identities, and low gender salient professional identities, they may have been particularly unlikely to notice the presence or absence of women, and even to have remained on unconscious principle gender-blind. They were not aware that they were not reproducing the presence of women in the field as they formed nearly all-male classes of trainees nor that conflicts between work and womanhood may have been particularly acute for those few women who did seek training.

We must ask, then, with Coser, whether, more generally, the full participation of women in professional life can be assured if it is not generated or monitored at least partly through intentional, gender-egalitarian consciousness and a feminist politics. When gender loses salience as a category for participants, there is the danger that discrimination or exclusion occurs and will not be noticed. Asking where all the eminent women psychoanalysts have gone provides insights into the study of women in the professions, generally — of the historical, organizational, and cultural conditions and prevalent gender-consciousness which affect women's ability to participate relatively fully in professional life.

Discussion

Second generation women analysts were able to become psychoanalysts because the profession was still in its movement phase, wanting adherents of either gender, and because it was marginal to, or lower status than, cognate fields, within medicine, for instance. But World War I turned people to psychiatry, even as it opened opportunities for women professionals. And World War II generated in the United States and in England a surge of psychiatric and social welfare interest in psychoanalysis, just as numbers of psychoanalysts were emigrating and as more women were being trained. There was thus a confluence of growth in the demand for psychoanalytic treatment and a rise in the status of the field just following a period favorable to the training of women.

More generally, my inquiry suggests, first, that women's professional identity will feel more secure and legitimate insofar as their field's theory is gender-inclusive — that it acknowledges the existence of two genders and accords women as well as men attention — and insofar as its form of practice does not make women feel, or label them as, masculine. It suggests that bureaucratization and centralization may not always work in women's favor, but rather that in some cases non-bureaucratized and institutionalized structures may provide more openings for women. Features of non-bureaucratization and centralization — a craft rather than professional character, multiple local centers, a centering of professional life in face-to-face processes, a few favorable creative or facilitative environments, a variety of valued professional hats — may sustain women's participation and enable their recognition and prominence. Such features of professional structure and process also enable women to practice as solo professionals in ways that mesh, rather than conflict, with their family obligations. My account also points to valuation of a core activity in which *all* practitioners participate, especially when that core activity is one in which women practitioners feel most confidently successful; to valorization of teaching and training, to professional generativity as a personal passing on of a craft; and to the universalizing of close mentoring or training relationships, as favorable to women's participation. All these structural and organizational features of professional life both enhanced women's participation and helped to generate a situation in which gender did not have to be salient to women practitioners.

But in the United States, at least, the early notable participation of women practitioners did not continue with succeeding generations, and even to some extent in Europe and England, as in the United States, it is largely the women of the second generation who are remembered and esteemed. As the field grew, it became formalized and bureaucratized, reducing, though not eliminating, the importance of personal relationships in training and the face-to-face quality of professional life. Universalistic rules favored traditionally trained men. In the United States, preprofessional requirements that psychoanalysts be doctors in a situation where medical schools discriminated against women and cultural and social pressures kept women out of medicine, ensured that most women did not and could not get the training that would allow them to become psychoanalysts. More than this, however, the same low gender salience — gender-blind professional principles — that eased the careers of women psychoanalysts who rose to the top may, paradoxically, have also been a major condition for women's professional demise.

Notes

1. A survey for *Refugee Scholars in America* (L. Coser 1984, p. 53) showed that American psychoanalysts rated four women among the top ten practicing analysts in this country over a fifty year period.
2. Compare, for instance, Epstein's early writings (1970) with her later ones (1981, 1988). See also Lorber (1984) and Walsh (1977).
3. McGovern (1984) focuses more on psychiatry than psychoanalysis, but she does note the relative prominence of women psychoanalysts during an earlier period in the United States. Her conclusions are supported by my own research.
4. During the early 1980s, I carried out open-ended interviews with eighty people in the United States, Great Britain, and the Netherlands. Forty-four of these were women psychoanalysts trained in the '20s through mid-'40s, the oldest born in 1894, the youngest in 1918, and most born between about 1900 and 1910. Eighteen were men of the same generations. Interviewees of these early generations have been members of the American, British or International Psychoanalytic Associations — in the U.S., this means "Freudian" analysts; in England, Freudian, Kleinian and "Independent." They have been lay and medical, and were born, trained and practiced — in a variety of combinations of mobility characteristic of their analytic generation — in the United States, England, Austria, Germany, Hungary, Czechoslovakia, the Netherlands, and elsewhere. About two-thirds of the women (and all the men) had married, and

about one-half had children. Ten interviewees were sons, daughters, and one a granddaughter of early women psychoanalysts, eight of whom are themselves practicing analysts or therapists. Six were analysts of the next generations (for the most part in their fifties and trained around the mid-1950s) who had had close relationships with particular early women psychoanalysts or were particularly knowledgeable about the history of psychoanalysis; and two were women married to men of the early generation, who participated in the interviews with their husbands. Thus, my interviewees were much more a set of ethnographic informants than a sociological sample, and I in addition, treated the research ethnographically, talking informally with analysts as well as historians, relatives of early women analysts, and staff of various analytic institutes.

5. Full-length accounts include: Carotenuto 1973; Roazen 1985; Westcott 1986; Quinn 1987; Meisel and Kendrick 1985; Bertin 1982; Grosskurth 1986; Gardiner 1983; Parker 1987; Lightfoot 1988; Burlingham 1989; Young-Bruehl 1988; Dyer 1983; and Peters 1985. Stepansky (1988) draws in part on my Mahler interview.

6. My membership figures are based on a subset of older, larger or more influential psychoanalytic societies and from rosters in the *International Journal of Psycho-Analysis*. In the United States, these societies include the Baltimore-Washington (subsequently Baltimore-D.C. and Washington), Boston, Chicago, Los Angeles (subsequently Los Angeles and Southern California), New York and San Francisco Societies. In Europe, they include the Berlin (subsequently German), British, Dutch (after World War II), Hungarian (through World War II), Paris-French, Swedish (after World War II), Swiss and Vienna Societies. Recent figures are also from rosters of the American Psychoanalytic Association, from surveys undertaken by the Workshop on Women's Issues in Psychoanalytic Education, under the aegis of the American Psychoanalytic Association's Committee on Psychoanalytic Education, and from the 1989 Roster of the International Psychoanalytic Association. As a result of feminism, varieties of participation and exclusion could be explored more fully for recent years, but the details of this exploration are beyond the scope of my inquiry.

7. Schuker (1985) suggests that women of the current generation may be very much influenced by expectations about appropriate feminine behavior and feminine role norms, and that traditional and conformist gender-role pressures on them may be greater than on women in other fields. I did not find that such issues were salient to the second and third generation women with whom I spoke. This could be a matter of forgetting, of choosing not to admit such limitations and potential discriminatory treatment, or, as I also think likely, of cohort and background differences: feminine role expectations were different in Europe than in the United States, and even American second-generation analysts were products of the pre-feminine mystique era. Schuker also notes that women are underrepresented as contributors to psychoanalytic journals, feel themselves to suffer from the "accumulation of disadvantage" in psychiatry and may not be mentored the way men are, and she assumes that there was no female-female mentoring and bonding in psychoanalytic history. Mayer and de Marneffe (forthcoming) report a survey demonstrating that both male and female analysts and non-analyst clinicians are reluctant to refer male patients to female analysts,

and that, consequently, women analysts receive relatively few adult male referrals. These findings and assumptions do not accord with my findings on an earlier period but do suggest a current climate of discrimination.

8. Helene Deutsch (1973) attributed her important clinic position during World War I to the absence of men as well.

9. European women with these professional backgrounds also became psychoanalysts, but there is some distinction between them and their English and American colleagues. As I indicate elsewhere, there seems to have been in the 1920s and 1930s a more receptive cultural climate in Central Europe, perhaps especially among Jews, both for women professionals and for psychoanalysis. Moreover, in contrast to their European colleagues, English women analysts were almost entirely Gentile. Americans were both Jewish and Gentile, including several mid-Western Protestants from upper-class families.

10. Ortner (unpublished) distinguishes between what she calls the "soft" or "external" role of culture in legitimating or accounting for history after the fact and the "internal" or "hard" role of culture as it more truly shapes history. According to this dichotomy, it may well be that women's sense of the compatibility between psychoanalytic concerns and feminine concerns was more external or legitimating, and even produced in response to my questions.

11. An eminent early woman analyst's written reflections capture the combination of qualities I refer to. Phyllis Greenacre (1971, p.xxi, xxiv) talks of having "aspects of the vision of both the hardcore scientist and the artist" and of her manner of making interpretations: "tentative, nonauthoritative, malleable, often admittedly imprecise and subject to correction," and of how the analyst's bodily and mental reactions interact and even fuse with a patient's unverbalized feelings and bodily communication from a preverbal era. These insights express a definition of psychoanalysis that suggests its compatibility with what we might think of as traditional feminine qualities or stances: the claim for psychoanalysis as a science and art, or what we might call a soft science that stresses tentative interpretation; an emphasis on feelings and on a person-to-person quality; and the reflexive importance of including the scientist in the inquiry. We also have Greenacre's sense of being able to understand the preverbal and nonverbal if only we pay attention and empathize intently enough. Greenacre is not a child analyst, nor has she been particularly concerned with the psychology of women. She is not talking about herself as a woman, but about her, or *the*, analytic stance; what she describes might well be the way a man would describe psychoaalysis. Similarly, I do not think that the women I have interviewed generally characterize or experience themselves first and foremost as *women* analysts. But this combination of qualities does emerge both in their general descriptions of psychoanalysis and when they are pressed to reflect on the specific role of women in the field.

12. Roazen (1971) makes the alternative suggestion that Freud was less threatened by women than by men.

13. On professions as movements, see Bucher and Strauss (1961). Anthropologist Meyer Fortes (personal communication) claimed that a similar situation was the case in anthropology — a field that was also relatively open to women from an

early period — in pre-World War II Britain. That field was also more a movement than a profession, and it attracted predominantly Jews, women and colonials. Self-respecting British gentlemen with anthropological interests were more likely to go into the colonial service. (McGovern [1984] makes the related point that hostility from without psychoanalysis created a need for unity within.)

14. As many histories of psychoanalysis indicate, this institutional independence also affected Jews, and increasingly so with the rise of fascism. Many interviewees linked the fate of women and Jews, pointing out that psychoanalysis not only had many women but also many Jews as well, and that "where they allowed Jews, they allowed women."

15. Although Boston Psychopathic Hospital was this same kind of generative prepsychoanalytic environment, and although a few women who became psychoanalysts trained there, Boston women psychoanalysts of the '20s-'30s generations were more likely to be European or, if American, trained in Europe.

16. McGovern (1984) contrasts institutional psychiatry in the 1880s, which all but kept women out of the hospitals or restricted them to work with women patients, with American psychoanalysis in the 1930s, pointing to the consequences for American women of entering the field during its preinstitutional period and therefore being able to participate in the creation of psychoanalytic institutions and to become elite as they did so.

17. What I am calling a craft here is closest to what Kernberg (1986) calls the "technical trade school" model of psychoanalytic training with an infusion of his "monastery" model.

18. One study suggests that analysts become partial to their own analysands in evaluating the success of their analysis and their suitability for further training (Klein 1965).

19. In this way, the field is somewhat like those of child development ad anthropology, which also had a fair number of early women practitioners. But these fields also form a useful contrast: their more established academic institutionalization meant that their practitioners, like Margaret Mead, or the leading child development researchers who had research affiliate appointments, often did not receive faculty positions. These fields, including psychoanalysis, contrast with less obviously gender-relevant fields like law or science, where it took the feminist movement to argue for women's inclusion and to demonstrate their gender-based assumptions and knowledge.

20. Interviewees sometimes gave this as a reason why women went into the field, but, as earlier, I would take this to be a legitimating cultural account rather than a causal explanation.

21. A quick perusal of recent journals reveals that the English *International Journal of Psycho-Analysis* has proportionately more women on its editorial board and women contributors than the American *Journal of the American Psychoanalytic Association* and especially than the almost entirely male editorial board of *The Psychoanalytic Quarterly*, in which major articles by women appear in less than half the recent issues.

22. That this lower status does not seem to have been as true in Boston may result from the fact that all the leading child analysts in that city with the

exception of Beata Rank were medical.
23. One thinks here also of the negative effect the Flexner report — which all but eliminated the medical schools that admitted women and the alternative homeopathic curing traditions in which women had participated.

References

Bernard, Viola. 1974. "Dora Hartmann, M.D., 1902-1974." *The Psychoanalytic Quarterly* 43:661-662.

Bertin, Celia. 1982. *Marie Bonaparte*. New York: Harcourt Brace Jovanovich.

Bucher, Rue and Anselm Strauss. 1961. "Professions as Process." *American Journal of Sociology* 66:325-334.

Burlingham, Michael. 1989. *The Last Tiffany*. New York: Atheneum.

Carotenuto, Aldo. 1973. *A Secret Symmetry: Sabina Spielrein between Jung and Freud*. New York: Pantheon.

Chodorow, Nancy. 1986. "Varieties of Leadership Among Early Women Psychoanalysts." Pp. 45-54 in *Women Physicians in Leadership Roles*, edited by Leah Dickstein and Carol Nadelson. Washington D.C.: American Psychiatric Press.

____. 1989a. "Seventies Questions for Thirties Women: Gender and Generation in a Study of Early Women Psychoanalysts." Pp. 199-218 in *Feminism and Psychoanalytic Theory*. New Haven: Yale University Press.

____. 1989b. "Toward a Relational Individualism: The Mediation of Self through Psychoanalysis," Pp.154-162 in *Feminism and Psychoanalytic Theory*. New Haven: Yale University Press.

Cohen, Mabel Blake. 1952. "Counter-Transference and Anxiety." *Psychiatry* 15:501-539.

Collins, Patricia Hill. 1990. *Black Feminist Thought: Knowledge, Consciousness, and the Politics of Empowerment*. Cambridge: Unwin Hyman.

Coser, Lewis. 1984. *Refugee Scholars in America*. New Haven: Yale University Press.

Coser, Rose. 1966. "Role Distance, Sociological Ambivalence and Transitional Status Systems." *American Journal of Sociology.* 72:173-187.

____. 1979. *Training in Ambiguity: Learning through Doing in a Mental Hospital*. New York:The Free Press.

____. 1981. "Where Have All the Women Gone." Pp. 16-33 in *Access to Power: Cross-National Studies of Women and Elites*, edited by Cynthia Fuchs Epstein and Rose Laub Coser. London: Sydney, and Boston: George Allen & Unwin.

____. 1982 "Stay Home Little Sheba." Pp. 153-59 in *Women and Work*, edited by Kahn-Hut et al. New York and Oxford:Oxford University Press.

____. 1984. "Authority and Structural Ambivalence in the Middle-Class Family." Pp. 362-73 in *The Family: Its Structure and Functions*, 2nd Edn., edited by Coser. New York: St. Martin's Press.

Coser, Rose Laub and Rokoff, Gerard. 1982. "Women in the Occupational World." Pp. 39-53 in *Women and Work*, edited by Rachel Kahn-Hut, Arlene Kaplan Daniels, and Richard Cloward. New York and Oxford:Oxford University Press.

Deutsch, Helene. 1973. *Confrontations with Myself*. New York: Norton.

Dyer, Raymond. 1983. *Her Father's Daughter: The Work of Anna Freud.* New York: Jason Aronson.

Epstein, Cynthia Fuchs. 1970. *Woman's Place: Options and Limits in Professional Careers.* Berkeley: University of California Press.

____. 1981. *Women in Law.* New York: Basic Books.

____. 1988. *Deceptive Distinctions: Sex, Gender and the Social Order.* New Haven:Yale University Press, and New York: Russell Sage Foundation.

Fortes, Meyer. 1978. "An Anthropologist's Apprenticeship." *Annual Review of Anthropology* 7: 1-30.

Freud, Sigmund. [1933] 1966. *New Introductory Lectures, Standard Edition of the Complete Psychological Works,* Vol 22, edited by James Strachey. New York: W.W. Norton.

Fromm-Reichman, Frieda. 1950. *Principles of Intensive Psychotherapy.* Chicago: University of Chicago Press.

Gardiner, Muriel. 1983. *Code Name "Mary": Memoirs of an American Woman in the Austrian Underground.* New Haven: Yale University Press.

Gifford, Sanford and Ann Menashi, eds. 1979. "In Memoriam, Edward Bibring, 1895-1959, Grete L. Bibring, 1899-1977. Boston: The Boston Psychoanalytic Society and Institute.

Greenacre, Phyllis. 1971. *Emotional Growth: Psychoanalytic Studies of the Gifted and a Great Variety of Other Individuals.* Vol 1. New York: International Universities Press.

Grosskurth, Phyllis. 1986. *Melanie Klein: Her World and Her Work.* New York: Knopf.

Harding, Sandra and Merill B. Hintikka, eds. 1983. *Discovering Reality: Feminist Perspectives on Epistemology, Metaphysics, Methodology, and Philosophy of Science,* Dordrecht: D. Reidel.

Harding, Sandra, ed. 1987. *Feminism and Methodology.* Bloomington: Indiana University Press.

Heimann, Paula. 1950. "On Counter-Transference." *International Journal of Psycho-Analysis* 31:81-84.

Horney, Karin. [1926] 1967. "The Flight from Womanhood." Pp.54-70 in *Feminine Psychology.* New York: Norton.

Jacoby, Russell. 1983. *The Repression of Psychoanalysis.* New York:Basic Books.

Keller, Evelyn Fox. 1983. *A Feeling for the Organism: The Life and Work of Barbara McClintock.* San Francisco: W.W. Freeman.

____. 1985. *Reflections on Gender and Science.* New Haven: Yale University Press.

Kernberg, Otto. 1986. "Institutional Problems of Psychoanalytic Education." *Journal of the American Psychoanalytic Association* 34:799-834.

Klein, Henriette R. 1965. *Psychoanalysts in Training.* New York: Columbia University Psychoanalytic Clinic.

Lightfoot, Sara Lawrence. 1988. *Balm in Gilead: Journey of a Healer.* Reading, MA: Addison-Wesley.

Little, Margaret. 1951. "Counter-Transference and the Patient's Response to It." *International Journal of Psycho-Analysis* 32:32-40.

Lorber, Judith. 1984. *Women Physicians: Careers, Status and Power.* New York and London: Tavistock.

Mayer, Elizabeth Lloyd and Daphne de Marneffe. Forthcoming. "When Theory and Practice Diverge: Gender-Related Referral Patterns to Psychoanalysts," *Journal of the American Psychoanalytic Association.*

McGovern, Constance M. 1984. "Psychiatry, Psychoanalysis, and Women in America: An Historical Note." *Psychoanalytic Review.* 71:541-552.

Meisel, Perry and Walter Kendrick, eds. 1985. *Bloomsbury/Freud: The Letters of James and Alix Strachey 1924-1925.* New York: Basic Books.

Ortner, Sherry. Unpublished. "Patterns of History: Cultural Schemas in the Foundings of Sherpa Religious Institutions."

Parker, Beulah. 1987. *The Evolution of a Psychiatrist: Memoirs of a Woman Doctor.* New Haven: Yale University Press.

Peters, Uwe Henrik. 1985. *Anna Freud: A Life Dedicated to Children.* New York: Schocken.

Quinn, Susan. 1987. *A Mind of Her Own: the Life of Karen Horney.* New York: Summit Books.

Reich, Annie. 1951. "On Counter-Transference." *International Journal of Psycho-Analysis* 32:25-31.

Reinharz, Shulamit. 1984. *On Becoming a Social Scientist.* New Brunswick: Transaction Books.

Roazen, Paul. 1971. *Freud and His Followers.* New York: Knopf.

_____. 1985. *Helene Deutsch.* New York: Anchor.

Schuker, Eleanor. 1985. "Creative Productivity of Women Analysts." *Journal of the American Academy of Psychoanalysis* 13:51-75.

Spiegel, Rose. 1977. "Freud and the Women in His World." *Journal of the American Academy of Psychoanalysis* 5:377-402.

Stepansky, Paul E. ed. 1988. *The Memoirs of Margaret S. Mahler.* New York: The Free Press.

Sterba, Richard. 1982. *Reminiscences of a Viennese Psychoanalyst.* Detroit: Wayne State University Press.

Tartakoff, Helen H. 1972. "Psychoanalytic Perspectives on Women: Past, Present and Future." Paper prepared for Radcliffe College Conference, "Women: Resource for a Changing World."

Tower, Lucia. 1956. "Countertransference." *Journal of the American Psychoanalytic Association* 4:224-255.

Valenstein, Arthur F. 1979. "Memorial Address for Grete Bibring. " Pp.6-8 in S. Gifford and A. Menashi, eds., "*In Memoriam, Edward Bibring, 1895-1959, Grete Bibring, 1899-1977.*" Boston: The Boston Psychoanalytic Society and Institute.

Walsh, Mary Roth. 1977. *Doctors Wanted: No Women Need Apply.* New Haven: Yale University Press.

Weigert, Edith. [1954] 1970. "Countertransference and Self-Analysis of the Psychoanalyst." Pp.239-248 in *The Courage to Love: Selected Papers of Edith Weigert,* New Haven: Yale.

Westcott, Marcia. 1986. *The Feminist Legacy of Karen Horney.* New Haven: Yale University Press.

Young-Bruehl, Elisabeth. 1988. *Anna Freud: A Biography.* New York: Summit Books.

12

Reshuffling the Social Deck: From Mass Migration to the Transformation of the American Ethnic Hierarchy

Andrea Tyree

For the past decade Rose Coser has devoted much of her energies to an ambitious project she calls World of our Mothers. She has collected structured oral histories with women who immigrated to the United States before the end of the mass immigration of 1880-1924. As this *Festschrift* comes out she is working with the data; they will provide the basis for her next major work. One premise of her project is that choices made when immigrants entered and settled had consequences and some of those consequences are visible today; to understand the multiethnic society in which we live one might sensibly look at the period in the past when some of the major ethnic pieces were being put in place. To get a fix on the world Coser means, you should know her own mother was born in 1891. I share her conviction that the experiences of the generation she has chosen to study are crucial to understanding what we are today. My skills are different from hers, running to assault on aggregate data, and in this piece I'll indulge my style of work in our continuing dialogue on a substantive interest we share.

Over the past decade sociologists have been coming aware that the social standing of persons in the United States today does not correspond to the ethnic hierarchy we had convinced ourselves was out there. The details of the current socioeconomic ranking of ethnic groups depend on what one takes to be an ethnic group and how one sorts people or households into categories, as well as what one uses as an indicator of hierarchy. However all this is done, one gets a basic picture pretty much like that in Table 1. The data in this Table come from the General Social Survey, the best data set for investigators who want to distinguish religion as well as national origin, to separate Catholics and Protestants and Jews from one another. The numbers are mean household incomes in constant 1967 dollars for the 13,626 respondents to the GSS between

TABLE 1. Ethnic Groups Ranked by Household Income in 1967 Dollars:
United States, 1972-1982

Ethnic Group	Income	Rank
Jews	12,463	1
British Catholics	10,433	2
Irish Catholics	10,280	3
Scottish Protestants	9,646	4
British Protestants	9,496	5
German Catholics	9,291	6
Norwegian Protestants	9,199	7
Italian Catholics	9,194	8
French Catholics	9,009	9
Other	8,938	10
French Canadian Catholics	8,910	11
Other Catholics	8,807	12
German Protestants	8,612	13
Polish Catholics	8,577	14
Dutch Protestants	8,338	15
Irish Protestants	8,231	16
Swedish Protestants	8,198	17
Other White Protestants	7,919	18
Black Catholics	7,655	19
Puerto Ricans/Other Spanish Spk	7,140	20
American Indians	6,864	21
Mexican Catholics	5,779	22
Black Protestants	5,429	23

1972 and 1982. Religion is the one reported at the time of the survey for
those who have one, and the one they report they had at age 16 if they
have none now. National origin is the response to a question about one's
"ancestors," which allows people of mixed ancestry a certain freedom to
decide which ancestors count.

In one sense what we have here is what we would expect on the basis
of newspapers and introductory sociology texts: a lot of different kinds
of whites arrayed above blacks, Hispanics, and American Indians (who
hold the bottom five ranks). The kinds of non-hispanic whites, however,
are ranked in an order which wreaks havoc on dearly held notions of
how ethnic hierarchy has come about in the United States.

A rank sequence rule, by which early arrivals enjoy a precedence of place, to be pushed on up by later arrivals who enter at the bottom, themselves to be pushed up later by the next group to arrive, fares poorly here. So does a vision of the United States as having a dominant Protestant majority with the clout to keep Catholics socioeconomically at bay. A third view of the British as a cultural core (see Neidert and Farley 1985) does not fare badly if one is willing to include Irish Catholics along with the British, but exclude Irish Protestants (an inclusion Irish Catholics themselves would doubtless reject as they did secular American schooling). The combination of Protestant majority and a British cultural core represented by the acronym WASP takes a lethal body blow here as a theory of ethnic stratification in the United States.

On the top of the hierarchy what we have are Jews and what are probably two varieties of Irish Catholics, those who stopped off in England for a generation or two and those who came directly. Toward the bottom of the non-hispanic whites are a couple of Northern European groups, Dutch and Swedish Protestants, whose ancestors mostly arrived before the mass migration of 1880-1924. In general, groups that arrived in this mass wave are doing as well as or better than those arriving before.

This is not to say there is no longer an ethnic hierarchy in the U.S. One is still there: ethnicity, as defined by the 23 categories in Table 1 is related to income, across individual respondents, by an eta of .213. When white Protestants are categorized by denomination rather than national origin, this eta goes up to .247. Ethnicity, all by itself, explains about 5% of the variance in household income of Americans. These may not be huge differences among all the various kinds of whites, but they are enough to be curious about; the top group, Jews, average 52% more income than Swedes, 57% more than "other" white Protestants, a category that includes Americans so unhyphenated (Lieberson and Waters, 1988) they cannot respond to the GSS question on ancestors.

The ethnic hierarchy revealed by Table 1 here and through other similar numbers coming to light poses a problem for students of ethnic stratification. We are short on theories or visions or ideas which can convincingly explain how we, as a multiethnic society, got to where we collectively are. If we assume our collective myths about ethnic hierarchy were at least true at some time in the past, we are led, when faced with the current reality of Table 1, to discard the history of our ethnic structure as of little relevance to the present and look to matters like differences in family formation and stability, childrearing practices, the intergenerational transmission of assets — cultural differences. While these may be informative, we also might expect more to be consequential about our ethnic history than who earned more than whom. We can expect that what was important about ethnicity at the turn of the century in America was more complicated than a single hierarchical dimension.

In seeking a fuller, more complicated picture of ethnicity at the turn of the century, I shall focus on immigrants and their children, the second generation then, all whites, all from Europe or Canada. I shall be looking for things about the tasks and places in which these people occupied themselves which bode well or poorly for the socioeconomic futures of their descendants. This inquiry is informed by a sense that ethnic stratification occurs in space and by some sort of industrial or occupational logic. The inquiry is also informed by a suspicion that if what we ultimately want to explain is between-group ethnic variability today, we should look to ethnic variability in the past on as many dimensions as we can interpret of what of socioeconomic significance people did then.

The Setting

In 1900 the tide of what the historians call the "New Immigration" was high. The immigrants were predominantly Eastern and Southern Europeans, a diverse lot in terms of their backgrounds, their plans,and what they took to be appropriate employment. They were not from some homogeneous European peasantry. Some groups were what Piore (1979) calls target workers, planning to return when their target was met; some had little attractive to return to even with fuller wallets; some followed earlier co-nationals to farms in the Midwest, others settled where they got off the boat. The matching of the resources of ethnic groups to available positions or the differential ability to create or adapt to new opportunities is an important feature of ethnic stratification. Ethnicity, especially among immigrants, then as now, was very much associated with occupation in the United States (Carpenter 1928; Hutchinson 1956; Duncan and Duncan 1968; Niedert and Farley 1985). Italians and Swedes and Jews did largely different things.

We know this is detail because the staff of the Dillingham Commission, among its other ventures (not always laudable to our sensibilities today), went to the trouble of analyzing previously unpublished 1900 census data on the occupational distributions of immigrants and their second generation children (United States Congress 1911). These analyses were published in Volume 28 of the Commission's reports, "Occupations of the First and Second Generations of Immigrants to the United States."

The data were made available in two forms. One is the percentage distributions within national origin/generation groups (first generation

Austrians, second generation Austrians. . . .) across the 140 occupations used by the 1900 census. In this form the data are full of blanks and notes indicating unspecified frequencies too small to amount individually to .1 percent. Collectively however, all these blanks amount to a lot of people, creating a sort of soggy indeterminacy for one wanting to analyze the data set as a whole.

The second form is an abbreviated percentage and frequency distribution across 35 distinct occupational categories, grosser categories than the 140 in the detailed version of the data. Enough detail is available here for the differences between groups to be accessible, while the system is compact enough that entering it into a machine-readable form is not daunting. The relative compactness also enables one trying to analyze the data to go back, when confused, and see what about the different occupational pursuits of the various groups has led to the confusion. The data in this form are manageable.

The people for whom all this is available are first and second generation members of 17 national origin groups, 15 European ones and two varieties of Canadians, the English and the French. All these people are white, though the numbers of nonwhites from these 17 origins were doubtless small. We shall restrict ourselves to male "breadwinners," for the socioeconomic diversity of female employment was not nearly so great as that of men at the turn of the century (nor is it so great today either). A parallel analysis of the occupational pursuits and labor force status of immigrant women should be able to add to the predictive uses we shall make of the male breadwinner data, but it must await another day. We have a data matrix defined by 34 ethnic-generation groups and 35 occupations. These data have been summed in Table 2, which presents the 35 occupations, along with their means and standard deviations. Numbers comparable to those in the first column, the percentages, describe the occupational distributions of both first and second generation members of each of the 17 national origin groups, with each of the 34 distributions summing to 100 percent.

The standard deviations in the second column of Table 2 assure us these 34 ethnic groups differ considerably in their occupational distributions. All we know about both ethnic and occupational stratification would lead us to suspect the variability not to be random, but to be orderly with respect to some underlying dimensions of occupational stratification in 1900. The position of each ethnic-generation group in the social structure of 1900 had to be largely a consequence of the ways its members participated in the labor force.

The task I propose is to reduce the occupational detail to the dimensions underlying it, dimensions which differentiate the ethnic-generation groups, identify these dimensions so we can talk about them,

TABLE 2. Mean Percent and Standard Deviation of Occupational Distributions of 34 Ethnic-Generation Groups in the United States in 1900

Occupation	Mean	S.D.
Agricultural laborer	11.3	9.6
Farmers, planters, & overseers	13.3	8.5
All others, agriculture	1.2	.8
Professional service	2.9	1.4
Laborers, not specified	11.6	6.6
Saloon keepers, bartenders	1.1	.6
Servants and waiters	1.0	1.0
All others, domestic and personal service	2.7	1.5
Agents	.9	.4
Bookkeepers and accountants	.9	.7
Clerks and copyists	2.8	2.1
Draymen and hackmen	2.1	1.1
Hucksters and peddlers	.7	1.1
Merchants, dealers, except wholesale	3.7	2.0
Messengers	.7	.9
Salesmen	2.6	1.8
Steam railroad employees	2.1	1.2
All others in trade and transportation	3.4	1.6
Carpenters, joiners	2.7	1.6
Masons, brick and stone	.7	.5
Painters, glaziers, and varnishers	1.3	.4
Others, building trades	.8	.5
Blacksmiths	1.1	.5
Boot and shoemakers, repairers	1.1	.9
Iron and steel workers	1.8	1.4
Machinists	1.6	.8
Manufacturers and officials, etc.	1.0	.6
Miners, quarrymen	4.7	5.9
Printers, lithographers and pressmen	.8	.4
Saw and planing mill employees	.7	.6
Tailors	2.2	3.4
Textile mill operators in cotton mills	.9	2.6
Textile mill operators in all other mills	1.1	1.1
Tobacco and cigar factory operatives	.6	.7
All others, manufacturing/mechanical pursuits	11.8	3.0

and explore how they are related to the hierarchic part of today's system of ethnic stratification revealed in Table 1. The tool we shall use will be the familiar data reduction machine of factor analysis. Before we turn the machine on, however, I'd like to take a moment to consider what we should expect to find.

Dimensions and Occupations

In much the way we accept the Weberian view of the social structure as multidimensional, one would get no contest from most sociologists in arguing that occupational structure is multidimensional. Much of the criticism of the early status attainment literature following the original Blau and Duncan monograph (1967) has been that it took an oversimplified view of occupational stratification. In their first volume on the OCGII data, Hauser and Featherman (1977) include a chapter by Hogan (Ch. 9) which makes a case for a two-dimensional status and situs structure, where the situses are industries. In several of the chapters of their second volume, the same authors (Featherman and Hauser 1978) adopt a methodology that frees them of the unidimensionality implicit in the original path analytic framework introduced by Blau and Duncan. There is apparent agreement now on the multidimensionality of occupational structures, but not the same degree of agreement on what the dimensions are or how important each might be (Kraus, Schild, and Hodge 1978; Goldthorpe 1966; Hope 1982). Additionally, while there is some agreement that a hierarchical dimension of prestige or socioeconomic status or income is everywhere important, it is not clear that the first principle of occupational differentiation is always the hierarchical one. Most dimensions orthogonal to the hierarchical one seem unique to the particular study (Blau and Duncan, 1967; Kraus et al. 1978). We can be open to the possibility that the characteristics of occupations determining the occupational structure at one time are not those of another, that the principles by which persons are routed to destinations change as the occupational distribution itself changes and as the aspirants for positions in it change. This does not mean we are at a loss as to what of note underlay the occupational differentiation of ethnic groups at the turn of the century. Two dimensions seem predictable, though their importance is not necessarily so: one is likely to have something to do with hierarchy; the other with space or geography.

Previous analyses of the characteristics of occupations have invariably revealed a hierarchical dimension as paramount (Hodge, Siegel, and Rossi 1964; Kraus et al. 1978).[1] We should expect a factor analysis of these data to yield a similar hierarchical dimension on which both occupations and ethnic groups can be ordered. In addition, the ethnic-generation groups residing disproportionately in rural areas where farming was a likely occupation were not the same as the groups preponderant in the cities, where industry and commerce were growing (Hutchinson 1956; Golab 1977; Dinnerstein et al. 1979). Groups with large representation in the states of the Confederacy got there prior to the Civil War, while groups disproportionately in the Northeast and North Central states were still getting there as the Dillingham Commission was compiling its report. Ethnic stratification occurs in space. In a country as large and diverse as the United States, all groups did not compete in any direct sense with all other groups. Since industrial and occupational differentiation also occur in space, we can expect ethnic differentiation when viewed from the perspective of the nation as a whole even if ethnic group members are assigned randomly to jobs within some reasonable commuting distance of their homes.

What other dimensions of occupational ethnic stratification might have been important is not so readily apparent. The great themes of the era provide a number of possibilities: the building of the twentieth century through the construction of subways, bridges, factories, homes; the union movement; the expansion of education; the decline of small farms. All of these differentially involved the occupations in Table 2, and differentially engaged the energies of immigrants and their offspring.

Ethnicity and Occupation in 1900[2]

It is now time to turn the factor analytic machine on. We take the 35 occupations in Table 2 as variables, the 34 European ethnic-generation groups as cases. Each case has a value on each variable, the percent of its members engaged in that occupation. The matrix of zero-order correlations between these variables across the 34 ethnic-generation cases becomes the input for the factor analysis. A varimax rotation should maximize our ability to identify the space, by maximizing variance in the columns of the factor matrix.

The decision to use the percentage distributions rather than the raw frequencies amounts to weighting each cell in the data matrix of frequencies by the reciprocal of the size of the particular ethnic generation group. In this sense, we have controlled for the size of the ethnic-generation group, a variable of potential significance to students of ethnic stratification. The correlation matrix produced by using the percentage distributions includes strongly positive and strongly negative associations. Some pairs of occupations are similar, some dissimilar, in the ethnicity of their incumbents.

TABLE 3. Factor Loadings for Occupational Distributions of 34 Ethnic-Generation Groups in the United States in 1900, Ranked by Loadings on the First Factor

Occupations	Factor 1	Factor 2	Factor 3
Bookkeepers and accountants	+.898	-.079	-.286
Professional service	+.857	+.199	+.143
Clerks and copyists	+.844	-.179	-.348
Printers, lithographers and pressmen	+.840	-.088	-.296
Agents	+.792	+.123	+.138
All others in trade and transportation	+.785	+.245	+.152
Other building trades	+.691	+.224	+.421
Salesmen	+.685	-.272	-.500
Manufacturers and officials	+.626	+.025	+.428
Messengers	+.579	-.395	-.479
Machinists	+.441	+.597	+.299
Draymen and hackmen	+.386	+.386	+.400
All others in domestic & personal service	+.247	+.002	+.687
Merchants and dealers, except wholesale	+.208	-.667	+.200
Painters, glaziers, and varnishers	+.175	+.567	+.174
Agricultural laborers	+.069	+.240	-.825
Blacksmiths	+.069	+.714	+.483
Saloon keepers and bartenders	+.048	-.177	+.449
Servants and waiters	+.032	+.146	+.354
All others in agricultural pursuits	-.020	+.660	+.252
Tobacco and cigar factory operatives	-.051	-.603	-.273
Carpenters and joiners	-.054	+.721	+.305
Textile mill operators, all other mills	-.069	+.173	+.556
All others in mfg./mechanical pursuits	-.072	-.313	+.516
Hucksters and peddlers	-.074	-.744	+.137
Steam railroad employees	-.129	+.150	+.541
Farmers, planters and overseers	-.174	+.663	-.225
Masons, brick and stone	-.181	+.294	+.730
Miners and quarrymen	-.186	-.547	+.187
Tailors	-.191	-.732	-.055
Textile mill operatives, cotton mills	-.283	+.233	+.275
Iron and steel workers	-.362	-.346	+.195
Boot and shoemakers and repairers	-.444	-.100	+.547
Saw and planing mill employees	-.480	+.543	-.190
Laborers, not specified	-.668	-.366	+.337

Three dimensions reduce this ethnic variability considerably, accounting for 55.7% of the original variance. The first two are almost equally important. accounting respectively for 22.6% and 20.6% of the variance. Interpreting them is a straightforeward affair. The third dimension, accounting for 12.5% of the variance, is more of a problem. I shall take a stab at making sense of it nonetheless, though I do so with less confidence than I'd like. Table 3 reports the rotated factor loadings of the 35 occupations on the first three factors. The occupations are listed as they are loaded on the first factor, from high to low. This first factor is apparently the hierarchical or up-down one we expected. A good deal of evidence supports this interpretation. Treiman's (1977, Appendix A) Standard International Occupational Prestige Scores (SIOPS) are correlated with these loading by a coefficient of .70, with significance at the .001 level. I do not feel comfortable in trying to specify whether the kind of up-down or hierarchy represented here is one of prestige or power or income or value to society or any of the other highly correlated variants that have been suggested in the literature as conceptually — and sometimes empirically — distinguishable.

For example, a good case could be made for calling the factor Literacy. Occupations loading high on factor 1 required incumbents to be literate. If incumbents were not literate in English, they surely had to be literated in some language. Occupations with negative loading did not require literacy. Bookkeepers and accountants; profesional service, clerks and copyists; printers, lithographers, and pressmen, and agents demanded considerable facility in some language, usually English. They should therefore have enjoyed greater prestige than occupations where literacy was not directly required for day to day performance of the job. All these occupations have high loadings on the first factor in column 1. Literacy — or education in more recent years — and prestige are know to have a strong positive association. Education was one of the two variables, the other being income, Duncan (1961) used to create his occupational socioeconomic status index — basically a predicted prestige scale — that has served us so well all these years.

Making a case for interpreting the first factor as literacy — or, indeed, using the evidence on literacy to make a case for the first factor as hierarchy — requires us to turn ahead a moment to Table 4, to the scores of the ethnic-generation groups on the first factor. Without paying any substantive attention for the moment to who is where on this factor, we want to use the numbers.

The first volume of the Dillingham Commission reports (United States Congress 1911) includes a table (Table 87) reporting the percent of the heads of household who could read and write for 10 of these 34 ethnic-generation groups. Correlating this measure of literacy with the factor scores in the first column of Table 4, we get r=.549, significant at the .05 level, but smaller than the association with Treiman's SIOPS.

Turning back to the loadings themselves in Table 3, we can test our hierarchical interpretation with recourse to two other pieces of information the Bureau of the Census collected and reported in 1900. These are not the direct matters one would like. Income and education would provide fairly direct validation, but alas were not collected in the 1900 census. Color and age, however, were collected and also reported as descriptive of occupations. Both Negroes and children, we can reason, were unlikely to be found near the top of the occupational hierarchy. Regressing the factor loading for factor 1 on the logarithm of the percent of incumbents in an occupation who are children and Negroes respectively,[3] we get

Factor 1 = -.350 LNCHILD -.536 LNNEGRO; R=.650.

This is a substantial multiple correlation and not all that different from the zero-order .70 we got with SIOPS. The prestige measure, indeed, absorbs most of the explanatory power here when it is added to the other two variables:

Factor 1 = -.076 LNCHILD -.186 LNNEGRO + .550 SIOPS; R=.710.

By adding the incumbency of children and Negroes to the prestige index with which we opened this discussion of validation, we have redistributed the explained variance, but have increased its total only trivially.

Before we try to interpret the second and third factors in Table 3, let us turn to the ranking of the ethnic-generation groups on the hierarchical factor in Table 4. The first thing we see here is that the second generation is doing better than the first. The bottom eight groups in the first column are first generation and eight of the top nine are second generation. Generation explains 30% of the variance in the factor scores, 41% of what it could be if all 17 top scores went to second generation groups and all 17 bottom scores went to first generation groups.

Generation, however, is not all that is here. One first generation group, Scots, scores a full 1.3 standard deviations above the mean.[4] A value in either Anglo-Saxon origins or English as a native language is suggested by the locations of three of the four English speaking immigrant groups (Scots, English and Welshmen, and English Canadians) at the top of their generation's hierarchy. All three of these groups were principally engaged in manufacturing occupations, were overrepresented in the professions and underrepresented in domestic

TABLE 4. Rankings of Factor Scores for 34 Ethnic-Generation Groups:
United States, 1900

Factor 1		Factor 2		Factor 3	
Hungarians(2)	+1.89	Norwegians(1)	+1.41	Irish(1)	+1.63
Russians(2)	+1.46	Eng. Canada(1)	+1.31	Italians(1)	+1.52
Scots(2)	+1.44	Danes(1)	+1.19	Scots(1)	+1.27
Irish(2)	+1.25	Swedes(1)	+1.18	Irish(2)	+1.19
Scots(1)	+1.13	Fr. Canadian(1)	+1.13	Eng./Welsh(1)	+1.15
Austrians(2)	+1.10	Scots(1)	+.86	French(1)	+1.12
Eng./Welsh(2)	+1.07	Danes(2)	+.82	Fr. Canadian(1)	+1.07
Italians(2)	+1.06	Fr. Canadian(2)	+.77	Italians(2)	+.94
French(2)	+.94	Eng. Canada(2)	+.69	Germans(1)	+.72
Eng./Welsh(1)	+.80	Norwegians(2)	+.66	Eng. Canada(1)	+.62
Germans(2)	+.73	Swiss(1)	+.61	Fr. Canadian(2)	+.47
Eng. Canada(2)	+.66	Scots(2)	+.50	Scots(2)	+.42
Eng. Canada(1)	+.55	Swedes(2)	+.50	Swiss(1)	+.31
Swiss(2)	+.19	Eng./Welsh(1)	+.41	Russians(1)	+.30
French(1)	+.13	Eng./Welsh(2)	+.39	Austrians(1)	+.25
Russians(1)	+.05	Swiss(2)	+.39	French(2)	+.21
Swedes(2)	-.05	French(2)	+.31	Eng./Welsh(2)	+.17
Irish(1)	-.09	French(1)	+.18	Poles(1)	+.10
Bohemians(2)	-.18	Irish(2)	+.09	Swedes(1)	+.09
Germans(1)	-.25	Germans(2)	+.06	Germans(2)	+.01
Danes(2)	-.27	Germans(1)	+.02	Hungarians(1)	+.00
Swiss(1)	-.59	Irish(1)	-.01	Danes(1)	-.11
Poles(2)	-.60	Bohemians(2)	-.18	Eng. Canada(2)	-.25
Norwegians(2)	-.65	Poles(2)	-.35	Bohemians(1)	-.40
Danes(1)	-.67	Bohemians(2)	-.38	Swiss(2)	-.68
Fr. Canadian(2)	-.79	Austrians(2)	-.59	Austrians(2)	-.83
Swedes(1)	-1.00	Italians(2)	-.85	Hungarians(2)	-.95
Austrians(1)	-1.08	Poles(1)	-1.14	Poles(2)	-1.04
Norwegians(1)	-1.11	Russians(2)	-1.32	Norwegians(1)	-1.16
Bohemians(1)	-1.17	Italians(1)	-1.44	Bohemians(2)	-1.36
Fr. Canadian(1)	-1.39	Hungarians(2)	-1.44	Swedes(2)	-1.42
Hungarians(1)	-1.40	Austrians(1)	-1.55	Danes(2)	-1.49
Italians(1)	-1.46	Hungarians(1)	-1.81	Russians(2)	-1.88
Poles(1)	-1.69	Russians(1)	-2.59	Norwegian(2)	-2.08

and personal service. Second generation French Canadians, stuck for whatever reasons in the textile and lumber mills of New England, trail socioeconomically behind all other second generation groups. Frenchmen whose forbearers did not stop off in Canada, on the other hand, are in the upper half of the ethnic hierarchy.

A note about the Russians, among whom both first and second generations appear to be doing well at the turn of the century. The ethnic composition of the immigrant generation is predominantly Jewish, while the second generation had a substantial proportion of gentile Ukrainians and Lithuanians. Prior to 1880 there was little Jewish immigration from Russia (Ross 1914, Dinnerstein, et al. 1979). The position of first generation Russians is high when compared to other first generation Eastern Europeans (Hungarians, Poles, Bohemians, and Austrians). Those mostly Jewish immigrants had more in common occupationally with English speaking immigrants than did any other group except the French.

This is not to discredit a long and elaborate Jewish folkmyth of a generation of struggle and poverty. To be well up the occupational hierarchy does not mean to earn what others earn in the same place, as women have been pointing out with respect to their earnings in recent years. While it is likely that Jewish immigrants were a bit better off than other immigrants in the same cities (such as the Italians with whom they lived in such proximity in New York) in the sense of having somewhat higher household incomes, it is also probable that they did not earn as much as the groups with which they were occupational peers. Position in the occupational structure of 1900 may predict economic status later better than it is descriptive of it at the time.

The second factor underlying the link between ethnicity-generation and occupation appears to be a rural-urban one. Occupations with loading above +.6 in column 2 of Table 3 were associated with farms, villages, and small towns (carpenters and joiners; blacksmiths; farmers, planters and overseers; and all others in agricultural pursuits). Those loadings below -.6 are for occupations based in cities or larger towns (hucksters and peddlers; tailors; merchants and dealers; and tobacco and cigar factory employees). Volume 1 (Table 19) of the Immigration Commission Statistical Reports provides information on the percent of each of the immigrant populations urban, in the sense of living in places of more than 25,000 inhabitants. The zero-order correlation between percent urban and the factor scores is -.732 (p<.01). Even the newer members of the "old" immigrant flow were settling on America's farms and smaller places, while the "new" immigrants were building the cities.

With positive (rural) scores above 1.0 we find all first generation Northern Europeans and Canadians. The first generations of Scots and

Swiss have scores above +.6, while the second generation of the Northern Europeans and Canadians have scores between +.82 and +.66. In contrast all the larger negative scores belong to first and second generation Eastern and Southern Europeans. Most negative of these by far are the first generation Russians. The occupations with the strongest negative loadings, hucksters and peddlers, -.744, and tailors, -.732, were dominated by Russian Jews (Hutchinson 1956; Golab 1977; Ross 1914, Dinnerstein et al. 1979), the most urban of all the "new wave" immigrants.

The literature on the occupational pursuits and regional distribution of immigrants is consistent with the outline available in these data. Hutchinson (1956) and Golab (1977) both report that Eastern and Southern Europeans were concentrated in the Northeast, where they were further differentiated with Russians and Italians in the cities and Hungarian, Poles, and Slovaks in the mining regions of Pennsylvania. The relative urbanization of the Northeast afforded employment in unskilled and semi-skilled jobs as well as low and middle level business opportunities, from peddling to merchants and manufacturers. French Canadians were overrepresented in cotton and other textile mills in rural areas of New England. Swedes, concentrated in midwestern states, followed occupational pursuits less agricultural than other Scandinavians in the same part of the country. They worked more often in saw and planing mills or in and around Chicago and Milwaukee than did the Danes and Norwegians. In general the scores on factor 2 are consistent with Hutchinson's more detailed descriptions of the geographical concentrations of the national-origin groups in 1900.

To this point we have found two interpretable and reasonable principles underlying the occupational structure of immigrants in 1900. A straightforward factor analysis, with an insistence on orthogonal factors, has told us that immigrant groups were different from one another in two important ways at the turn of the century. First, substantial hierarchical socioeconomic diversity already existed among them. Second, they differed from one another in the urbanness of their occupational pursuits.

A third factor emerges from the factor analytic machine; the loading of the occupational variables on it are reported in the third column of Table 3. It is a problematic factor to interpret. There are only nine negative loadings in the column, of which only one, that for agricultural laborers, is substantial (-.825). The only other moderately high loadings are positive, those for brick and stone masons (+.730) and all others in domestic and personal service (+.687). It is not immediately apparent what of importance distinguishes agricultural laborers on the one hand from masons and personal service workers on the other.

TABLE 5. Variance Explained by the First Two Factors and Factor
Loadings as a Percent of Their Potential Maximum

Occupations	% of Variance Explained	Factor 3 Loading/Max
Agricultural laborers	.06	-.851
Farmers, planters and overseers	.47	-.309
All other agricultural pursuits	.44	.337
Professional service	.77	.298
Laborers, not specified	.58	.520
Saloon keepers, bartenders	.03	.459
Servants and waiters	.02	.358
All others in domestic and personal service	.06	.709
Agents	.64	.230
Bookkeepers and accountants	.81	-.656
Clerks and copyists	.74	-.682
Draymen and hackmen	.30	.478
Hucksters and peddlers	.56	.206
Merchants and dealers, except wholesale	.49	.280
Messengers	.49	-.671
Salesmen	.54	-.737
Steam railroad employees	.04	.552
All others in trade and transportation	.68	.269
Carpenters and joiners	.52	.440
Masons, brick and stone	.12	.778
Painters, glaziers and varnishers	.35	.216
Other building trades	.53	.614
Blacksmiths	.51	.690
Boot and shoemakers and repairers	.21	.615
Iron and steel workers	.25	.225
Machinists	.55	.446
Manufacturers and officials, etc.	.39	.548
Miners and quarrymen	.33	.228
Printers, lithographers, and pressmen	.71	-.550
Saw and planing mill employees	.53	-.277
Tailors	.57	-.084
Textile mill operators in cotton mills	.13	.295
Textile mill operators, all other mills	.03	.565
Tobacco and cigar factory operatives	.36	-.341
All others in mfg./mechanical pursuits	.10	.544

The fact the other loadings are weak, however, is largely due to the amount of variance in these occupations already explained by the first two factors. Variance in a variable held in common with factors 1 or 2 is no longer available to be loaded on factor 3. As column 1 of Table 5 indicates, communalities after the extraction of the first two factors are as high as .81, with approximately half the total variance or more in almost half the occupations already gobbled up by the prior factors. There is not enough variance in these occupational distributions for them to "define" further factors. How their residual variance is distributed, however, can help us *understand* factor 3, help us figure out what descriptive words to attach to it.

Looking at the second column of Table 5 we see the factor loadings as a percent of their potential maximums, the variance unexplained by the first two factors. Agricultural laborers are joined on the negative end of the factor by salesmen (-.737), bookkeepers and accountants (-.656), messengers (-.671), clerks and copyists (-.682), and printers, lithographers and pressmen (-.550). Strong positive loadings have been augmented in this view as a percent of their maximum: to masons (+.778) and other domestic and personal service (+.709) are added other building trades (+.614), blacksmiths (+.690), boot and shoemakers (+.615), and other textile mill employees (+.565). Men who worked in "other domestic and personal service" were mostly watchmen, firemen and policemen; soldiers, sailors and marines; and barbers. Other textile workers were mostly in woolen mills. We have a group of blue collar craftsmen and industrial workers on one end of the factor, with agricultural laborers and a collection of white collar and service occupations on the other.

There are two things that differentiate these two groups of occupations. It is difficult to choose between them in interpreting the factor. First, the occupations with strong negative loadings tend to be the province of second and later generation men; those with strong positive loadings tended to be held by the immigrant generation, though there are significant exceptions to this. The relationship between the generational composition of the occupations and the values in column 2 of Table 5 is only .461. From the factor scores in Table 4 we see that two second generation groups, the Irish and the Italians, were particularly likely to be employed in what we are calling immigrant generation jobs. Similarly, immigrant generation Norwegians were disproportionately employed in the occupations most often held by the second generation or natives of native parentage. While generation is associated with this factor, generation does not seem to be what is crucial about it.

The other way these two groups of occupations differ is in what happened to them in the first half of the century. The union movement proceeded through blue collar occupations, leaving both agricultural laborers and most white collar occupations untouched. Masons, the building trades in general, blacksmiths, boot and shoemakers — occupations with high factor loadings — were all going to be organized soon. Agricultural laborers, bookkeepers, accountants, messengers, clerks were not going to unionize.

The important matter here is not what or who was already organized, but what and who were going to participate in the expansion of union membership in the 1930s and 1940s. These were largely the second generation children of the first generation groups with high scores on factor 3. These were not printers, lithographers, and pressmen, whose trade union history dates back to the Revolutionary period. By 1902, before the rapid expansion of trade union membership in the United States, 46.4% of printers, lithographers and pressmen were already organized.

There are two views of the role of immigration in the development of unionization in the United States. By focusing on different periods they reach different conclusions. One looks at the last quarter of the 19th century. Many of the original craft trades in building construction, manufacturing, and transportation were proletarianized in the years between 1800 and 1900. Here the rapid spread of modern industrial techniques, what in today's jargon is called deskilling, produced a phenomenal rise in labor organization. The mass arrival of immigrants, whose goal was to save money quickly and return home, provided an abundance of strike breakers, a new supply of labor for whom the new technology was more tolerable, and the sharp decline of the Knights of Labor in the late 1880s (see Rosenblum 1973 for a detailed presentation of this argument). By this view, the major role of immigration was to defeat the labor movement.

A second view, promoted by Piore (1979) and others, sees the mass immigration of the same period as producing the huge population of mostly second generation workers who made large scale growth of unionization possible in the 1930s and 1940s. To Piore (1979), a population of first generation target workers was succeeded by their second generation children — in the same jobs their parents had held, jobs with characteristics that had already proved unsatisfactory to native workers. Unionization is cast by Piore as "endogenous to the immigration process, a product of the stabilization of the immigrant communities" (1979, p. 157).

At issue here is not the second generationness of the workers, but residential intentions and industrial locations. First generation immigrants whose intention was to stay, such as Jews and the Irish, could be expected to behave with the same vigor in organized attempts to alter working conditions as the second generations of other groups who initially did not, such as the Italians. In addition, location in unskilled jobs, brutish, boring, without prospects of advancement is taken by Piore (1979) as central to creating the impetus to the kind of ameliorative union activity that emerged. By this criterion Jews in particular (best represented by Russians 1 in Table 4) are not likely candidates for an extremely high score on factor 3. More frequently professionals than most immigrant groups and with far the highest percentage of merchants and dealers, Jews were weakly represented in manufacturing, the construction trades, and transportation, the areas that unionized rapidly later. With more tailors and people with needle skills assembled in New York and New Jersey than the world had probably ever seen in so small a space, Jews did build the ready-to-wear clothing industry, though Jewish men graduated from the sewing machines fairly rapidly to be replaced by Jewish then Italian women.

The two second generation groups that most resemble their first generation brethren are the Irish and the Italians. For the Italians, a good deal of this occupational similarity between first and second generations can be traced to the padrone system and the dominance of Italians in public works projects in the cities of the Northeast. Most of these city construction trades were substantially unionized by 1910. The second generation Irish were also heavily represented in the building trades, though usually in more prestigious positions within them than those of the Italians.

Discussion

The current socioeconomic hierarchy of white ethnic groups has been puzzling many of us. It is clear there has been a considerable reshuffling of the social deck during this century. I have argued here that one place to look for circumstances at force in that reshuffling is to principles underlying the occupational differentiation of those same white ethnic groups at the turn of the century. This analysis of the Dillingham Commission data is designed to provide us such a view, at least for first and second generation men. The match between the present data and the past is not neat. For one thing, for 1900 we have omitted all native men of native parentage, men still likely to have had ethnic identities they could pass on to whatever descendants of theirs responded to the General Social Survey in recent years. For another, the 17 national origin groups recognized by the Dillingham Commission match only imperfectly the ethnic groups we have constructed for the more recent period. Nevertheless, attempting to match the two can be informative.

Eleven turn of the century groups can be matched with eleven of the contemporary groups: five predominantly Protestant groups (the English and Welsh, Germans, Norwegians, Scots, and Swedes), five predominantly Catholic groups (the French, French Canadians, Irish, Italians, and Poles), and one group of Jews, taken to be best indicated at the turn of the century by Russians.[5]

We want to see how well we can predict the current socioeconomic position of these eleven groups, as indicated by the income data in Table 1. We know the social deck has been substantially reshuffled. We are asking here if some of the precursors of the reshuffling were already in place in the ethnic-occupational differentiation of the turn of the century, differentiation we have reduced to three underlying factors. The degrees of freedom are few, the parameter estimates can be expected to be unstable, varying substantially when single groups are dropped from the equation. For the eleven groups we get

Income = .530 HIERARCHY -.734 RURAL -.211 UNION, R^2=.628.

In this equation the current ranking of white ethnic groups is a positive function of hierarchical position at the turn of the century and a strongly negative function of working in the kinds of occupations rare in cities, and no function at all of the factor we have interpreted as incipient unionization. The fact that hierarchical position persists across generations is expected; that the persistence is only modest we knew simply by looking at the current income data in Table 1 in light of the lore of our collective past. The powerful effect of the spatial factor, the one we are calling a rural-urban dimension, recalls the real estate adage that what matters for the price of houses is "location, location, and location." The equation is also astonishingly stable, as one assesses it by dropping each of the individual cases from its estimation one at a time — with one devastating exception. The value of urbanism and irrelevance of unionization reverse when Jews/Russians are dropped from the calculations. In this case we get

Income = .499 HIERARCHY -.033 RURAL + .266 UNION, R^2=.409

Here hierarchy at the turn of the century remains important, but the role of rural-urban differences has totally collapsed, while that of incipient unionization is weakly asserted. The parameters for HIERARCHY and RURAL are stable, as this equation is assessed by dropping additional groups one at a time; the parameter for UNION varies little except when Norwegians are dropped, when it bounces up to .656, a bounce which alters nothing else except the R^2, which rises to

.820. Thus with Jews (and Russians) in the equation we get something very much like the first equation, no matter what other group is dropped out; with Jews out we get something very much like the second equation, no matter who else is also dropped out. The underlying problem is that the zero-order correlation between 1972-1982 income and the rural-urban factor is about -.62 with the Jews/Russians in and about .00 with them out — whoever else is in or out of the estimating. The zero-order correlation of recent income with the union factor is about +.12 with the Jews/Russians in and about +.45 with them out — again no matter who else is left out.

I find it difficult to trumpet the importance of the rural-urban second factor in the transformation of the ethnic hierarchy since the turn of the century, since the evidence for it rests on only one group, an outlier on that factor as well as the top of the distribution on the dependent income variable. Jews were both distinctively urban at the turn of the century and have been distinctively successful, but their urbanness is a poor candidate as an explanation for the success since urbanness did not seem to benefit, nor rural occupational pursuits hamper, any other group here. I am distressed at this finding, for the conviction I brought to this work was that being in the right or wrong place, an expanding or contracting place, is consequential. I wish I had the nerve to simply present the first equation above and proclaim the importance of geography, but with so few degrees of freedom one must assess the stability of parameter estimates. Perhaps my prior conviction is justified on some ground, but apparently not on the ground of occupational differentiation characteristic of rural and urban places at the turn of the century.

The case for the long term benefits of the union movement to the specific ethnic groups most involved in it is stronger, though the parameter estimates are not real strong. They are real persistent and are kept as modest as they are only by the Norwegians, who were extremely overrepresented among agricultural laborers at the turn of the century, work they would have to abandon along with the locales in which they pursued it. Agricultural laboring had already declined as a stepping stone to status as a farmer; it was soon to declined as an occupation at all. With Jews/Russians and Norwegians out we get

INCOME = .487 HIERARCHY -.071 RURAL +.656 UNION, R^2=.820.

That the union movement benefitted workers in general in the United States is so familiar an argument as to amount to a truism. That its success was facilitated by the increasingly restrictive immigration laws of the 1920s is also plausible. Restrictive legislation reduced the ability of employers to find new target earners, new immigrants who viewed their stay in America as temporary. It also influenced the immigrants already here to redefine their presence as permanent, hence increase their interest in union activity they could see as designed to ameliorate working conditions tolerable only temporarily. These are the senses in which unionization was endogenous to the immigration process.

We have seen here that unionization was also consequential for ethnic stratification. The ethnic groups that worked at the turn of the century in those industries that were going to be unionized after the restrictive immigration laws made unionization easier have done better over time than have ethnic groups who worked in other industries. It does not appear to be a strong effect, but then it is an effect that has had to reach over three generations.

Notes

1. A clearly hierarchical first canonical variate also emerges from the matrix of occupations by national origins for relatively recent immigrants (1976-1978) to the United States. (Tyree, 1980)
2. I am indebted to Deborah Biele for running this factor analysis and for considerable input in the process of interpreting the factors and to Yael Har-Even for the calculations assessing the stability of the equations in the Discussion section.
3. These equations omit other domestic and personal service, servants and waiters, and messengers. The first two categories had extremely high percentages of blacks, while messengers had a similarly high percentage of children, making these occupations such extreme ouliers even the logarithmic transformation could not bring them in to approximate conformity to the assumptions of regression.
4. As with all factor scores these three sets of values in Table 4 are in standard form, with means of zero and unit variances.
5. The matches are:

Dillingham	*General Social Survey*
English and Welsh	Protestants, England and Wales
Germany	Protestants, Germany
Norway	Protestants, Norway
Scotland	Protestants, Scotland
Sweden	Protestants, Sweden
French	Catholics, France
French Canadian	Catholics, French Canadian
Ireland	Catholics, Ireland
Italy	Catholics, Italy
Poland	Catholics, Poland
Russian	Jews

Estimates for factor scores on the three factors are made by weighting the first and second generation scores in Table 4 by the proportions of the group in each of the two generations.

References

Blau, Peter M. and Otis Dudlay Duncan. 1967. *The American Occupational Structure*. New York: Wiley.

Dinnerstein, Leonard, Roger L. Nichols and David M. Reimers. 1979. *Natives and Strangers*. New York: Oxford University Press.

Duncan, Beverly and Otis Dudley. 1968. "Minorities and the Process of Stratification." *American Sociological Review* 33:356-64.

Duncan, Otis Dudley. 1961. "A Socioeconomic Index for All Occupations." in Albert J. Reiss, *Occupations and Social Status*. New York: The Free Press of Glencoe.

Featherman, David L. and Robert M. Hauser. 1978. *Opportunity and Change*. New York: Academic Press.

Golab, Caroline. 1977. *Immigrant Destinations*. Philadelphia: Temple University Press.

Goldthorpe, J.H. 1966. "Social Stratification in Industrial Society." Pp.648-59 in *Class, Status, and Power*, 2nd ed, edited by Reinhard Bendix and Seymour Martin Lipset.

Hauser, Robert M. and David L. Featherman. 1977. *The Process of Stratification*. New York: Academic Press.

Hodge, Robert W., Paul M. Siegel and Peter H. Rossi. 1964. "Occupational Prestige in the United States, 1925-1963." *American Journal of Sociology* 70:286-302.

Hope, Keith. 1982. "A Liberal Theory of Prestige." *American Journal of Sociology* 87:1011-31.

Hutchinson, E.P. 1956. *Immigrants and Their Children, 1850-1950*. New York: Wiley.

Kraus, Vered, E.O. Schild and Robert W. Hodge. 1978. "Occupational Prestige in the Collective Conscience." *Social Forces* 56:900-18.

Lieberson, Stanley and Mary C. Waters. 1988. *From Many Strands: Ethnic and Racial Groups in Contemporary America*. New York: Russell Sage.

Neidert, Lisa J. and Reynolds Farley. 1985. "Assimilation in the United States." *American Sociological Review* 50:840-49.

Piore, Michael J. 1979. *Birds of Passage: Migrant Labor and Industrial Societies*. Cambridge: Cambridge University Press.

Ross, Edward A. 1914. *The Old World in the New*. New York: Century Co.

Treiman, Donald J. 1977. *Occupational Prestige in Comparative Perspective*. New York: Academic Press.

Troy, Leo. 1965. *Trade Union Membership 1897-1962*. New York: National Bureau of Economic Research.

Tyree, Andrea. 1980 "Determinants of Immigration to the United States: 1968-1977." Final Report, Select Commission on Immigration and Refugee Policy.

United States Congress. 1911. *Immigration Commission Abstracts of Reports. Reports of the Immigration Commission*. Vol 1, Senate Doc No.7. Washington: Government Printing Office.

____. 1911. *Occupations of the First and Second Generations of Immigrants* in the United States. Reports of the Immigration Commission. Vol 28, Senate Doc No. 282. Washington: Government Printing Office.

PART FOUR

Role Realignments and Structural Change

13

Ambiguity and Dysfunction in the Training of Physicians

Ellen C. Perrin and James M. Perrin

Rose Coser writes of life in the ward and the socialization of physicians mainly in the context of hospital settings. Hospitals have indeed been the focus through which physicians at most stages of training have received their clinical education. Training programs in internal medicine or pediatrics typically include an extensive series of rotations through different in-patient units, interspersed with variable amounts of clinical care in office or other out-patient settings. Yet, the emphasis on training in hospitals leaves physicians less well prepared for clinical care in office settings, and recent changes in the organization and funding of graduate medical education threaten further the quality of training available.

Dysjunction and Dysfunction

In *Training in Ambiguity*, Rose Coser (1979) described some of the basic structural problems involved with hospital-based training in all medical specialties: (1) the conflict between professional and student roles, (2) aspects of physician-nurse relationships, (3) the tension between educational and patient care goals, (4) the differences between training experiences and clinical problems encountered in real world practice, and (5) the complex conflicts when multiple professionals are involved in inpatient care. While some of these issues are inherent in the process of professional training, others are amenable to changes (for better or worse) through manipulation of training programs. Several key changes have occurred over the past decade, dictated by educational, administrative, financial, and political constraints.

A primary issue that Rose Coser describes is the expectation that physicians perform in the role of the professional at the same time that they are learning to become professionals. This contradictory definition of their role causes considerable ambivalence and anxiety for residents and leads to tensions in interpersonal interactions. The ambiguity is especially difficult in a system so intensely complicated and hierarchical as a hospital (Coser 1962). The potential confusion in the resident's status and responsibilities complicates the relationship of resident physicians to nurses. Residents — physicians — have more power and authority than nurses. However, it is nurses who are in charge of the wards; residents are in a sense only visitors, and this gives nurses a great deal of implicit power over the residents. Head nurses are responsible for allocating work to be done, assigning particular nurses to particular patients and making decisions regarding whether and when to call the resident at night. Nurses can also affect the tasks of the resident's life by how they present information to the senior physicians and by how much work they allocate to the resident.

The fact that until recently most nurses were female and most resident physicians male strengthened the formal hierarchical arrangement. The relationship of female residents to female nurses is in some ways even more complicated. Women are particularly uncomfortable with rigid hierarchies in which all players are women. Rose Coser's relevant books (1962, 1979) were published before recent demographic changes in American medical students resulted in equal numbers of male and female residents in many specialties.

Residents in all disciplines have multiple goals (the most clearly stated being their education and the care of their patients) that may conflict. What happens when an important teaching conference conflicts with an urgent request from a patient? How do residents justify ordering additional laboratory tests to help them understand a person's disease when the additional tests have no direct benefit to the patient and cause both physical and fiscal discomfort? The ambiguities associated with having to make decisions involving conflicting goals produce considerable tension in the physician.

An issue that transcends the training of many different sorts of physicians is that what the resident does and learns to do is substantially different from what most of them will do after they graduate from the training program. It has been said, for example, that residents completing pediatric training are superbly prepared to be chief residents in pediatrics but not to practice pediatrics in a community setting. Hospital-based training experiences tend to be acute, intensive, and technology-dependent. Community practice needs tend to be long term, low in intensity, and require less technological than interpersonal and interviewing skill. The hospital environment imposes specific opportunities and constraints that are very different in nature from those imposed by the more "real life" situation in which physicians will soon work.

For psychiatric residents in a mental hospital such as the one described in *Training in Ambiguity* (Coser 1979), one of the physician's jobs is to define the appropriate level of freedom of movement and of activity of the patients. In a general medical hospital, residents in pediatrics and internal medicine must decide on the appropriate level of visiting, nutrition, and activity. None of these is a central function of the physician in an outpatient setting. The physician and nurse "team" truly do "care for" patients in the hospital setting. In the outpatient setting, the patient and the family care for the patient; the physician and nurse (and other professionals who participate in the patient's care) are, in fact, only consultants or advisers to that care. In the hospital, the physician's responsibility is circumscribed by the length of time of the patient's admission; in the "real world" of practice, the physician has long-term responsibility for patients' well-being. These considerable differences in the terms and types of responsibility result in a large body of important learning that does not occur during the time of the residency but that is critical for later professional roles. Coser writes about how difficult it is to learn the limits of "the use of authority over patients," and these limits vary tremendously from hospital to community care.

During the period of training, residents must learn to work with multiple other professionals whose skills and roles overlap with the physicians' and who intermingle power and authority with the physicians as well. Intrinsic contradictions in status relationships are introduced when multiple professionals with overlapping and interrelated roles work together in both educational and patient care contexts. Hospitals are complex institutions that may employ nutritionists, nurses, health aides, psychologists, social workers, record room personnel, laboratory technicians, and many others. These professionals each have autonomous but interrelated responsibilities. Physicians are a part of a complex team; roles and responsibilities may require frequent negotiation and clarification. In contrast, office-based physicians may find only secretaries and nurses in their immediate environment, and they are usually expected to take a supervisory rather than a collaborative role.

An obvious problem common to the training of physicians in all specialty areas is that of having insufficient data on which to make clinical decisions but having to make and to justify those decisions anyway. In this case, the resident encounters ambiguity that is intrinsic to the professional role of "medicine man," with which the resident must learn to become comfortable in order to practice successfully in any medical specialty. On the other hand, the expectations of patients, their families, and many of the professionals with whom the resident works within the hospital, are inconsistent with this experience of reality by the resident. The expectation of most non-physicians is that if the physician is "good enough" or "senior enough," he or she will be able to amass sufficient data to make a scientific and unequivocally "right" decision. Yet, uncertainty is a constant companion in health care, both because of the great biologic variation in individual differences in the course of illness and the response to treatment and because many health conditions are quite rare with insufficient cases to provide enough information on which to make informed judgments. In an age of escalating technology, this uncertainty becomes more complex and results in considerable tension for residents in hospitals where they are always prone to be judged in comparison to other residents and more senior physicians.

Changes in the Patterns of Health Care

Patterns of hospitalization have changed dramatically in the past decade, reflecting not only changing incentives for reimbursement for in-patient care, but also consumer preferences for more care out-of-hospital than in the past. The federal government pays for a large proportion of in-patient hospitalization in all parts of the country, mainly through the Medicare program, which covers the cost of hospitalization for most people over age 65 (a population that utilizes a disproportionately large percentage of all hospitalization). Further federal support for hospitalization comes through the Medicaid program, although this program supports a much smaller percentage of all U.S. hospitalizations.

In the 1980s, the federal government instituted a program of reimbursement according to diagnostic-related groups (DRGs), in which a hospital was paid a lump sum for a given hospitalization based on the diagnosis (or DRG) of the patient. Prior to the institution of the DRG system, hospitals tended to be reimbursed on a daily rate and thus received more dollars for increasing numbers of hospital days. Further, insofar as the intensity of hospitalization (and thereby the resources needed to care for the patient) was typically higher at the beginning of hospitalization, hospitals made more money (because they used relatively fewer resources) in later days of a person's hospitalization and thereby had incentives to keep patients in longer. The DRG approach changed these incentives dramatically. Hospitals now have incentives to discharge patients early, since they accrue the same amount of money regardless of the number of days a patient is in the hospital; more days cost hospitals money. The growth in the DRG system has been accompanied by the growth of prepayment systems (such as HMOs), where again the incentives are either to keep people out of hospital or to limit the length of stay once they are in.

These changing incentives have led to decreased rates of hospitalization in all age groups and have markedly shortened the average number of days for hospital stays as well (Kozak et al. 1987; Perrin, Valvona, Sloan 1986). Far more acute health care problems are treated in out-of-hospital settings than was true in the past. Further, much long-term and convalescent care for severely ill, disabled, and elderly patients is now provided in home or community-based settings (Perrin, Shayne, Bloom 1992). The brevity of most hospital stays also means that physicians in training have an even narrower view of a specific illness episode than in years past. The result may be less opportunity to develop skills important for diagnosis and early treatment. Physicians in surgical training now commonly meet their patients for the first time on the operating table, with the preoperative evaluation and diagnostic work occurring in the attending senior surgeon's office rather than in an in-patient setting. Thus, the surgeon may learn the technical aspects of an operative procedure well but learn less well the types of events that typically lead up to these surgical interventions or the natural history of health conditions that may lead to surgery. Similarly, with earlier discharge in the postoperative period, physicians have less experience with the normal patterns of recuperation and the common complications of surgery.

These changes generally benefit consumers and help to control inflation in health care costs, but they also greatly affect the education of the next generation of health professionals. Almost all health care now occurs outside of hospital settings, yet physicians in training have little experience in these settings. Their brief in-hospital encounters with patients continue to be the central focus of their education. This tendency is dysfunctional for their future practice of medicine both in the sense that most health care is not hospital-based and in the sense that it provides little opportunity to learn the continuity of person and health condition that exist jointly over a longer period of time (Rabkin 1985).

Changes in the Financing of Graduate Medical Education

The major portion of funding for stipends for resident trainees has come from revenues generated through delivery of inpatient services. For most hospitals, these stipends have been incorporated into the calculated daily patient room rate for in-patient care at the hospital, paid either by

Medicare or by private insurers for hospitalized patients. In-patient care, therefore, forms not only the educational but also the financial backbone of postgraduate training in medicine. Medicare has traditionally paid teaching hospitals a premium over their reimbursement to non-teaching hospitals (that is to say, hospitals without residency programs), providing explicit Federal (public) support for the postgraduate teaching function of these hospitals.

Two policy changes in the past decade have greatly eroded this financial support. The GMENAC report of 1981 was designed to develop a physician manpower policy for the United States (GMENAC 1981). It carefully examined ways of determining the need for services in different realms of health care and the numbers of health providers needed for these services. It attempted to predict changes in the epidemiology of health conditions, to examine areas where there is over- and under-utilization of specific health services, and to predict areas where non-physician providers might well replace physicians. These tasks are admittedly all very complex, and some perspective comes from recognizing that AIDS had not even been described as a health condition at the time of the preparation of the GMENAC report. Thus, the authors had no way of predicting the tremendous demands on internal medicine providers (among others) and the markedly expanded need for their services resulting from the AIDS epidemic (Harris 1986). Nevertheless, the GMENAC report furthered the notion that the nation faced an oversupply of physicians, especially in higher technology specialty areas. Whereas much of public policy in the 1970s encouraged expanding the supply of physicians, the main impact of the GMENAC report was to diminish public support for medical education. One key result has been that the federal agency responsible for Medicare rate setting has initiated a program to phase out the educational premium to teaching hospitals.

In addition to changes in the Federal reimbursement scheme, increasing competition at the community level has led to similar changes in reimbursement patterns from private insurance (such as Aetna or Prudential) as well as the nonprofit insurers (Blue Cross and Blue Shield). These insurers, in order to stay competitive, have strong incentives to utilize less expensive in-patient facilities wherever possible. If it is less expensive to have a gallbladder removed at a hospital without a surgical training program, an insurer has a strong incentive to encourage hospitalization in the less expensive institution. Thus, both private and public funding in support of graduate medical education is much less available than in years past.

Whether there is an advantage to receiving medical and surgical care in a hospital that has a residency program remains somewhat controversial (Luft, Bunker, Enthoven 1979; Sloan, Perrin, Valvona 1986).

In general, the additional costs involved in providing care in teaching hospitals compared to that in non-teaching hospitals have been addressed (Sloan, Feldman, Steinwald 1983; Sloan and Valvona 1986). Care in teaching hospitals is clearly more expensive than in non-teaching ones. But the data are difficult to interpret insofar as teaching hospitals tend to get more complex cases, at least for certain conditions, than do non-teaching hospitals. In the area of surgical proficiency, there is reasonable evidence that greater experience with a surgical procedure is associated with better outcomes; a team having done hundreds of open-heart procedures is likely to be more skillful than one that has done three in the past year. How does this notion affect teaching hospitals? On the one hand, as institutions, they are likely to have a record of performing much larger numbers of specific surgical procedures. On the other hand, partly because of their training mission, it is not uncommon for a surgical procedure to be carried out by a junior person to get his or her first experience with this specific surgical procedure. In general, the evidence does weigh in favor of improved outcomes in teaching hospital settings, although the results are indeed mixed. Teaching hospitals provide less independence with more surveillance and accountability, elements likely to improve outcomes.

Increasingly, the driving force behind all experiences in resident education, as a result of the erosion of other types of financial support for graduate medical education, has been whether the specific effort produces income rather than whether it promotes education. Medical faculty in almost all institutions face demands to see more patients or to produce more funded research rather than to participate in educational activities for which the ratio of financial support to time expended is likely to be unfavorable.

Tentative Solutions and the Need for Action

A few training programs for physicians have responded to changing needs and practices. Changing standards of practice, economic complexities and pressures, and new understanding of the pathophysiology and treatment of many diseases have altered social and professional expectations of the physician's role in providing care to patients and thus of the training appropriate to that role. More health care is being provided outside of hospitals, making it necessary for physicians to collaborate more actively and effectively with patients' families and with many other disciplines of helping professionals.

Rapidly increasing understanding of the behavioral and psychological aspects of health and disease, and of the complex interrelationships that exist among biomedical and psychosocial factors, have forced significant changes in clinical assessment and intervention techniques. There has been an increasing attempt to integrate teaching about these issues into training programs, with a recognition that this teaching is best done outside of the hospital and in the context of long-term relationships with both senior practicing physicians and patients.

Training located entirely in the hospital has thus become increasingly dysfunctional and inappropriate. A few residency education programs are experimenting with locating a portion of the resident's education outside of the hospital, emphasizing that part of the educational curriculum that is intended most directly to prepare the resident for later practice of the clinical specialty. For example, the departments of pediatrics at the Universities of Utah and Massachusetts currently designate a practicing community pediatrician as a clinical preceptor for each resident throughout the three years of the residency. The resident spends one full month each year with this preceptor, initially observing the operation of the practice and then working as a junior colleague in it. In addition, the resident spends between one half and one full day every week working in the practice setting, essentially as an apprentice to the practicing pediatrician, taking on increasing responsibility and a larger panel of patients for whom he/she is responsible, as the preceptor allows.

This innovative model for residency training addresses some of the problems encountered in training that is located entirely in hospital settings. It allows residents to interact with senior physicians as teachers who are performing the roles for which the resident is training. Residents can begin to understand and develop relationships with patients and with other members of the office staff that are long-term and collaborative in nature. The outpatient office environment is characteristically less hierarchical in nature, and it allows the resident to move in as a "student physician" in much the same way that student teachers and craftsmen's apprentices do. While the ambiguity regarding how much he or she is a student and how much a physician remains, the clearer definition of the resident's status in the functioning of the office results in less discomfort with conflicting roles than is experienced in the more formal and ingrained hospital system. Furthermore, it is clear who is responsible: the practice is an ongoing system that functions without the resident; he or she is only an adjunct to the practice and takes on only the level of responsibility that makes sense educationally and that is assigned to him or her by the responsible nurse and physician. The residents's function is to learn, not to provide primary patient care. This definition allows for a more carefully graded system of increasing responsibility than is possible in the hospital where residents are the "front line" staff in charge of key and critical patient care decisions. The office environment, and the clear role definition provided therein, further encourages the resident to be observed and his or her performance in particular tasks or interactions to be criticized. Because the resident isn't "supposed to" be the expert in this setting, the uncertainty and insecurity associated with inconsistent expectations is minimized.

The increasing dysjunctions we have described in the training of physicians call for a major reorganization in the methods, places, and financing of graduate medical education. More specifically, there is a need for greater emphasis on longitudinal care of patients and for greater opportunities for experience in out-patient and community-based settings. To a degree, a return to an apprenticeship activity may be appropriate, linking a resident in training with, for example, a surgeon and having those two work together for an extended period of time. Apprenticeships lost favor in the training of physicians after the turn of the century and with publication of the Flexner Report, which was a key element in improving the scientific base of medical education, partly by linking it to other university-based educational activities. Although no one would propose returning fully to pre-Flexnerian modes of physician education, recognition of the predominance and the importance of non-hospital-based medical care and non-inpatient training requirements may require further distance from the university setting as the main locus of training.

Bringing these changes about will require a radical change in how graduate medical education is financed. Dependence on in-hospital revenues will need to be replaced with some other form of payment. To a degree, the continuing (although diminishing) public investment through Medicare does nevertheless reflect a national public commitment to the support of graduate medical education. It may be important to reexamine the source and the distribution of these funds. Some specific Federal grant programs, such as those from the Bureau of Health Manpower to improve training in general medicine, general pediatrics, and family medicine, have led to increased training in community settings. These experiments have generally gone well and could be followed by more extensive redistribution of current funds through the Medicare program to support out-of-hospital education. Doing so will, however, require more public acknowledgement of the subsidy by taking it out of hospital reimbursement and allocating it clearly as an investment in the training of physicians.

Summary

Changing patterns of health care and of its financing are having significant effects on medical education in many disciplines. Some of the ambiguities and conflicts that are unique or exaggerated when postgraduate medical education occurs exclusively in hospital settings may be dealt with better in apprenticeship-like training models using out-of-hospital settings. Since most funding for postgraduate medical education has traditionally come through hospital care expenditures, supplemental support for broadened aspects of medical education will have to be sought from new governmental or private sources responsive to the increasing need for and amount of care that is provided outside of hospitals, and to the need therefore for training sensitive to the long-term comprehensive care of patients in the contexts of families and communities.

References

Coser, Rose L. 1962. *Life on the Ward*. East Lansing: Michigan State University Press.

_____. 1979. *Training in Ambiguity*. New York: Free Press.

GMENAC. 1981. *Report of the GMENAC to the Secretary*. Department of Health and Human Services Publication Number (HRA) 81-652; Washington, D.C.: U.S. Government Printing Office.

Harris, Jeffrey E. 1986. "How Many Doctors Are Enough?" *Health Affairs* 5:73-83.

Kozak, Lola Jean, Catherine Norton, Margaret McManus, and Eileen McCarthy. 1987. "Hospital Use Patterns for Children in the United States, 1983 and 1984." *Pediatrics* 80:481-90.

Luft, Harold S., John P. Bunker, and Alain R. Enthoven. 1979. "Should Operations Be Regionalized? The Empirical Relation Between Surgical Volume and Mortality." *New England Journal of Medicine* 301:1364-9.

Perrin, James M., May W. Shayne, and Sheila R. Bloom. Forthcoming. *Home and Community-Based Care for Chronically Ill Children*. New York: Oxford University Press.

_____, Joseph Valvona, and Frank A. Sloan. 1986. "Changing Patterns of Surgical Hospitalization for Children." *Pediatrics* 77: 587-592.

Rabkin, Mitchell T. 1985. "The Teaching Hospital and Medical Education: One-room Schoolhouse, Multiversity, Dinosaur?" *Journal of Medical Education* 60:92-7.

Sloan, Frank A., Roger D. Feldman, and A. Bruce Steinwald. 1983. "Effects of Teaching on Hospital Costs." *Journal of Health Economics* 2:1-28.

_____, James M. Perrin, and Joseph Valvona. 1986. "In-hospital Mortality of Surgical Patients: Is There an Empirical Basis for Standard Setting?" *Surgery* 99: 446-453.

_____ and Joseph Valvona. 1986. "Uncovering the High Costs of Teaching Hospitals." *Health Affairs* 5:68-85.

14

Role Protection in an Era of Accountability: The Case of the Medical Profession

Donald W. Light

During the thirty years since Rose Coser completed her seminal research on role protection in medical settings, the environment of medicine has changed. Since about 1970, federal and state governments, together with a growing number of major employers, have instituted one wave of measures after another to restrain the rise of medical expenditures. During the 1980s, these measures became more stringent and demanded accountability. Payers wanted to know not only if their bills were accurate and fair, but also if the services were necessary and effective. Thus, medicine has entered an era of accountability (Relman 1988). The vast majority of hospital care and even a majority of ambulatory care is now "managed," that is, reviewed and monitored (Light 1991). What are the implications of the scholarship of an easier time, when medical educators worked with sociologists to think about role distance, evasiveness, and insulation from observability? Even then, laughter was honored with the professional attention it deserves (Coser 1960).

The Civilities of Role Distance

Re-entering that time through the seminal work of Rose Coser makes one realize how relatively stable basic arrangements were, and why not? Organized medicine and the hospital industry had structured the American health care system to suit their values and priorities (Light 1991). The post-War economy and new federal programs benefitted medicine immensely. Some call it the "Golden Age of Medicine." Others might call it "Pride before the Fall," because more of medicine's ills today are of its own making than most accounts recognize.

Within this historical haven, there is much to be learned and much to contemplate for the current period. One realizes how little the social interaction of colleagues is examined today by comparison; most current research involves is based on large data sets without qualitative analyses. By contrast, we have in 1960 an analysis of humor and laughter among colleagues, done at the invitation of Alfred Stanton, the co-author of *The Mental Hospital* (1954). Still more interesting for my purposes is Coser's article in the *American Sociological Review* on insulation from observability, which was published in 1961. Like the classic article on laughter, this one concerns rituals of civility to handle delicate and sometimes trying circumstances. When role demands clash with status differences or values, people create buffers to minimize interaction and observability (Coser 1961, p.32).

Coser observed that those in power keep a distance, in part not to see too much and always to have the right to deny what they see. Inappropriate but unreported actions observed by subordinates of superiors or by superiors of subordinates means they participate in guilty knowledge. Quoting Moore and Tumin (1949), Coser wrote ". . . . quilty knowledge further insulates the actors against observability by the public and assures the 'quotient of ignorance that all social groups require to preserve *esprit de corps.*'"

In a subsequent pair of articles on handling sociological ambivalence, Rose Coser (1966; 1967) further developed the thesis that full visibility is a source of strain. People need role distance, evasiveness, denial, role segmentation, and periods of withdrawal to cope. In addition, people co-operate to maintain pluralistic ignorance (1967). Forms of evasion, pluralistic ignorance, denial are all institutionally structured to help deal with the strains of full visibility.

These particular articles of that period exemplify a larger literature that emanated from studies of medical training and which drew from that setting more universal inferences by Merton and his students (Merton, Reader, and Kendall 1957) and by Hughes and his students (for example, Becker et al. 1961). Their underlying perspective and micro focus, as I have pointed out elsewhere (Light 1989), is more rooted in an historical period than their universal generalizations would suggest. This is also true of my own earlier work with Renée Fox, in which the analysis of uncertainty was extended to identify several new clinical dimensions of uncertainty and the techniques for controlling them (Light 1979). The underlying perspective changed radically when Eliot Freidson (a student of Hughes) boldly opened a new avenue of thinking (Freidson 1970a, 1970b), though that work too was more time-bound than its sociological sweep suggested (Light 1989).

Historical Forces Demanding Role Scrutiny

Ironically, Freidson put forth his thesis of professional dominance just as countervailing forces began to change the structure of medicine so that insularity from observation, role protection and role segmentation became less possible. My thesis is that Rose Coser's research and insights provide an important framework for understanding the distress which physicians feel and actions which they take in the current era of intense scrutiny.

The breadth and intensity of attack was palpable (see, for example, Ribicoff 1972; Greenberg 1971; Kennedy 1972; Bodenheimer, Cummings & Harding 1972; *Fortune* 1970). In a speech actually written by young men who would emerge later as a leader of the buyers' revolt, President Richard Nixon (1971) outlined the malaise of American medicine and proposed solutions to it that are still being digested. Senator Edward Kennedy and others ushered in a decade of systemic efforts to rein in medicine's dominance through national health insurance and more modest measures such as a national system of rational planning, a national system of peer review, a national system for rationing capital expenditures, and the promotion of prepaid group plans as rational delivery systems rechristened as "health maintenance organizations" or HMOs (for a synopsis of this new history, see Light 1991).

As the decade wore on, a growing number of leaders concluded that regulatory efforts were not working, largely because the medical profession either co-opted them or frustrated them. Medical services in the United States had evolved to reflect the professional priorities of providing the best clinical medicine to every sick patient, located where doctors practice and able to pay. Complementary goals included developing scientific medicine to its highest level and protecting the autonomy of physicians. These goals, worthy in their own right, have led to overspecialization, to increasingly fragmented and depersonalized care, to maldistribution, to the whims of charity care in lieu of universal insurance, to hi-tech acute intervention, iatrogenesis, and to rapidly increasing expenses. The complementary deficiencies include a neglect of prevention, wellness, chronic conditions, public health, and the obvious mirror sides of the excesses like integrated services, primary care, rural and inner city services, universal insurance, and the like (Light 1991).

Those paying for services concluded that "regulation doesn't work," and launched into the current era of buyer revolt. Corporations and government, particularly Medicare, began to take control of their medical budgets. These institutional buyers demanded an exact account of where the money was going and thus launched an entire secondary industry of computer-based utilization analysis. Focusing initially on hospital expenditures, they instituted reviews to screen admissions, to monitor each day's decision to keep a patient in the hospital, and to analyze retrospectively the patterns of hospitalization. Greatly assisted by a huge number of beds and of physicians, institutional buyers have put parts of their budget out for competitive bid or offered a fixed price to any provider who wants the business. ("Provider" is a generic term for physicians, hospitals, clinics, nursing homes, and a growing variety of combinations or services institutions.) Although this is passionately advocated as "competition," it is competition among providers in a buyer-driven market. This has set off a fundamental restructuring of providers into horizontally and vertically integrated combinations that can best compete for the business. Those managing the combinations must now look upon physicians and their work with the critical eye of a manager responsible for quality and budget.

The law, a lagging indicator of social and political values, also changed in ways that shook the profession. Virtually all of the elaborate legal protections which medicine had built up since the end of the nineteenth century, except licensing, were torn down in less than a decade. The U.S. Supreme Court opened in 1975 with a ruling that professions were businesses and therefore no longer exempt from the Sherman-Clayton anti-trust laws (Havighurst 1980; Weller 1983). The Federal Trade Commission quickly responded, and each year since 1975 it has begun or completed a score of major actions to end anti-competitive practice in the medical profession. Subsequent court decisions or FTC actions have brought to an end restrictions on advertising, discrimination against non-physician health care providers, monopoly control of Blue Cross and Blue Shield boards, discrimination against HMOs and other managed care systems not based on fee for service, and a number of other manifestations of professional dominance. In addition, many states have removed anti-competitive laws and written new ones to encourage the development of HMOs. Even licensing has changed considerably. Essentially, certification in one's specialty (on which professional work depends) is no longer presumed for life as physicians must take a certain number of courses and pass recertification exams.

Institutional buyers have also changed incentives for the individuals they represent, be they employees or recipients of Medicare (Hewitt 1988). These include making patients pay more of their bills through higher deductibles and co-payments, making them pay some of the insurance premium through co-insurance, offering them more coverage or less cost if they sign up for HMOs or other managed care systems that limit choice but promise to control expenditures, and shifting payments to favor non-hospital services over hospital services. At the same time, a large number of corporations have developed wellness programs, which include programs for substance abusers, new menus in the cafeteria, exercise centers with professionally trained staff, safety programs, counseling services and classes to help employees control obesity, hypertension, stress, smoking.

In terms of the medical profession, these changes are captured in Table 1. Perhaps most fundamental is a distrust of the doctor as the patient's agent. The excesses of the 1960s and 1970s, together with virtually no quality controls after graduation or cooperation in voluntary efforts to restrain costs, has led to many of the changes summarized above. These have not softened after a decade of buyer-oriented efforts to restrain expenditures. Medicare and Congress instituted the most far-reaching changes of the 1980s and succeeded in reducing hospital expenditures. However, physicians have responded quickly by circumventing the hospital payment system, increasing non-hospital expenses so rapidly that overall medical costs have not slowed down. Congress now has two decades of frustrating experience, and its target for the 1990s is doctors.

The Era of Accountability

My particular focus here is on the radical change from American doctors being among the least scrutinized of professions to being among the most. This raises basic questions ripe for research about all the ways Coser and others identified that physicians protect themselves from full visibility. If such ways of protection are now less possible, are there new ways of coping — which would imply that the insights of the 1960s are time bound — or is their inability leading to various forms of pathology — implying that such protections are universally needed and their removal produces other, unanticipated costs? To what extent are there cohort differences, so that physicians trained before 1980 and used to working on their own are outraged and revengeful, while physicians trained after 1980 and used to working in managed care systems tend to accept review of their work as normal?

The following pages describe the extent to which external accountability is breaking down insularity from observation. In hospitals, every test and procedure is supposed to be noted in a patient's chart. However, while charts were a form of dead storage before the late 1970s — to be pulled out for malpractice suits or reviewed when a patient returned — charts and the record department are now the object of scrutiny. Since hospital payments increasingly come in prepaid forms,

TABLE 1. Dimensions of change in the American Health Care System

Dimensions	Provider driven	Buyer driven
Ideological	Sacred trust in doctors	Distrust of doctors
Economic	Carte blanche to do what seems best. Power to set fees. Incentives to specialize, develop techniques. Insurer as providers' agent	Fixed prepayment or contract. Accountability for decisions and their efficacy. Insurer as buyers' agent
Political	Extensive power to define and carry out professional work without competition, and to shape the organization and economics of medicine.	Replacement of professional with buyers' legal and administrative power to define and shape medical services.
Clinical	Exclusive control of clinical decision-making. Emphasis on state-of-the-art specialized interventions. Disinterest in prevention, primary care, and chronic care.	Close monitoring of clinical decisions, costs, quality, and efficacy. Emphasis on prevention, primary care, and functioning. Minimize high-tech and specialized interventions.
Technical	Political and economic incentives to develop new technologies in protected markets.	Political and economic incentives to develop cost-effective technologies.
Organizational	Cottage industry	Corporate industry
Potential Disruptions and Dislocations	Overtreatment Iatrogenesis High cost Unnecessary treatment Depersonalization Fragmentation	Undertreatment Neglected problems Reduced access Reduced quality Depersonalization Much paperwork

whether by diagnosis or contract, charts provide vital information about costs, utilization, and quality. From these charts, institutional buyers extract comparative information on the performance of physicians and hospital units. The latter are now called "cost centers" and are closely monitored.

The most detailed accounting is provided by MediScripts and APACHE, which are systems that integrate clinical signs of progress or regress with an inventory of procedures that were carried out. Their use is spreading, and there are basic forces driving this development further. Quite simply, institutional buyers want to get good value for their money. Reducing services is politically unacceptable among employees or the elderly; so the institutional buyer needs to acquire information on comparative performance. Crude comparisons, like the mortality rate for hospitals, do not help much since they do not take into account diagnosis, severity, and other variables. Physician-researchers have played a central role in developing refined systems. They believe in cost-effective medicine and the need to identify which procedures are unnecessary or inferior to alternate ones. Physician profiling and comparative data on departments of hospitals means that HMOs, insurers, and institutional buyers have statistical profiles of each physician's patterns for diagnosing and treatment patients with similar disorders. They therefore *know more about a physician's practice patterns than the physician does.*

The largest single watchdog system is PROs, Professional Review Organizations, instituted by the largest single buyer, Medicare (Office of the Inspector General 1988; Kusserow 1989). Their job is to examine records for evidence of unnecessary or inappropriate treatment, principally in hospitals. Thus, they are concerned about quality, but they primarily put pressure on hospitals or physicians who do more operations or admit more patients than average, and they can deny a Medicare payment for services already rendered if they think they are inappropriate. Unlike the physician-friendly PSROs that preceded them, PROs bid competitively for contracts covering every region of the United States. In these contracts are specific targets of bed days or procedures which the federal government identifies from huge data sets as overused in the area. In other words, the buyer is knowledgeable and tough. The PROs have a detailed, three-stage system for review, beginning with aberrant patterns picked up by the computer and ending with a detailed review of the suspect procedure or a medical action. In some regions academic physicians dominate the review committees and therefore apply academic standards to the work of community physicians, a new and more threatening manifestation of town-gown conflicts that sociologists have noted for decades.

A number of investigations and challenges trouble the work of the PROs, but my emphasis here is on the unwavering resolve of the Congress and Medicare's administrator, HCFA (Health Care Financing Administration), to scrutinize everything they pay for. Congress has expanded the scope of work and range of power of the PROs. In addition, PROs have increasingly contracted with other large buyers to monitor their claims, and they have expanded from just hospital claims to HMOs, home health agencies, skilled nursing homes, ambulatory surgical centers, and imaging centers. To get a sense of their scope, PROs hand-reviewed four million hospital charts in 1987 (Newhouse 1989). In addition, there is a SuperPro to evaluate the work of the PROs. It too has its problems, but its very existence is indicative of how much times have changed. Thus, in less than a decade the dominant purchaser of medical services has institutionalized a detailed system of accountability and is constantly elaborating it.

Twenty-four states had established statewide data organizations as of 1988, and seventeen have established state data commissions that require by law that hospitals, physicians, and nursing homes submit their financial and clinical records to the commission (National Association of Health Data Organizations 1988). (Exactly what each commission requires varies by state.) These commissions in turn publish periodic comparative analyses. Most of them are rather crude, and funding for the commissions is typically modest. But all signs point to their expansion from inpatient to all forms of care, and to their increasing technical sophistication.

In addition, a number of large companies and business health coalitions have established large data sets for comparing and selecting the most cost-effective hospitals and providers. Of particular interest (because of the Big Brother implications for employees) are "integrated data management systems" that combine employees' health risk profile, their use of substance abuse services, their use of health prevention programs, their clinical records, disability records, accident records, and workers' compensation records. These are cheerfully seen as providing the basis for compassionate, informed programs to minimize illness, disability, and accidents, while providing the most cost-effective care possible. However, they can be used for determining who receives various rewards in the company, and they can be used as criteria by another company for not hiring a person. Although "confidential," they are accessible to management, that is, to those with the power to affect a person's occupational life. Among corporate buyers, about two-thirds of all mid-size and large corporations require a second opinion on surgery, and a third of them penalize an employee for going ahead if the second opinion does not confirm the need for surgery (Hewitt 1988; *Health Care Benefits Survey* 1988). These numbers are steadily rising. Two-thirds of the largest firms require preadmission review before a doctor can admit a patient to a hospital and concurrent review day by day in the hospital, declining to a third of firms with 500-999 employees. Two-thirds of large employers and one-third of small employers provide management of catastrophic cases, the five percent of cases that consume 30 to 40 percent of all costs. The number offering HMOs ranges from over ninety percent for the largest firms to over half of the small ones. While a fifth of the employees had signed up by 1986, that figure had risen to 32 percent by 1988 (*Health Care Benefits Survey* 1988). About a third of the firms offer a preferred provider organization (PPO) and negotiate discounts averaging ten percent. All of these figures are approximate and reflect the reports of corporate officers.

The point for our purposes is that about two-thirds of all the HMOs and a majority of the PPOs do physician profiling. In addition, four-fifths of the largest firms and two-fifths of firms with 500-999 employees audit their claims. About half actually compare institutional providers and forty percent compare individual providers (Higgins 1988). These practice profiles become more refined with each year.

Besides the extensive efforts to monitor and profile clinical work, a minor research industry has arisen around the work of John Wennberg, a physician-researcher at Dartmouth who in 1973 published a revolutionary study ((Wennberg and Gittlesohn 1973), showing that if one controlled for almost all reasonable variables regarding patient diagnosis, physicians' training, insurance coverage, medical resources, and the like, there still remained within small geographical areas large unexplained variation among physicians in the frequency with which they admitted patients to hospitals and operated on them. Extensive research and research tools have developed that allow corporations and state agencies to analyze small area variations. This research has led to specialty societies, HMOs and other organizations, to reduce the variation by establishing norms of practice. Meanwhile, on the national scale, the longstanding large variation among regions of the United States are the object of reduction by HCFA and national corporations with facilities in many locations. Thus rationalization and normative medicine is moving apace.

Most radical of all is the new *outcomes research* (Tarlov 1989). It has naturally evolved from the monitoring discussed above to address the question, "Which provider, or procedure, is most cost-effective?" The answer requires an unprecedented shift from input measures (licensing, certification) and throughput measures (detailed review of whether the "proper" tests, medications, and procedures were done) to outcome measures (how much better did the patient get in one, three or six months)? Outcomes research is developing a variety of measures by which surgical teams, procedures, hospitals, and other provider units can be compared systematically. From a patient's point of view, these measures are heartening, because they consist not just of the usual clinical and laboratory signs of biomedical status, but they also focus on social, physical and even psychological functioning. They also include a number of measures from the patients themselves — how well they feel, how much pain they perceive to have, and the like. Thus, outcomes research is bringing the patient back in and redefining what medicine is.

If outcomes researchers have their way, medicine will consist of those ministrations that most effectively restore patients to the highest physical, social and personal functioning they are capable of attaining (Tarlov 1989). The research is also being conducted without regard to a physicians' specialty, so that it will settle a number of turf battles between overlapping specialties. Outcome measures could in time make licensing obsolete. Already the body that has long certified hospitals is committed to evaluating them in terms of outputs rather than inputs (for example, ratio of RNs to beds). Given the number of studies showing few or no measurable differences between the performance of physicians and other clinicians in primary care settings (Light 1983), outcomes research may redefine what it means to be a professional. Most impressive is the depth of commitment to this work. The Congress is so keen on it (especially in its role as the payor of Medicare debts) that it has created a separate budget just for this work, and several top researchers have left prestigious jobs to form a critical mass in Boston to carry out this work for Congress.

Research on Role Scrutiny

Although experts in the field will find the description above overdrawn because of all the technical problems and obstacles that have accompanied accountability, they may agree that the degree of scrutiny which has developed in about ten years is remarkable and that major forces drive these developments still further with each passing year. If so, then it is the senior members of the role set who are the most scrutinized, and insulation from observability becomes increasingly more difficult. How do people in the role set respond? Of course, there are efforts to manipulate the codes or "doctor" the charts, and indeed hospitals pay consulting firms millions of dollars a year to teach staff how to get the maximum payment out of the patients they treat through "chart management." But these efforts soon run their course, and in the case of Medicare, Congress has responded quickly by reducing the annual inflation factor to "correct" for "code upgrading." Then what? Rose Coser's classic research identifies the issues. Denial and insulation from observability seem almost impossible, as do periods of withdrawal. Role segmentation certainly happens, but that does not *per se* reduce scrutiny. Collective maintenance of pluralistic ignorance appears to be replaced by collective maintenance of good records.

Rose Coser begins her article on insulation from observability (1961, p.28) by stating that "The extent to which role performances within an organization are open to observation by others is structurally determined." The new structural arrangement make role performances very open to observation, and they also are beginning to tie those observations to payment, renewal of contract, and promotion. One doubts that nurses complain that physicians do not read their records; on the contrary, they probably work together to produce "good" ones. Very little research is being done on these matters, even though they are of great importance to the clinicians involved.

How, then, are professionals coping with these new structures? Rose Coser's seminal articles suggest that the loss of role protection is a major new source of stress, discontent, and anger observed among physicians. This implies a basic tension between the desire to spend limited funds wisely and effectively and the need for professionals to have their own space in their work. Or are the insights from this research time-bound? Perhaps it is just as plausible to conceive of professionals as interacting with reviewers and critics — learning, negotiating, correcting, revising. That is what academic researchers do, especially those on soft money from grants. They experience a never-ending life of peer reviews, pink slips, applications and drafts, reapplications and drafts, some successes, and some failures. Clearly the high observability of their work and its financial consequences are stressful, but thousands keep doing it for years without mental breakdown.

We need, then, to begin comparative research on the work started by Rose Coser and her contemporaries on evasiveness, insulation, pluralistic participation in ignorance or guilty knowledge, and denial. This research will benefit from a differentiated analysis of accountability that distinguishes, for example, between institutional forms of accountability that allow informal types of insularity, from collegial forms of accountability that are negotiated (Blau, personal correspondence). Thus work begun over forty years ago by Rose Coser has, if anything, more salience and immediacy for our time than ever before.

References

Becker, Howard S., Blanche Geer, Everett C. Hughes, and Anselm L. Strauss. 1961. *Boys in White: Student Culture in Medical School.* Chicago: University of Chicago Press.

Bodenheimer, Tom, Steve Cummings, and Elizabeth Harding, eds. 1972. *Billions for Bandaids.* San Francisco: Medical Committee for Human Rights.

Coser, Rose. 1960. "Laughter Among Colleagues: A Study of the Social Functions of Humor Among the Staff of a Mental Hospital." *Psychiatry* 23:81-95.

_____. 1961. "Insulation from Observability and Types of Social Conformity." *American Sociological Review* 26:28-39.

_____. 1966. "Role Distance, Sociological Ambivalence, and Transitional Status Systems." *American Journal of Sociology* 72:173-187.

_____. 1967. "Evasiveness as a Response to Structural Ambivalence." *Social Science and Medicine* 1:203-218.

Fortune (entire issue) January 1970.

Freidson, Eliot. 1970a. *Profession of Medicine: A Study of the Sociology of Applied Knowledge.* New York: Dodd, Mead.

_____. 1970b. *Professional Dominance: The Social Structure of Medical Care.* New York: Atherton.

Greenberg, Selig. 1971. *The Quality of Mercy: A Report on the Critical Condition of Hospital and Medical Care in America.* New York: Atheneum.

Havighurst, Clark C. 1980. "Antitrust Enforcement in the Medical Services Industry: What Does It All Mean?" *Milbank Memorial Fund Quarterly* 58:89-123.

Health Care Benefits Survey. 1988. Princeton, NJ: Foster Higgins.

Hewitt Associates. 1988. *Salaried Employee Benefits Provided by Major U.S. Employers in 1982-1987.* Chicago: Hewitt Associates.

Kennedy, Edward 1972. *In Critical Condition.* New York: Simon & Schuster.

Kusserow, Richard P. 1988. "*The Utilization and Quality Control Peer Review Organization (PRO) Program: An Exploration of Program Effectiveness.*" Washington, D.C.: Office of the Inspector General.

Light, Donald W. 1979. "Uncertainty and Control in Professional Training." *Journal of Health and Social Behavior* 20:310-322.

_____. 1983. "Is Competition Bad?" *The New England Journal of Medicine.* 309:1315-9.

_____. 1985. "Comparing Health Care Systems." Pp. 429-442 in *Sociology of Health and Illness: Critical Perspectives,* edited by Peter Conrad and R. Kern, 2nd edition. New York:St. Martin's Press.

_____. 1989. "Social Control and the American Health Care System." Pp. 456-474 in *Handbook of Medical Sociology,* edited by Howard E. Freeman and Sol Levine, 4th edition. New York: Prentice-Hall.

_____. 1991. "The Restructuring of American Health Care." In *Health Politics and Policy,* edited by Theodor J. Litman and Leonard S. Robins, 2nd edition. New York: John Wiley.

Merton, Robert K., George Reader, and Patricia Kendall, eds. 1957. *The Student-Physician.* Cambridge, Mass.: Harvard University Press.

National Association of Health Data Organizations. 1988. *NAHDO Resource Manual.* Washington, D.C.: NAHDO.

Nixon, Richard Milhous. 1971(1972). *Public Papers of the Presidents of the United States: Richard Nixon 1971,* Item 63. Washington, D.C.: U.S. Government Printing Office.

Office of the Inspector General. 1988. *"The Utilization and Quality Control Peer Review Organization (PRO) Program: Sanction Activities."* Washington, D.C.

Relman, Arnold S. 1988. "Assessment and Accountability: The Third Revolution in Medical Care." *New England Journal of Medicine* 319:1220-2.

Ribicoff, Abraham (Senator), with Paul Danaceau. 1972. *The American Medical Machine.* New York: Saturday Review Press.

Stanton, Alfred H., and Morris S. Schwartz. 1954. *The Mental Hospital.* New York: Basic Books.

Tarlov, Alain. 1989. *Journal of the American Medical Association.*

Weller, Charles D. 1983. "The Primacy of Standard Antitrust Analysis in Health Care." *Toledo Law Review* 14:609-637.

Wennberg, John and Alan Gittlesohn. 1973. "Small Area Variations in Health Care Delivery." *Science* 182:1102-8.

15

A Margin of Difference:
The Case for Single-Sex Education

David Riesman

During this past academic year, 1989-90, national publicity attended the effort of Mills College undergraduates to keep their institution as an option of a women's college in the face of the reluctant decision by the President and the Board of Trustees that there was too limited a market for such an institution. The Trustees decided that Mills had to follow the road to coeducation taken in recent years by Goucher in Maryland, Wheaton in Massachusetts, Colby-Sawyer in New Hampshire, and ever so many others, some more and some less eminent. The combination of market pressures and the unwillingness of adolescent girls to identify themselves as preferring a single-sex education (either as a statement that they love other women "too much" and are perhaps lesbian, or fear boys and men "too much" and are cowards) means that at both the precollegiate and the college level coeducation has become the overwhelming American norm.

The enthusiasm for their particular option exhibited by the Mills College students (and with less national visibility, and unsuccessfully, by undergraduates at Goucher College and at Wheaton College) illustrates the problems the women's colleges face, namely, how to persuade high school graduates to consider them seriously; it is only after these students have been recruited that they may become enthusiastic about what they find available to them in a supportive yet demanding locale, where they come to feel assured that they can obtain jobs and enter careers with confidence that they can compete, as well as cooperate, with men.[1] Trustees of Mills agreed to give the College a five-year period to see whether or not it could make a go of it. The President has resigned, to be replaced by someone who would accept this challenge. The Mills

I would like to acknowledge the contribution made by the comments and criticisms of Jeanne Chall, Jill Conway, Donna Eder, Alice Emerson, Martha Fuller, Carol Gilligan, Norman Goodman, David Karen, Mary-Linda Merriam, David Mittelberg, and Cornelius Riordan. In addition, I gratefully acknowledge the support of Lewis A. Dexter, Stimson Bullitt, and Michael Maccoby.

drama appeared in an arena where virtually all the pressures favor diversity, by which is meant active recruitment of people of color, in some cases students from abroad, the poor as well as the well-to-do, and of course both sexes. But the diversity prized within each institution can come at the cost of diversity among them. My thesis in this essay is to show why it matters that single-sex options survive.

When it comes to girls' schools and women's colleges, the observation is often made by feminists and others concerned with the fate of girls and women that we must reform our coeducational institutions to make them more supportive or at any rate less likely to defeat girls' and women's aspirations. I myself belong to this class of reformers in terms of seeking to improve teaching and learning in coeducational settings (Riesman 1988, pp. 10-11). However, I am inclined to think that in the United States, in part because we are so egalitarian — a theme to which I shall return — we are unlikely to reach the point at which single-sex enclaves will have no redeeming value.

Looking at the academic landscape, the Trustees of Mills College will have noted the overwhelming number of men's colleges which quickly became coeducational, increasing their attractiveness for men while competing at every level of academic selectivity with the declining number of women's colleges. In the last three decades, the majority of the women's colleges, public, Catholic, Protestant, secular, have become coeducational — although hardly ever attracting the hoped-for equal number of men. Mills can look to an unusual example of resuscitation of a failing women's college. In 1979 the trustees of Wilson College in the small town of Chambersburg, Pennsylvania, which currently enrolls 191 students in the College for Women and in the Division of Continuing Studies 752 students part-time, three-quarters of them women, decided to close the college, since they saw no prospect for maintaining it as a women's college, and to give its remaining endowment for the furtherance of women's education. A group of alumnae mobilized and took the trustees to court. Mary Patterson McPherson, the nationally visible President of Bryn Mawr College, was one of the trustees. The judge concluded that she had an interest in closing down a competitor college (an unrealistic charge, even if McPherson were a less scrupulous person, given Bryn Mawr's exalted test scores — 650/630 — and high academic seriousness, and Wilson's combined SATs in the low 900's). The judge, illustrating the increasing readiness of courts to intervene in academic governance and other academic issues, ordered the board replaced, the college reopened. Mary-Linda Merriam, who had worked under the entrepreneurial and fierce John Silber at Boston University, came in as president and set to work to find a market niche for Wilson. One way she has succeeded is in programs for adults both on the home campus and elsewhere in the south central Pennsylvania region, and by increasing the already mobilized alumnae support — energies reflected in the listing of Wilson in the top ten regional liberal arts colleges in the North in *U.S. News & World Report* in 1990.

However, Chatham College in Pittsburgh, which also provided adult programs for older women students, offering mothers an opportunity to live with their children on campus, has decided that it can no longer maintain itself as a single-sex college and has announced that it will become coeducational.[2]

The assumption that coeducation is the norm is not only that of student peer groups, but of the wider society. James S. Coleman addresses himself to the paucity of research concerning the assumption that coeducation is better for both sexes in school and in college. He writes: "Like other institutions held in place by conventional wisdom, coeducation is held to be right in part because of its contribution to other, more strongly held values." One of these values, he notes, is that of educational equality for women on the assumption ". . . that single-sex education is inherently unequal." A second value results from the replacement of values now labeled "Victorian" by precepts based on psychology: "That replacement of values occurred through a conflict, and single-sex schools were on the losing side of the conflict. The interest of the winning side in eliminating all the institutions connected with the Victorian values added force to the elimination of single-sex schools" (Coleman 1990, pp. ix-x).[3]

I do not believe that a case can be made for single-sex education beyond the baccalaureate degree. It is in the earlier periods of schooling that I believe that coeducation has triumphed in spite of empirical observation that boys and girls develop differently, with great individual differences, making it likely that, at various stages in one's schooling, each sex can profit from having some settings free of the pressure resulting from the presence of the other. Depending on interest and background, it would seem that boys are most at risk through the presence of girls in elementary school. In the debate "Co-education or Separate Schooling?" held at the all-girls Brearley Day School in New York City several years ago, Brian Walsh, Headmaster of the Buckley School, a boys' school, described differences in the behavior of boys in a coeducational school he headed on the North Shore of Boston vis-à-vis the Buckley School, which carries boys through the ninth grade: boys ordinarily do not even try to sing in a coed school, whereas they love choral singing in a boys' school; in the coed setting they make fun of French pronunciation, whereas in the single-sex setting they enjoy becoming fluent in French; in drama, they muck up or clown to avoid seeming imperfect, in contrast to the girls in a coed setting, whereas they excel at drama when by themselves. Walsh believes that boys from a single-sex school can enter, as most of the Buckley School graduates do, coeducational day or boarding schools at the ninth or tenth grade, without the slightest impairment, but with greater confidence than if they had been in coed settings all along (Brearley School 1989, pp. 10-12).

On the same panel at Brearley School, Ellen Stern, of the coeducational and progressive Fieldston School, spoke in favor of coeducation. She recognized the gains girls make in single-sex schools in academic achievement, especially in mathematics, but insisted that women must be educated with people of all colors, cultures, and genders, to prepare for habituation to the wider worlds of diversity (Brearley School 1989, pp. 10-12).[4] The case for single-sex education for boys in secondary school is much more difficult to make. However, some of the observations of Brian Walsh of the Buckley School would still apply. In the academic year 1970-71, when I was on leave at the Institute for Advanced Study, Lawrenceville School, near Princeton, was debating whether or not to become coeducational. Reading the excellent poetry in the school magazine and observing the capable work in the arts, I concluded that when the school admitted girls (which it has now done), the likely outcome would be that the boys will be in the shop and the girls in the studio. Still, it is on the whole girls who suffer more from the presence of boys in terms of academic performance.

On the one hand, for a large number of boys in junior and senior high school, girls are commonly a sideline, a sometime thing; on the other hand, for most girls, boys are not a sometime thing. This situation does not appear to have been changed by the women's movements, even if these have affected the mothers and sometimes also the fathers of girls who are in school during their increasingly early adolescence. To put it differently, the self-consciousness of the enlightened, genuinely two-parent families can have little impact prior to college entry, save in the rarest instances.[5] Donna Eder (1985), Professor of Sociology at Indiana University, observed girls in middle school in order better to understand findings of earlier research that, to quote Eder: "While boys' self-esteem is tied to achievement, girls' self-esteem is tied to their interpersonal relationships" (p. 154). Her research reports her ethnographic observations in a coeducational middle school and many interviews with seventh and eighth grade girls. The focus was on their relations not with boys but rather with one another. Girls were popular with other girls if boys liked them; the "drips" were ignored by the boys and rejected by other girls. Girls wanted to be with the popular girls, thus crowding the latter with a network wider than they could manage. Having in effect to fend off their own "groupies," the popular girls would begin to be disliked as snobbish, high-hat, and stuck-up. Not being sociometrists, these girls found it hard to understand why they evoked such envy and dislike. Often their popularity would wane without winning them an increase in same-sex friendship. Eder (1985, p. 161) writes, "Popular people were disliked not only by former friends but by many of the students in the school. . . . Again, it is likely that interaction with popular students was so salient that being ignored by them was also particularly salient. Many students took the snobbery of popular people very seriously, as if it automatically implied that they were not as good." One of the most interesting findings was that it was difficult for shy girls to make friends because they, too, were seen as snobs and stuck-up when their shy behavior was misinterpreted as rejection. As others have noted, the most popular girls were the cheerleaders. The "fear of success" among the girls Donna Eder observed was not so much oriented by fear of surpassing the boys at what might be defined as boys' games, as out of the strong feeling that if one is to be accepted among girls, one cannot afford to surpass them — even, in the long run, in popularity (Eder and Parker 1987).

In the fall of 1984 I had the opportunity to supervise an independent study project by Eri Iwakuni, a Japanese student brought up primarily in England and a senior in Harvard College. She had attended a girls' boarding school in the United Kingdom and then came for four years to Choate Rosemary Hall in Wallingford, Connecticut — a school created by the merger of two outstanding single-sex schools in 1977. Shy in the Japanese fashion, she was enthusiastic about her secondary school, believing that had she come directly from a girls' boarding school in England, she would not have been able to cope with the coeducational milieu in Harvard College. I did not ask her to surrender this judgment, which made sense to me, but rather to see her project as an exploration of differences between Choate Rosemary Hall and Westover School in Middlebury, Connecticut, which has remained a small girls' boarding school — 50 students in the senior year. I suggested that she focus in the first instance on the teaching of mathematics in the two settings. At the school she had attended, even if there was a woman teacher, a girl who did reasonably well in mathematics was praised, whereas when she visited mathematics classes at Westover School, she found that expectations were higher: there was no assumption that a particular level was acceptable for a girl. The other arenas on which her observations focused were those raised by the Donna Eder study. At Choate Rosemary Hall, as in the middle school in Eder's research, girls whom boys liked were popular. "Drips" were rejected. At Westover School, whatever jealousies there might be about weekend dates and vis-à-vis cliques, there was a strong sense of camaraderie which embraced everyone in the senior class; girls did not stay away from those whom boys did not like because there were no boys around.

Not all girls need the temporary benefits of a single-sex setting — far from it. A recent Australian study presents somewhat fragmentary evidence that girls benefit from single-sex schools in wealthy, urban Victoria, although there is no comparable benefit in the more remote state of Queensland.[6]

A glance at Australia brings up questions of class and culture. There are a few women's colleges in Japan, some of them initiated by Christian missionaries, and a few girls' schools, but most schools are coeducational. Parental pressure, the "infernal examination system," the authority of teachers as well as of parents, create a milieu in which most students work hard (although there is more vandalism and bullying among students in recent years than the stereotype calls for). It is still true that Japanese women for the most part have jobs rather than careers: careers are for the boys and men, but the girls and women must be highly skilled and literate for the level of jobs they have prior to marriage, and also later, if marriage or family life fails them.

We can understand our egalitarian American attitudes a bit better by looking at problems of coeducational schooling on the Israeli kibbutz, as illuminated for me in discussions with Professor David Mittelberg, who was in 1989-90 Visiting Professor for Kibbutz Studies at Harvard, on leave from the University of Haifa in Israel, and a visiting lecturer in Sociology. It is hardly news that the kibbutz is defiantly egalitarian — and secular Jewish women are not notable for being shy. In the agrarian kibbutz, the sexual division of labor did not work to the serious disadvantage of women. But in the kibbutz of today, grounded in manufacturing and high technology, lack of skill in mathematics, science, and related engineering technologies leaves women at the bottom of the occupational order.[7] Mittelberg concluded that this situation, aggravating and against the grain for the men as well as the women of the kibbutz, could only be altered by providing single-sex education in mathematics and science for the girls in the kibbutz schools. He wanted to try some experiments in tutoring girls, or otherwise providing special courses for them. But in kibbutz discussions both sexes refused to believe that there are *really* any differences by gender, or at any rate differences that good will cannot overcome. The attitude bears resemblance to that of a number of American feminists with whom I have discussed single-sex education, who contend that girls and women should everywhere be where men are, because that is where power lies. In vain Professor Mittelberg argues that women will continuously lack access to power in manufacturing if they are not willing even experimentally and tentatively to surrender their ideology of equality in every realm at every single stage in human development.

At the college level there is a modest amount of evidence concerning the difference women's colleges make in comparison with coeducational ones. Mirra Komarovsky's (1985) cohort study of freshmen re-interviewed as sophomores and then as seniors at a college that is clearly Barnard is splendidly illuminating concerning the dilemmas of career-oriented college women in a world where men as dates and boy friends still hold much of the initiative. Many shared the experience of a premed student who in sophomore year had said she preferred coed classes, but by graduation had noted discrimination against women in some of those same classes and in her future profession, and as a result had become more sympathetic to a women's college. Other seniors attributed to the college their support for the women's movements, although of course such support occurs in coeducational colleges also.

The most sustained research is that of M. Elizabeth Tidball, Professor of Physiology at The George Washington University Medical School and a graduate and former Trustee of Mount Holyoke College. Her work builds on earlier work to highlight the achievements in terms of post-baccalaureate scholarship and other careers, such as being included in *Who's Who in America*, by graduates of women's colleges (Tidball 1986, 1989). Since even the topflight women's colleges have become less selective, as the vast majority of young people have chosen coeducational institutions, the comparative studies done by Tidball and others are less determinative of what the future holds.[8]

Moreover, even if it should be shown that in terms of opportunities for women to pursue careers in mathematics and the sciences, they stand a better chance if they graduate from a women's college (Mount Holyoke is notable in this respect), this would say nothing directly concerning women's general satisfaction and personal development in a single-sex setting. Furthermore, in the many segments of the women's movements there are some feminists who see the assumption that women *should* go into the sciences as itself a reflection of "male" values. This outlook is discussed at length in "Feminist Critiques of Science" in *Notices of the American Mathematical Society* (1989). While some scholars have seen male bias against women in science, one wing of the women's movement (whose work is discussed in "Feminist Critiques of Science") sees science as hard, mastery-oriented, and in general unnatural — some of these judgments have drawn on Carol Gilligan's *In a Different Voice* (1982) to restate in contemporary terms some earlier views of women's place.[9] I am reminded of the marvelous words of Diana Trilling many years ago, referring to the "Seven Sisters" colleges, that women had to get an education at least as bad as men were getting in order to feel they were getting as good a one!

Diana Trilling's ironic conceit brings to mind the experience of David Karen, Assistant Professor of Sociology at Bryn Mawr College, who had done his graduate work in sociology at Harvard, specializing in the sociology of higher education. He reported that it took him a while to realize that Bryn Mawr College students, unlike those he had taught as a Teaching Fellow at Harvard College, usually took reading lists seriously. At Harvard College he had been accustomed, as is in fact the norm, to assign huge amounts of reading on the assumption that students might do a mite of it. (I think that there is a subsidiary intention which originally contributed to this giantism at Harvard, namely the desire to impress one's colleagues.) When in the first several weeks at Bryn Mawr he realized that his students were very sleepy, it dawned on him that they had stayed up all night to do *all* the reading!

Tidball disaggregates her research by type of coeducational institution. She takes note of those institutions which began as coeducational, Oberlin the first among them, Carleton and Reed, and most state universities in the Middle West and West. She discusses what she terms the men's-change colleges, which include all the Ivy League (other than Cornell, created according to its founder, Ezra Cornell, for "any person, any study") and the many top-flight primarily undergraduate colleges such as Wesleyan, Williams, Amherst, Bowdoin, Lafayette (Swarthmore became coeducational in the 1920's), and ever so many Catholic or once-Catholic institutions. Then there are the women's-change colleges, which in the private sector include Vassar, Skidmore, Connecticut College,[10] and many Catholic and once-Catholic colleges; also, of course, many state institutions in the South, such as Mary Washington College in Virginia; Florida State University (now thoroughly coeducational); the University of North Carolina at Greensboro.

When Wheaton College in Massachusetts became coeducational, its President, Alice Emerson, and the many active feminists on the administration and the faculty, expressed their aspiration that Wheaton would still be a college offering notable support for women in and out of the classroom, even though it would now be in a coeducational setting. In one effort to chart progress in espousing an alternative form of education, Wheaton hired Catherine Krupnick of the Harvard Graduate School of Education, formerly director of the Harvard-Danforth Center for Teaching and Learning, to come to the Wheaton campus to videotape some freshman classes in the first half year of men's presence so as to provide a baseline view of what the dynamics were in the coed classroom. Not surprisingly, despite the small number of men in the four individual classes thus recorded, the women spoke less frequently than the men. Moreover, in the second year the sophomore men, fewer than one in five, were elected to all the positions on the judicial board which examines alleged violations of the Honor Code. While the first reaction to these latter bits of news was one of surprise, a more reflective response was based on the judgment that both politics and law had combative elements which may be more attractive to men than to women.

Indeed, a critic could argue that my own concern that women develop their gifts in mathematics, the sciences, and engineering could be seen as a preoccupation with American competitiveness vis-à-vis the Japanese and other countries where students in school, if not always at university, work with great seriousness and parental and even peer support in that seriousness. Of course I have in mind what matters for the United States as a whole, but in this essay my focus is primarily on individual girls and women, and what in the long run is best for them. The women's movements and the state of the economy, the instability of marriages along with the perils of divorce for women, and the assumptions we all make as to what is a proper standard of living combine to tell girls and women that they cannot count on support by a man, but must be prepared at any point to make their way on their own. For most of those aspiring to college and also post-baccalaureate education, that means a career, turned part-time, perhaps, for a spell of motherhood and perhaps not, but not a job or a series of jobs. Hence academic seriousness, being stretched to their limit, is important for them as well as for the country.[11]

My understanding of these matters has gained from exchanges with my colleague Carol Gilligan. She herself is a graduate of the Swarthmore College Honors Program. Swarthmore is now so thoroughly egalitarian that many people are surprised to realize that it began as a men's college and that it still has fraternities. In the Honors Program (where the examinations are given by invited outsiders) one must for every session prepare a paper and distribute copies to the instructor and the seven other members of the seminar and read it aloud, eliciting responses. As Carol Gilligan has commented, there are days when what one has done is inadequate, even embarrassing; yet, with grading and evaluation removed from the classroom by the use of the outside examiners, one learns to proceed; one has to learn in the course of things that one can live with awkwardness, live with public performance at least in the milieu still somewhat influenced by Quaker tradition. As one endures in the Program, one's self-confidence grows; one discovers that it is not lethal to have bad days, bad performances. ("Bad" at any rate by Swarthmore's exalted standards.) Now doing field studies at Emma Willard School in Troy, Carol Gilligan has come to appreciate single-sex education more than she had earlier, when she was less cognizant of the specialness of the Swarthmore Honors Program in her own development.

I need hardly remind readers that Swarthmore-style seriousness can be found by those who seek it out in many research universities and liberal arts colleges, even where the general temper is often to act "cool." Three colleges come to mind: Reed, Carleton, Oberlin, all coeducational since their founding, where women have never been "coeds," where there are no fraternities or sororities, and where women quite as often as men go on to further professional and graduate studies in a wide variety of fields. Oberlin admitted women in 1833 on the basis of the argument that they, too, would be going out on mission overseas with their husbands, and would need to understand the background of their faith if they were to become adequate partners. Carleton opened its doors to men and women in 1866, and its tradition, like that of Oberlin, has been assertively egalitarian. In 1986 I asked Diane Harrison, who after majoring in sociology-anthropology had become assistant to Carleton's President Robert Edwards, to look at the fields in which women were majoring; she reported that there were as many women in mathematics as there were men, and that a greater number of women majoring in chemistry went on to Ph.D. programs than did men, who more often chose the medical school route. Carleton then had women who were majoring in geology, and so on around the orbit of the natural sciences. Even so, although Carleton is not a chilly climate for women, there appeared to be some women who nevertheless might have fared better at a women's college of comparable academic quality. One student who had transferred to Carleton from Bryn Mawr College reported that she felt somewhat inhibited, less free, less capable of whimsical intellectual forays in the presence of men than she did at Bryn Mawr College, where there were also a few men — Haverford men — but the latter were not her fellow students in the same way.

By the time one reaches graduate and professional school, no one, and certainly not this writer, makes a case for single-sex education. However, there are better and worse locales: for example, women feel cramped at Harvard Law School in a way that is not true at Yale or Stanford; women in engineering at Tufts are numerous and feel supported in a way that is much less the case at, for example, California Institute of Technology. Such observations, as well as what has been said earlier about Swarthmore and other outstanding colleges where women were never "coeds," raise by implication the question of whether women's colleges should be seen as, at best, transitional, perhaps necessary concessions to the way things are now: at the majority of institutions the women are still "coeds" and class leadership, both in the classroom and in student government, is generally in the hands of the men. The argument could also take the form of contending that if the women's liberation movements were still more potent, the young woman transfer from Bryn Mawr College to Carleton would have felt entirely uninhibited — Bryn Mawr must have coddled rather than liberated her if she was not prepared for the Carleton milieu.[12]

In the heady early days of the women's movements that exploded in the 1960's, it was believed that differences between women's and men's wages, statuses, and performances in their years of schooling and thereafter were the result of a potentially curable sexism on the part of men, and inhibition and lack of raised consciousness on the part of women. Even now, many women active in the Women's College Coalition, the organization of many of the remaining women's colleges, believe that these colleges are needed for a transitional period, and that we are moving toward a time when either gender differences will become minimal, or when such differences will not produce great differences in outcome.

Claire Guthrie, former Chairman of the Board and Acting President of Chatham College, now Assistant Attorney General of the State of Virginia, believes that this outlook asks for Affirmative Action concessions to favor women to overcome previous handicaps. She concludes that this demeans the differences between men and women and joins other members of the Women's College Coalition who insist that in the United States, whatever might be the situation worldwide, there will remain in the best of circumstances differences according to gender — differences with wide overlap but differences nonetheless. In sharing this latter position, I do not write from an orthodox Freudian perspective — far from it — when I note that women continue to be the ones to bear children and to nurse them and in most homes, even in the most enlightened homes, to be around them more than fathers are. I think the Oedipus complex is a fairy tale; yet boys brought up by mothers have a different relation to them than do girls brought up by mothers. This is so despite the fact that each of us has cross-sex as well as same-sex components and that these may well change with development, so that many of us become more androgynous as we age (Gell 1989). This is not to argue for, using the title of Steven Goldberg's book, "The Inevitability of Patriarchy." In the occupational worlds that lie ahead for America, as I have already suggested, women's options for success and corresponding security will be greater if they are comfortable with numbers and spatial concepts, in architecture as in astronomy or in musical composition. Girls' schools and women's colleges at their best provide models of how women's horizons for the future can be enlarged, without using the masculine occupational models as necessarily paramount.

Those models are often referred to as the "real world." The many feminists who oppose women's colleges want girls and women to enter that world at an earlier age. In the United States, girls and young women are vulnerable in middle school and high school years in part because they are more mature emotionally and more alertly connected to their peers of both sexes than boys of the same chronological age. In a more aristocratic society, upper-class girls and women would be less subject to the egalitarian fear of being thought snobbish and aloof; they would be less susceptible to generalized peer pressure. But even in more egalitarian America, there are different degrees of susceptibility that girls experience, depending on ethnicity, social class, and parental bent. Stages of development, as already indicated, also vary; for some girls a single-sex high school would be much more important than a women's college, analogous to the common statement at Harvard Business School that Wellesley College graduates do particularly well there despite the notoriously combative, grade-conscious classrooms.

All of us in the United States are in some sense in the "real world," in the media around us and in our imaginations, and that of course is coeducational. None of my argument is intended to resist present efforts by women and men to make workplaces more commodious for women, including mothers, than they are now, which will surely not make them less comfortable for most men. Women differ, and their timetables differ. After a chance for single-sex education, I am all for girls and women plunging into the coeducational worlds their previous experience has made available to them. And if, as is less common today than a few years ago, they emerge "more macho than thou," that is their privilege. That mode of being feminine is legitimate.

I was astonished to learn from Nancy Bekavac, President of Scripps College, the women's college in the Claremont College Consortium, that during the uproar created by the Mills College students' protesting the College's decision to admit men, the *Los Angeles Times* and other West Coast newspapers were filled with irate letters from men, attacking these same women (comparable in some respects to the venom released on a number of Wellesley College seniors for raising questions about having Barbara Bush, no achiever in her own right, as Wellesley's Commencement speaker). The letter-writers complained that it was unfair for women to keep enclaves to themselves while insisting on admission to previously all-male enclaves such as clubs and fraternal orders, and indeed all men's single-sex organizations. I had not fully appreciated the depth of the backlash among men against what they see as preferential treatment for women.

In part, this is an aspect of the backlash against all Affirmative Action, and to the extent that girls' schools and women's colleges are seen as a form of Affirmative Action, that is, of preferential treatment, they run not only the political and cultural hazard of backlash, but also, as indicated earlier, the hazard of being deemed unnecessary, for enough compensation has already been provided to make up for past discriminations (would, indeed, that this were so!).

I hope I have made clear that my own defense of single-sex education is based on a belief in maintaining the American heterogeneity — private and public, religious and secular, single-sex as well as coeducational — that has of course its negative aspects, but that is almost universally admired by countries with more unitary educational systems. American egalitarianism has in the past permitted these differences, even while often being uneasy about them, and even though we sometimes recognize that all of us, women and men, are in this country and on this planet together so that what helps strengthen the intelligence and self-confidence and also the scrupulousness of each of us can benefit all of us. Something is lost, quite possibly irretrievably, when the residual boys' schools and men's colleges take to the overwhelmingly majoritarian, coeducational road, thanks to market pressure, juridical pressure, or political attack. In the rare instances where it still continues, enhancing single-sex education for girls and women deprives some boys and men of a traditional, still extant, periodically threatened easy superiority — and this only during the seasons when schools are in session — and not even that entirely. American society as it is today gives both sexes ample, and in the judgments of people like myself, often premature time for "playing the field." Boys and men lack many things, but opportunities for cross-sex interaction is not invariably the most visible deficit! As already suggested, those interactions are not quite so mediated by social class as in many other countries of the world. On the contrary, what many otherwise advantaged Americans, women perhaps more than men, lack is privacy, chances to appreciate same-sex camaraderie in non-combative settings, and supportive yet challenging teaching, including opportunities for learning with older persons of all gender orientations and a certain measure of wisdom.

Notes

1. When in 1962 I gave a convocation address at Mount Holyoke College, some of the seniors complained about their being sequestered in academic settings away from men. I asked for a show of hands of those who had attended summer school, and about 80 per cent had, in settings that were invariably coed. Mount

Holyoke recently was cited by the Council on Undergraduate Research for having the largest and best-equipped chemistry building of U.S. four-year undergraduate institutions (*U.S. News & World Report* 1988, p. C-8). In another ranking of national liberal arts colleges in the same issue, based on reputation, Wellesley comes out at the very top, followed by Smith, with Bryn Mawr and Mount Holyoke in the ninth and tenth positions, and Barnard twentieth (p. C-12).

2. Chatham's President, Rebecca Stafford, had in her earlier career as a sociologist studied microclimates on the Harvard College campus, in collaboration with Charles Bidwell, discovering at a time when Harvard College was exclusively for men, although Radcliffe women attended the same classes, that the residential Houses had, despite the lotteries involved in selecting students for them, developed distinct climates, reflecting the Master and the Tutors associated with the House. Having previously been President at Bemidji State College and Executive Vice President of Colorado State University, her experience persuaded her of the benefits for some women of single-sex education, but the task of making that case among high school seniors alert to the judgments of their peers was, she concluded, insuperable. As a result of the national publicity surrounding the decision of Mills College to remain at least for five experimental years a women's college, alumnae mobilized also at Chatham College and helped force the resignation of Rebecca Stafford, whose decision to make Chatham coeducational had been supported by the board of Trustees. What the future holds at Chatham is still unclear.

3. I am indebted to James Coleman for discussions concerning single-sex versus coeducational schools at the time when he was working on his book, *The Adolescent Society*, and when we were colleagues at the University of Chicago in 1955-58.

4. I do not have space in this essay adequately to explore the bases for my judgment that the case for boys' elementary schools and also high schools is stronger for black Americans than it is for white Americans. Having held this view for several decades against much opposition, I was encouraged when I read that William Raspberry, the hardy black columnist of *The Washington Post*, has proposed that the District of Columbia create separate elementary schools for boys and for girls. He notes that girls at that age are less unruly than boys and have a quicker way with words. (The same is true among whites, on the whole, but the white boys catch up and marginally even overtake the girls in verbal ability, not to speak of mathematical ability, by the end of the high school years.) Interesting material on this issue may also be found in Holland and Eisenhart (1990), a study of women students at a predominantly black and a predominantly white university in the American South.

5. Alice Elizabeth Stone, for her honors thesis in Social Studies at Harvard, "Learning to Put Your Foot Down — Gently: The Subculture of Working-Class Girls" (1985), studied 15-year-old girls in a parochial school in Boston which had once been a girls' school and had become, like ever so many others, coeducational. The Sisters sought in vain to discourage girls from smoking; the boys were into sports and did not smoke. The girls thought it was cool to smoke and that it would make them more attractive to the boys, who, however, paid

only occasional attention to them whether they smoked or not. (Sisters were reported to have had considerably greater success in warning the girls against too-easy sex with boys who would love them and leave them, pointing to many examples in the neighborhood of unwed but still teenage mothers. Passively, they appear to have supported contraception where other cautions failed.)

6. Peter Carpenter and Martin Hayden (1987 pp. 156-167) suggest that in Victoria, although not in Queensland, attendance at a single-sex school improves girls' academic achievements, holding parental education and social class constant. Since Carpenter and Hayden note that in England parental "cultural capital" is more important than the gender composition of the school, I might tentatively interpret the finding to suggest that Australia is so egalitarian and, on the side of the boys, so "matey" that girls cannot benefit as fully as in England from the boundaries erected by parental social class position. However, although many scholars and novelists have written about the continuing male hegemony in Australia, a study of campus culture at the University of Melbourne seemed to me to indicate a fair degree of equality, once students were at university. See Little (1975) and my Foreword to the book.

Jill Ker Conway's *The Road From Coorain* (1989) is a work of magnetic autobiography; it presents a fine portrait of Abbotsleigh School, a girls' day and boarding school outside of Sydney, where girls in the 1940's were held to the strictest standards of academic and personal discipline. Of her time at the University of Sydney in the mid-Fifties, she writes, "I was used to concealing how well I did academically when in male company, and to feigning interest in explications of subjects about which I knew a great deal more than the speaker. This was required conduct for women in Australia. It didn't do to question male superiority in anything. One learned early not to correct mistakes in a male companion's logic, and to accept the most patent misinformation as received truth" (p. 178). She goes on to report her delight in meeting an upper-class Australian, Peter Stone, educated at Harrow: "In his company I enjoyed the experience an intellectual woman needs most if she has lived in a world set on undermining female intelligence: I was loved for what I was rather than the lesser mind I pretended to be" (p. 179). She became an historian and later President of Smith College.

7. Mittelberg, commenting on the text, writes: "Women, however, were a minority in the early kibbutz and those who wished to struggle against physical hardship could and did work in all agrarian branches — the egalitarian ethos worked in their favour as the sexual division of labour was seen as existentially temporary. Neither was it seen as all that problematic as all labour was ideologically regarded as equal in intrinsic worth and indeed earned identical life rewards. Moreover, all work shared a common denominator of menial suffering though sanctified. . . . the movement from agriculture to industry found women with a paradoxically higher rate of education than men but rarely in maths and sciences, a *sine qua non* for economic leadership thence power and control" (1990).

8. Problems of comparison are complicated by the fact that women in higher education, down to recent years, generally came from higher social strata than men (Coser 1973, p. 471). Today, in contrast, more women than men go on from

high school to college, thus somewhat diluting the previous advantage of women in their verbal scores vis-à-vis men in the SATs, in addition to other factors that might also be lowering women's scores. The issues of these tests, and allegations that they are biased by gender and race, are too intricate for me to develop here. (See, e.g., Riesman 1980 pp. 123-136).

9. Commenting on some of this discussion, Sheila Tobias (1986) observed that women and men who claim that women cannot (or should not) do mathematics suffer from "'mathematics anxiety,' which consists not just of inability to do mathematics, but of worrying about this incapacity. . . . Why are people so defensive about their mathematical deficiencies?"

10. Vassar, Connecticut, and Skidmore colleges have all reached the proportion of two-fifths men, reflecting their traditional eminences in the arts and other areas and vigorous recruiting enhanced by renovated athletic and other facilities. Many women's-change colleges, Catholic and other, have recruited male commuters while maintaining dormitories primarily for women — on the whole the situation of the women's-change colleges is radically different from that of the men's-change colleges, all of which have been enhanced in recruiting men by the presence also of women.

11. Of course I recognize that discipline and seriousness are found in schools and colleges, often to the very highest extent, outside the curriculum: notably in sports for both sexes, in the band and the orchestra, in the student magazine or paper or dramatic performance. Many coaches have a better experience with those whom they serve as mentors than the academic teachers do. For an evocative account by a high school teacher of his observations of girls and boys, blacks and whites, at T.C. Williams High School in Alexandria, Virginia, see Welch (1986). See also my discussion in Introduction to Jessie Bernard, *Academic Women* (1964), p. xxiii.

12. On the whole, the problems Bryn Mawr and other women's colleges have today do not arise from heavy attrition on the part of women wanting to transfer to coed schools (the student who transferred from Bryn Mawr to Carleton is not unique, but such shifts are rather uncommon). Bryn Mawr graduates 83 per cent of its students in five years, Mount Holyoke 82, per cent, Wellesley 85 per cent, and Carleton 80 per cent.

References

Brearley School. 1989. "Co-education or Separate Schooling? A Brearley Alumnae Day Panel." *Brearley School Summer Bulletin* 65 (no. 2): 9-15.

Carpenter, Peter and Hayden, Martin. 1987. "Girls' Academic Achievements: Single Sex vs. Coeducational Schools in Australia." *Sociology of Education* 60: 156-167.

Coleman, James S. 1990. "Foreword." Pp. ix-x in Cornelius Riordan, *Girls and Boys in School: Together or Separate?* New York: Teachers College Press.

Conway, Jill Ker. 1989. *The Road from Coorain*. New York: Alfred A. Knopf.

Coser, Rose. 1973. Review of *Changing Women in Changing Societies, Science* 182 (no. 412): 471.

Eder, Donna. 1985. "The Cycle of Popularity: Interpersonal Relations Among Female Adolescents." *Sociology of Education* 58: 154-165.

____ and Parker, Stephen. 1987. "The Cultural Production and Reproduction of Gender: The Effect of Extracurricular Activities on Peer-Group Culture." *Sociology of Education*, 60: 200-213.

"Feminist Critiques of Science." 1989. *Notices of the American Mathematical Society* 36 (no. 6): 669 et seq.

Gell, Alfred. 1989. "Cross-sex and Single-sex Transactions." Review of Marilyn Strathern, *The Gender of the Gift* (Berkeley: University of California Press, 1989), in *Times Literary Supplement* June 16-22: 663.

Gilligan, Carol. 1982. *In a Different Voice: Psychological Theory and Women's Development*. Cambridge: Harvard University Press.

Holland, Dorothy C. and Eisenhart, Margaret A. 1990. *Educated in Romance: Women, Achievement, and College Culture*. Chicago: University of Chicago Press.

Komarovsky, Mirra. 1985. *Women in College: Shaping New Feminine Identities*. New York: Basic Books.

Little, Graham. 1975. *Faces On the Campus: A Psycho-Social Study*, Melbourne University Press.

Mittelberg, David. 1990. Letter to David Riesman from University of Haifa, December 20.

Riesman, David. 1988. "On Discovering and Teaching Sociology: A Memoir." *Annual Review of Sociology* 14:1-24.

____. 1964. Introduction to Jessie Bernard, *Academic Women*. University Park, Pennsylvania: Pennsylvania State University Press.

____. 1980. *On Higher Education: The Academic Enterprise in an Era of Rising Student Consumerism*. San Francisco: Jossey-Bass.

Stone, Alice Elizabeth. 1985. "Learning to Put Your Foot Down — Gently: The Subculture of Working-Class Girls." Honors thesis, Department of Social Studies, Harvard College.

Tidball, M. Elizabeth. 1986. "Baccalaureate Origins of Recent Natural Science Doctorates." *Journal of Higher Education* 57: 606-620.

Tidball, M. Elizabeth. 1989. "Women's Colleges: Exceptional Conditions, Not Exceptional Talent, Produce High Achievers." Pp. 157-172 in *Educating the Majority: Women Challenge Tradition in Higher Education*, edited by Carol Pearson, Donna Shavlik, and Judith Touchton. New York: Macmillan.

Tobias, Sheila. 1986. *Newsletter of the Association for Women in Mathematics* (November-December): 10.

U.S. News & World Report. 1988. "America's Best Colleges," (October 10): C-8.

Welch, Patrick. 1986. *Tales out of School: A Teacher's Candid Account from the Front Lines of the American High School Today*. New York: Viking Penguin.

16

Marriage and the Family in the United States: Dying Institution?

Norman Goodman

"The family has become a problem" is the opening line of a book by Brigitte and Peter Berger (1983) entitled, *The War Over the Family*. Actually, as Rose Coser would immediately point out, concern about the family is nothing new, though there does seem to be an urgency about it at the present time that stems from the increasing drive for equality in relationships between men and women. The central issue currently is whether the family is still (if it ever was) useful in the contemporary world in which a growing number of people seek to promote different, more equal, roles for men and women than had been previously typical in marriage. Additionally, questions have been raised as to whether there is a *future* for the twin institutions of marriage and the family in the United States. Even more pointedly, some have posed the question in its normative form: *should* there be a future for them? Cadwallader (1975), for example, sees contemporary marriage as a "wretched institution." Cooper (1970, p. 140) calls for the "death of the family" because he sees it as destroying "autonomous initiative." And Thamm (1975, p. 4) believes that in monogamous marriage "Needs for prolonged intimate association are not met and free expression of affection is curtailed." On the other hand, O'Brien (1981, p. 13) believes that "marriage may be as close to what living intimately with other people on this small planet is all about: loving, touching, hoping, caring." Finally, we have the view of Douvan (1980) that "if we didn't have the family we would probably have to invent it."

To a large degree, most of these statements reflect the unique, personal experience of those making them; and that is not necessarily the best basis for attempting to understand whether there is a future for marriage and the family as major social institutions in the United States. This task — an extremely important one — is more appropriately approached by examining the available relevant data from recent census and survey research. Data from these sources on eight important aspects of contemporary marriage and the family life will serve as a basis for projecting the likely future of these two institutions. In many ways, the thread that is woven throughout the fabric of the following discussion is Rose Coser's (1964) view that the family is an adaptable and resilient institution that can only be understood in the context of the larger social order in which it is embedded.

Important Aspects of Marriage and Family Life

The Viability of Marriage and the Nuclear Family as Social Institutions

Despite media hype to the contrary, careful examination of the relevant evidence clearly indicates that both marriage and the nuclear family are still going strong in the United States today. Specifically, with respect to the nuclear family, not only are there considerable data to demonstrate its resiliency over historical time and geographical space (see, for example, Murdock 1949; 1955), but in the past two to three decades it has been put to some severe tests in the United States and elsewhere, and it has survived (although with some important changes, a point I will take up shortly). This survival, despite clearly challenging circumstances, is probably the best indication of the nuclear family's continued underlying strength and viability.

As for marriage, it too continues to be a popular institution. Take, as an example, the turbulent 1960s and 1970s during which several social trends were evident that seemed at the time to pose a serious threat to the institution of marriage and the continuity of the nuclear family as a major social form: (1) a proliferation of communes (often organized along familial lines and including a range of sexual relationships); (2) an increase in non-marital cohabitation as a proposed *alternative* (rather than just a prelude) to marriage; (3) a growing number of gay and lesbian relationships with increasing tolerance for them though perceived now with greater ambivalence since the AIDS "epidemic") and (4) an increase in the social and geographical mobility of young people. Yet, recent census data indicate that most people are still getting married, and most couples are still having children. Marriages increased in 1985 for the tenth straight year, though it decreased slightly over the next three years, from 2,450,000 to 2,389,000 (U.S. Bureau of the Census, July 26, 1989, p. 4 Table D). It should also be pointed out that about 90 percent of all marriages are formal affairs, tied to a religious and/or civil ceremony (up from 83 percent in 1960).

On the other hand, there has been an increase in the percentage of the population under age 30 who have never married. In 1980, 48 percent of males and 36 percent of females had never married; by 1989, those figures were 66 percent for males and 48 percent for females (U.S. Bureau of the Census, March 1989, p. 4). These statistics have been taken by some to denote a changing, less positive, view of marriage among contemporary young adults. However, there is an alternative explanation possible: these figures may well reflect a tendency to delay the age at first marriage (for a variety of personal and career reasons) rather than signifying an actual reduction in the number of people who will eventually marry. Furthermore, those claiming that these projections for "never married" signal the demise of the nuclear family should note that the 1989 figures are virtually identical with the percent of "never married" in 1890. In line with the alternate interpretation of a delay in first marriage, is the fact that the contemporary rate of *first marriages* is also quite close to that which existed in 1890.

The comparison between 1890 and the contemporary scene points to the importance of keeping our eye on long-term trends instead of on short-term fluctuations. Cherlin (1980) is even more specific about this caution when he points out that most contemporary analyses of the family take the 1950s as their base; yet, he notes, the 1950s should be seen as an unusual period exhibiting quite untypical patterns of American family life. The American people turned inward after the upheaval of World War II, Cherlin argues, investing their physical and emotional energies into family life. These were the Eisenhower years, when the mood of the country — both socially and politically — was moderately conservative. In short, this period was disjunctive with the hectic 1930s and 1940s that preceded it and the turbulent 1960s and 1970s that were to come. Thus, Cherlin points out, family structure and family life in the 1980s, rather than reflecting a major change from the past — what some have said signals the beginning of the end of the nuclear family — is quite in line with more long term trends.

Divorces began to decline in 1982 for the first time in two decades (from 1.21 million to 1.18 million, or from 5.3 to 5.1 per 1,000 population) and continued to do so between 1985 and 1988 when they fluctuated yearly. In 1988, there were 1.18 million divorces, for a rate of 4.8 per 1000 population (*Monthly Vital Statistics Report*, July 26, 1989, p. 5, Table F). Again, the decrease in the beginning of the 1980s or the later fluctuations may be the pattern of the future. Only time will tell.

Even though divorce has become more common than in the past, so has remarriage and the establishment of second families. More than three-quarters of women and over four-fifths of men remarry after divorce, and about one-half do so within three years of the dissolution of their earlier marriage. Recent research indicates that for every person who was divorced and had not remarried, there were ten persons in an existing intact marriage. Moreover, during the 1980s, attitude surveys (e.g., Thornton and Freedman 1982), various public opinion polls and census data show clearly, as Mary Jo Bane (1978) termed it, "the persistence of commitments to family life" of most Americans. Thus, an increasing divorce rate — which may be slowing down or abating — does not necessarily signify increasing unhappiness with the *institution* of marriage, only with a specific partner; this view is supported by the relatively high remarriage rate and the surveys mentioned above.

Taking all of these data together, it seems quite clear that the nuclear family is still going strong and will continue to do so into the foreseeable future. There may well be continuing pressure on it to adapt to changing circumstances, but past experience suggests that it will do just that.

Changes in the Structure of the Nuclear Family

The fact that the nuclear family will, I believe, survive into the foreseeable future does not mean it will do so unchanged. For example, earlier "straight line" projections to 1990 suggested that the number of married couple households will decrease from 65 percent in 1975 to 55 percent in 1990. In fact, the 1989 figure was quite close to this projection: 56 percent (U.S. Bureau of the Census, March 1989, p. 4 Table 1). In part, changes will be due to several factors. First, changes will result from a likely increase in single adult-headed households with children; the percent of male-headed households, increased from 2.9 percent in 1980 to 4.3 percent in 1989; and female-headed households increased from 14.6 percent to 16.5 percent over the same period (U.S. Bureau of Census, March 1989, p. 5 Table 4). Changes in the number of cohabiting couples will also contribute to the decrease projected for married couple households. Living together (without marriage) will continue to increase not only as an alternative to marriage for some, but as a prelude to (or between marriages) for many others. The actual number of cohabiting couples has increased threefold (to about 2.6 million) in the past decade; however, these couples still only constitute a small fraction (about 5 percent) of all households in America (U.S. Bureau of the Census, March 1988, p. 2) media coverage notwithstanding.

Over the past fifty years, there has been a notable reduction in average family size (3.76 in 1940, 3.58 in 1970, 3.29 in 1980 and 3.16 in 1989) and an increase in the incidence of "partial" (e.g., childless/childfree couples), "fragmented" (e.g., single-parent, widowed) and "modified extended" families (more than two generations living together). In an earlier analysis that still seems relevant today, Westoff (1978) points to several demographic changes that have influenced the form and structure of the nuclear family: (1) people are getting married later, often after some years of childless/childfree cohabitation; (2) women are, on the average, bearing fewer children and are having their first child later in life; (3) a larger number of children are being raised in single family settings, at least for some period of time; (4) fertility is on the decline, and we will have occasional years in which we will experience negative population growth as fertility falls below the replacement level — however, this change would have to continue for a considerable period of time for it to have any noticeable effect upon the United States' population distribution, an unlikely event.

Such changes as those discussed above will undoubtedly continue, and others as yet unforeseen will occur; and these will obviously alter the form of the contemporary nuclear family in the United States. But, an historical perspective suggests that despite this, the nuclear family will not be so distorted in form as to be unrecognizable.

Family Size, Family Stability and Marital Happiness

Important social and attitudinal changes that have occurred in the United States have made it easier and more acceptable for a couple to remain childless/childfree. Safe, inexpensive, and effective contraception is generally available for both men and women; abortions are widely and legally performed, though the political climate has made the continuation of this practice somewhat problematic; and an increasing number of women now pursue — with considerably less negative social sanction than previously — a career in lieu of, or prior to, bearing children. Does this mean that more and more couples are actually childless/childfree? Poston and Gotard (1977) found this to be the case for an increasing number of couples. In their words, this change is probably "linked to broader societal changes regarding fertility, control contraceptive technology, female work preferences and patterns, and sexual and family norms" (p.212). On the other hand, Levitan and Belous (1981) do not believe that we are currently experiencing a new and major shift in family size. They point out that the increase in children as a result of the post World War II "baby boom" temporarily interrupted a steady, long-term decline in the birthrate. Also relevant here is the report by Mosher and Bachrach (1982) that only about 2.2 percent of married women of childbearing ages expect *not* to have children, though that number has increased to 5.4 percent in 1988 (U.S. Bureau of the Census, June 1988 Table 10). Thus, it seems that smaller families were already part of an historical trend of modest proportions. The important contemporary change in this realm is not total family size; it is the *timing* of births to take account of women's career interests.

Reproduction was always an important function of the family (see, for example, Murdock 1949). Nowadays, a childfree/childless marriage is more likely to be a considered and socially tolerated option than at any other time in American history for at least four reasons: (1) better, more effective, and more easily available methods of birth control; (2) more career and educational opportunities for women who, only a few short years ago, would have had little choice but to bear children soon after marriage; (3) increasing societal acceptance of the legitimacy of childless/childfree marriages; and, finally, (4) the mundane fact of the dramatic rise in the costs of raising a family in contrast to just being a married couple (and by being a large family rather than a small family). This is not to argue that all or even most couples will not have children (recall Mosher and Bachrach and the Census data on this issue cited earlier); rather, it is to suggest that couples now have more of a choice than they had in the past. For many couples, the decision to have children (and, if so, when) has become and will continue to be more carefully thought out than it had been earlier. Most families today still do have children, and all studies of future childbearing intentions suggest a continuation of this pattern, though with fewer children and more deliberate planning in the timing of their births.

There has been considerable speculation about how this increase in childless/childfree couples will affect the institution of marriage which, it is suggested, has been in large part designed for the rearing of children. While some people believe that childfree/childless marriages tend to be unhappy (and old stereotype that it is believed was perpetuated to encourage people to have children), there is some evidence to the contrary. Renne (1976), for example, investigated the over-all physical health and dimensions of marital satisfaction for married couples with children and those without children. She concludes that for some, "parenthood detracts from the health and morale of husbands and wives, particularly among younger couples" (p. 196). Specifically, she points out that parenthood detracts from the physical and psychological health of both husbands and wives, particularly among younger couples. Rates of joint marital satisfaction were lower for "active" parents than for "former" parents and childless/childfree couples, regardless of the duration of the marriage and the wife's age and employment status.

Renne's (1976) results need to be replicated before they are accepted as established fact; but they at least raise some serious questions about the effect that children are presumed to have on marriage. If these findings hold up, it still does not automatically follow that we should literally "throw out the baby with the bathwater;" rather, the creative task becomes one of the changing conceptions of marital and gender (and, one might add, occupational) roles so as to increase marital satisfaction for families with children.

Changes in the Roles of Nuclear Family Members

The traditional nuclear family in which the husband/father works full time, the wife/mother is a "homemaker," and there are one or more dependent children at home, is found in only about 11 percent of American families; in about 21 percent of American families, both mother and father are contributing wage earners (Friedan, 1981, pp. 106-107). In 1990, the comparable figures were projected to be 14 percent and 31 percent respectively. These variations from the stereotypical view of the nuclear family have led some scholars to suggest throwing out the concept of the nuclear family in research and policy analysis (e.g., Bernardes 1986). That strikes me as naive and unnecessary. One can recognize diversity in how the various roles within the nuclear family are played without denying the existence of widespread consistency in its general structure. Another version of this argument is that there is no single, universal structure that can be called "the nuclear family" (see, for example, Barrett and McIntosh 1982, p. 81ff) since it differs even in the contemporary world by race, ethnicity and socio-economic status. Once more, I see this more as difference in role performance than in social structure.

Significant role changes *have* taken place in the family. Clearly, the most pronounced change in this area involves the role of women. As the social and personal expectations of women have risen over the past decade, along with their level of education and economic attainment, the role of housewife and mother is now one of several options available to girls who enter womanhood. Some will choose a career followed by marriage and, for some, motherhood; others will elect a career and family simultaneously; still others will choose not to marry at all, and some of these women will also decide to have children. This last pattern does not involve an easy decision; there is still an palpable degree of social pressure on women to have children, and to do so within the context of marriage. But, more women than before are exercising their right to break with past convention, and, it seems to me, their numbers will increase. In any case, because for the contemporary American woman, the wife/mother role has become but one option among several viable alternatives, she is likely to regard it differently than women in the past for whom this was the *only* socially legitimate "choice." Since family roles — like many roles within a defined social structure — are complementary, changes in women's roles have necessitated changes in the roles of men. And that is the hard part in many families!

For most working wives there is both good news and bad news! The bad news is that at present there is little evidence as yet of relief for them from what has been traditionally defined as *their* responsibilities for household and childrearing tasks. Since relatively few husbands apparently share necessary domestic family responsibilities, many working wives simply have to forego carrying out many of these tasks (to the detriment of the quality of family life in many cases) or they have them added on to their outside job responsibilities. In an increasing number of families, commercial help is used: fast food (and other type of) restaurants for dinner, domestic help, day care, etc.; clearly, these alternatives are more likely to be available to those with sufficient income to pay for these services.

However, there is also some good news! It does appear that while the number of husbands who view domestic tasks as a joint, shared responsibility of marriage is relatively small, their number does seem to be increasing. Put differently, the full impact of the evolving consciousness of the importance and necessity of equality in marriage, childrearing responsibilities, domestic tasks and other aspects of family life will not be felt for several years yet. Though these changes will not occur in all families, those that have already taken place in the behavior of many couples and in the normative culture are being transmitted to future generations through socialization. Consequently, the present trend toward equality in adult family roles seems likely to continue — even be enhanced — *as long as the pressure for these changes are maintained.*

The sexual roles of spouses are also undergoing changes. The wife's traditional position as a sexual subordinate, whose job it is to please her husband, has come under sustained attack. Women, both married and single, show a greater willingness to speak out for *their* sexual needs and desires, and this has influenced men's sexual attitudes and practices. In an increasing number of marriages, the husband is less likely to be viewed as the sole or even primary sexual force, the only one whose sexual needs have to be satisfied; in these families, a man's role increasingly includes the responsibility of pleasing his wife — a decided change for many husbands. While this change has put an additional burden on many couples, it has also opened up greater possibilities for the satisfaction of *both* partners. For example, Blumstein and Schwartz (1983) find that equality in "initiating" or "refusing" sexual acts between them was associated with reports by both husbands and wives (and women and men "cohabitators") of considerable satisfaction with the quality of their sex life. This is but one of the tangible benefits that seem to flow from the changing family roles currently taking place.

The Relationship Between Family Roles and Work Roles

Since family roles are not independent of work roles, changes in one will inevitably affect the other. Nowhere is this seen more clearly than in the case of dual-career couples, whose number has approximately tripled over the past decade. (It should be pointed out that many working class wives have always worked, due to economic necessity; the present change results largely, though not exclusively, from the influx of middle-class wives into the work force. In fact, the term used in this literature, "dual-career couple," signifies a distinctly middle-class bias, emphasizing a "career" rather than a "job"; more recently, the term "dual-earner families" has become more frequent reflecting, I believe, a decrease in the class bias in these analyses).

Earlier literature — popular and professional — suggested that if wives went to work outside of the home, they would do so to the detriment of family (e.g., Parsons 1954). More recent studies have led to the contrary conclusion: dual-career couples function at least as well as "traditional" couples, and in some areas (such as flexibility in problem solving) possibly better. Nor does having a family seem to be detrimental to a woman's career, as Parsons (1954) argued, at least for the special case of sociologists married to other sociologists (Goodman, et al. 1984; Martin, Berry and Jacobsen 1975). But a recent study by Blumstein and Schwartz (1983) makes it clear that happiness and good marital functioning depend on *agreement* between a husband and wife about the wife's working.

Even a cursory glance at recent relevant research will show support for the earlier view of Hopkins and White (1978) that in the 1980s "the dual career family is an emergent family form in our society that offers new satisfactions [and] also presents new types of problems for families (p. 253)." Just how these problems are resolved will significantly influence the strength and viability of the new types of roles played by family members. Problems to be considered here include: day care on and off the job site, flexible work times, parental (maternal *and* paternal) leaves, more equal allocation of household tasks, separations due to job requirements, etc. The 1980 White House Conference on the Family considered many of these issues. Unfortunately, however, it got embroiled in political and ideological battles and was unable to develop the kind of coherent and pragmatic approach necessary to provide sustained political and economic support for addressing the identified problems. It was left to *ad hoc* groups and existing organizations to generate the required political pressure that was necessary to get many of these issues onto the national agenda. But the opportunity to use the forum and leverage of the White House Conference, and all the political muscle that would have entailed, was lost. Thus, many of these problems will take longer to solve, and there is less certainty of including them into a consistent national policy to effect necessary change.

Divorce and the Reconstituted Family

If the divorce rate continues to rise while the marriage rate remains relatively stable or even decreases slightly (as seems likely), we may well see as typical a pattern of sequential marriage. That is, some time in the not too distant future, there may be as many men and women in their second (or subsequent) marriage as there are in their first marriage. As a sign of that possible trend, note that while in 1980 almost one-third of all new marriages were remarriages, in 1985 that figure reached 45.8 percent (U.S. Bureau of the Census, 1989, p. 85, Table 124).

Many of these remarried couples will bring together in a new family children from their previous marriage(s), establishing what has been called a "reconstituted" or "blended" family — two parents, at least one of whom brings to this new unit one or more children from a previous marriage (or relationship). There is a dearth of societally agreed upon and well understood social definitions of family roles and responsibilities for those adults and children involved in the increasing number of reconstituted families. Specifically, there is little consensus or consistency about how to deal with many of the questions that arise in these relationships in contrast to those in primary families (e.g., the distribution of assets each party brings to this new relationship; "her" children, "his" children, "their" children; relations with former spouses and in-laws; relationship of child to step-parent and to the non-custodial "biological" parent; relationships among step-siblings). These are serious issues for which society as yet provides no real help for those reconstituted families having to deal with them. However, given the increasing frequency of such families, it seems likely that new roles, norms, and social conventions will evolve to fill the social vacuum; that, in fact, has been the history of social change. To the extent that this social process can be speeded up, fewer reconstituted families will have to suffer the consequences of the lack of social definitions and support available to primary families. This is especially important since it appears that reconstituted families may become the modal form some time in the not too distant future.

Changes in Non-marital Sexual Attitudes and Behavior

Research between the late 1940s and the present have identified significant changes and some surprising stabilities in the sexual attitudes and behaviors of adolescents and young adults. Clearly, there has been an increase in permissive attitudes and the frequency of non-marital sex. Also, over past half century, out-of-wedlock births have increased significantly, so that in 1988 they were 606,000 of 3,667,000 or 16.5 percent of all births (U.S. Bureau of the Census, June 1988. p. 5 Table D). Interestingly, so has the number of adolescents using contraceptives. These facts apparently reflect an increase in teenage sexual activity. Moreover, though the rate of abortion is difficult to measure since illegal abortions in earlier years went largely unreported, the legalization of abortion in the early 1970s led to an increase in its use as a method of birth control; this suggests that the "illegitimacy" rate is an underestimate of the number of out-of-wedlock *conceptions*, one estimate of non-marital sexual activity.

These reported levels of non-marital sex are undoubtedly related to the fact that the mass media of communication offer a more open, less inhibited view of sexual behavior than in the past, though a precise cause-and-effect relationship is easier to assert than to prove. But, the media have been shown to be an important agency of general socialization for young people (e.g., Goodman 1985, pp. 109-110), and there is no reason to expect the sexual sphere to be exempt from its effect.

I should point out that the so-called "sexual revolution" of the 1960s and 1970s was not the first time there was a reported sharp increase in the level of non-marital sexual attitudes and practices in the United States. As the Kinsey (1948; 1953) data and Shorter's (1977) analyses make clear, there was a substantial increase in the rates of both during the 1920s (the "roaring twenties"). Moreover, civil and church records from the colonial period indicate a relatively high rate of "premature" births, suggesting that permissive sex did not begin with the "roaring twenties" either (Reiss and Lee 1988, pp. 76-77).

While the "sexual revolution" of the 1960s and 1970s clearly led to more permissive attitudes and behavior on the part of many young people, a large number still adhere to more traditional values. And this is particularly true for a modified form of the earlier double standard (termed "transitional double standard" by Reiss, 1968, pp. 115-116). For example, in a national study, Zelnik and Shah (1983) showed that while the age at which girls first engage in sexual intercourse was a little over age 16, most adolescent girls (about 60 percent) still associate sexual activity with a serious "steady" relationship; and the large majority maintain for some time a monogamous relationship with the boy with whom they had their first sexual encounter. Boys, on the other hand, begin having sexual intercourse slightly younger (at about 15 1/2 years of age) and, more importantly for the purpose at hand, report less concern with the stability and seriousness of the relationship with their first sexual partner. As we saw earlier with the domestic responsibilities of husbands and wives, though general social change in these spheres is occurring, gender differences seem to change more slowly.

It is evident that there are elements of both change and stability in sexual attitudes and practices. Though there is a generally moderately conservative mood in the U.S. on political and economic matters, in the social sphere I believe that we will see continued diversity as a consequence of increasing tolerance of differences; moderate sexual permissiveness will be the general rule, with a substantial minority continuing to adhere to more traditional sexual values. However, it should be noted that the increased concern over AIDS is a new element whose precise effects on both marital and non-marital sexual relationships are somewhat unclear at this point. Growing alarm — and that seems the proper term — over the spread of AIDS will almost certainly reinforce more traditional values about non-marital sex; how long and how pervasive this will be depends on a number of factors, most especially on whether there will be a medical breakthrough on the prevention or successful treatment of AIDS. The present concern also deeply affects the marital relationship in general by heightening the importance of trust in marriage since infidelity has now become more than an ethical issue; it is now, literally, a potentially communicably fatal intrusion into marriage.

Changes in the Preparation for Marriage and Family Life

In the past, Americans by and large learned about marriage and family life primarily through informal observations of their own family (and occasional direct instruction by parents regarding specific relevant skills — e.g., cooking, sewing, carpentry work around the home, changing the diapers of a sibling), from the families of relatives, from neighbors and friends, and from the mass media. While these sources of information continue, others have also emerged as important in recent years. For example, there has been a growing emphasis on institutionally supported preparation for marriage and parenthood. Schools, civic, and religious organizations increasingly provide information in this area; and reading material to help teenagers and young adults understand and assess their future marital and parental roles is more readily available than in the past.

An increasing number of high schools, colleges, and universities offer courses that emphasize effective communication and an understanding of the nature of marital and parental roles. Many of these courses have a practical orientation, focusing on issues of problem solving. They deal with such potential conflict areas as: premarital sex, birth control, extra-marital entaglements, financial management, working wives and their earnings, and alcohol problems. Recently, concern over AIDS has given impetus to the inclusion of discussions of human sexuality in Family Life curricula in very pragmatic and "down to earth" terms. Initial reports suggest that discussions with young people have engendered affirmations by them of more conservative and restrictive sexual attitudes; but such statements are easier said in an educational context than done in a "romantic" situation, as many a youth has remarked.

This kind of preparation, along with the attitudes and specific skills required of parents that are now taught in many high schools and colleges, provide young people more relevant information and guidance on marriage and family life than was available to most of their parents. And the most effective of these programs involve the parents in this learning process (Goodman and Goodman 1976).

The present national administration and, more importantly, the generally conservative mood of decision makers at the local and state levels, however, do not auger well for the maintenance, much less extension, of family life education programs — particularly in the public school system. These types of programs have been under severe ideological, political, economic, and religious attack at both the national and local levels for several years; many still are. This sustained attack has threatened not just the expansion, but the very existence, of many of these programs. The changed political tone hinted at by the 1988 elections and the present mobilization around the issue of abortion, may offer a ray of hope for the continuation and expansion of family life education in the school, if it also reflects change at the local level as well.

For various reasons — the decrease in the pervasive cynicism of the 1960s and 1970s, the fact that many of those currently entering marriage are increasingly acquainted with people who are getting divorced, and because they no longer see marriage as inevitably and automatically permanent — more young people today are aware that hard and continuous work is necessary to make their marriages succeed. There is a growing realization that any intimate relationship, particularly marriage, requires ongoing effort and adjustment; more young people are aware of the fact that there is no "natural" path to lifelong happiness that routinely occurs when one marries. Many recognize that a "good" marriage is not made in heaven, but here on earth; not through the forces of nature or some supreme being, but through their own efforts — a point made by the astute sociologist Willard Waller (1938) more than half a century ago. The recognition of this essential fact is one of the positive consequences of the more realistic assessment of marriage that has emerged in the past fifteen to twenty years.

At the same time, however, the easing of legal and social constraints against divorce have made it easier to avoid dealing with the sometimes difficult process of marital adjustment. For many, divorce has become an earlier rather than a later (or ultimate) option in the face of marital difficulty. But, mechanisms to aid couples in the critical process of marital adjustment continue to grow. There is, for example, an increasing availability of couples' groups, growth groups, encounter groups, self-help groups, marital and family therapy counsellors and programs, books and popular articles on making marriage succeed.

These conflicting trends — the ease and greater social acceptance of divorce, and the more realistic assessment of and support for marriage — have yet to be completely played out in American family life. Both currently affect the nature of contemporary American marriage and family. I believe that the evident reduction, or at least fluctuation, in the *rate* of divorce will continue, and marriage will be put on a more realistic basis than it has in the past. And this will be, in part, a result of the change in the preparation for marriage and family life that has occurred in American society over the past two decades.

The Likely Future of Marriage and the Family in the U.S.

Having reviewed — though somewhat sketchily — some aspects of the present state of marriage and the family in the United States, it seems to me that these twin social institutions are still strong and viable — and will continue to be so for at least the foreseeable future. Clearly, they will be somewhat different institutions from what they have been in the past. They will be marked by more equality between men and women, greater flexibility in marital and family roles, and contain more opportunity and support for re-evaluating and negotiating changes in this relationship. The transition to the present state has been — and will continue to be — difficult and even painful in many families, as is so often the case during rapid social change. Unfortunately, these difficulties have fallen disproportionately on women. For example, the recent easing of divorce and spousal and child support laws have actually exacerbated the problems of divorced women and their children: fewer and lower financial settlements, and for shorter time periods, coupled with low rates of actual payments by men of these court-ordered awards, have increased the "feminization of poverty" (see, e.g., Hewlett 1987). The key to smoothing the way toward a more useful system for *both* men and women — argued more than three quarters of a century ago by George Bernard Shaw in his 1908 play, *Getting Married: A Disquisitory Play*, and echoed recently by many feminists (see, e.g., Segal 1983) — is to make women economically independent of men, thereby helping to equalize power in the family. But even this is not enough. As Barrett and McIntosh (1982) so clearly and succinctly put it, "The experience of many women has. . . . proved that even when two partners in a marriage bring in similar incomes the man retains his domination in all sorts of non-economic ways. The structure of domination and submission go far beyond the material facts of providing and depending. . . . " (p. 70). The thrust of their argument is that there is a "culture of masculine domination" that is not amenable to the quick economic fix — even if that were easier to accomplish than currently seems possible. Barrett and McIntosh (1982) argue for societal change (specifically, the creation of a socialist state) as a necessary prelude to changing the normative system. One need not endorse their particular solution as the sole, or even, primary, strategy for facilitating a more egalitarian relationship between men and women. The already changing patterns reported above need to be buttressed; and further changes in this same vein encouraged; supportive social structures have to be developed; and the fruits of these endeavors transmitted to future generations through the socialization process.

As I indicated earlier, marriage and the nuclear family have proved to be resilient institutions in the past, and I see no reason why they will not continue to be so in the future. As Rose Coser (1964) would undoubtedly agree, they will continue to adjust to the changing social circumstances noted earlier, and are likely to adapt similarly to the as yet unclear changes likely in the near future. That is not to say that an enlightened "social engineering" approach to help shape the nature of these adaptations would be amiss. Rose Coser has never been a passive person; letting something as important as marriage and family life just drift or change aimlessly is not in her nature. She would do what she could — and would urge others to do likewise — to influence the way in which these two important social institutions respond to the changing social and ethical environment.

Perhaps the best summary statement on this topic I can make is captured in the title of a book by Mary Jo Bane (1978) that indicates that the American family, though changing, is "here to stay" — though its shape and form, as well as the lived experience of its constituent members, will depend on the social context, presently in a state of transition; but clearly this is not news to sociologists.

References

Bane, Mary Jo. 1978. *Here to Stay: American Families in the Twentieth Century*, N.Y.: Basic Books.

Barrett, Michele and Mary McIntosh. 1982. *The Anti-Social Family*. London: NLB.

Berger, Brigitte and L. Peter. 1983. *The War Over the Family: Capturing the Middle Ground*. N.Y.: Anchor/Doubleday.

Blumstein, Philip and Pepper Schwartz. 1983. *American Couples: Money, Work, Sex*. N.Y.: William Morrow.

Cadwallader, Mervyn. 1975. "Marriage as a Wretched Institution." Pp. 26-31 in *Current Issues in Marriage and the Family*, edited by J. Gipson Wells. New York: Macmillan.

Cherlin, Andrew J. 1981. *Marriage, Divorce, Remarriage*. Cambridge, MA.: Harvard University Press.

Cooper, David. 1970. *The Death of the Family*. N.Y.: Vintage (Random House).

Coser, Rose (ed.). 1964. *The Family: Its Structure and Functions*. New York: St. Martins.

Duberman, Lucile. 1975. *The Reconstituted Family: A Study of Remarried Couples and Their Children*. Chicago: Nelson-Hall.

Friedan, Betty. 1981. *The Second Stage*. London: Michael Joseph Ltd.

Goodman, Barry and Norman Goodman. 1976. "Effects of Parent Orientation Meetings on Parent-Child Communication about Sexuality and Family Life." *The Family Coordinator*, 25 (3): 285-290.

Goodman, Norman. 1985. "Socialization II: A Developmental View." Pp. 95-116 in *The Foundations of Interpretive Sociology: Original Essays in Symbolic Interaction*, edited by Harvey A. Farberman and Robert Perinbanayagam. Greenwich, CT.: JAI Press.

_____. Edward Royce, Hanan C. Selvin, and Eugene A. Weinstein. 1984. "The Academic Couple in Sociology: Managing Greedy Institutions." Pp. 240-61 in *Conflict and Consensus: Essays in Honor of Lewis A. Coser*, edited by Walter W. Powell and Richard Robbins. New York: Free Press.

Hewlett, Sylvia Ann. 1987. *A Lesser Life: The Myth of Women's Liberation*. London: Michael Joseph Ltd.

Hopkins, J. and P. White. 1978. "The Dual-Career Couple: Constraints and Supports." *The Family Coordinator* 27 (3): 253-259.

Huser, W. R. and C.W. Grant. 1975. "A Study of Husbands and Wives from Dual-Career and Traditional-Career Families." *Psychology of Women Quarterly* 3 (1): 78-89.

Hymowitz, C. and M. Weissman. 1978. *A History of Women in America*. New York: Bantam.

Levitan, Sar A. and Richard S. Belous. 1982. *What's Happening to the American Family?* Baltimore, MD.: Johns Hopkins University Press.

Martin, Thomas W., Kenneth J. Berry, R. Brooke Jacobsen. 1975. "The Impact of Dual-Career Marriages on Female Professional Careers: An Empirical Test of a Parsonian Hypothesis," *Journal of Marriage and the Family* 37 (4): 734-42.

Masnick, George and Mary Jo Bane. 1980. *The Nation's Families: 1960-1990*. Boston: Auburn House.

Mosher, William P. and Christine A. Bachrach. 1982. "Childlessness in the United States: Estimates from the National Survey of Family Growth." *Journal of Family Issues* 3 (4): 517-43.

Murdock, George P. 1949. *Social Structure*. New York: Macmillan.

_____. 1957. "World Ethnographic Survey." *American Anthropologist* 59 (4): 664-687.

O'Brien, Patricia. 1981. "Staying Together: Marriages that Work." Pp. 11-13 in *Confronting the Issues: Marriage, the Family and Sex Roles*, edited by Kenneth C.W. Kammeyer. Boston: Allyn and Bacon.

Parsons, Talcott. 1954. *Essays on Sociological Theory*. Chap. V. Glencoe, IL.: Free Press.

Poston, D.L. and E. Gotard. 1977. "Trends in Childlessness in the United States, 1910-1975." *Social Biology* 24 (3): 212-224.

Reiss, Ira L. 1960. *Premarital Sexual Standards in America*. New York: Free Press.

_____ and Gary R. Lee. 1989. *Family Systems in America* 4th Edition. New York: Holt, Rinehart and Winston.

Renne, K. S. 1976. "Childlessness, Health and Marital Satisfaction." *Social Biology* 23 (3): 183-197.

Segal, Lynne (ed.). 1983. *What is to be Done about the Family?* London: Penguin.

Thamm, Robert. 1975. *Beyond Marriage and the Nuclear Family*. San Francisco, CA: Canfield.

U.S. Bureau of the Census. 1989. *Monthly Vital Statistics Report* Vol. 37 No. 13. Washington, D.C.: U.S. Government Printing Office.

_____. 1989. *Marital Status and Living Arrangements* P.-20 Series, Advance Reports Washington, D.C., U.S. Government Printing Office.

_____. 1989. *Statistical Abstracts of the United States, 1989*. 109th Edition. Washington, D.C.: U.S. Government Printing Office.

_____. 1988. *Households, Families, etc.* P.-20 Series, Advance Reports Washington, D.C.: U.S. Government Printing Office.

_____. 1988. *Fertitity of American Women*, P.-20 Series, Washington, D.C.: U.S. Government Printing Office.

Waller, Willard. 1938. *The Family: A Dynamic Interpretation*. New York: Dryden.

Westoff, C.F. 1977. "Some Speculations on the Future of Marriage and Fertility." *Family Planning Perspectives* 9 (4): 153-157.

Zelnik, Melvin and Farida K. Shah. 1983. "First Intercourse Among Young Americans," *Family Planning Perspectives* 15 (2): 65-70.

Selected Bibliography
of Rose Laub Coser

Books

In Defense of Modernity: Complexity of Social Roles and Individual Autonomy. California: Stanford University Press, 1991.

The World of Our Mothers. New York: Russell Sage Foundation, forthcoming.

Access to Power (editor, with Cynthia Fuchs Epstein). Cambridge: Allen and Unwin, 1981.

Training in Ambiguity: Learning Through Doing in a Mental Hospital. New York: The Free Press, 1979.

The Family, Its Structure and Function. Revised edition with new Introduction. New York: St. Martin's Press, 1974.

Life Cycle and Achievement in America. Edited with Introduction. New York: Harper Torchbooks, 1972.

The Family: Its Structure and Functions. Edited with Introduction. New York: St. Martin's Press, 1964.

Life in the Ward. East Lansing: Michigan State University Press, 1962.

Papers and Chapters

"Reflections on Merton's Role-Set Theory," and "Coser Replies to Hilbert." Pp. 159-74 and 187 in *Robert K. Merton, Consensus and Controversy*, edited by Jon Clark, Celia Modgil, and Sohan Modgil. London: Falmer Press, 1990.

"Power Lost and Status Gained: A Step in the Direction of Sex Equality." Pp. 71-87 in *The Nature of Work: Sociological Perspectives*, edited by Kai Erikson and Steven P. Villas. Connecticut: Yale University Press, 1990.

"Reflections on Feminist Theory." Pp. 200-07 in *Feminism and Sociological Theory*, edited by Ruth A. Wallace. Newbury Park: Sage Publications, 1989.

"Machtverlust und Statusgewinn: Ein Schritt zur Gleichstellung der Geschlechter." *Koelner Zeitschrift fuer Soziologie und Sozialpsychologie* (1987):1-14.

"Cognitive Structure and the Use of Social Space." *Sociological Forum* I (1986):1-26.

"The Greedy Nature of *Gemeinschaft*." Pp. 221-40 in *Conflict and Consensus*, edited by Walter W. Powell and Richard Robbins. New York: The Free Press, 1984.

"The American Family: Changing Patterns of Social Control." Pp. 187-203 in *Social Control: Views from the Social Sciences*, edited by Jack P. Gibbs. Beverly Hills: Sage Publication.

"On the Reproduction of Mothering: A Methodological Debate" (with Judith Lorber, Alice Rossi, and Nancy Chodorow). *Signs: Journal of Women in Culture and Society* 6 (1981):482-514; Rose Laub Coser's discussion on pp. 487-92.

"Where Have All the Women Gone? Like the Sediment of a Good Wine, They Have Sunk to the Bottom." Pp. 16-33 in *Access to Power: Cross-National Studies of Women and Elites*, edited by Rose Laub Coser and Cynthia Fuchs Epstein. London: George Allen and Unwin, 1981.

"Women and Work." *Dissent* (Spring 1980):158-63.
      Reprinted: *Sociology*, edited by Kurt Finsterbusch. Gifford,
      Connecticut: Dushkin Pub., 1984.

"Jonestown as Perverse Utopia" (with Lewis A. Coser). *Dissent* (Spring 1979):158-63.
      Reprinted: *Sociology*, edited by Kurt Finsterbusch. Gifford,
      Connecticut: Dushkin Pub., 1984.

"The Principle of Patriarchy: The Case of the Magic Flute." *Signs: Journal of Women in Culture and Society* 4(1978):337-48.

"Pockets of Poverty in the Salaries of Academic Women." *AAUP Bulletin* 64 (1978):26-30.

"Why Bother: Is Research of Women's Health Issues Worthwhile?" Pp. 3-9 in *Women and Their Health: Research Implications for a New Era, Proceedings of a Conference,* edited by Virginia Oleson. DHEW, Publications No. (HRA) 77-3138.

"Das Maennerreich Universitaet: Diskriminierungen in den USA und in der Sowjetunion." *Giessener Universitaetsblaetter* 9 (1976):38-49.

"A Conservative Critic of Affirmative Action." Essay review of *Affirmative Discrimination, Ethnic Inequality, and Public Policy,* by Nathan Glazer. *Dissent* (Summer 1976):318-320. See also further discussion and rejoinder in *Dissent* (Winter 1977):110-11.
> Reprinted: Pp. 289-295 in *The New Conservatives,* edited by Lewis A. Coser and Irving Howe. New York: New American Library, 1977.

"Suicide and the Relational System: A Case Study in a Mental Hospital." *Journal of Health and Social Behavior* 17 (1976):318-27.

"The Complexity of Roles as a Seedbed of Individual Autonomy." Pp. 237-63 in *The Idea of Social Structure: Essays in the Honor of Robert K. Merton,* edited by Lewis A. Coser. Harcourt Brace Jovanovich, 1975.

"Stay Home Little Sheba: On Placement, Displacement, and Social Change." *Social Problems* 22 (1975):470-80.
> Reprinted: Pp. 153-59 in *Women and Work,* edited by Rachel Kahn-Hut, Arlene Daniels and Richard Colvard. New York: Oxford University Press, 1982.

"Affirmative Action: Letter to a Worried Colleague." *Dissent* (Fall 1975): 366-69. See also "A Debate." *Dissent* (Spring, 1976):207-10.
> Translated. "L'Action Positive." *Problemes Politiques et Sociaux* 3 (September 1976):236-39. France: Secretariat General du Gouvernement, Direction de la Documentation.
> Reprinted: Pp. 117-21 in *Point-Counterpoint: Readings in American Government,* edited by Herbert M. Levine. Glenview, ILL: Scott, Foresman Co.

"The Housewife and Her Greedy Family" (with Lewis A. Coser). Pp. 89-100 in *Greedy Institutions,* by Lewis A. Coser. New York: The Free Press, 1974.
> Reprinted: Pp. 208-16 in *Relationships: The Marriage and Family Reader,* edited by Jeffrey P. Rosenfeld. Glenview, ILL: Scott, Foresman and Co., 1981.

Reprinted: Pp. 378-84 in *Social Interaction,* edited by Howard
Robboy, Sidney C. Greenblatt and Claudia Clark. New
York: St. Martin's Press, 1979.

"The Principle of Legitimacy and Its Patterned Infringement" (with
Lewis A. Coser). Pp. 119-30 in *Cross-National Family Research,* edited by
Marvin B. Sussman and Betty Cogswell. Leiden, the Netherlands: E. J.
Brill, 1972.

"Women in the Occupational World." *Social Problems* 18 (1971):535-54.
Reprinted: Pp. 39-53 in *Women and Work,* edited by Rachel Kahn-
Hut, Arlene Daniels, and Richard Colvard. New York:
Oxford University Press, 1982.
Reprinted: Pp. 218-37 and 446-63 in *The Study of Society,* edited by
Peter I. Rose. Third and fourth edition. New York: Random
House, 1977.
Reprinted: Pp. 45-65 in *The Substance of Sociology: Codes, Conduct
and Consequences,* edited by Ephraim Mizruchi. New York:
Appleton Century, 1973.

"On Nepotism and Marginality" (Communication). *The American
Sociologist* 6 (1971):259-60.

"Evasiveness as a Response to Structural Ambivalence." *Social Science and
Medicine* 1 (1967):203-18.

"Role Distance, Sociological Ambivalence, and Transitional Status
Systems." *American Journal of Sociology* 72 (1966):173-87.
Reprinted: Pp. 318-35 in *Sociological Theory,* edited by Lewis A.
Coser and Bernard Rosenberg. New York: Free Press, 1969.

"Authority and Structural Ambivalence in the Middle Class Family." Pp.
370-83 in *The Family, Its Structure and Functions,* edited by Rose Laub
Coser. New York: St. Martin's Press, 1964.
Reprinted: Pp. 566-76 and 508-19 in *Sociological Theory,* edited by
Lewis A. Coser and Bernard Rosenberg. New York: The
Free Press, 1974, 1976, 1980.

"Keni to Kozoteki anbibarensuas — Chukankaiso no Kazolu." Pp. 146-63
in *Kaoku no shakaigaku riron* (*The Theory of Sociology of the Family*), edited
by Tsuneo Yamane. Tokyo: Sheishin Shobo, 1971.

"Alienation and the Social Structure." Pp. 231-65 in *The Hospital in
Modern Society,* edited by E. Freidson. New York: The Free Press, 1963.

Reprinted: Pp. 213-22 in *Basic Readings in Medical Sociology*, edited by David Tuckett and Joseph M. Kaufert. London: Tavistock Publications, 1978.

"Time Perspective and the Social Structure" (with Lewis A. Coser). Pp. 251-65 in *Modern Sociology: An Introduction to the Study of Human Interaction*, edited by Alvin M. Gouldner and Helen P. Gouldner. New York: Harcourt Brace Jovanovich, 1963.

"Insulation from Observability and Types of Social Conformity." *American Sociological Review* 26 (1961):28-39.

"Laughter Among Colleagues: A Study of the Social Functions of Humor Among the Staff of a Mental Hospital." *Psychiatry* 23 (1960):81-96.
> Translated: "Das Gelaechter der Geschlechter" in *Humor und Macht in Gerspraechen von Frauen und Maennern*, edited by Helga Kotthoff. Frankfurt: Fischer, 1971.
> Reprinted: *The Hospital Digest Yearbook* 1 (1963):134-38.
> Reprinted: "Some Social Functions of Laughter: A Study of Humor in a Hospital Setting." *Human Relations* 12 (1959):171-82.
> Reprinted: Pp. 292-305 in *Social Interaction and Patient Care*, edited by James K. Skipper and Robert C. Leonard. New York: Lippincott, 1965.

"Authority and Decision-Making in a Hospital: A Comparative Analysis." *American Sociological Review* 23 (1958):56-63.
> Reprinted: Pp. 54-62 in *Sociological Observation*, edited by Matilda W. Riley and E. E. Nelson. New York: Basic Books, 1974.
> Reprinted: Pp. 174-84 in *Medical Men and Their Work*, edited by Eliot Freidson and Judith Lorber. Chicago: Aldine, 1972.
> Reprinted: Pp. 119-30 in *Comparative Studies in Administration*, edited by James D. Thompson. Pittsburgh: University of Pittsburgh Press, 1959.

"The Dangers of Hospitalization" (with Leon Lewis, M.D.). Pp. 303-32 in *Hospitals and Patient Dissatisfaction*, by Richard H. Blum. San Francisco: The Medical Review Board of the California Medical Association, Technical Report, 1958.

"A Home Away from Home." *Social Problems* 4 (1956):3-17.
> Translated: Pp. 63-80 in *Medecine, Maladie et Societe*, edited by Claudine Herzlich. Paris, France: Ecole Pratique des Hautes Etudes and Mouton, 1970.

Reprinted: Pp. 154-72 in *Sociological Studies of Health and Sickness,* edited by Dorian Apple. New York: McGraw-Hill, 1960.

"Political Involvement and Interpersonal Relations." *Psychiatry* 14 (1951):213-22.

Reviews

"The Women's Movement and Conservative Attacks." Essay review of *A Lesser Life,* by Sylvia Hewlett. *Dissent* (Spring 1987).

"The Women's Movement and Conservative Attacks." Essay review of *Myths of Gender,* by Anne Fausto-Sterling. *Contemporary Sociology* 16 (1987):281-282.

"Women in American Society." Essay review of *More Work for Mother,* by Ruth Schwartz Cowan. *Dissent* (Fall 1984):499-510.

Essay review of *Parenthood and Social Reproduction,* by Esther N. Goody. *Contemporary Sociology* 13 (1984):187-89.

"American Medicine's Ambiguous Progress." Essay review of *The Social Transformation of American Medicine,* by Paul Starr. *Contemporary Sociology* 13 (1984):9-11.

"Portrait of Bolshevik Feminist." Essay review of *Bolshevik Feminist: The Life of Aleksandra Kollontai,* by Barbara Evans and *Aleksandra Kollontai: Socialism, Feminism and the Bolshevik Revolution,* by Beatrice Farnsworth. *Dissent* 29 (1982):235-39.

"Why do Women do the Mothering?" Essay review of *The Reproduction of Mothering: Psychoanalysis and the Sociology of Gender,* by Nancy Chodorow. *Contemporary Sociology* 8 (1979):537-38.

"Freud and Feminism." Essay review of *Psychoanalysis and Feminism,* by Julia Mitchell. *Partisan Review* 44 (1977):152-56.

"Women's Liberation: The Real Issues." Essay review of *The New Chastity and Other Arguments Against Women's Liberation,* by Midge Decter and *The American Woman, Her Changing Social, Economic, and Political Roles, 1920-1970,* by William Chafe. *Dissent* (Spring 1973):224-230.

"Humor is Serious Business." Essay review of *Laughter: A Socio-Scientific Analysis,* by Joyce D. Hertzler. *Contemporary Psychology* 16(1971):585-86.

"Anti-Semitism Re-examined." Essay review of *Christians and Jews*, by Rudolph M. Loewenstein. *The New Leader* (May 28 1951).

"Prejudice and Personality." Essay review of *The Authoritarian Personality*, by T. W. Adorno, Else Frenkel-Brunswik, Daniel J. Levinson and R. Nevitt Stanford; *Dynamics of Prejudice*, by Bruno Bettelheim and Morris Janowitz; *Anti Semitism and Emotional Disorder*, by W. Ackerman and Marie Jahoda; *Prophets of Deceit*, by Leo Lowenthal and Norbert Guterman. *The New Leader* (Feb. 19 1951):22-24.

Essay review of "L'Angoisse et al Pensee Magique," by Charles Odier Neuchatel; Delachaux et Niestle, 1947. *Psychiatry* (February 1950) 13:122-26.

"A Social Disease." Essay review of *Anti-Semitism, a Social Disease*, by Ernst Simmel, M.D.Ed. (*International Universities Press*). *Modern Review* 9(November 1947):714-19.

About the Contributors

Judith R. Blau, professor of sociology at the University of North Carolina at Chapel Hill, is the author of *Architects and Firms*, *The Shape of Culture*, and co-editor of *Professionals and Urban Form*, *Remaking the City*, and *Art and Society*. Recent published articles deal with the ecology of contemporary cultural organizations, and she is currently collaborating with Kenneth C. Land on research in historical sociology.

Peter M. Blau is Robert Broughton distinguished research professor, University of North Carolina, and Quetelet professor emeritus, Columbia University. His major current interest is macrostructural theory. He recently participated on a collaborative research project with the Tianjin Academy of Social Sciences, which resulted in two coauthored papers that compared Chinese and American social mobility and core networks, respectively. He is probably the contributor to this *Festschrift* who has known Rose longer than any other (except, of course, Lew and, possibly, Ellen), since she and he were fellow graduate students.

Nancy J. Chodorow is in the sociology department at the University of California at Berkeley. Her paper in this volume builds on earlier work dealing with the relevance of psychoanalysis for the sociology of gender. Other publications are *The Reproduction of Mothering* and *Feminism and Psychoanalytic Theory*.

Lewis A. Coser is distinguished professor emeritus at the State University of New York at Stony Brook and adjunct professor of sociology at Boston College. He has published books and articles on a wide range of topics, including theory, intellectual history, power and conflict, organizations, work, and gender.

William V. D'Antonio is the executive officer of the American Sociological Association and professor emeritus from the University of Connecticut. D'Antonio has been active in a large number of professional associations and currently is president-elect of the District of Columbia Sociological Society, vice president of the International Institute of Sociology, and the chair of the Executive Committee of the Consortium of Social Science Associations. He is an author or co-author of four books in the fields of family sociology, sociology of religion, and political sociology. He has co-edited three other books and has published articles and chapters, and continues to do research on ethnicity and religion.

Arlene Kaplan Daniels received her Ph.D. from the University of California, Berkeley in 1960. Presently she teaches at Northwestern University where she is a professor in the department of sociology. Her edited books include *Academics on the Line* (with Rachel Kahn-Hut), *Hearth and Home: Images of Women in the Mass Media* (with Gaye Tuchman and James Benét), *Women and Work* (with Rachel Kahn-Hut and Richard Colvard), and *Women and Trade Unions in Eleven Industrialized Countries* (with Alice Cook and Val Lorwin). Her co-authored book (with Teresa Odendahl and Elizabeth Boris) is *Working in Foundations: Career Patterns of Women and Men*. Her most recent book is titled *Invisible Careers: Women Civic Leaders in the Volunteer World*.

Cynthia Fuchs Epstein is distinguished professor of sociology at the Graduate Center, City University of New York. She received her Ph.D. from Columbia University in 1968. She has held a Guggenheim Fellowship and was a fellow at the Center for Advanced Studies in the Behavioral Sciences. From 1982-88 she was a resident scholar at the Russell Sage Foundation. She has been a consultant to the White House and co-directed two research programs on gender issues at Columbia University and the Graduate Center. Her work has focused on theoretical and structural issues in the analysis of gender and she has conducted research on women in the professions, business and politics, on gender ideology and on workplace culture. She is the author of numerous articles; her books include *Deceptive Distinctions: Sex Gender and the Social Order* (1988); *Women In Law* (1981); *Woman's Place* (1970); *Access to Power* (1981), edited with Rose Coser; *The Other Half* (1971), edited with William J. Goode; and a forthcoming book, *Boundaries: On the Meaning of Work, Workplace and the Self*.

Norman Goodman is distinguished teaching professor and distinguished service professor in the department of sociology at the State University of New York at Stony Brook. His is the co-author of *Personality and Decision Processes: Studies in the Social Psychology of Thinking* (Stanford University Press, 1962), *Society Today* (3rd and 4th edition; Random House, 1978 and 1982), *Marriage, Family, and Intimate Relationships* (Rand McNally, 1980), and the author of the forthcoming *Introduction to Sociology* (Harper Collins, 1991). His articles have been published in the *American Sociological Review*, the *Journal of Marriage and the Family*, the *Journal of Social Psychology*, other journals, and edited volumes of original articles. He is currently working on a volume on marriage and the family.

Donald Light left the University of Chicago to complete his training with Everett C. Hughes, Morris Schwartz, Lewis Coser and other members of the Brandeis faculty. He met Rose Coser as she was conducting her study of training at McLean Hospital (*Training in Ambiguity*) and he was completing similar research that resulted in *Becoming Psychiatrists: The Professional Transformation of Self*. They soon established a lively relationship which has grown with the years. Professor Light now does comparative studies of relations between professions, the state, and the economy, with particular focus on health care. He has appointments at the University of Medicine and Dentistry of New Jersey and at Rutgers University.

Helena Znaniecka Lopata was born in Poznan, Poland. She obtained her Ph.D. from the University of Chicago in 1954. Many of her studies and writing have focused on social roles in the occupational world and in the lives of American women. Examples include *Occupation: Housewife* (1971); *City Women: Work, Jobs, Occupations, Careers* (1985) *Women as Widows: Support Systems* (1979) and *Women's Social Roles, Women's Life Spaces* (1991). Current research focuses on the social integration of suburban women, 1956-1992; wars and families; and, the retirement of university professors.

Robert K. Merton is university professor emeritus, Columbia University.

Helga Nowotny is professor at the University of Vienna and director of the newly founded Institute for Theory and Social Studies of Science. She was the founding director of the European Center in Vienna, a position she held from 1974 to 1987. Among her major publications in the fields of social policy and social studies of science and technology are several books published in English, including *Counter-movement and the Sciences, Science Between Utopia and Dystopia, and In Search of Useable Knowledge*. She has held various teaching and research positions, including King's College, Cambridge; University of Graz; and the University of Bielefeld.

Ellen Coser Perrin has a B.A. from Barnard College, and M.D. from Case Western Reserve University School of Medicine, and an M.A. in developmental psychology from the University of Rochester. She has been a member of the faculty in the department of pediatrics at the University of Rochester, Vanderbilt University, and the University of Massachusetts Schools of Medicine. Her interests are in the teaching and practice of developmental and behavioral pediatrics, and the psychosocial implications of chronic illness for children and their families.

James M. Perrin has an A.B. from Harvard College and an M.D. from Case Western Reserve University School of Medicine. He is currently associate professor of pediatrics at Harvard Medical School, director of the Division of General Pediatrics at the Massachusetts General Hospital, and a member of the Division of Health Policy at Harvard. His research has examined issues in clinical and behavioral pediatrics and in health services and child health policy. He trained in pediatrics at the University of Rochester and has held faculty appointments there and at Vanderbilt University.

David Riesman came to Harvard University in 1958 as Henry Ford II Professor of the Social Sciences; he is now an emeritus professor in the sociology department. *On Higher Education: The Academic Enterprise in an Era of Rising Student Consumerism* (1980) is the final volume in the series published by the Carnegie Commission on Policy Studies in Higher Education. Judith Block Mclaughlin and David Riesman, *Choosing a College President: Opportunities and Constraints* was published by Princeton University Press in 1991.

Jeff Rosenfeld took his doctorate in Sociology at SUNY Stony Brook where he studied with Rose Coser. His first research on inheritance appeared in Rose Coser's *The Family: Its Structures and Functions*, 2nd ed., and he has continued to write on the benefactor-beneficiary relationship. He is a regular contributor to *Probate & Property*, and to *Trusts & Estates*, and he frequently testifies in estate litigation. Since 1984 he has been an advisor to the Intergenerational Wealth Study, an Internal Revenue Service project based upon Estate Tax returns. Currently he is investigating the social and inter-generational impact of will-contests. Jeff Rosenfeld is professor of sociology at Nassau Community College, SUNY.

Gladys Rothbell received her Ph.D. in sociology in 1989 from SUNY at Stony Brook. Rose Coser was her advisor. Her dissertation is on the stereotype of the Jewish mother. She has been working with Rose Coser on a study of the acculturation processes of immigrant women who came to the U.S. before 1925. Her current position as director of the Emigre Program (Institute for Children and Families, New York City) centers on the acclimation of contemporary refugees in the United States.

Andrea Tyree is professor of sociology at the State University of New York at Stony Brook. She received her B.A. at Antioch College (1962), M.A. at the University of Hawaii (1964), and Ph.D. at the University of Chicago (1968). As a social demographer with underlying concerns with processes of population transformation and replacement, she has worked primarily in social stratification, status attainment, and international migration. This line of work was initiated by her role as a collaborator on *The American Occupational Structure* (for which she shared the Sorokin Award) while a graduate student. She has recently been dividing her research time between work on international migration (into the U.S. and in and out of the Middle East) and a longitudinal project on spouse abuse with K. Daniel O'Leary, a psychologist at Stony Brook.